THAILAND AND THE
UNITED STATES

A Study of the East Asian Institute, Columbia University

ROBERT J. MUSCAT

THAILAND
AND THE
UNITED STATES
DEVELOPMENT, SECURITY,
AND FOREIGN AID

COLUMBIA UNIVERSITY PRESS
NEW YORK

Columbia University Press
New York   Oxford
Copyright © 1990 Columbia University Press
All rights reserved

Library of Congress Cataloging-in-Publication Data

Muscat, Robert J.
Thailand and the United States :
development, security, and foreign aid
Robert J. Muscat.
p.   cm.
(A Study of the East Asian Institute, Columbia University)
Includes bibliographical references (p.   ).
ISBN 0-231-07144-2
1. Economic assistance, American—Thailand.
2. Economic development projects—Thailand.
3. Military assistance, American—Thailand.
4. Thailand—Economic policy.
5. United States—Relations—Thailand.
6. Thailand—Relations—United States.
I. Title. II. Series.
HC445.M87   1990   338.9'1730593—dc20   89-28811
CIP

Casebound editions of Columbia University Press books are Smyth-sewn
and printed on permanent and durable acid-free paper

∞

Printed in the United States of America

c 10 9 8 7 6 5 4 3 2 1

to
Dr. Puey Ungphakorn
and to the memory of
M. L. Dej Snidvongse
and
Khunying Suparb Yossundara

THE EAST ASIAN
INSTITUTE
OF COLUMBIA UNIVERSITY

The East Asian Institute is Columbia University's center for research, education, and publication on modern East Asia. The Studies of the East Asian Institute were inaugurated in 1962 to bring to a wider public the results of significant new research on modern and contemporary East Asia.

CONTENTS

PREFACE

Foreign aid has been a controversial subject in the United States. This is a study of the role of the U.S. foreign aid program in the development of one country—Thailand. The program began in 1950 and has continued, with ups and downs, through the succeeding thirty-eight years. During this period Thailand has racked up one of the strongest sustained growth records of the Third World. What can be said, with any authority or presumption, about the impact of the aid program on this experience and on the social and political evolution of Thailand in its post–World War II history?

Because of the nature of the program, an assessment of the impact of U.S. aid to Thailand must often rely on qualitative judgment rather than on quantitative evidence. For this reason I must say a few words about my personal involvement in Thailand. I do this partly to explain references to personal knowledge and assertions that do not always correspond to assertions of similarly placed authors; and partly to let readers, especially skeptics, be aware of a possible bias in this treatment of the subject of U.S.–Thai relations. I first went to Thailand in 1957 as an economist with the U.S. foreign aid program in the International Cooperation Administration (ICA), predecessor to the present aid agency, the U.S. Agency for International Development (USAID). I remained there until 1962 and subsequently earned my doctoral degree in economics from Columbia University with a dissertation on Thailand, which then appeared as a book. After a career with AID and a few years with the World Bank and the UN Development Program, including work in other countries, I returned in 1985 to serve with the Thai Government's National Economic and Social Development Board (NESDB) as an economic advisor. This study is written under funding from AID. Meanwhile I am still working for the Development Board as well as being a visiting scholar at the East Asian Institute of Columbia University.

Foreigners who live in Thailand for long periods almost invariably develop an affection for the Thai people. I am no exception. Affection does not necessarily distort one's ability to be objective. On the contrary, such feelings can sharpen one's disappointment over programs that fail to produce their putative benefits for a people whose welfare has become a matter of personal concern. I have been conscious throughout of the need to sustain objectivity, especially in a subject, foreign aid, surrounded by conflicting views. In the end it is up to the reader to decide if I have succeeded.

The economic aid program has been an important component of Thai–U.S. relations and a significant factor in Thailand's economic development. On both counts, however, this study is not a comprehensive treatment. As far as Thai–U.S. relations are concerned, the security dimensions, U.S. military operations and military aid, and the range of regional conflicts and major power interests extend far beyond the content of the development aid effort. I will examine these relationships where their pertinence to development aid has been direct, in the process hoping to provide enough information to put the development assistance program in proper perspective. Differences of view within the U.S. government (between the Embassy and the AID mission, for example, or between the mission and AID headquarters in Washington) are recounted where they are pertinent to an understanding of some of the activities and problems I examine. For the most part, however, I have focused on the aid program as it was in fact and have not extended the analysis into an exploration of the internal workings of the policymaking and implementation machinery behind the aid program.

I adopt a similar approach towards a treatment of Thailand's economic development as a whole. The focus is on the problems addressed by the aid program. Of course, the individual sectoral problems, bottlenecks, and other issues addressed by the program are significant aspects of the general development process; to draw some conclusions about the program's cumulative impact, these activities also need to be seen against the background of their most broadly defined objectives and of the economy's overall performance. At the same time it would take a much more extensive study than can be attempted here to do justice to that performance. My approach is to provide a minimal framework, though I hope it is sufficient to serve the purposes of the study. (Given the considerable changes that have taken place in Thai political and economic affairs in recent years and the country's rapid emergence in one of the world's important regions, full-scale study of the recent history of socioeconomic change in Thailand is overdue.)

My study makes no effort to do justice to the substantial development assistance provided by other countries and the international aid and finance agencies. The occasional references to the programs of other donors should be taken as reminders of their importance, especially as the U.S. program declined over the years in relative and absolute size, as I shall spell out.

Many aid projects I will discuss ran into delays in day-to-day implementation, failures to meet specifications, realization of mistakes in project design requiring midcourse correction, misunderstandings and problems of poor communication, and so on. These are normal difficulties found in any complex human endeavor. It is not surprising to find such problems more acute in foreign aid programs than at home; the aid technicians and administrators work in an environment where the whole technological and institutional framework, the ecology, and the language and culture are usually very different from the home conditions in which they learned their professions and work habits. In most cases a recounting of details of implementation problems would be tedious and would add little to an understanding of the essential purposes and outcomes of the program. In some cases, however, these details are significant and need to be spelled out to explain project results or some general characteristics of the program. Occasional details will also give the unfamiliar reader some feel for what the ordinary business of foreign aid is like.

Since July 1, 1961, the aid program has been administered by the U.S. Agency for International Development, known as USAID or AID. There are significant differences between the roles of the Washington headquarters and of the field offices; for ease of distinction, the former is commonly referred to as AID/W, while the field office (or "mission") is called, in the case of Thailand, USAID/Thailand, or USAID/T. Prior to 1961 AID had predecessor agencies established under successive aid legislation. While their names varied (Economic Cooperation Administration, Mutual Security Agency, Foreign Operations Administration, International Cooperation Administration), the aid organization continued on through the several configurations with many of the same personnel. The Bangkok mission was first established in 1950 as the Special Technical and Economic Mission (STEM), but soon had a name change to United States Operations Mission (USOM). The acronym USOM became so well known in Thailand that AID/W allowed the mission to retain USOM for several years after the rest of its field missions had adopted USAID. USOM then became USAID in 1977. On the Thai side, the mission has a counterpart agency, the Department of Technical and Economic Cooperation (DTEC). Originally set up as a counterpart to STEM in 1951 (with a slightly different name), DTEC became the coordinating agency for the Royal Thai Government (RTG) for all grant aid.

The reader unfamiliar with Thailand's geography should examine the map. The basic facts of the country's location and configuration are important to fix in mind since they have been primary determinants of the conditions shaping the aid relationship: the long border with Laos and Cambodia that circles the Northeast plateau region of the country (the poorest and largest region in area and population); the mere seventy miles (of Laotian territory) separating the northeastern corner of Thailand from Vietnam; the one hundred miles between northern Thailand and China; Thailand's central position in Southeast Asia; the focal position of Bangkok at the head of the Gulf of Thailand for the movement of the bulk of the country's trade with the rest of the world; the extreme northern provinces that form part of the drug-producing Golden Triangle area (which includes parts of Burma and Laos). North of Bangkok stretches the large Central Plain region, a rice-growing alluvial plain watered by the Chao Phrya River and its tributaries. The North and the long peninsular South are fragmented by chains of hills. Thailand is about the size of France (or four-fifths of Texas), around 200,000 square miles. It lies fairly close to the equator (Bangkok is near the fourteenth parallel) and enjoys a warm monsoonal climate. The population is about 55 million.

Thai is a tonal language and does not transliterate easily into English. The spelling of the few Thai words used below conforms to standard practice. In some cases the current standard English spelling is not the same as standard practice years ago, as will be evident from occasional quotations from earlier sources.

Much of the information and many of the insights in this book were obtained from interviews with Thais and Americans personally involved with the activities of the aid program or the development problems addressed. I owe special thanks to Dr. Snoh Unakul, former Secretary-General of the National Economic and Social Development Board, to Dr. John R. Eriksson, currently Director of the AID mission in Bangkok, and to Professor William Klausner, Professor John P. Lewis, Robert Halligan, Frederick F. Simmons, and David I. Steinberg for many fruitful encounters on the subjects of this book over many years before the idea of doing such a study arose and for their close reading of the manuscript and their many helpful comments and challenges. I learned much and made many corrections from readings of the whole or portions of the manuscript by Sunthorn Hongladarom, Professor Medhi Krongkaew, Krisda Piampongsant, John Bresnan, Robert A. Ralston; by Kamol Chantanumate, Thongkorn Hiranraks, Narintr Tima, David A. Delgado, Douglas J. Clark, Dr. Gary Suwannarat, Lawrence M. E. Brown, Willy D. Baum and other members of the AID staff in Bangkok.

There were many who gave generously of their time and their judgments, without whose help this study could not have been accomplished. Deserving particular thanks are M. L. Pin Malakul, Dr. Boonrod Binson, Apilas Osatananda, M. R. Chandram S. Chandratat, Chavalit Thananchanand, Dr. Virabongsa Ramangkura, Dr. Bunyaraks Ninsananda, Kittipan Kanjanapipatkjul, Dr. Kor Swasdi-Panich, Nikhom Chandravitoon, Dr. Pramukh Chandavimol, Prasong Sukhum, Dr. Viwek Pangputhipong, Vice Admiral Wirul Kongcham, Anek Laothamatas and Barnett Baron, Roger Berthelot, Roger Ernst, Jeffrey W. Evans, Philip A. Fishman, Philip-Michael Gary, William Gilmartin, Billy Gregg, Mintara Silawatshananai, James L. Sloan, and Lee Twentyman.

I owe a special debt to Vimol Thammamongkol for her invaluable help in extracting old financial data from USAID's files and explaining their almost forgotten accounting mysteries; to Khunying Kanitha Vichiencharoen and her staff at the Thai-American Technical Cooperation Association for the use of their files on trainees; and to Major R. J. Dunn of the Armed Forces Research Institute of Medical Sciences, Pauline Tallman, CINCPAC Command Historian, and Julie A. Martin of the Overseas Private Investment Corporation. Thanks also go to the Asia, Ford, Rockefeller, and Winrock/ADC foundations and to the Population Council for materials from their files; and to Ayesha Pande for preparing the manuscript. Finally, I want to thank Professor James W. Morley and Professor Gerald L. Curtis of the East Asian Institute of Columbia University for their generosity in providing me a research home and support facilities.

For all the debts owed, responsibility for error is my own, and my judgments and conclusions do not necessarily reflect those of either the U.S. Agency for International Development or the Thai National Economic and Social Development Board.

ABBREVIATIONS

ADB   Asian Development Bank
AID/T   Agency for International Development/Thailand
AID/W   Agency for International Development/Washington
ARD   Accelerated Rural Development
ASEAN   Association of Southeast Asian Nations
BAAC   Bank for Agriculture and Cooperatives
BOI   Board of Investment
BOT   Bank of Thailand
CINCPAC   Commander in Chief, Pacific Area Command
CIP   Commodity Import Program
CPT   Communist Party of Thailand
DA   Development Assistance
DOLA   Department of Local Administration
DTEC   Department of Technical and Economic Cooperation
EEC   European Economic Community
ESF   Economic Support Fund
FAA   Foreign Assistance Act
FY   Fiscal Year
IBRD   International Bank for Reconstruction and Development, also
           known as the World Bank
ICA   International Cooperation Administration
IFCT   Industrial Finance Corporation of Thailand
IIE   Institute for International Education
IMET   Institute for Management Education for Thailand
JPPCC   Joint Public-Private Sector Consultative Committee

Abbreviations

JUSMAG	Joint U.S. Military Advisory Group
MAP	Military Assistance Program
MSA	Mutual Security Agency
NESDB	National Economic and Social Development Board
NIC	Newly Industrializing Country
OICC	Office in Charge of Construction
PRC	People's Republic of China
PVO	Private Voluntary Organization
RTG	Royal Thai Government
SEATO	Southeast Asia Treaty Organization
TDRI	Thailand Development Research Institute
U.N.	United Nations
UNDP	United Nations Development Programme
UNESCO	U.N. Educational, Social, and Cultural Organization
USOM	U.S. Operations Mission

Thai Terms

amphur	district
baht (B)	Thai currency unit
changwat	province
rai	0.16 hectares, or 0.4 acres
tambon	subdistrict village group

CHRONOLOGY OF THAI–U.S. RELATIONS

1821 First Amerian ship reaches Bangkok.

1831 First American missionary arrives in Thailand.

1833 First Thai-American treaty, Treaty of Amity and Commerce, signed in Bangkok.

1856 Townsend Harris negotiates second treaty.

1894 Standard Oil (New York) opens a branch in Bangkok.

1902 King Vajiravudh (then Crown Prince) visits the United States.

1903 First American adviser, E. H. Strobel, appointed as General Adviser.

1920 Thai–U.S. Treaty abolishes extraterritoriality for American subjects.

1921 Minister of Education requests medical education assistance from the Rockefeller Foundation.

1926 Treaties with all European countries concluded along lines of the 1920 Thai–U.S. treaty.

1927 Future King, Bhumibol Adulyadej, is born at Mt. Auburn Hospital, Boston

1941 Japanese troops occupy Thailand, December 8.

1942 Thai Government declares war on the United States. Thai Ambassador M. R. Seni Pramoj announces that his legation is independent of the Bangkok Government. The United States refuses to recognize the declaration of war. Overseas Thai establish Free Thai movement.

1945 U.S. Secretary of State Byrnes accepts Thailand's Peace Proclamation. The United States supports position of RTG against peace terms and financial reparations proposals advanced by the British.

1950 Korean War begins. Prime Minister Pibul sends four thousand troops to support UN effort in South Korea. Economic and Technical Co-operation Agreement and Military Assistance Agreement are signed.

1954 Manila Pact is signed and SEATO is formed.

1960 Their Majesties King Bhumibol and Queen Sirikit visit the United States.

1962 Rusk-Thanat Agreement signed.

1964 U.S. aircraft and first military detachment are based in Thailand.

1966 President Johnson and Vice President Humphrey visit Bangkok.

1967 Royal Family visits the United States a second time.

1969 President Nixon visits Bangkok.

1975 The *Mayaguez* incident: U.S. marines use Thai airbases without prior Thai consent.

1976 The United States completes military withdrawal from Thailand.

1979 Prime Minister Kriangsak Chomanan visits Washington, D.C.

1980 President Carter orders airlift of weapons to Thailand.

1981 Prime Minister Prem Tinsulanonda visits the United States.

1986 U.S. Farm Bill enacted subsidizing U.S. rice exports. Agreement is reached on U.S. military material stockpiles in Thailand.

THAILAND AND THE
UNITED STATES

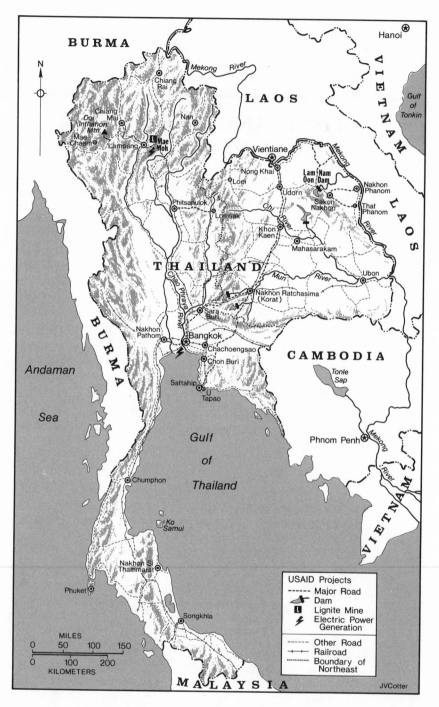

THAILAND

ONE

BACKGROUND

DEVELOPMENT AND MODERNIZATION

In a resurgence of growth in the two years 1987 and 1988, the Thai economy expanded over 18 percent. The flush of optimism was constrained only by signs that the demands of the private sector for power, transport, and other services of the country's infrastructure were straining the limits of the economy's ability to realize the growth in construction, investment, and the movement of goods that the marketplace was driving to achieve. One of the most widely discussed topics became the notion that Thailand would soon become a "NIC," a newly industrializing country, or alternatively, would soon join South Korea, Taiwan, Hong Kong, and Singapore as a fifth "Asian Tiger" economy. It is interesting to recall that in the 1950s, following the end of the Korean War, the consensus view saw a bright economic future for Thailand and a dim one for South Korea. Although Korean development has outpaced Thailand's by a considerable margin, the record of Thai economic growth has borne out the confidence that the World Bank, AID, and other observers had in the late 1950s when modern Thai development was just gathering steam.

During the 1950s the economy grew by an average of more than 5 percent per annum. In the '60s the average rate rose to 8.4 percent. Growth was slowed by the oil price rise of 1973, when Thailand was heavily dependent on petroleum imports for its commercial energy supply; but the economy quickly recovered as the world prices of the country's major export commodities also rose, and it managed to achieve an average growth rate over 7 percent for the 1970s. The second oil "shock" in 1979 had an even stronger negative impact, and in 1983–1985 the economy went into a severe slump. Despite these setbacks, economic growth continued at rates surpassed in the Third world by only a handful of countries. When Thailand's national income accounts were first being estimated in the 1950s, they yielded per capita income figures of well under $100 a year. Per capita income numbers at such low magnitude can only be used as notional indications of the status of largely subsistence economies, a reflection of the relative importance of only partially monetized agriculture and the low state of development of manufacturing, transportation, electrical, and mechanical power and urbanization. By 1986 per capita income had risen to over $800, well into the World Bank's middle-income category, thanks to the combination of economic growth and a substantial slowing in the rate of population growth.

As the economy expanded over these decades, it became increasingly diversified. Dependence on the production and export of a narrow range of primary commodities (mainly rice, rubber, teak, and tin) became a thing of the past as agriculture diversified and the manufacturing sector grew to equal agriculture in contribution to GNP (one of the rules of thumb for eligibility as a NIC) in the mid-1980s. The development of domestic energy sources lowered the country's dependence on petroleum imports and its susceptibility to the balance of payments effects of high oil prices. Tourism also became a major industry, the largest earner of foreign exchange by 1987. In the rising protectionist atmosphere of the 1980s the country's penetration into world markets for textiles, processed foods, and other products also began to draw attention to Thailand as an emerging economy and to generate occasional frictions (to which I will return below). Meanwhile the development and modernization that was taking place was accompanied by (or better, made possible by) a vast expansion of the country's human capital, its intellectual and skill resources, and the institutional infrastructure supporting and mobilizing these human resources. And by the conventional measures of human well-being, such as life expectancy at birth, infant and child mortality rates, the health status of the population, levels of literacy and educational achievement, and economic and social mobility, the economic expansion over these three decades has been generating substantial dividends.

It is important to keep these accomplishments in proper perspective. Thailand's economic status and the living standards achieved thus far by the majority of its population are still quite modest, middling by world averages and poor in comparison with the United States and other industrially advanced countries. By Thailand's own standards poverty remains a serious problem. Roughly 10 million people, or 20 percent of Thailand's population, still live below the government's poverty line. Levels of education and technology lag substantially behind that of the four Tigers. While alleviating many problems and creating a stock of material and human capital, development has also created new social, environmental, and economic problems. Although the government's development policies deserved the highest marks generally accorded by the World Bank and other development agencies, they have also been deficient in important respects at various times. Thais often refer to the comparison with Korea, noting that Thailand's per capita GNP was higher than Korea's in 1965, but that it was only one-third of Korea's in 1985. Another view, expressed to me by one of my most thoughtful Thai interlocutors, sees Thailand's more moderate success, its less than headlong plunge into industrial transformation and change in the material character of everyday life, as a blessing; Thailand's social fabric and culture have been subject to less pressure for change than would have been the case if economic growth had been more rapid.

In sum, AID and the other official and private American (and other donor) agencies that have been helping the Thais achieve their own development and change objectives have been associated with a successful experience. There are many qualifications to this success, and Thailand still has some distance to go before it reaches levels of economic, technological, and institutional self-sufficiency that would translate into full graduation out of the international development system's network for advancing the progress of relatively poor nations. Nevertheless, the Thai experience thus far has been very positive. It remains now to attempt to identify in exactly what respects and to what degree of effect, the American involvement contributed to this experience.

A FOREIGN AID PRIMER

In the jargon of economics, "foreign aid" is an unrequited transfer. The country providing the aid, the "donor," transfers resources (money, goods, food, and so on) to the "recipient" country and gets back little or nothing, or certainly less than originally transferred. The use of the term "unrequited" is not very apt in fact, since unlike the forlorn and hopeless figure conjured up by the more common image of the luckless unrequited lover, the donor of foreign aid expects the largesse to be returned. If the aid has been transferred in loan form, there is an expectation that it will be repaid, albeit at rates of interest and payback periods less onerous (that is, more "concessional") than if the same funds were acquired from commercial sources. If transferred in grant form, the donor hopes at least for good will. Whatever its components or form, the donors—the relatively rich industrialized countries—have been providing these more or less unrequited transfers for most of the post–World War II period. These donors must believe they are getting sufficient compensation, whether cast in terms of their relations with individual recipient states or with the Third World at large or in terms of the long-run benefits that are presumed to flow from economic and social advance in all countries, rising popular hopes, or strengthened mutual security in a regional or global context.

Foreign aid comes in several forms. It can be a straight cash transfer, which adds to the recipient country's foreign exchange reserves and is available immediately (mixed as it is with the country's total foreign exchange holdings) to finance general imports. Or it may be provided to finance imports in a restricted format—for example, to buy imports only from the donor country (it would then be called "tied aid")—or to finance those imports designated as eligible (that is, anything except items specified on a "negative list"). Aid for general imports that are restricted in some manner is normally called a "commodity import program" (CIP in U.S. aid terminology, also called a "program loan" if loan-financed) and is usually administered through normal commercial bank trade financing procedures.

A more restricted or targeted form of aid is the "project." Funds are allocated as a project when donor and recipient agree on detailed uses of the funds for specific activities. Capital projects finance investment costs of physical goods, construction, and other inputs that go to make up a particular facility, say a road or an irrigation system. Technical assistance projects usually comprise training, technical expertise and advice, and relatively modest amounts of equipment (perhaps for demonstration purposes); they aim to create or strengthen institutional capacity (educational, governmental, scientific, and so on), transfer and develop technology, or strengthen the recipient country's human resources. The distinction between capital and technical assistance projects often is not sharp, and many capital projects have technical components, just as technical assistance projects may have physical commodity components.

Background

Although one might expect that foreign aid would finance only identifiable goods and services not available in the recipient country (as in imports of such goods or services), there is no inherent logic in restricting aid this way. One of the common characteristics of developing countries is an inability of the government to generate enough revenue (to acquire sufficient domestic resources) to provide the complementary local inputs needed by aid-financed projects (and public sector development programs generally). Aid can help to ensure that all the resources, imported and local, can be assembled if the project financing includes some funds allocated to buying resources (such as manpower or cement) available from the domestic economy; normally dubbed "local cost" financing, this form of aid uses the dollars to buy the equivalent in the currency of the recipient country (usually bought from the country's central bank). Thus, local cost financing, in its initial step as a form of resource transfer, has the same effect as a cash transfer, adding to the recipient's import capacity.

Foreign aid may also be used by the donor for purposes other than those mentioned above, ranging from the humanitarian granting of food, medicine, and other commodities for famine, other relief, or immediate succor to the most disadvantaged poor in developing countries to the most self-serving commercial purposes of the donor. Aid that is tied only to the acquisition of goods from the donor economy or that has little provision for local currency financing has traditionally been considered less than optimal in its potential transfer size and usefulness to the recipient. It may even be harmful to the recipient, depending on the terms applied to servicing the debt (in the case of tied loan-funded projects) and on the degree to which the tying donor is not one of the more competitive or technologically suitable source countries for the equipment or technologies involved. The tying of aid can be carried to extremes in terms of the effort to extract commercial advantages. For example, during the 1960s American CIP program loans to a number of countries were administered in a way that was designed to channel importers in the recipient country to buy things from the United States they would not have bought otherwise (if accomplished, this was called "additionality"). Since then the United States has been less prone than some other donor countries to bend development assistance for commercial advantage.* (By common agreement among the donors who form the Development Assis-

---

*U.S. aid is too small to be a serious policy tool for coping with the U.S. trade deficit problem of the 1980s, and its purposes are utterly different. It is to the credit of AID administrators since the days of "additionality" that they have resisted pressures to use aid for what would be marginal additions to the volume of American exports. Aid authorities in some of the other donor countries (such as the United Kingdom) have tried to resist similar pressures.

tance Committee of the Organization for Economic Cooperation and Development [OECD], technical assistance is normally tied, while tying of loan-funded economic aid is viewed with disapproval but widely practiced.)

So far I have been speaking about aid appropriated by donor country legislatures in the form of money to be administered by their development aid agencies. Substantial amounts of aid are also authorized in the form of food (which may also be associated with funds required for shipping and handling the food). The most important foods for aid purposes have been grains because of their relatively long storage life, their basic role in the diets of most countries, and the salient economic fact that domestic agricultural support policies in many of the donors have made it profitable for their farmers to grow more grain than can be absorbed in the world's commercial grain markets. Dried milk and a few other commodities have also figured in food aid. For the United States, the title "food aid," or the legislated category of Food for Peace, is not quite accurate, since the enabling legislation (Public Law 480) has also been used to finance concessional sales of cotton and tobacco. This is a minor point in U.S. aid, but I mention it because most of the PL 480 sales to Thailand have been for tobacco. PL 480 aid can be transferred in grant or loan form, with the loan terms very concessional.

A major aid distinction is between "bilateral" and "multilateral." Bilateral aid is provided directly from a donor to a recipient country. Multilateral aid is provided by the donor country to an international development agency, such as the U.N. Development Programme of the United Nations system, the World Bank, or regional development banks. These institutions in turn use the donor financial contributions (the international banks also borrow from world capital markets for relending to developing countries) to fund technical assistance or capital (or program) loans to their developing country members. Small donor countries with relatively large aid programs (large relative to their GNP) and small aid implementing organizations (like the Netherlands) tend to put a larger proportion of their aid into the multilateral system. Food aid can also be provided bilaterally or through the multilateral UN organization, the World Food Program.

Although some technical assistance activities were conducted in Latin America during World War II, we normally think of foreign aid as having originated in 1947, when President Truman extended aid to Greece and Turkey, and in 1948, when the United States launched the Marshall Plan to revive the economies of Western Europe. This was soon followed by a general program for developing countries under

Truman's Point Four concept, which was oriented toward technical assistance rather than being a replication of the massive resource transfer concept of the Marshall Plan. Partly in response to U.S. prodding in the 1950s as the industrial countries of the West recovered their economic strength, all the OECD countries gradually began to develop aid programs. Between the growth of the U.N. development agencies (some, like the World Health Organization and the International Postal Union, preceded the United Nations by many years), the World Bank and regional development banks, the bilateral aid programs and the emergence of substantial aid from the major oil exporting countries, a vast and complex aid system has come into existence.*

ON DEFINING OBJECTIVES AND EVALUATING RESULTS

With so many donors and recipients, multilateral agencies, aid bureaucracies, and domestic interests with large stakes in how aid is used, foreign aid has also become very politicized in many of the donor countries, a highly symbolic and substantively important instrument of international relations, and an important factor in the economic development and immediate welfare (in some cases, the immediate survival) of many developing countries. Not surprisingly, there are widely conflicting views over the effects of foreign aid and its efficacy for helping to achieve the purposes for which it is appropriated and for which the general public is taxed (the proportion of total tax burden going to foreign aid is actually very small in all donor countries).

One of the results of the years of debate over foreign aid has been rising pressures in some legislatures and among professional and general public groups interested in aid substance for improved evaluation and analysis of aid projects and programs. Much work by aid practitioners has gone into the development of elaborate analytic frameworks for improving project design and for evaluating the effects of projects, both in midcourse, for making necessary changes while a project is still in progress, and after completion, to learn

---

*The Soviet Union and other socialist countries also have aid programs, but these are typically, except in a handful of countries (as in Cuba and Vietnam), quite small and are not integrated or even coordinated with the institutional arrangements that form the international aid system. The developing countries contribute modest sums to the budgets of the U.N. development agencies, and in some cases (such as India and Thailand) they have modest aid programs of their own.

lessons that can be applied to future projects. Although the United States was a leader in developing evaluation systems and urging their general adoption, even USAID's project evaluation literature does not date much before the 1970s.

The evaluation of the broad impact of an entire country aid program, stretching over many years, is much more complex than the evaluation of single projects and has been tried in very few cases, chiefly Taiwan and South Korea.[1] The "classic" first major effort was done by Neil H. Jacoby in 1966 on the economy of Taiwan and the impact of U.S. aid to Taiwan over the period 1951–1965. Jacoby found that U.S. aid had made a substantial contribution to an outstandingly successful development performance. The continuing record of economic growth of Taiwan since then is well known. In some respects the aid programs in Taiwan and Thailand were similar. Both put the bulk of the aid funds into infrastructure and human resource development, in a framework of general agreement over broad economic policy that (a) promoted monetary stability, (b) avoided detailed central planning or any U.S. pressure to bring about changes in domestic political affairs, and (c) gave wide scope for private enterprise.

In two respects however, the programs were very different. The amount of aid the United States provided to Taiwan was very much larger in relation to Taiwan's economy and population than the volume of aid to Thailand. In Taiwan aid averaged $10 per capita per annum for many years. In Thailand it was seldom over $1 per capita. In Taiwan U.S. aid made up 34 percent of gross investment; in Thailand seldom 1 percent. U.S. aid averaged 6.4 percent of Taiwan's GNP — 10 percent in the initial years. In Thailand between 1950–1970 the U.S. aid flow averaged 0.7 percent of GNP and was exceptionally high (at or near 2 percent) in only two years (1957 and 1959).[2] Only about one-fourth of U.S. aid to Taiwan was in the form of projects; the rest was in the form of nonproject aid, or general imports. In the Thai case nonproject aid has been a small portion of the total. These differences mean that in the Taiwan case, the examination of the impact of U.S. aid focused on the quantitative effects on Taiwan's macroeconomic performance. In the Thai program, the magnitude of the U.S. aid transfers was relatively small, and a search for quantitative relationships would not be a useful approach.

These differences are reflected in the previous study of U.S. aid to Thailand up to 1970 by J. Alexander Caldwell.[3] In his book Caldwell records the relatively small economic magnitudes of U.S. aid to Thailand and examines the program by reviewing the content of individual projects and the specific objectives or problems the program tried to address. Some of the issues Caldwell reviewed in detail seem less worth pursuing nearly twenty years later (such as the history of the aid mission's internal reorganizations); others have remained important in subsequent years and can now be reconsidered in the light of hindsight (such as the counterinsurgency efforts).

The Thai aid program has been made up of over 350 "projects," which are defined as separate, formal financial accounting units. Many of these individual projects comprised several subprojects. Additional activities have been funded out of project accounts held in AID/W and thus do not appear in the Thai mission's books. Many projects can be viewed as clusters of activities aimed at a common objective. Others represented one-time efforts to assist in some problem or subsector— in some cases very minor efforts in terms of funds, training, or expertise. The clusters form obvious subjects for a systematic review of the program's history. Among the variety of one-time projects, I have tried to identify those of significance and have left encyclopedic completeness to the program tables in the annex. If it were possible to count individual activities that were separate "units of management," which together have made up the totality of the aid program in Thailand, this complete universe of activities would probably add up to over five hundred components.

My study of the effects of U.S. development assistance to Thailand will not address certain of the big foreign aid issues that have been debated over the years for several reasons:

1. U.S. aid to Thailand was not large enough in relation to Thailand's own resources to be relevant to the hoary debates over whether or not aid was truly incremental, either as an addition to the country's net savings rate, as a reliever of balance of payments pressures, or as an addition to the public sector's investment levels. In cases where the volume of resource transfer has been "large" relative to these economic magnitudes, critics of aid have claimed that aid succeeds only in allowing the recipient government to continue unwise economic policies affecting these magnitudes, which they would have otherwise been forced to put right. In other words, according to this view, aid has permitted, if not encouraged, bad policy. Less severe criticism has maintained that because resources are interchangeable, the recipient economy and society make adjustments that in effect enable consumption to rise, while the aid is used to substitute for investment that would have been financed in the absence of aid, albeit with more immediate belt-tightening. The U.S. aid experience in Thailand does not speak to such questions. In this respect Thailand is more typical of U.S. aid practices than the handful of cases (Korea,

Taiwan, Israel, Egypt, Bangladesh, and other countries for short periods) where the aid volume has been large relative to the recipient economy. For a few years in particular, as we shall see, the volume of U.S. aid to Thailand was large in some sectors for some purposes, but it was not in total of orders of magnitude for significantly long enough periods to be classified as having enduring macroeconomic impact through the sheer additionality of the resources made available to the country.

2. Thailand has received very little food aid. In only two years was the aid received under PL 480 not "negligible," and even then the commodity provided was mainly tobacco. Thus none of the classic food aid questions arises in the Thai case (disincentive effects on local farmers through the depressing of local food grain prices; disincentive effects on government food policies by allowing governments to avoid taking tough production-augmenting decisions or on tax policies by allowing the government to earn substantial revenues through the local sale of the food aid).*

3. The Thai aid program has been composed largely of projects. Grant financing for general imports (in earlier years "program" assistance was called "nonproject" aid) was provided to Thailand between 1955 and 1962. In the peak year of 1961 nonproject aid was only $18.4 million. These funds were used to generate local currency (deposited into a counterpart fund) to help finance the domestic costs of projects, mainly civil and military construction. The amounts were small (2–3 percent) in relation to Thailand's total imports and were not associated with macropolicy change (as is often the case with large program aid). Thus the standard issues that have been associated with nonproject aid from time to time in other countries (CIP administration and additionality, economic policy dialogue) do not arise in the Thai case as an aspect integral to the resource transfer process itself.

There are many aid issues to which the Thai program experience does speak: the efficiency with which aid is administered; the effectiveness of aid as an instrument of U.S. foreign policy; the effectiveness of aid for promoting economic advance in a poor country; and some of the distributional questions (does aid just tax the poor in the rich countries for the benefit of the rich in the poor countries?). The Thai program also may have some relevance to aid critics on the Left, who argue that aid creates enhanced "dependence" of the recipient country on the more powerful economy of the donor and that the aid

---

*The classic food aid question of the impact of the PL 480 sales on normal commercial marketing did arise in Thailand's case when the RTG viewed occasional sales of rice to Indonesia as injurious to normal marketing of Thai rice exports.

relationship's a wedge for donor "intervention" into the domestic affairs of the recipient. The harshest criticism on the Left is that aid is an instrument of imperialism, used by the donor to persuade (or entrap or force) a recipient government to adopt policy positions it would not pursue otherwise. The harshest criticism on the Right is that aid is detrimental to development because aid agencies deal mainly with government, put aid resources into the government sector, and thereby weaken the private sector that is a much more powerful engine for growth. This study is not a general treatment of foreign aid, American or otherwise. But on many of these issues the Thai case is pertinent and should be taken into account in any discussion that pretends to take empirical instances seriously. My conclusion is that the Thai aid experience cannot be used to support any of the above assertions.

FOREIGN AID OBJECTIVES
AND CONSTRAINTS

In order to understand the role of the Thai aid program and be in position to reach some conclusions and judgments, it is necessary to know what the objectives of the program were, what the program did to reach those objectives, and what the results were.

To be clear about the objectives, it is helpful to distinguish between the primary, or ultimate, goals and the numerous instrumental, or subsidiary, objectives that are expected to contribute toward achievement of the primary purposes. Foreign aid is an instrument of foreign policy for the United States and for all other donor countries. The primary objectives must be seen (and are so described in the justifications presented to the Congress by successive U.S. administrations) in terms of overall U.S. national interests, in this case in Southeast Asia and in the relationship between the United States and Thailand. These primary objectives concerned no less than the integrity of the Thai state in the face of regional threats and the internal stability and economic development that have been judged by successive Thai and American governments as essential conditions for maintaining Thailand's external security. There were significant changes in the sources and nature of the threats to Thai security over the period I am examining and concomitant changes in Thai government policies and in the aid and other efforts of the United States to support those policies.

To help achieve the primary objectives, the aid program set up a number of sectoral or problem-solving goals: specific improvements in living conditions, better access to isolated regions, more effective and responsive government administration, and so on. These specific objectives were adopted because they appeared to be essential instrumental conditions, directly determining the ability of the Thai government to meet the challenges to Thai security. Given the politics of foreign aid in the United States, intensive Congressional oversight, and the pressures within AID (and its predecessor agencies) to raise the effectiveness of the program's performance (and the ability of the agency to document that performance), foreign aid has left a long, public paper trail that describes the objectives in each country year by year and how the program relates to these objectives, project by project.

The objectives and program content in any one country are set through a complex process of interaction between the recipient government and the AID mission in the country and between the AID mission and the agency's headquarters in Washington. Within the framework of the legislation as it stands in any one year, Washington develops general guidelines within which the field missions, in dialogue with their counterparts in the host government, develop their program proposals. The general guidelines are modified by additional guidelines written in AID's separate regional bureaus, more tailored to the conditions of each respective region. The field proposals are reviewed and modified by AID/W, put together into an integrated agency budget proposal, and brokered out with the Department of State, the Office of Management and Budget, and, where necessary, the White House. The final administration foreign assistance budget proposal, with volumes of program and project detail, is then submitted to Congress. The appropriations that result from the congressional process are reprogrammed (to take account of the actual funds made available, changes in legislation or statements of congressional intent, and changes in recipient country circumstances during this lengthy process) and allocated to missions (or Washington-based units of the organization that have programs managed from headquarters). The actual allocation of funds to the missions, along with authority to implement any individual project, is made only after each project has passed through a lengthy process of project development and review.

The annual planning guidelines and instructions the agency sends out to the field missions and the standard guidelines prepared annually by the agency's lawyers contain a mixed bag of legislative and executive branch constraints and heterogeneous and not necessarily consistent goals. In the overhaul of the aid legislation in 1973, Congress attempted to draw a sharper line between development and foreign policy. Different criteria were applied to funds appropriated under various development categories than were applied to security-oriented appropriation categories, although the different categories continued to be appropriated under the umbrella Foreign Assistance Act (FAA), which has remained the basic legislation, though it was subsequently amended. Thailand, like many recipient countries, has received a changing mix of Development Assistance (DA) and Economic Support Funds (ESF), the two categories of monies (and earlier different appropriation categories) applied toward different kinds of problems and objectives. Under the 1973 legislation, the primary objective for DA funds became economic development—more precisely, the alleviation of poverty. Given USAID/T's long focus on poverty alleviation as one factor determining loyalty and security conditions in rural areas in Thailand, it may seem that the 1973 emphasis on equity introduced a distinction in philosophy with no difference in program content. In fact, the distinction did affect the content of the program in Thailand quite fundamentally because of the way the congressional instructions were interpreted by AID. Thus the security-development link remained at the heart of the rationale for the aid program, but the redefinition of appropriation categories and purposes and the agency's interpretation of how to carry out the congressional intent led to substantial changes in the program's content.

The aid programs in virtually all countries are also affected by a large number of constraints that are either imbedded in the legislation or imposed by agency (or administration) policy. For example, the law mandates that aid funds cannot be used to promote the production of any commodity that might then be exported by the developing country in competition with U.S. exports. This constraint was introduced in FY 1988.[4] If it had been operative in the 1950s, it would have hobbled the ability of the program to help achieve what turned out to be significant advances in Thai agriculture and in the incomes of poor Thai farmers.

The law also imposes a host of constraints on the way AID does its business, constraints that reduce the agency's operational flexibility. Whether or not these "barnacles," as they are called, are assets or liabilities depends on one's point of view, of course. One provision, for example, requires AID to ship at least 50 percent of all aid-financed commodities in U.S.-flag ships.* This provision throws some business

---

*Section 603 of the Foreign Assistance Act provides only very limited exemption to the requirement of the Merchant Marine Act of 1936 that at least 50 percent of cargo financed by the U.S. government should be shipped in privately owned U.S. flag vessels. The cost of shipping in U.S. vessels is higher than in foreign flag ships. The difference "represents a

to the U.S. maritime, though of marginal size for the objective of helping to sustain the shipping industry for its potential role in national security; but the higher cost of shipping in U.S. bottoms reduces the size of the resources the aid program can actually make available to the recipient countries. In this case, aid is being made to serve two different objectives, one at the cost of the other. A second example is a provision requiring AID to allocate at least 10 percent of its procurement (from the Development Assistance and Sahel funding accounts)* to minority firms and organizations and to "historically black" colleges and universities.[5] The search for minority firms with the relevant capabilities can add delays to the project implementation process, as has occurred in the Thai program in connection with a recent project concerning rural industrialization. Affirmative action is well established as an instrument of U.S. domestic social policy, but can increase the costs and administrative complexities for achieving the objectives of foreign aid to poor countries.

Finally, if we are to reach some conclusions about the program's successes and failures in terms of its primary objectives, if we try to make the connections between instrumental and final targets and achievements, we need to put all this activity in its relevant context. What was Thailand like when the program began? What progress has been made in overcoming the problems addressed by the program? How has the economy performed, and what economic development has been achieved over the thirty-eight years? How has Thai external and internal security evolved? From the vantage point of 1988, what conclusions can be drawn regarding the role of the U.S. aid program and the other major American development programs as factors in Thailand's postwar experience?

In trying to form a judgment about the impact of American involvement in Thai development, it will also be important to look for effects that were not intended, especially effects on the country's political evolution. Economic development and political change are closely linked. The AID program could not possibly have been conducted as if economic development were an independent track of

---

substantial subsidy to U.S. vessel operators and reduces the funds that would otherwise be available to AID recipient countries for the purchase of commodities. . . . These direct costs have been running in the range of $100 to $200 million per year in the 1982–1984 period." It is ironic that the economic justification for subsidy to the U.S. maritime appears "quite dubious," while the national security rationale (namely to help sustain a maritime capacity for potential wartime use) is also weak ("There is virtually no military sealift requirement for dry bulk carriers [and] roughly two thirds of the cargo preference costs are associated with shipments on dry bulk carriers.") This analysis includes shipments of food aid under PL 480. See "Report on Cargo Preference," prepared by IPAC, Inc. (International Planning and Analysis Center), for AID (Washington, D.C., September 1985), from which these excerpts are drawn.

* Sahel refers to countries along the semi-arid strip of Africa south of the Sahara Desert.

activities with no significant political interactions. Quite apart from the minor politics of daily project implementation or the more important politics of program design, aid allocation, and the effects of the aid process and resources on the distribution of power within the Thai bureaucracy, there are larger questions concerning effects on aspects of Thai political processes, such as those concerning the decentralization of power and the evolution of democratic forms during this period. Since at certain stages the AID program included internal security as one of its primary objectives, actually cofinanced military facilities in its early years, reached into virtually every corner of the country and every sector of economic activity, and carried out a number of projects with explicit political implications, an examination of the program's economic development role alone would ignore some of the principal reasons for providing the assistance. However, while I will examine the impact of the aid program on Thailand's internal security problems, I make no original research in this respect. I believe the conclusions with respect to this very important piece of the aid program's history are firmly based, although a full treatment of this now completed episode in Thailand's history would take much more extensive analysis.

Finally, I make no attempt to explore the history of American assistance to the Thai police (first from the Central Intelligence Agency beginning in 1957 and subsequently from AID's Office of Public Safety) or to review the literature on the effectiveness of this aid. The AID projects assisted both normal police functions (crime suppression, fingerprinting, railway police, marine policing to reduce smuggling in the Bangkok port, and so on) and intelligence and paramilitary functions. The latter were related to the broad AID effort to assist Thai counterinsurgency programs, which I will examine below. But a review of the effectiveness of execution of the security and policing functions themselves would be beyond the scope of this study or my competence.

TWO

THAI-AMERICAN RELATIONS: SECURITY AND DEVELOPMENT

The governments of Thailand and the United States have had formal relationships since 1833, initiated with a Treaty of Amity and Commerce. The relationships were cordial up to World War II, perhaps for the very reason that they were distant. That is to say the Thais saw the United States as one major Western country that had no imperial designs in Southeast Asia (the Philippines not withstanding) or on Thailand in particular. In fact, the Thais employed an American, Francis B. Sayre, as advisor to their Foreign Office between 1920 and 1927. Sayre, who was President Wilson's son-in-law, helped Thailand (then called Siam) renegotiate the country's nineteenth-century treaties to eliminate the extraterritoriality and other provisions that had infringed on Thailand's sovereignty in its relations with Western powers, including the United States. Since the end of World War II the relationship has developed into a close one of complex economic and security interests.

On the economic side, the United States has become Thailand's largest export market. In 1986 U.S. imports from Thailand reached $1.9 billion. With exports to Thailand of over $900 million, the United States ran a deficit that year of around $1 billion in the bilateral trade account. (Thai trade data is based on a different accounting system and shows smaller figures for the value of Thai exports to the United States and for the size of the resulting U.S. bilateral trade deficit.) Among the leading commodities Thailand supplies to the United States are apparel and textiles, canned tuna, integrated circuits, canned pineapple and juice, jewelry and precious stones, rubber, tin, tobacco leaf, artificial flowers, and frozen marine products. Thailand's imports from the United States include cotton, tobacco, wheat and other agricultural commodities, fertilizer, machinery, chemicals, and office equipment. The United States is the largest foreign investor in Thailand, with the value of total cumulated private American investment in the country estimated at over $4 billion. Nearly half of this investment is in oil and gas production and distribution, one-quarter in banking and finance, the rest in manufacturing and trade. Given the relative sizes of the two economies, it is not surprising that these economic relationships are asymmetrical, much more important relatively for Thailand than for the United States. Thus Thai exports to the United States represented 18 percent of total Thai exports in 1986, but only 0.5 percent of total U.S. imports. The relatively large U.S. investment in Thailand amounts to less than 2 percent of total U.S. investment in other countries.

For Thailand the United States emerged after World War II as the principal guarantor of the country's independence against hostile regional powers. For the United States, Thailand became an important regional ally, a "front-line state" in an area threatened both by overt Communist Chinese and Vietnamese expansionist policies and by domestic insurgencies aligned with revolutionary Communist regimes. Thailand was a pro-Western, strongly anti-Communist country, with a history of cautious adjustment and deliberate modernization aimed at integration into the world economy of the market-oriented Western powers.

The basis for this new relationship was set in the events surrounding Thailand's wartime position and the conditions of settlement of World War II hostilities in Asia. In 1940 Thailand had approached Britain and the United States for assistance (oil, armaments, and airplanes) in the face of a possible Japanese attack. The RTG even attempted to get a declaration from the two countries that they would consider such an attack as an act of aggression against themselves. Although the British Government did issue a statement to this effect, the United States, not yet at war and advised by the ambassador in Bangkok who was apparently distrustful of Thai policy, was not responsive. Three months before the Japanese attack on Pearl Harbor, the U.S. position was turned around by a new ambassador, but the United States had neither the ability nor the time to translate this sympathy for Thailand's exposed situation into concrete support. Japanese troops landed at six points along Thailand's coast on December

8, 1941, the day after Japan declared war on the United States. The Thai armed forces were in no position to offer serious resistance. After three days the RTG signed a treaty of alliance with Japan that, among other things, gave the Japanese military transit rights in Thailand and left the governing of the country in the hands of the Thais.

The transit rights allowed the Japanese army to attack Malaya and Singapore by land from the north, a contingency for which the British had not prepared. As a result, Britain considered Thailand a belligerent power and accepted the declaration of war issued by the Thai Prime Minister, Field Marshal Pibulsonggram, as defining Thailand's status in the conflict. In Washington, by contrast, the Thai ambassador, M. R. Seni Pramoj, refused to accept the legitimacy of his government's treaty with Japan or the declaration of war on the United States and formed the Free Thai resistance movement to work with the Allied powers. By the end of the war, Pibulsonggram (commonly referred to as Pibul) had been forced out. Immediately after Japan's surrender the new Thai government repudiated the declaration of war on the United Kingdom and the United States as having been illegal and contrary to the will of the country. On August 21, 1945, Secretary of State Byrnes accepted this position. The British Foreign Secretary, Ernest Bevin, responded with a statement calling for Thai reparations and saying that the British attitude would depend on how Thailand met "the requirements of our troops now about to enter their country."

The stage was now set for a confrontation between the United States and Britain over the economic and political conditions of Thailand's reentry into the postwar world. The events that followed are familiar to every Thai schoolchild, but probably known by few Americans. Over several months of difficult negotiations, the British attempted to secure Thai agreement to a peace treaty that would have severely compromised Thai sovereignty and imposed heavy reparation payments. According to one account, "Largely due to the United States government's objections to the original proposal, Thailand escaped becoming a quasi-British colony."[1] I need not go into the details of U.S. involvement in these negotiations. The essential point is that if the United States had not played the role it did, the integrity of the Thai state—the central object of Thai foreign policy and domestic modernization for the previous hundred years—would have been substantially compromised.

THE SECURITY RELATIONSHIP AND ITS DEVELOPMENT DIVIDEND

A two-pronged economic and military aid relationship between the United States and Thailand developed surprisingly quickly starting in 1950, reversing a brief cooling in relations that had been precipitated by a military coup in Thailand in 1947 and the return to power of Prime Minister Pibul. Reflecting U.S. concern over the regional implications of a rising Communist China and insurgencies operating in several countries, Ambassador-at-Large Philip C. Jessup was sent on a fact-finding mission in early 1950 to explore the needs of countries in the region for increasing their economic and military strength. Acting on Jessup's recommendation, a second mission arrived in April 1950 to examine Thailand's economic needs more closely.* By September both the Fulbright education exchange program and the economic aid agreements had been signed. The sudden North Korean invasion of South Korea in June 1950 propelled both governments into the security relationship that has continued ever since, despite a near interruption in the mid-1970s. Between 1950 and 1980 about 18,000 Thai officers had received training in the United States. American military equipment has been provided to the Thai armed forces under various loan and grant programs administered by the Department of Defense. American combat units have been stationed in Thailand at various times, in strengths and configurations reflecting changing conditions in Southeast Asia and the mutual perceptions of the two governments regarding their regional security requirements. And Thailand sent combat units to fight alongside U.S. troops in both the Korean and Vietnam wars.

Almost immediately after the Korean War broke out, Pibul announced the Thai government's support of the United Nations' effort to repel North Korean troops and the dispatch of a 4,000-man contingent of Thai soldiers to fight under the U.N. command, A month after the economic aid agreement was signed, a military assistance agreement was initialed under which the United States would provide equipment and training for the Thai armed forces.

Under the military assistance agreement, a U.S. military mission was established in Bangkok, subsequently called the Joint U.S. Mili-

---

*The chief of this mission, R. Allen Griffin, saw his objective as "formulating 'a constructive program of aid' to help prevent in Southeast Asia a repetition of the circumstances leading to the fall of China." In 1951 the U.S. Ambassador to Thailand Edward Stanton said he expected China to try to take over several countries in the region "sometime this year," including Thailand "sooner or later." Cited in Caldwell, *American Economic Aid to Thailand,* p. 39.

tary Advisory Group (JUSMAG). To meet both economic and security objectives, assistance for strengthening the surface transport systems between Bangkok and Northeast Thailand had begun by 1954 under the economic aid program (described in more detail below) in the wake of the Geneva accords under which France withdrew from Indochina and the separate North and South Vietnamese states were established. A parallel program to construct military support facilities was initiated in 1955 under the administration of a second U.S. military organization called the Office in Charge of Construction (OICC), which was headed by U.S. Navy Corps of Engineer personnel. The OICC had a staff of about one hundred persons of whom two-thirds were Thai and the rest U.S. civilians, apart from the three-man Navy management team.

The history of U.S. military construction in Thailand falls into two periods that track the changing security circumstances between the years 1955 and 1975.[2] During the first period, from 1955 to about 1963, there was an $18 million program of limited airfield improvements, installation of a military communications network between Bangkok and the Northeast, and construction of contingency-oriented facilities at the Sattahip naval base on the eastern coast of the Gulf of Thailand. In addition, alongside Royal Thai Army engineering battalions, U.S. Navy Seabee units built a road to connect Sattahip with the Northeast gateway town of Korat, bypassing Bangkok. As with the AID highway projects on the route connecting Bangkok with Nongkai, these military aid projects were designed to strengthen Thailand's internal military mobility in the face of possible threats from the People's Republic of China (PRC) or from North Vietnam, emanating through a weak and unstable Laos. The facilities at Sattahip and the improvements of the Northeast airfields were intended to increase Thailand's ability to receive and deploy military reinforcements from the United States in the event it became necessary for the two countries to act under the terms of the formal mutual security arrangements established in September 1954 with the initialing of the SEATO treaty.

The second period of military construction projects began in the wake of the crisis in Laos in 1960–1961 and the beginning of the U.S. build-up in South Vietnam in early 1962. In Laos a civil war broke out between the rival left and right factions supported by the North Vietnamese and the Thais, respectively. The war was resolved at the Geneva conference on Laos in July 1962, which installed a coalition government in Vientiane. By then there were clear indications that the Communist Party of Thailand (CPT) had launched an insurgency movement in the Northeast, supported by North Vietnam and the PRC. The Thai Government had declared the CPT illegal in the Anti-Communist Act of 1952. The party had spent the next several years building up cadre and organization in the Northeast, following a Maoist rural strategy and sending people to the PRC and North Vietnam for training. Although the CPT formally adopted a policy of armed revolution in 1961, the first clash did not come until August 1965. Meanwhile, Thailand's relations with Cambodia were deteriorating as Cambodia's Prince Norodom Sihanouk tried to strengthen his position by developing closer ties to the PRC. And to the east of Cambodia and Laos the struggle between North and South Vietnam had opened up, ending the peace of the 1954 Geneva accords.

In the face of the rising threat from North Vietnam, the fragility of the Laotian neutralist settlement and the Cambodian buffer, and the incipient domestic insurgency supported by both Vietnam and the PRC, the Thai government saw the country confronted by profound threats to its integrity. The Thais turned to the United States to strengthen the security relationship.

Although the underlying mutuality of interests was strong, the Thais sought further reassurance of the U.S. commitment. Their concern over the extent of overlap of Thai and U.S. interests arose from their misgivings about the Kennedy Administration's policy to pursue a neutral coalition government solution in Laos that would include the Communist Pathet Lao faction. The United States provided the desired reassurance through a visit to Bangkok in early 1962 by Attorney General Robert Kennedy and through the joint statement issued in March 1962 by Foreign Minister Thanat Khoman and Secretary of State Dean Rusk. The statement asserted that the U.S. "regards the preservation of the independence and integrity of Thailand as vital to the national interests of the United States." It also removed a constraint in the terms of the SEATO treaty by affirming that the U.S. commitment to help Thailand meet any aggression was "individual as well as collective"—that is, the United States would act even without consensus to do so on the part of the other SEATO members.[3] The statement issued by Thanat and Rusk has stood as a commitment of American policy for twenty-seven years. It has been reaffirmed time and again by subsequent U.S. administrations.

The second phase of military construction in Thailand was designed to expand the network of Thai airbases that could be used for American air operations. U.S. involvement in the Vietnam conflict was growing, and Thailand offered direct military participation. The first deployment of U.S. combat units in Thailand had occurred as a show of force in March 1961 in connection with the Laotian crisis. When the threat appeared to abate within a few months, the units were withdrawn. By May 1962 the situation had deteriorated again, and the two governments agreed to move U.S. units back into Thailand. By the end of that year the Laotian coalition settlement had been negotiated, and all American combat units were withdrawn a second time. The big build-up of U.S. forces in Thailand began in 1966, when the Sattahip port, the nearby U Tapao airfield (the biggest in Southeast Asia), and the other jet fields being installed under the military construction program became operational. U.S. Airforce units remained in Thailand until 1975, although some force withdrawals began immediately after the cease-fire in Vietnam in June 1973. By December of 1975 the last U.S. combat aircraft were withdrawn, and all facilities turned over to the Thai government. The last airforce personnel left Thailand in July 1976. The only U.S. military personnel remaining in Thailand were the 270 advisors in the JUSMAG mission and a small joint medical research unit. The work of the medical unit continues and is described below. The JUSMAG has also continued in operation to administer U.S. military assistance programs. The American staff has declined to about thirty-five.

Much of the U.S. investment in the supportive military infrastructure in Thailand was purely military in character—barracks, radar, communications, and so on. But the program also included substantial construction of transportation facilities that were either immediate additions to the country's economic infrastructure or may yet revert to general use. The individual civil works projects are listed in table A.19. The most important dual-use projects to date have been the asphalt roads. As the reader will see from the map, the 264-kilometer Route 304 between Chachoengsao and Korat and the 127-kilometer Route 331 from Sattahip to Chachoengsao are north-south roads located in the central cone of the country, while Routes 22 and 223 are provincial roads on the periphery of the Northeast. The first two (the so-called Bangkok bypass) provided direct connection between the Sattahip port–U Tapao airbase complex and the Northeast highway system so that military traffic between the main entry complex and the Northeast could avoid having to circle through Bangkok.

Before Highway 304 was constructed as a modern road, built to U.S. specifications, it was a narrow laterite trail. It traversed a densely forested and very sparsely inhabited area. A study of the effects of the new roadway on a 540-square-kilometer area a mere two years after its completion, showed very rapid change.[4] There was a substantial increase in traffic, some of which was heavy trucking diverted from the Friendship Highway, a major AID project opened in 1957–1958 in order to relieve the vehicular load on the latter. Extensive areas in the zone of influence of Highway 304 had been cleared and thousands of migrants from other provinces had moved in and settled as home-steaders. The highway had opened up a new area for settlement by farm families leaving other areas under rising population pressure. The land that then came under active economic use was yielding timber, wood for charcoal, corn for export to Japan, and other minor crops. These benefits, however, were being wrung from a fragile envi-ronment. The soils in the area are poor in structure and low in nu-trients. Some of the settlers had come from upland areas and were accustomed to a rotational (slash and burn) system, under which any one plot was cultivated one year in ten and allowed to undergo a natural nutrient regeneration during the nine fallow years. These settlers might have established a sustainable system that would have maintained yield levels. Other settlers had come from lowland areas where the annual flooding had sustained the natural nutrient levels of the soil and were unaccustomed to a rotational regime. As the popu-lation rose rapidly, it was already apparent in the early 1970s that the rotational settlers were being crowded into shorter fallow periods and that yields were falling. Other problems were appearing because the absence of previous development meant that there was little in the way of government institutional framework, especially concerning land claims and titling. Responding to the pressures as they emerged, various government services (such as schools) were moving in and the settlers themselves were undergoing rapid adjustments (of technol-ogy, settlement patterns, abandonment and out-migration, and the like).

Altogether we have a mixed picture of economic benefits, new opportunities for populations from areas under land pressure, and increased access for the Northeast region through a new route alter-native to the Friendship Highway, along with environmental costs, conflicts among settlers competing for lands with ill-defined claims, and pressures on government for new services. Unfortunately, I know of no study of the same area that describes the outcome of this, in effect, pioneering process, what sort of ownership pattern developed among the settlers, and how successfully they adapted their technol-ogies to the characteristics of the soil. Heng Liong Thung's early impact study does serve to give some idea of the complexity of impact from highway penetration of previously unoccupied land and of the care an observer must exercise in an attempt to understand, let alone judge, the development process such interventions initiate.

While the current traffic levels of the Bangkok bypass roads do not place them among the major arteries of the road system, they are important routes and are likely to become more so as the Eastern Seaboard area at the head of the Gulf of Thailand develops as another regional focus for urban and industrial activity, second to Bangkok. There are no studies of the impact of the other OICC roads. Route 22 connects the provincial capitals of Sakon Nakhon and Nakhon Phanom and forms a last 54-kilometer leg of the main highway traversing the northern half of the Northeast region of the country. At around 6,000 vehicles a day (including motorcycles) in 1986, it is relatively well traveled. Route 223 extends southwest 70 kilometers from Sakon Nakhon to That Phanom on the Mekong River and was carrying about one-fourth the traffic of Route 22 in 1986. The fifth and last military road built was Route 1009, a 48-kilometer side road constructed to give access to the top of Doi Inthanon, the highest peak in Thailand, where the United States sited a radar installation. This road climbs through very picturesque mountain country and has become a tourist attraction for visitors to northern Thailand. The identifiable cash cost of the five roads has been put at around $15 million, excluding the regular operating costs of the Thai Army engineering battalions and the U.S. Army engineer and Naval Seabees units involved.

Eight airfields (U Tapao, Tahkli, Korat, Udorn, Ubon, Nam Phong, Kamphaeng Saen, and Chiangmai) were brought up to combat standards under the military construction program; three of these were entirely new facilities. Two of the fields, Udorn and Ubon, were for many years after the only Northeast locations with scheduled civil airline service. After recent terminal expansion, Chiang Mai has become an international airport. Medium-sized jets now serve this increasingly popular tourist destination. Korat has had occasional civil air service, while the giant runway at U Tapao has served as a backup to Bangkok's Don Muang airport for bad weather or other emergencies. In late 1987 the Thai Cabinet instructed the Ministry of Communication to draw up plans to restore unused U.S.–built airfields for commercial traffic. The Cabinet also revived the idea of developing U Tapao for international commercial use, one of the options for the early 1990s, when Don Muang is projected to reach capacity utilization.[5]

The largest program of the entire U.S. military construction effort was the building of the Sattahip–U Tapao complex. Sattahip was first designated as a naval district in 1914 and became an operational base for the Royal Thai fleet in 1922. Before the U.S. construction program, however, the navy had installed only minor facilities. In the first phase in 1961–1963, only limited facilities were installed as part of the contingency planning at that time. During the second phase, 1963–1969, a complete operational port was built, including a 3,600-foot quay wall, a dredged harbor, nine-berth docks, POL pier and loading and storage space. At its peak use, the port/airfield complex was served by a force of 10,000 U.S. and Thai military and civilian employees. In recent years the port has been open for limited civilian shipping use but seldom actually utilized. With constraints imposed by the Royal Thai Navy, limitations of access to the port area and of storage facilities, and the level of fees charged by the Port Authority of Thailand, there has been little incentive for private shippers to use Sattahip despite the growing problems and costs of the main Bangkok port on the Chao Phya River. Although there is much room for improvement in the efficiency of operation of the Bangkok port, there is no doubt that the country's growing international trade requires substantial augmentation of port capacity on the Gulf of Thailand coastline. While some more southerly minor ports are being expanded down the peninsular region, the RTG has for several years been developing the deepsea port potential of the Eastern Seaboard coastal area running southeast of the Bangkok area (at locations above and below Sattahip) as the major alternative port complex for the country's trade. It is in this context that the potential use of Sattahip for civilian commercial shipping has been hotly debated from time to time.

In mid-1988 the surge of commodity trade movement through the port of Bangkok brought to a sudden head both the need to break the bottlenecks constraining commercial use of Sattahip and the urgency of correcting some of the management problems of Bangkok port (which I need not detail here). The measures adopted to cope with the Bangkok port congestion crisis included a reduction in Sattahip port fees, the first significant step reflecting the pressures on the RTG to exploit Sattahip's economic potential. Thus, after twenty years, it appears that the U.S. construction project for military shipping to Thailand may also begin to yield economic benefits.

The close links between the security and development objectives of both governments and between the U.S. military and economic assistance programs are well illustrated by these dual-use facilities, especially the roads increasing access to and mobility within the Northeast. Over the years, in response to the changing threats to Thailand's security as seen by succeeding U.S. and Thai governments (namely, the PRC, Pathet Lao, CPT insurgents with North Vietnamese backing, then North Vietnam's southern expansion and subsequent occupation of Cambodia), mobility for Thai armed forces, access to remote areas, bases for U.S. air operations, and development programs in the Northeast have been basic ingredients of Thai policy and of U.S. aid. Both the economic and military aid programs constructed major access highways and local access routes. These were designed for use by Thai security forces, by government economic and social services personnel previously absent from these areas, and by merchants who could extend the money economy into isolated areas. As noted below, some of the local currency for financing OICC construction projects was generated by nonproject aid appropriated to AID (ICA) and has been carried on U.S. books as economic aid. The USOM held these funds in the counterpart account and transferred them to OICC as needed. The total amount of such counterpart financing was about $35 million, roughly 7 or 8 percent of the total OICC construction program cost.

The OICC projects as a group, and the Sattahip–U Tapao complex in particular, comprised the largest and most complex civil engineering program ever undertaken in Thailand up to that time. The total cost of all OICC projects has been put at nearly $500 million. Unlike Highway 304, which had been constructed by Thai and U.S. military engineering units, the OICC projects were built by U.S. and Thai private contractors. More than 40,000 Thais were employed on these projects. For both the individual workers and the Thai contractors the OICC projects provided on-the-job training experience in construction, engineering, and design on a scale the country had never seen before. Combined with AID engineering projects underway during the same years, these activities created the first major demand for a Thai private engineering and construction sector and provided the engineering and management oversight that sector needed to respond to an unprecedented opportunity.

Returning to the chronology of the framework of Thai–U.S. relations, the mid-1970s was a period of strain in which Thailand had to adjust its foreign policy to take account of the impact of the Vietnam withdrawal and President Nixon's opening of American relations with China. Political upheaval in Thailand (described below) had forced out the country's military regime and ushered in a three-year period of civilian rule and open democratic politics. These years were marked by considerable unrest, even anti-American feeling among university students. The United States was criticized as having drawn Thailand into antagonistic relationships with its neighbors and then having left Thailand to cope with the consequences. Criticism of the United States also served as an attack on the military regime with which the United States was associated. The students were particularly strident in their calls for immediate withdrawal of U.S. troops. The troops were withdrawn on schedule, as already noted, although the JUSMAG remained. (It was noteworthy, however, that the anti-American demonstrations were never directed against USOM or the development aid program.)

The nadir in the relationship came in May 1975. The Khmer Rouge had just seized power in Cambodia. When American marines were mobilized in response to the seizure of the U.S. vessel the *Mayaguez* by the Khmer Rouge, they landed at Thai airbases without prior notification or consent from the Thai government. The RTG recalled its ambassador in protest. To cope with the new alignment of power in Southeast Asia, especially after the Vietnamese occupation of Cambodia in 1979 (in which Vietnam replaced the hostile Khmer Rouge with a Cambodian government of its own creation), Thailand turned to its refashioned and now cordial relationship with the People's Republic of China and to the regional support it derived from its fellow members of the Association of Southeast Asian Nations (ASEAN). Relations with the United States warmed again shortly. The United States expressed support for ASEAN's opposition to the Vietnamese occupation of Cambodia and provided substantial aid for the flood of refugees that had begun to pour into Thailand from Cambodia. In February 1979 Prime Minister Kriangsak Chomanan made a state visit to the United States, during which President Carter reaffirmed the U.S. commitment to Thailand as embodied in the Rusk-Thanat statement of seventeen years before.

The return to close relationships of mutual security was relatively swift and has been marked in recent years by annual joint military training exercises in Thailand and by an agreement in 1986 under which U.S. military supplies are being prepositioned in stocks in Thailand in order to provide both the U.S. and Thai military with ready resupply facilities. The agreement is unusual in that the United States has similar arrangements only with other countries with which there are formal military alliances and in which there are U.S. bases.

The reader will appreciate that this very brief account of the course of overall U.S.–Thai relations is intended to serve only as a framework for an examination of the aid relationship. It omits a wealth of detail that can be found in other sources but is not of close relevance to this subject. Where such detail is pertinent below, especially in chapter 5, it will be included. At this point, I add only two further observations.

First, the restored security relationships of the 1980s are obviously quite different from those of the Vietnam War years. The relative geopolitical simplicity of earlier years, with Communist powers of the region aligned on one side in a context of clear-cut adversarial challenges and the United States being given extensive military operational license in Thailand (the two countries never developed a formal status-of-forces agreement to define the legal framework, the usual practice where American armed forces are stationed in foreign jurisdictions), has given way to a very different and more complex regional configuration along with a diminished Thai reliance on U.S. military support. The easing of tensions between China and the Soviet Union, the prospects for withdrawal of Vietnamese forces from Cambodia, the diversification of Thai military equipment purchases to include tanks and other items from China, the emergence of Japan as the overwhelmingly large source of foreign aid in the region, and the role of the ASEAN nations as a diplomatic bloc are among the key changes in recent years that have widened the options for Thai regional foreign policy and security arrangements and reduced the former centrality of the U.S. relationship.

Second, to describe the relationships between Thailand and the United States (or indeed between any two countries) as if the events took place between two unitary players is obviously an oversimplification. At various times on both sides there were conflicting views and interests at work. One aspect of the dynamics behind Thailand's interest in close military relationships with the United States merits mention here, although I cannot do justice to its importance or complexity. I refer to the asymmetry between the domestic political ramifications of the relationship in the two countries. The military aid relation and even the direct military operational role in Thailand during the Vietnam War years has had no, or only very marginal, impact on domestic U.S. politics (the U.S. military role in Thailand was only an appendage to the main Vietnam theater of operations as far as the politics of the Vietnam War were concerned). In Thai politics, on the other hand, according to many political analysts, the flow of materiel and the close military relationship strengthened the domestic political position of commanding officers of the Thai armed forces (mainly the army) and lent added weight to the proponents of a strong anti-Communist foreign policy. In my view the historical analyses of the impact of the military relationship are frequently overdrawn, especially in their (usually unstated) assumption that the interests of the country as a whole (apart from the personal interests of successive military leaders during their relatively short periods of political ascendancy) would have been better served if Thailand had attempted to steer an alternative course in Southeast Asia by eschewing the military relationship offered by the United States. With due regard to the importance of these issues, I can only note them, since any attempt to do justice to their complexity would draw this study away from its main objectives.

In the last couple of years, trade issues have become troublesome problems and irritants to Thai–U.S. relations. They are widely discussed in Thailand but remain relatively obscure to the American public. Thai reactions to U.S. legislation and to executive branch decisions regarding textiles and other Thai exports to the United States and affecting Thai rice export earnings as a whole have ranged from puzzlement and dismay to outrage. How could the United States impose economic hardship on its most consistent ally in Southeast Asia through both the Korean and Vietnamese wars? These issues will be discussed later. For the moment it is worth noting that the joint military exercises and other components of the security relationship have not been raised by the RTG as a relevant issue in the midst of these trade tensions, in the sense of any calling for a reevaluation. Nor did these problems touch the long-run development aid program, to which I now turn, starting with an overview of its size, composition, and major objectives.

THE DEVELOPMENT RELATIONSHIP: COMPONENTS AND BASIC NUMBERS

The United States has provided Thailand around $1 billion of development aid. (Different definitions and accounting sources yield varying estimates of the amount of aid, as explained below.) This does not put Thailand in the big league of foreign aid recipients. I have already noted the difference between the aid given to Thailand and Taiwan in absolute and per capita terms. Some additional country comparison data is shown in table 2.1. In the forty-year period 1946–1986* Thailand received 3 percent of the aid extended to all the countries of the East Asian region, with the five larger recipients having been allocated between 2.3 and 7.3 times as much as was Thailand. Nonetheless, the Thai program has not been a minor one, having cumulated to larger amounts than any African recipient for example (Egypt aside). The "middling" character of the Thai program is perhaps better illustrated by a per capita comparison. On this basis Thailand's $0.62 per capita aid level in 1985 was in the mid range of the region

---

*Official U.S. economic aid includes a postwar rehabilitation loan of $6.2 million in 1946, which preceded the launching of the foreign aid program in 1950.

TABLE 2.1.

U.S. Economic Aid, 1946–1986

Country	Amount ($ million)	Regional Share (%)	Ratio to Thailand	1985 Aid per Capita ($)
East Asia	29,284	100		
South Viet Nam	6,949	24	7.3	—
Republic of Korea	6,063	21	6.4	—
Indonesia	3,428	12	3.6	0.38
Philippines	3,053	10	3.2	2.98
Taiwan	2,207	8	2.3	—
Thailand	952	3	—	0.62
Others	6,632	23	—	0.62
Other Major Recipients				
Egypt	13,082		13.7	21.96
Israel	12,700		13.3	464.29
India	11,415		12.0	0.11
Turkey	4,217		4.4	3.49
Bangladesh	2,205		2.3	1.01
Kenya	667		0.7	0.90
WORLD TOTAL	196,477			

SOURCES: AID, "U.S. Overseas Loans and Grant," 1986; AID, Congressional Presentation, 1988.
NOTE: Country figures exclude regional and centrally funded projects. Percent shares do not total 100 due to rounding

and lower than a large number of African countries, where relatively modest country allocations translate into high per capita amounts because of relatively small populations.

To put the official U.S. aid program in proper perspective, I have listed in table 2.2 virtually all the official and private American programs that have been financing development (or development-related) activities in Thailand in the postwar period. The table excludes some nongovernmental organizations conducting programs in Thailand with funds additional to what they may have received from one or more of the funding sources listed in the table. To complete this raw list, the table also shows U.S. military aid and base construction.* The right-hand column lists the annex table for each program category for which I am providing detailed data.

---

* A complete study of the economic impact of the U.S. military relationship with Thailand would have to take account of the local expenditures in connection with the operation of the air bases used during the Vietnam War and the expenditure of U.S. military personnel on R&R in Thailand during that conflict. Caldwell cites U.S. Embassy estimates of the balance of

TABLE 2.2.

American Programs: Thailand, 1946–1988[a]

	Amount ($ million)	Table
USAID/T Mission-Funded Program	907.3	A.1
(Counterpart Account—nonadd)[b]	(375.3)	A.1a
(U.S. Local Currency Loans—nonadd)[b]	(7.8)	A.1b
Regional Economic Development Program	58.1	A.1.1
Centrally-Funded Projects	33.8	A.1.2
American Schools & Hospitals Abroad (ASHA)	9.6	A.1.3
Trade Development Program (TDP)	5.5	A.1.4
Housing Guarantees (HG)	10.0	——
TOTAL USAID	1,024.3	
Peace Corps	48.5	——
Food for Peace (PL 480)	37.2	A.1.5
Drug Enforcement Agency (DEA)	35.8	A.15
Fulbright Academic Exchange Program	N/A	——
Export-Import Bank loans	239.6	——
Other U.S. loans	34.1	——
Asia Foundation	10.0[c]	——
Overseas Private Investment Corp.—Insured American Investment in Thailand (nonadd)	(362.0)	——
TOTAL USG & USG-related (excluding military appropriations)	1,429.5	
Ford Foundation	17.8	A.3
Rockefeller Foundation	17.0[c]	A.4
Winrock/ADC	2.1	A.5
Population Council	N/A	——
Military Assistance Programs	2,163.3	A.21
OICC Road/Airfield Construction	500.0[c]	A.19
TOTAL	4,129.1	

[a] Years for individual programs are shown in referenced Annex tables.
[b] Thai currency accounts are nonadd funding sources in this table because they comprise Thai government funds and local currency "generated" (as explained in the text) by U.S. funds included already under "USAID/T Mission-funded Program." Inclusion of local currency generation would entail double-counting of the dollar value of these funds.
[c] Rough estimates.
N/A = not available.

I will cover most of these programs in the subsequent chapters. A brief review at this point will be useful to give a picture of the scope and composition of the entire complex of the development relationship between the two countries. The largest component has been the "mission-funded" program of USAID and its predecessor agencies. By and large, the mission-funded program comprises projects that are designed and implemented by the resident aid mission and funded from allocations made to and administered by the mission. As can be seen from annex table A.1, the total mission-funded program has cumulated (as of this writing)* to $907.7 million through an uninterrupted sequence of annual aid levels of varying amounts and composition. The program's high funding years ran from 1955 to 1959 and from 1966 to 1969. The aid levels dipped sharply in 1964–1965 and remained well below the peak 1960s years during the whole 1970s decade. Aid levels recovered again in the 1980s. Although the figures accounted for by fiscal year do not track closely the actual level of disbursements and program activity, the ups and downs do broadly reflect the changing U.S. government perceptions of Thailand's aid requirements as driven by a mix of regional and domestic security challenges and by considerations of the country's economic position. Over the entire period the United States viewed Thailand's economic prospects as strongly favorable; the corollary judgment was that Thailand had less of a need for concessional aid—on purely economic and financial grounds—than many of the countries among which scarce concessional funds had to be divided. Nonetheless, although the country's growth performance has fulfilled these expectations, the rise of per capita income over this period has been into the range still described by the World Bank as "lower middle," an economic position that leaves Thailand with a substantial poverty problem. While the security-based aid allocations have varied greatly depending on the circumstances, there has been a continuous underlying rationale for U.S. aid to Thailand—namely, that Thai and U.S. regional interests have remained mutual for the long run and that these interests will be promoted if Thai economic strength grows.

The nonproject column in annex table A.1 gives the numbers showing the relatively minor role of general import financing in the Thai

---

payments effects of these expenditures for the years 1965–1971 (*American Economic Aid to Thailand*, p. 173).

*As explained in the notes to table A.1, the figures on aid amounts are recorded by U.S. fiscal year of legal obligation; as active projects funded in prior years are gradually closed out and any unspent funds are returned to the U.S. Treasury, the aid levels recorded for those years decline until all the books have been closed. These downward adjustments normally are not large.

aid program. The uneven loan numbers reflect several factors: (a) accidents of timing of the preparation process of individual loan-funded projects; (b) occasionally large reductions (rather than over-runs!) in the size of loans, especially in the earlier years, as some components of projects were not carried out as planned; and (c) changes in legislative provisions and in AID policy with respect to the grant/loan mix in the aid program as a whole and as applied to Thailand.

Referring back to table 2.2, there I have listed five other program categories that, together with the mission-funded program, make up the complete set of AID programs that have operated in Thailand. (The annex tables give the amounts by year for four of three programs as indicated.) The Regional Economic Development program ran between 1968 and 1981, was administered by a separate regional AID office in Bangkok for much of that period, and appears in USAID/T accounting. Although all the program's activities involved several countries of the area, Thailand appears to have been the main beneficiary. Inclusion of the program amounts thus overstates the level of aid to Thailand by an amount that cannot be sorted out but which is minimal as a fraction of the total aid and development-related American programs over the period. In contrast, the figures for centrally funded projects understate the amounts allocated to Thailand since only partial information is available except for very recent years.

The relatively small allocations to projects in Thailand under the American Schools and Hospitals Abroad (ASHA) and the Trade Development programs are centrally funded but are shown separately because they have separate identities with their own annual appropriations in the Foreign Assistance Act. The ASHA program extends grants to overseas schools and hospitals that are affiliated with American institutions. As shown in table A.1.3, three institutions in Thailand (two private colleges and the Seventh Day Adventist Hospital in Bangkok) have received ASHA grants totaling $9.6 million since 1978.

The Trade Development Program (TDP) finances feasibility studies of projects for which, if implemented, American suppliers would be in a good competitive position to obtain contracts and/or equipment supply orders. These TDP study grants qualify as aid even though any resulting American business might be contracted entirely as a commercial transaction. The eighteen TDP studies financed between 1984 and 1987 at a total cost of $5.5 million (table A.1.4) covered projects in electric power, communication, transportation, flood control, hazardous waste and computers.

The FAA/USAID picture is completed with the addition of the Housing Guarantee program under which private American funds (from U.S. private financial institutions) are invested (under U.S. guarantees) in housing projects in developing countries. This program is normally considered part of the foreign aid program as a whole, although the economic transfer being effected by this AID activity involves private funds on nonconcessional terms (and a small amount of technical assistance on grant terms).

In addition to official aid, the U.S. government has been conducting several programs that have direct developmental impact, even though their primary purposes have been framed in nondevelopmental terms or, especially in the case of military aid, have had no developmental dimension to their rationale or authorizing legislation. The Peace Corps, like many other country volunteer programs it has inspired, is conceived as a people-to-people program that serves as a learning experience for the volunteers and a demonstration of international concern and goodwill. As pointed out below, the Peace Corps operates at a micro level and on a scale that is not intended to have general leverage on the development process. Nevertheless, the content of Peace Corps activities is certainly developmental in substance. The Peace Corps program has been working in Thailand since 1962. In its first decade 80 percent of the volunteers were teaching English in Thai schools, from the primary to the university level. In the mid-1970s the RTG and the Peace Corps agreed to shift the emphasis of the program, assigning the majority of volunteers to work in rural areas in health, agriculture, and other aspects of rural development. All told more than 3,500 volunteers had served in Thailand by the end of 1986, at which time the current number of volunteers was about 175. (There are also volunteers working in Thailand under similar British, New Zealand, German, and Canadian programs.)

The U.S. Information Agency has been bringing Thais to the U.S. under its International Visitor Program since 1950. These are short visits designed to promote Thai–U.S. relations and to give Thai leaders, future leaders, and professionals an opportunity to acquaint themselves with American life and meet Americans working in the same professional areas. Between 1950 and 1986 a total of 845 Thais visited the United States under this program. This, however, is not called a development program and is not included in the tables.

Since 1974 the United States has been assisting the Thai government in virtually all aspects of RTG efforts to deal with narcotics production, traffic, and addiction. Three U.S. agencies have been involved. AID projects have addressed several aspects of the narcotics problem. The activities assisted by the Drug Enforcement Agency (DEA) have been confined to law enforcement and traffic interdiction.

The American Embassy administers a State Department program (financed under FAA) aimed primarily at developing income sources to substitute for narcotics production in areas populated by Thailand's northern Hill Tribe minorities. Roughly one-quarter of the narcotics assistance has been allocated to the alternative income projects. The DEA enforcement and interdiction activities from table 2.3 are excluded, although all of these narcotics programs can be considered developmental in the broad sense that everything that typically surrounds and flows from the existence of a narcotics "industry' is destructive and corrupting to the governmental and legal frameworks of developing countries where this industry has become entrenched.

The Fulbright Academic Exchange Program (funded under appropriations to the U.S. Information Agency) is not limited to developing countries, nor was it conceived as a developmental instrument. It warrants inclusion (although I have no dollar value estimate) as an important component of American developmental relationships with poorer countries, however, thanks to the central role of the foreign higher education experience in the development of countries like Thailand.

To finish the picture of all U.S. *official* programs affecting economic development in Thailand, table 2.2 also includes Export-Import Bank loans that provide (nonconcessional) credits for Thai imports of U.S. civil aircraft and other manufactures and the volume of American direct investments in Thailand that have been facilitated by (noncommercial) risk insurance coverage extended to more than eighty U.S. firms by the Overseas Private Investment Corporation.

To complete the list of American development programs, five nongovernmental organizations are shown with their estimated resource inputs. The Ford, Rockefeller, and Asia foundations and Winrock/Agriculture Development Council (ADC) have operated programs with significant development impact, described in the text and summarized in the tables. The work of the Population Council (which, unlike the first four organizations, is not a funding source but an operating technical assistance source using funds from AID and the foundations) is also covered below. A number of American private voluntary agencies (such as CARE and Helen Keller International) have been working in Thailand, some receiving AID grants. Data on the expenditures of these agencies from non-U.S. government funding sources is incomplete, but the amounts appear to run less than $1 million a year. Although the Asia foundation is funded by congressional appropria-

TABLE 2.3.

U.S. Aid Components and Categories: 1946–1988

	$ million
A. Official Aid	
Economic (B)	1,127.2
Military	2,163.3
TOTAL	3,290.5
B. Official Economic Aid	
FAA/USAID (C)	1,005.7
Food for Peace	37.2
Narcotics Assistance Unit (FAA/Embassy)	35.8
Peace Corps	48.5
TOTAL	1,127.2
C. FAA/USAID	
Mission-funded	907.7
Regional	58.1
Centrally funded	33.8
ASHA	9.6
TDP	5.5
TOTAL	1,005.7
D. Official Economic Transfers	
Official economic aid (B)	1,127.2
Export-Import Bank loans	239.6
Other USG loans	34.1
TOTAL	1,400.9
E. Development Aid	
Official economic aid	1,127.2
Less AID-financed military and police projects	−98.0
TOTAL	1,029.2
F. Aid Having Development Impact	
Development aid (E)	1,029.2
Civil use military construction	
AID-financed 4.3	
DOD-financed 500.0 (?)	504.3
TOTAL	1,533.5

TABLE 2.3. (continued)

U.S. Aid Components and Categories: 1946–1988

	$ million
G. Total Resources Available for USAID Projects	
FAA/USAID (C)	1,005.7
Counterpart fund (baht 7,694 million)	375.3[a]
TOTAL	1,381.0
H. Total Resources Available for USAID Development Projects	
Development aid (E)	1,029.2
Counterpart fund less military/police project allocations	296.3
TOTAL	1,325.5
Plus other RTG contributions	N/A
I. Private American Investment Effected/Assisted by USG Programs	
Housing Guaranty loan	10.0
OPIC-insured investment	362.0
Other U.S. investment effected by USAID "private sector" projects	N/A
J. American Development Aid	
Official development aid (E)	1,029.2
Foundations	46.9
Other NGO additional resources	N/A
TOTAL	1,076.1

NOTE: Not all components are as of 1988.
[a] Dollar figure based on exchange rate prevailing in years of largest counterpart expenditures ($1 = baht 20.5). Overstates nominal dollar equivalency.
N/A = not available.

tion (through the State Department), it is an independent organization.

These various components of official and nongovernmental programs are listed a second time in table 2.3, rearranged to illustrate different categories and definitions of aid and nonaid transfers from the United States to Thailand. Table 2.3 should be read more for the concepts illustrated than for the numbers, which are intended as orders of magnitude indicating relative sizes of the programs and concepts involved. Total U.S. official economic and military assistance from 1946 to 1988 amounted to roughly $3.3 billion (item A). The economic aid (of $1.1 billion) is divided into Foreign Assistance Act and other legislative components in item B. U.S. government assistance under FAA is broken down into separate components in item C. Item D adds nonaid U.S. official financial flows to item B to get a total figure of $1.4 billion of official economic transfers.

Not all labeled economic aid has been for development, however. In earlier years appropriations for military and police were included under programs administered (or accounted) by USAID (and predecessor agencies). The development/nondevelopment distinction is not all that clear, however, since some of the projects assisting the Thai police included rural development components ("civic action" was the popular American term) that were clearly developmental in content, and some of the AID military projects were for construction of airfield and naval facilities that have served civil traffic subsequently. AID-funded military projects (mainly construction in the 1950s) amounted to $11.2 million (plus $34.2 million of counterpart funds). Public safety projects amounted to $86.8 million (plus $44.5 million of counterpart funds). As an approximation, however, taking the military and police categories at face value, item E deducts these amounts from official economic aid (item B) to get a net development aid figure of a little over $1 billion. A further step would be to take account of the military aid–financed construction of transport facilities open for civilian use. The amounts are uncertain, but the facilities are significant, as I have indicated. Item F adds the civil-use facilities to development aid (item E) to derive a figure representing all U.S. aid "having development impact."

Items G and H add the value of counterpart availabilities gross (a rough dollar equivalent) to get a figure representing the total resources (U.S. plus local) that have been available for USAID projects (item G) and net resources for development projects (item H) after deducting the military and police allocations from both the dollar and counterpart funds. The baht components of virtually all projects were financed from the counterpart fund. Given the importance of the counterpart fund as a source of finance for the aid program, it merits a brief explanation. Total resources of the fund have amounted to about $375 million. A little more than one-third of this comprised deposits "generated" by the nonproject aid the United States provided between 1952 and 1962, the dollar allocations for which appear in table A.1. The remaining two-thirds derived from RTG budget contributions and small miscellaneous (non-U.S.) fund income. As noted above, nonproject aid normally finances general imports for a country's economy rather than commodities needed as inputs into specific aid projects. In the Thai case nonproject aid financed imports of petroleum products. The local currency generated by the domestic sale of these imports was deposited into the fund. Petroleum products were chosen for their administrative convenience, involving only a few transactions a year with the supplying American oil companies. The annual contribution by the RTG to the fund was calculated on several bases: a "commensurate value" concept (1951–1954); fixed yearly amounts (1955–1960); rising annual deposits and additional occasional contributions for individual projects (1961–1976). No deposits into the fund have been made since 1976. The fund has continued to earn some income from investment of balances in short-term obligations, but the size of the fund has been diminishing as project disbursements have exceeded these interest earnings. A few of the annex tables show counterpart in addition to the dollar funding figures, mainly for groups of projects using major local currency funding. No effort is made to identify separately the project allocation of the counterpart generated by the nonproject aid, which in fact was utilized largely for the road-building and other engineering projects discussed below. Finally, I have made no attempt to collate the figures, listed separately in every project's documentation, that were intended to represent additional cash and in-kind contributions made by the RTG agencies or departments involved in each project through their respective budgets, but were not folded into the project financing through the counterpart fund. The determination of these additional RTG costs (no doubt substantial) followed no common definitions.

Item I represents American private investment funds flowing to Thailand as a result of U.S. official programs. Item J derives a figure for total American (public and private) development assistance to Thailand by adding U.S. foundations; no figures are available for NGO resources not derived from the U.S. government or, as noted above, for the Fulbright program.

One further adjustment is needed to put this whole picture into proper perspective. The aid numbers stretch across nearly four decades, during which time both the dollar and baht lost substantial purchasing power. Thus, the $30.9 million aid provided in 1986 (table A.1) could buy about the same quantity of U.S. goods and services as the $8.9 million aid level in 1951, the first year of the program. If the entire series up to 1986 is deflated to 1951 prices (using the U.S. GDP deflator series), total *real* aid provided amounts to the equivalent of about 645 million 1951 dollars, or less than two-thirds of the nominal total.[6]

TIME PERIODS AND OBJECTIVES

In reviewing the history of the Thai aid program in detail below, it is helpful to divide it into several periods of different character and size. Before doing so however, I should note by way of qualification that the history of the Thai aid program, as with most aid programs, cannot be divided into time periods of very sharp delineation in program content for several reasons. The basic security rationale for U.S. aid to Thailand was set out from the start and has remained a consistent theme ever since, albeit changing over time as the nature of the region's security problems have changed. Supportive objectives concerning economic development and poverty were also set forth at the inception of the program and have also remained basic themes. In addition, the program's content has not been sharply differentiated from one period to the next; the policy goals of security and development were interdependent and broadly conceived so that many of the specific activities appeared to be sensible regardless of which policy theme was being emphasized during any one period.

There have also been practical reasons for the program's continuity and slow response to the occasional perception of a need to shift direction. The long sequence of field mission planning, agency review, and congressional appropriation, and several years of actual project implementation means that the aid program's content and its operational objectives during any one year comprise an overlay of responses to problems and perceptions of several previous years. Only emergency relief delivered in the form of food and other commodities and nonproject aid that consists of a check or a line of credit for general import financing can be transferred quickly enough to be a fine-tuned and rapid response to a specific aid need. The Thai program has consisted largely of projects. With capital projects typically having a five-year implementation period and full-scale institution-building projects often taking up to ten years, a project-based aid program is not likely to change content much from year to year.

AID's funding procedures also act as a drag on the speed with which a country program can respond to a change in conditions or objectives. Capital projects financed by loans generally have been fully funded at the start under the loan agreement that legally obligates the monies. Projects funded by grants and technical assistance projects, whether loan- or grant-funded (technical assistance projects being more easily cut back in scope then capital projects if the availability of funds is cut back in midproject), can be financed in partial slices in successive fiscal years. Partial funding does not lock in funds up front to cover expected future years' expenditures: this permits a given year's allocation to be spread over a larger number of projects. By the same token, partial funding puts claims on future years' allocations ("mortgaging" in AID parlance) and restricts an AID mission's ability to make major changes in program content except over several years as mortgage requirements are met and decline. The Thai program has comprised mainly technical assistance and partially funded projects, contributing to the lack of sharply defined periods in its history. Finally, year to year changes in the level of new funds (obligations) may not follow an intended change in program level or indicate deliberate U.S. intent to alter the size of the program as a matter of policy. Obligations for one year may be larger than in the previous year merely because signing of a loan agreement may have slipped from the end of one fiscal year to the beginning of the next. (The details of accounting concepts behind the aid numbers are given in the notes to the funding tables.)

Caldwell divided the first two decades of the aid program up to 1970 into four periods of nearly equal length: (a) "Point Four," 1950–1954, during which the program followed the general lines of President Truman's Point Four concept of technical aid; (b) "Nation-Building," 1954–1959, characterized by a large increase in funding and a shift to emphasis on capital projects to build roads and other economic infrastructure; (c) "Phasedown," 1960–1964, reflecting a decline in U.S. concern over Thailand's security position and a judgment that the country's economic progress would enable the United States to terminate economic aid altogether within a fairly short period of time; followed by (d) a major expansion of the program in 1965–1970 to help the Thai government mount a counterinsurgency effort as security once again appeared threatened.

The "Counterinsurgency" period actually extended until 1974 (beyond the time Caldwell was writing his book), when public safety assistance was ended and the last funds for Accelerated Rural Development, the major insurgency-oriented development project, were allocated. In the fifth period, extending roughly from 1975 to 1981, poverty alleviation was the dominant theme. While projects to help reduce some of the causes and effects of poverty have continued as important components of the AID program to the present, the current period, since 1982, has seen the emergence of a parallel orientation that is likely to become the central theme of any future aid relationship between Thailand and the United States—namely, transition to middle-income status. Thailand is one of a number of aid recipients that are still at modest levels of per capita income by industrial country standards, where a continuing aid relationship with the United States could be mutually beneficial, but where the increasing institutional strength and technical capabilities of the country are changing the mix and substance of activities that would be most relevant and beneficial to their development and most suitably obtained from the United States. Policy research, science and technology, and environment and resource problems are examples of the issues that have surfaced under this latest perspective.

The text of the *Congressional Presentation* for fiscal year 1952 contains a succinct statement of the U.S. view of Thailand's economic position when the aid program began, its security relationship with the United States at that time, and how the substance of the aid program was expected to contribute to the mutual objectives of the two governments:

> Thailand's resources are substantial and increasing. It has a good credit rating and has received IBRD loans. There is nevertheless an urgent need for technical assistance, accompanied by moderate grant aid to help secure prompt and practical application of all resources available to the Thai economy.
>
> Thailand's economy is based on the production of food, which engages the activities of 90 percent of the working population. Despite relative prosperity in Asian terms, most Thai live at or near subsistence level. Their productivity is greatly restricted by wide incidence of malaria and other diseases. Their access to markets is severely limited by inadequacy of transportation. The assurance of regular crops is lacking because droughts and floods are insufficiently compensated by modern irrigation. Their food processing, mining and other industries are handicapped by inadequate electric power. The [aid] program in Thailand in FY 1952, as in FY 1951, is chiefly directed toward helping find remedies for a number of these situations.
>
> While Thailand receives, in the FY 1952 proposal, the smallest grant of any Southeast Asia country, this aid covers equitably the requests and need of the Thai Govern-

ment for such aid, supplementing the utilization of its own resources and IBRD loans. The socioeconomic improvement that can be achieved through the aid program will tend to sustain the present intimate political alignment with the United States. The stability, cooperation and economic progress thereby induced could well provide a clear example to all Southeast Asia. Moreover, this joint effort will create more rice for deficit areas and more tin and tungsten for the free world generally. . . . Though small, Thailand is a staunch and stable outpost of the free world in a threatened and turbulent area.[7]

Compare this view with the following excerpt from the AID *Congressional Presentation* for FY 1988:

Thailand's economy is undergoing rapid transition. With a per capita income of $860 (1984), Thailand is approaching middle income status. . . .

The United States has a fundamental interest in the stability and independence of Thailand as a contributor to peace and regional cooperation in Southeast Asia. As a "front line state," in concert with its Association of Southeast Asian Nations (ASEAN) partners, Thailand is central to the preservation of regional security. In support of this goal, U.S. economic policy in Thailand is directed toward the use of trade and investment to help sustain broad-based economic development, with continued reliance on the private sector and openness to the world trading system. The continued cooperation of the RTG is also essential to several U.S. foreign policy objectives, including refugee programs, antipiracy activities, the control of illicit narcotics trafficking from Southeast Asia, and support of U.S. security objectives in the region. . . .

A.I.D.'s development strategy for Thailand is undergoing a transition in approach. For the last 15 years the program has focused on agriculture, health and family planning. Thailand has made impressive strides in these areas, and during the FY 1986–1987 period many of A.I.D.'s ongoing projects in these fields will end. A new A.I.D. strategy, approved in February 1985, represents a marked departure from earlier analysis, programs and projects. This revised approach to Thai development reflects the Kingdom's evo-

lution toward "middle income" status as Thailand under-
goes transformation from an agrarian society to a semi-
industrialized state.[8]

In 1951 Thailand's modern economic development had not yet
begun. Low productivity agriculture occupied and supported the bulk
of the population. The economic infrastructure was very limited in
extent, and rail transport in particular had been bombed repeatedly
during World War II. Nevertheless, by Asian standards Thailand's
position at the time was relatively favorable, and its prospects appeared good. Thanks to Thailand's strong credit rating and access to
other aid sources, the U.S. administration saw a need for only a
relatively small aid effort. The text implies that the RTG was satisfied
with the aid level proposed. The socioeconomic improvement that
was expected to result (partly) from the effects of the aid program
would help sustain stability and "intimate political alignment" with
the U.S. Thailand was a "stable outpost" in a "turbulent" area of
concern to U.S. interests.

In 1988, after thirty-seven years of turbulence in the region and
profound changes in geopolitical relationships in Southeast and East
Asia, Thailand has undergone substantial development, is becoming
a semi-industrialized state, and remains a country in which the United
States has a "fundamental" interest for the role Thailand plays at the
center of regional security.

In a world grown used to a seeming relentless unfolding of the
unexpected, to vast and unpredictable change in the course of a single
generation, the two statements about Thailand and its relationship
with the United States, made by administrations three and a half
decades apart, make remarkable reading. While neither Thailand's
economic course nor its domestic stability nor the state of U.S.–Thai
relations has been without periods of stress, the prognosis for economic progress has been borne out, and the political and security
relationships between the two countries remain intimate.

A recent Thai summary of the economic course of the past quarter
of a century will suffice as an introduction for the development context of this study:

> In the 1960s, with a favorable world economic situation
> and domestic policies promoting private enterprise, Thai-
> land's real GDP grew at an average rate of 7% a year with
> an inflation rate of less than 2%. The major policy at that
> time was to encourage private investment with very mod-

erate government involvement in economic activities. During the period, savings and investment relative to GDP also increased at rates above those of other less developed countries (LDCs). Exports of Thai primary commodities expanded but imports of capital goods and raw materials increased more rapidly. The industrialization policy of the period was to promote import-substitution industries.

In the 1970s, there were oil crises and the world economy was less stable. In Thailand, the inflation rate quadrupled and the average annual growth rate of real GDP declined from the previous decade to 6.6%. However, the growth rate was still relatively high compared to other LDCs during the same period. This was partly due to the more outward-looking policy of export promotion implemented by Thai authorities since the early 1970s. Although most policies initiated in the 1960s were maintained, the emphasis previously put on import-substitution was shifted over to export promotion. As a result, the economy was more open to international trade and foreign investment. The gains from the freer trade enabled the country to recover quickly from the mild recession in the mid-1970s and hence the average growth for the decade did not decline much.

Nonetheless, the fact that a relatively small country like Thailand became increasingly [oriented] to world trade made it more susceptible to the changing world economic situation. The impact of the volatile world market and economic conditions the domestic economy was quickly noticed during 1979–82. During that period, the world economy was buffeted by a deepening recession, another oil crisis, increasing interest rates, declining commodity prices, and rising protectionism on the part of the [developed countries]. In Thailand, the average annual growth rate of real GDP during 1979–82 was low and the unemployment rate was high. In 1979–81, the domestic inflation rate was a record high. Meanwhile, import costs increased and export growth slowed, resulting in widening trade and payments deficits. From 1981, various short-run policies were attempted to cope with the problems. These included devaluation, spending reductions, flexible energy prices, and energy conservation. Later on, investment and savings were also stimulated. During 1983–84, Thailand recovered from the economic slowdown as the world economy improved. But in 1985, hit by another world recession and restrictive domestic policies, investment was reduced and real GDP grew at the lowest level in the past 25 years. There was a slight upturn in 1986 as the economy benefitted from much lower world oil prices.[9]

The recovery in 1986 and the surge into high growth again in 1987–1988 (the economy grew around 7 percent in 1987 and 11 percent in 1988) have been accompanied by factors giving rise to a widespread view that Thailand could well join the ranks of the so-called NICs or newly industrializing countries* by the end of the 1990s.[10] The propelling factors at this stage of the country's development include remarkable expansions in tourist earnings, diversified agricultural products, nontraditional manufactured exports, and foreign investment (especially from Japan, but also from the Asian NICs and the EEC and United States), all benefiting from a sound economic policy framework, sustained domestic stability, and the apparent waning of any security threat from Vietnam for the foreseeable future.

Thus, it is fair to say that both the broad security and development objectives of the U.S. aid program in Thailand and many of the component objectives (in health, population growth, poverty alleviation, infrastructure, institution-building, and so on) have been or are in the process of being realized. What role has U.S. aid and the American development connections generally played in these achievements? I will attempt to answer this question by assembling and examining pertinent evidence respecting many of the specific problems and individual projects that have comprised the development relationship.

THE GEOGRAPHIC DIMENSION

Over the thirty-seven years of the aid program, project activities have reached every part, probably every province, of the country. I am unable to disaggregate the funding geographically because many projects covered more than one area of the country without disaggre-

---

*The NIC sobriquet is misleading. Thailand will continue to have major comparative advantage in agriculture for the foreseeable future, service industries are growing rapidly, and agriculture-based industries form an important part of the industrial sector. Because the Thai economy is unlikely to resemble the typical NIC, alternative acronyms are frequently suggested by after-dinner speakers, such NAC, for newly agro-industrializing country, and NISE, for newly industrializing and service economy.

gated bookkeeping. Furthermore, much of the allocations to projects in Bangkok went to develop institutions with national responsibilities and activities whose beneficiaries lived in the provinces. Nonetheless, it is clear that the Northeast region of the country has been the priority area for the aid program since its inception.

The Northeast's priority has stemmed from its geographic position and the relative severity of its internal security problems. The region has Thailand's longest border with Indochina, is inhabited by people who are ethnically different from the Central Plain Thai, and has long been the poorest area of the country. In the 1950s the Northeast economic infrastructure was rudimentary. It had only a few miles of paved road. Travel on the limited network of washboard, laterite roads was arduous at best and virtually impossible in the rainy seasons. Only the provincial and district capitals had electricity and then usually only a few hours a day from small and unreliable town generators. Health services were very limited and inadequate, as were the schools and agricultural and other economic services of the government. Few villages had radios, and telecommunications service was skeletal.

The relative isolation of the Northeast and the limited opportunities for educational advance reinforced the fundamental causes of the area's low-income and premodern subsistence economy—its poor natural resource base and water regime. Northeast soils are generally poor in nutrients and inferior in physical agronomic characteristics, making them relatively unresponsive to chemical fertilizers. The monsoon rains fall in concentrated brief periods and are followed by long dry spells. Rains are late in many years and drought is a recurrent problem as is seasonal shortage of drinking water.

The history of Thai efforts to cope with this daunting set of problems and of the United States' (and other donors') attempts to help and to find "answers" make up a good portion of the history of foreign aid to Thailand.

THREE

TRAINING

When one asks Thais in business, government, or academia what they think has been the most important contribution of the U.S. aid program to the country's development, the answer virtually always is the same: training. It is easy to see why Thais come to this common-sense judgment. Large numbers in the senior ranks of government, the professions, the modern corporate sector, and increasingly in smaller family enterprise have studied abroad. These are the people who have to a large extent designed and implemented government development policies and programs, run the state utilities and other major state enterprises, put in place the country's education system, and managed the evolution of the private sector. If one agrees with the broad conclusion that Thailand's economic development performance ranks high in Third World experience, there is a prima facie case for giving substantial credit to the people whose decisions and careers have had a major role in guiding this performance and to the education and training that have given them the tools for carrying out this function. I agree with this judgment, although it is not possible to describe the development impact or effectiveness of this training with any precision.

In the AID lexicon a person sent abroad (to the United States or a third country) for education or training is called a "participant." The training may be long term, usually for graduate education in the United States, or short term (one year or less) for special courses, on-the-job training, or observation tours. Participants are usually selected in the context of a project. For example, the director of a government unit responsible for a project in rural sanitation might be sent to the U.S. Bureau of Public Health, while the capability of the unit in the long run to implement the project and continue its activities after the aid project concludes might be built up by sending more junior staff for a Master's in Public Health or degrees in sanitary engineering. Training grants have also been provided by AID through general training "projects" that were not linked to a particular sectoral development activity and its implementing unit.

The aid program began sending participants to the United States right from the start, with an initial 14 in 1951 and 77 in 1952. The numbers rose rapidly and reached a cumulative total of nearly 8,000 by 1970. According to what appears to have been the aid mission's first formal review of participant training, conducted in 1969, about 25 percent had gone to the United States for long-term training, mostly for graduate degrees. About 62 percent of the total had been sent to the United States, taking long- and short-term training together. By 1979, in the program's twenty-ninth year, 4 percent of the participants were deceased, 10 percent had already retired, and another 10 percent had left government employment. Of the remaining 6,000 (nonpolice) participants, about one-third had received degree training under the program.[1]

Participant training reached its high point in 1970, when over 900 Thais were in the program, amounting to over half of the aid-financed scholarships available to Thailand from all aid sources. The U.S. aid program declined rapidly thereafter as a financier of training for Thai academics and civil servants. The number of trainees fell to less than half by 1973 and to a low of 29 by 1979. Since 1980 they have fluctuated between 50 and 150 a year. In 1985 U.S. participant training stood at 3 percent of all aid-financed external training provided to Thailand.[2] As of September 1987, the cumulative total of participants was 11,181. (As I will show below, substantial additional numbers of Thais received training grants over the years for study in the United States under auspices other than AID, including programs of other U.S. government agencies and of American foundations and nongovernmental organizations.)

There are several reasons for the decline of AID training, the most important being the sharp contraction in the overall aid level. Participant training costs also started rising in the 1970s after many years of only very slow increase. Thus, in 1951 the first year's costs were budgeted at $5,000 for one training year. In 1960 the figure was still

$5,000. By 1970 it had risen to $6,500, a 30 percent rise over the decade. By 1985 the annual cost of a trainee in the United States had risen to $21,000 (excluding international travel, which was funded by DTEC).[3]

Another problem was that degree training came under a cloud after the 1973 aid legislation was enacted. To meet AID's legal requirement to refocus the program on the poor, field missions had to specify who were the target beneficiaries when they submitted new project proposals to Washington. Advanced training was stigmatized as elitist and had to be justified by demonstrating its essentiality for the conduct of any poverty-oriented proposals that contained higher education components. General training projects not linked to specific poverty alleviation activities also became unfashionable. A third factor was the progress Thailand had made in developing its domestic education system, thereby reducing the country's dependence on external training. The 1969 participant study reexamined the need for foreign training in the light of this growth of domestic capabilities. The study reached the limited conclusion that there was no further justification for participant undergraduate education (which had always been very minor) and that in a few selected subjects the masters degrees offered by Thai universities obviated any need for participant grants in those fields.

We can see a decline in the need for overseas training more clearly in specific subjects where participant training had been concentrated for several years to help the Thais build up their own institutional strength and professional personnel. For example, in demography and the medical and administrative disciplines needed for planning and implementing Thailand's population and family planning programs, the period of major institutional development was the decade between 1965 and 1975. Participant training in population skills had been minor in earlier years, when population was just emerging as a subject of public policy and private health sector activity. When Thailand determined that population was an important aspect of the country's social and economic development, the Ministry of Health and the universities turned to AID, the Population Council, and other agencies to help develop the staff capabilities of the fledgling Thai institutions involved. This object was accomplished, and participant training in population-related subjects then declined. There have been similar periods of concentrated training in engineering and other subjects during initial years of institutional capacity building, followed by declining need for external education.

The successful efforts to develop domestic capabilities in specific

TABLE 3.1.

Distribution of AID Participants by Field of Study
(as of 1980)

Field	Number of Participants	Percent
Social Sciences & other	2,094	20
Agriculture	1,925	18
Education	1,525	14
Engineering & technology	1,442	13
Medicine & public health	1,253	12
Police	1,092	10
Business administration	787	7
Sciences	595	6
TOTAL	10,714	100

SOURCE: USAID/Thailand.

disciplines do not add up to a decline in the overall need of a developing country for external education, especially advanced education and training in specialized subjects in which the creation of domestic capacity is not yet feasible or may never be sensible as a means of educating the small numbers of specialists the country needs. And, as recognized in the 1969 study, differences in content and quality between domestic and foreign education in the same discipline may persist and remain good justification for a country to continue to educate some professionals abroad. In fact, large numbers of Thais continue to seek their education in other countries, even for secondary education under private family funding. In mid-1987 there were about 2,650 Thai government officials and King's scholars studying abroad, of whom about 1,950 were in degree training, about 40 percent in the United States.[4] The total number of Thais studying overseas is not known, but it is commonly believed that the number of Thais studying abroad in recent years under family or other private auspices dwarfs the number under official programs.

The aid program has financed training over a wide range of disciplines relevant to the development process. Table 3.1 shows the cumulative distribution by major field of study as of 1980. While training in agriculture (both basic science and applied specialties like extension and crop management), medicine and health, and engineering (such as civil and electrical, related to the road-building and power systems projects) were obvious subjects given the importance of the institutional and infrastructure projects in these areas, the fields that might be characterized as broad development management subjects—economics, other social sciences, management—were well represented at 27 percent of the total. The importance of the anti-insurgency projects in the late 1960s and early 1970s is reflected in the 10 percent share of police training participants. (None of the additional 467 participants between 1980 and September 1987 are police trainees.)

Needless to say, the importance of participant training cannot be drawn from a mere toting of the numbers. For one thing, any effort to identify the returns to investment in education runs into difficult problems of measurement and concept. When these efforts are applied to the special case of aid-financed training, the problems are multiplied. Participant training may be a neat category as far as aid administration is concerned, but it is a program component, an educational function, too heterogeneous for easy generalization. The impact of training (and the possibility of measuring such impact) varies from disciplines that can be measured and evaluated with some precision (road building, for example) to disciplines inherently very imprecise (public administration, say, or agricultural extension). In addition, an impact evaluation would have to examine separately the doctorate and master's degrees students and observation tour and short course trainees, all with very different educational experiences. It would also be necessary to separate the educational experience from a number of other factors that are known (from studies of the determinants of differential income status in the United States, for example) to interact and jointly determine career outcomes and performance (individual personality aside), such as family background or prestige ranking of schools attended.

One should not dismiss such considerations as academic quibbles. In the Thai bureaucratic elite, achievement of high rank has been shown to be strongly associated with middle- and upper-class family background, including families with a tradition of government service.[5] Educational attainment is also a powerful determinant of elite status but cannot be considered an independent factor since the Bangkok-based families of wealth or government service also have been highly overrepresented among the university population, although this predominance has been declining in recent years with the establishment of open universities.

There are other problems as well in trying to specify the long-term effects of training programs for government officials who have been selected because they hold particular jobs in programs being assisted by specific projects. After a few years they are often moved to other positions, usually up the ranks of the same program, but sometimes to an activity or unit not directly related to the original project. After more time has elapsed, they may leave that ministry or the government altogether or get further training that leads to a shift in their discipline or expertise. Or the activities of the original project may be discontinued, policy may change, and the former participants may be assigned to new programs. Such problems do not translate into a cancellation of the value of the original training. It is reasonable to assume that over their careers the participants try to maximize their private returns to the investment they (and the RTG and AID) have made in their education, whether they remain in the functions for which they were trained or move elsewhere. In a bureaucracy that puts significant weight on merit and allows considerable scope for individual career maneuver, it is reasonable to conclude that the participants are likely to succeed in their efforts and that the investment in human capital will continue to pay off through their careers. When an aid program has invested in the training of officials on the scale AID has, one needs to look for impact on two levels: the specific institutions and functions for which the training was provided and in which many participants have continued to work; and the overall performance of departments and agencies of government in which large numbers of former participants are scattered in influential positions.

I will return to both these levels repeatedly in this study. The reader should be aware, however, that although training has been an important element of all aid programs in Thailand and elsewhere, there have been very few attempts to evaluate its impact in the face of these difficulties of tracking and of defining and measuring impact. In short, the effects of training as an input into a project to build an institution or to overcome some specific problem can be identified when one evaluates the immediate, proximate results of the project as a whole. What is more difficult and seldom tried in the aid literature is to evaluate the long-run and more subtle effects on entire career paths of large cohorts of trainees, including both their behavior as economic or development actors and their orientation toward the donor and country of training, a not insignificant factor in the sponsoring programs.

Now that some of the difficulties of judging the impact of aid-financed training have been put up front, what can be said initially about the second level or broad impact of the participant training? After examining the evidence on the aid program's activities in some detail, I will take a second look at overall impact and the role the training has played. So far I am addressing only the training that took place in the United States and elsewhere outside Thailand. The numbers of Thais trained inside Thailand under aid-related projects has been vastly greater than the number of participants, but this domestic training role of AID has been sufficiently different in character to warrant separate treatment.

What has happened to these 11,000 persons? Unfortunately only limited records are available on the participants. They are kept by the Thai-American Technical Cooperation Association (TATCA), an organization that publishes a regular bulletin on participant news and undertakes other activities to foster continuing contacts among participants and with such RTG agencies as DTEC and to a lesser degree with the AID mission. Use of the records for analysis of the long-run track of the participants awaits computerization of TATCA's information and would need to be supplemented with special surveys. To get some idea of the extent to which former U.S. participants are found in senior reaches of the Thai government (excluding military and other security related positions), TATCA combed its records to identify which of the individuals occupying 411 senior administrative and decision-making positions in the government had received external training under AID. The results are shown in table 3.2.

Senior positions have been defined as all permanent secretaries, directors-general, secretaries-general, governors, and their deputies, plus the governors of the country's seventy-three provinces. In the Thai government the permanent secretary is the top subcabinet civil servant in each ministry. Directors-general form the next rung as heads of departments, and in some ministries have more authority than the permanent secretary. Secretaries-general and governors head various offices and agencies that are not constituted as departments. Provincial governors are the senior officials of the bureaucratic system outside Bangkok and report to the Ministry of Interior.

In 1986, 163, or nearly 40 percent, of these positions were held by former AID participants. About 40 percent of the provincial governors had been participants, mainly for long-term training. Of the 130 former participants in the seat of national government in Bangkok, 91 had earned graduate degrees under their training, including 15 doctorates. Several had been participants two or three times, including long-term education and subsequent short training opportunities. While some of the former participants had had only short-term training under the aid program (as brief as two months), they comprised only a minor fraction.

TABLE 3.2.

Senior RTG Officials Trained Under the U.S. Aid Program (as of February 1986)

Ministry	Senior Officials	Participants
Office of the Prime Minister	54	17
Finance	24	10
Foreign Affairs	17	0
Agriculture & Cooperatives	43	16
Communications	25	7
Commerce	20	4
Interior	46	24
Justice[a]	8	0
Science, Technology, & Energy	17	7
Education	46	29
Public Health	19	10
Industry	16	5
University Affairs	3	1
Governors of Provinces	73	32
TOTAL	411	162

SOURCE: Thai-American Technical Cooperation Association.
[a] Excludes courts.

In addition to these top-layer jobs across the ministries, there are many units in the Thai government and among university faculties where AID participant training was concentrated for several years and where cadres of former participants now hold many of the senior and middle ranking positions. Between the large number of exparticipants in top government positions, the especially heavy representation in the so-called "core" agencies of the Prime Minister's Office and the Ministry of Finance, and the concentration in the powerful Ministry of Interior, the universities, and in ministries with major development functions, it is easy to see why the Thais themselves view the training as the most pervasive long-run contribution the United States has made to Thai development, and a contribution in which the U.S. numbers have cumulated to levels that far outdistance other aid programs. This impression of a predominant American role is substantially enhanced when one takes account of the additional numbers of Thais, especially in the medical and academic realms, who have been trained in the United States under other American program auspices. These numbers are summarized in table 3.3.

TABLE 3.3.

Foundation Fellowships for Study in the United States: 1951–1985

	Fulbright[a]	Population Council[b]	Ford[c]	Rockefeller	ADC/Winrock
1951–1955	142	——	——	——	——
1956–1960	113	1	——	96[d]	5
1961–1965	159	6	——	24[e]	12
1966–1970	175	9	——	133	12
1971–1975	99	13	62	86	5
1976–1980	118	4	37	33	3
1981–1985	118	3[f]	12	6[g]	1
Year Undetermined	——	3	——	——	——
TOTAL	924	43	111	378	38

Total Fellowships = 1494

[a] A few grantees received two scholarships at different times for different degree studies; thus the number of scholarships shown slightly exceeds the number of individual grantees.
[b] The Population Council has been funded by Ford, Rockefeller, USAID, and other sources and is not itself foundation.
[c] Includes a few grants for conducting doctoral research work in Thailand.
[d] 1922–1963.
[e] 1964–1965.
[f] Through 1983.
[g] Includes 1986.

The largest of these other American programs, in terms of numbers of Thais trained in the United States, has been the Fulbright. The Fulbright Educational Exchange Program was legislated by Congress in 1946. The program extended its first grants for study by Thais in the United States in 1951. By 1985 the number of Thai Fulbright scholars had reached 924, of whom 786 had received grants for study towards graduate degrees. Their fields of study covered virtually every discipline, with education the main area (25 percent of the scholars), followed by the humanities and the social sciences (15 percent each). (The program has also financed study and teaching in Thailand by over 200 U.S. scholars, a few of whom have joined the small ranks of American specialists with long-term interest in and expertise on Thailand.) While most of the Thai scholars have made academic careers in Thai universities, several have gone into government and the private sector and have risen to senior positions.[6]

The Rockefeller Foundation did some of its earliest overseas work in Thailand, starting in 1916 on problems of hookworm and environmental sanitation. Beginning in 1963 the Foundation chose Thailand as one of its countries for concentrated assistance under a major University Development Program. Seven developing country institutions were included in this program, of which three were in Thailand —Thammasat, Kasetsart, and Mahidol universities, the country's leading universities in the social sciences, agriculture, and medicine and public health, respectively. Most of the Foundation's grants for study in the United States went to faculty members of these three schools. The bulk of the 378 recipients appear to have remained with their institutions since. Some have left for careers elsewhere, and several of these individuals have achieved prominence as development technocrats.[7]

The Ford Foundation first opened an office in Bangkok in 1967. In addition to extending over $18 million of grants to various Thai academic and research institutions, which have supported the work of many Thai scholars, Ford also has granted about $1.5 million for external study and travel to 360 individual Thais between 1971 and 1987. Some 111 of these individual grantees worked towards graduate degrees, about one-third in countries other than the United States. In both the individual and institutional grants, the Foundation covered a wide range of social and humanities subjects (such as human rights, archeology, temple art preservation, museums, and literature) in addition to standard economic development disciplines. The Foundation has focused (not exclusively) on specific faculties such as (in recent years) the Khonkaen Faculty of Agriculture and Engineering and the Chiengmai Faculty of Agriculture and Forestry.[8]

The Agricultural Development Council (ADC), recently merged into Winrock International Institute for Agricultural Development, is an American foundation specializing in training and agricultural institution-building in developing countries. ADC's work in Thailand began in 1955 and has concentrated since then on the establishment and support of the Faculty of Economics and Business Administration of Kasetsart University. From a staff with three Ph.D. professors in 1957, the faculty grew to 31 Ph.D.'s and 84 M.A.'s and M.S.'s in 1985. Undergraduate students in agricultural economics at Kasetsart grew from 16 in 1957 to 277 in 1985, graduate students from zero to 100. Over the whole period ADC has had resident American economists on the faculty. Through 1985, a total of 63 Thais from Kasetsart and other institutions received graduate economics degrees with ADC support, of whom 38 studied in the United States. ADC's total resource input into its Thai activities, which has also included research and seminar support, amounted to about $2.1 million by 1985. (The Population Council training is discussed below.)

The Asia Foundation has had a resident program in Thailand since 1954. Although the Foundation financed only small numbers of Thais undertaking long-term training in the United States (or elsewhere), it has extended grants for numerous observation tours in the United States and to many Thai educational institutions. The Foundation's work is not easily summarized since the organization's policy has been to limit individual grants to an average of $5–7,000 and many fields have been eligible for support over the past three and a half decades. In the early years the Foundation focused on Buddhist and cultural institutions and supported programs of Chinese and other minority groups. In the 1960s it added areas such as rural and urban community development, then health and population. In the 1970s education, law, and public administration received significant support. Grants in recent years have also been made in such areas as science and technology, computers, business, and linkages with Asia and the United States. The distribution of English language books (mainly to institutions and libraries) has always been an important part of the Foundation's programs, with the total number of books distributed in Thailand having now reached over 700,000. Since 1969 the Foundation has spent $8.6 million in its Thai program (I do not have the figures for the earlier years); in 1986–1987 the program was running at about $800,000 a year.

The mid-1950s to mid-1970s were decades of substantial USAID participant training and fellowship activity of the foundations (and other smaller American sources). During this time institutional financing accounted for a major fraction of government and academic long-term training in the United States. Compared with the total Thai higher education student body in the United States in those years, however, these trainees comprised 10 percent or less. Data on foreign students in the United States is gathered annually by the Institute of International Education, located in New York. The IIE figures for the Thai student body in selected years are shown in table 3.4.[9] (The IIE data show the Thai students in most years comprising about 2 percent of the total foreign student population in the United States.) After a sharp rise in the late 1960s and early 1970s Thai students have remained around the 6,000–7,000 mark. I have not tried to get a precise picture of the numbers of Thai students financed by other American institutional sources, but they would not raise the totals significantly during those peak years. (According to the Thai Civil Service Commission, those other sources supported about 130 fellows in 1986.) Well

TABLE 3.4.

Thai Higher Education Students in the United States

Academic Year	Total Number of Students
1950–1951	234
1954–1955	586
1959–1960	1,006
1964–1965	1,630
1969–1970	4,372
1974–1975	6,250
1979–1980	6,500
1984–1985	7,220
1985–1986	6,940
1986–1987	6,480

SOURCE: Institute for International Education.

over 5,000 and perhaps over 6,000 of these students are thus financed privately.

The total number of Thais who had long-term training in the United States under these official and institutional American auspices over this long period—roughly 4,500—is not large compared with the entire ranks of Thais with higher education or the total civil service. But in a meaningful sense these Thais can be described as a cohort that has had distinguishing common characteristics and has played a role in Thai development much greater than the numbers themselves might imply. This group can be distinguished first by the competitive selection procedures each member had to undergo. The selection process was not the same for each agency, nor was it uniform for all AID projects. But the language, academic record, personal interviews, and other criteria and procedures were sufficiently rigorous and even-handed to ensure that the trainees were a cohort of above-average ability and prospects. AID's much larger scale of overseas training and very wide institutional coverage probably made it more difficult for AID to screen out candidates who had been proposed for reasons of favoritism than for the foundations to do so. However, while some diminution of candidate quality was unavoidable, it was probably minor given the gauntlet of DTEC, AID, and (for long-term training) university screening through which each candidate had to pass.

Projects that trained a large fraction of the staff of any one office or agency would inevitably end up sending the less capable along with the obviously outstanding. Quality diminution from such agency or functional saturation training was at least offset, however, by the added benefits of concentrated training on the performance of the institution as a whole. The qualitative differences between highly selective individual training and a concentration by institution pose more of a dilemma or option for the foundations than for AID, where the training has usually been a component of a functional or institutional project. Looking back over its University Development (UD) Program approach, in which the three Thai universities figured prominently, the Rockefeller Foundation summed up the problem in its 1986 *Annual Report:*

> One disadvantage of the institution-building focus as compared to the individual-scholar focus . . . is the forced recruitment of candidates from a much smaller pool. Some Rockefeller Foundation officers with comparative experience argued that there was a discernible decline in the overall quality of candidates after the Foundation's shift to institution-building under the UD . . . program. The disadvantage of the individual approach is the production of a group of stranded individuals without institutional affiliation.[10]

The Foundation may be overstating the disadvantage of the individual focus since most grantees, even under the relatively unstructured approach of the Fullbright Foundation, had an institutional base both before and after their training. The difference is sharper between the training of (affiliated) grantees as individual fellows versus the training of groups of (affiliated) grantees as part of a structured institutionally based project.

In fact—and this constitutes in my view a second characteristic behind the high impact of these training programs—the Thais trained under both AID and foundation auspices have been relatively concentrated institutionally both in the universities and in the functions and government agencies that have been major recipients of AID assistance. As we shall see below, the structure of development institutions in Thailand includes many that are well staffed with American trainees, quite apart from the top layers of the Thai government. The concentrated training has enabled these institutions (not all were successful, of course) to assemble the variety and quality of skills they needed (the phrase "critical mass" captures this motion) to achieve organizational viability and an acceptable level of effectiveness. The greater efficiency of providing training (and other technical cooperation, or TC) within institutional development frameworks was stressed by a World Bank evaluation of its technical aid activities in Bangladesh which concluded that the Bank's technical assistance had done little to strengthen the institutions involved because the assistance, attached to capital projects, had not been designed to achieve institutional development goals.[11]

A third factor has been the prestige accorded to foreign training, especially foreign academic degrees. For many years the Thai Civil Service Commission gave formal recognition to the qualitative differences between Thai and foreign universities by establishing a dual-entry system under which foreign degree holders were hired into government employment at a salary at least 50 percent higher than holders of domestic degrees. (This practice was rightly criticized for failing to take into account the wide variations in quality among foreign universities, and for several reasons, including the growing strength of Thai universities, was discontinued in 1975.) In 1977 the advantages of the foreign degree were described by a Thai political scientist, Likhit Dhiravegin, as follows:

> In Thailand, education (especially Western education) plays a significant role in determining one's mobility. Once a higher education degree is obtained, the future elite status of the individual is almost assured. . . . One [reason] is the simple law of supply and demand. The percentage of the population having a graduate degree is quite small. College enrollment is small in proportion to the total population. [Likhit put this proportion at less than 1 percent.]
>
> Location of the elite's training is important. . . . A foreign degree especially that of the West, is considered of better quality. This is not just considered from the educational qualifications but also the social implications that follow. A Western-trained person is either believed to be smart enough to earn a scholarship or to be from a wealthy family. . . . A person who has a M.A. or Ph.D. from say, England or the United States would be given respect.[12]

The prestige bestowed by Western education on those who could obtain it was evident already after World War I. As Walter Vella notes, "Upon return to Siam they would expect to attain relatively high official positions at an early age. Their technical and professional skills were a source of power and the prestige attached to things Western gave additional weight to their ideas."[13] The prestige of the

Western degree was enhanced further for the individuals who were recipients of training grants, since the sponsoring foreign organizations carried their own additional prestige.

The timing of the training programs was a fourth and very important factor in their impact. When the U.S. programs were launched, there were very limited numbers of Thais with advanced education in the skills required for modern economic development. Postwar Thailand faced critical shortages of people with development management skills—engineers, administrators, statisticians, economists, and the like. The development management problem Thailand faced in the 1950s and the role of foreign training at that time were described by the World Bank team writing its major development review in Bangkok in 1958:

> Stated very broadly, the principal need of higher education in Thailand is a rise in its quality, so as to provide the opportunity for developing the talents of the numerous able young Thai who cannot afford to attend foreign universities or who cannot share in the limited program of assistance for foreign study. High quality at home would also reduce the cost of that program.
>
> Other sections of this report call attention to the need in Thailand for trained administrators, engineers, agricultural experts, economists, statisticians and other types of technically skilled personnel. At present, these needs for special training are being met largely by sending Thai nationals abroad. This solution is expensive, as well as self-perpetuating.[14]

AID and other donors agreed with the Bank that high priority should be given to development of Thai educational institutions capable of meeting these requirements, and much of the training has in fact has been devoted to helping build up teaching staffs of both the major universities and the teacher training colleges that were turning out the primary and secondary school instructors. The Thai education system was unable then to meet these needs, having limited training capacity in most disciplines (the problems of educational quality aside). Both advanced training and specialized short course opportunities were very limited. The development of the institutional structures of a modern economy was just getting started. Outside of medicine, virtually no graduate education was available in Thailand in the 1950s. By 1967 Thai institutions of higher learning were graduating only about 150 master-level students a year, of whom about 50 were medical. Even today doctorates are offered in few subjects, although the quality and scope of undergraduate and master-level education has developed very substantially.

The American training program burgeoned during a period when Thai development was most heavily dependent upon overseas education and training and when only the American programs offered training on a scale commensurate with the needs. The cumulative impact on the Thai Government by the mid-1970s is reflected in Likhit's data. Of the one-third of highest ranking officials (then called Special Grade) who were foreign-trained, 71 percent had received this training in the United States. Among the next rank (First Grade officials), 19 percent had been trained abroad, of whom 78 percent went to the United States.[15] The American training also came at a time when the prestige and economic predominance of the United States was at its height. Combined with the role the United States was playing as guarantor of the integrity and independence of the Thai state, the training programs were also seen—again by the Thais themselves, as best as one can judge on such an uncertain proposition—as having profound impact on Thai elite orientation towards the United States and on their values and their effectiveness and behavior as professionals and members of the governing elite.*

I cite these elusive qualities of behavior and attitude as the fifth factor that has contributed to setting the U.S. trainees apart and giving them the opportunity to play a disproportionate role in Thailand's development. The sense that Thais exposed to, or better, immersed in American life return with new perspectives and an altered frame of mind is not likely to apply to trainees who have had only short courses or observation tours, although even casual foreign travel can widen the outlook of an alert observer. That Thais who have undertaken long term study in the United States (and elsewhere) return perceptibly different from other Thais is a commonly held and voiced belief. Likhit writes that "it is believed that a foreign-trained individual is cultured, and understands the 'high civilization' of the west. He is different from others in terms of outlook, values and tastes."[16]

---

*The prevalence of American education among the Thai elite goes well beyond government circles. No less than 70 percent of the 1,210 persons in an early 1980s Who's Who in Thailand had studied or trained overseas, 24 percent for bachelor degrees and 36 percent for graduate degrees. Sixty-one percent of the overseas study had been in the United States, followed by 17 percent in the United Kingdom. About one-fourth of those who studied in the United States had attended six universities—Indiana, Pennsylvania, Harvard, Radcliffe, Michigan, Illinois, and Cornell. See G. W. Fry, "The Economic and Political Impact of Study Abroad."

To an American who has lived and worked in Thailand, the differences between Thai and American culture appear substantial. In their temperament, interpersonal interaction, etiquette, and organizational behavior and in their characteristic methods of coping with issues of power and conflict, the Thais tend to conduct themselves in ways strikingly different from Americans or Europeans. At the same time, the Thais have shown great tolerance towards other cultures and have been comfortable and adept at absorbing and harmonizing influences from outside. Thus, the American-trained Thais in government, business, and academia appear to have internalized many values learned in the United States in a manner that seldom results in alienation or other indications of psychological disjuncture. They are certainly a transitional generation, in the vanguard during an era of great change in their society. The American professional finds his or her Thai counterparts fully recognizable and knowledgeable as fellow members of an increasingly international culture of professionals, based on shared higher education and common language, competence, and membership in international economic and institutional networks. Nevertheless, on their home ground, the Thai "new" men and women remain powerfully attached to a culture for which they feel great pride.The impact of the U.S. educational experience has unquestionably been strong. But these impressions, common as they are, must remain elusive and anecdotal until systematic social study in Thailand catches up with elite change.*

A Thai educator has observed that "it has become almost proverbial that those Thais found in elevated government positions, in commerce or in banking, at universities, and even in the military, have received at least part of their education in the United States. For a Thai to have attended an American university, or to have been trained at an American institution for a short term, is of immense practical value."[17] To a considerable extent, the Thais who could be identified today as comprising the country's intellectual class are found in these same elevated ranks of the government, business, academic, and even military establishments. Thai intellectuals as a recognizable and well-

---

*One of the rare efforts to identify nontechnical effects of foreign training under an aid program happens to have been conducted in Thailand. It covered 92 of the 454 Thais who studied in Israel between 1976 and 1982 under the Israeli aid program. These participants all had college degrees, were mostly early and mid-career civil servants and university faculty, and went to Israel for short courses in agriculture, community development, and public health. Despite the brevity of the training, the evaluation attempted through questionnaire and interviews to find out if the experience had affected attitudes toward change, initiative, cooperation, and other aspects of work orientation deemed characteristic of the Israeli environment. While the authors believed attitudinal changes were discernible, they found that the evaluation in this respect was inconclusive. See the Israel Association for International Cooperation, *Thailand Country Evaluation Report*.

defined class numbering more than a handful emerged only in the 1960s, when small groups of social science–trained individuals began to hold occasional meetings.* By the 1980s the intellectuals were a large group whose members appeared often in the media and whose views on social problems and economic policy could be heard at open seminars that had become almost a daily feature of life in Bangkok. The numbers of Thai intellectuals are still small enough for personal knowledge and networks that enable the individuals to know a great deal about each other, from schooling to career to personal affairs. The names of a large number of these individuals can be found among the lists of AID and American foundation grantees who have taken their higher education in the United States.

I do not want to exaggerate the extent or depth of the effects of this permeation of American education among Thai intellectuals. Many of them have been trained in other countries as well, increasingly so in recent years. Since Thai intellectuals have yet to develop an interest in analyzing themselves as a class, we have no ready literature on the development of Thai thought, apart from occasional pieces on Thai economists and the more considerable work that has been on the writers and students whose ideas were central to the student rebellions and political turbulence of the mid-1970s. Still, the perceptions of the Thais themselves and the sheer weight of the numbers would appear to warrant a supposition of substantial American intellectual impact on Thais with high education, on Thais in government and the major universities, and on Thai intellectuals—three groups that to a considerable extent overlap. Backing for this supposition is certainly less elusive than the effects of the American experience on their professional behavior, values, and tastes. In the course of undertaking this study, I have gathered some impressions and examples of how the training and a number of particular institution-building and technical assistance projects have served as transmittal experiences through which American ideas have influenced Thai intellectual orientation. These influences are clear in some realms, ambiguous in others.

Foreign training under aid programs has been criticized on several

---

*Noted in William J. Siffin, *The Thai Institute of Public Administration, A Case Study in Institute Building*, p. 265. Initially these meetings were often lunches to which the younger intellectuals were drawn by the opportunity to hear Dr. Puey Ungphakorn speak informally about current issues. Puey was the leading Thai economist for over twenty years from the mid-1950s to the mid-1970s and one of the leading Thai intellectuals of his time. In the late 1950s I participated occasionally in a regular lunch held by a group of young Thai intellectuals, mostly economists who had returned recently from long-term study abroad and who were protégés of Puey. The group included most of the initial professional staff of the National Economic Development Board, and most of them subsequently rose to senior policy responsibility in the Thai government. At the time of these lunches they formed a considerable fraction of all the postwar foreign-trained Thai economists; the group numbered eleven.

counts. One of the earlier problems to arise, already evident in the mid-1950s, was "brain drain." Large numbers of trainees under U.S. and other aid programs and private auspices were not returning to their home countries after completion of their overseas education. This posed a serious issue for the developing countries concerned and for the effectiveness of aid programs that were training many people who ended up putting their new skills to work in the donor country instead.[18] In the case of Thailand this appears not to have been a significant problem overall, certainly not among AID participants of whom only five have failed to return. There has always been a compulsion to return, of course, since Thai government employees are obliged, after completion of any training under government sponsorship, to continue working for the government (two years for each year of training received) or refund the cost of the training. Other countries experiencing brain drain of participants presumably had similar requirements or binding arrangements, but these were apparently less effective. Since we have no follow-up survey information since 1970, we do not know how many may have subsequently left the country, how many years of work the government got from such people before they left, whether they tended to repatriate, and so on. Between the impressions one gains from the numbers and knowledge of the role of former participants and the apparent absence of any Thai concern over outmigration of professionals until 1988, one can probably put the matter aside.

Has foreign training been a cost-effective way of meeting developing country skill requirements? As the World Bank study on Thailand noted in 1959, overseas training is expensive, and it is more cost effective to develop domestic institutions capable of providing the same training. There are several factors to take into account here. One is the time frame. As a rule of thumb in the development literature, it is commonly observed that a donor agency starting on a project to build up a university faculty that is merely nascent in size and quality should plan to carry through for at least ten years before the faculty is in a position to produce the qualitative equivalent of foreign training. Even so, the equivalency attained is not likely to put the faculty on the same level as the very top-ranking institutions of world quality, and arrangements should be in place for further specialized assistance to ensure an adequate level of institutional exchange and other linkages that will help the aided institution to keep abreast of the state of the art in its field.The heaviest years of participant training took place during years when few Thai educational or training institutions had reached such equivalency levels. Indeed, much of the participant training was an integral part of projects designed to bring Thai educational and research institutions up to standards and capacities that would obviate the need for further overseas training, with the exception of the residual requirements for intellectual exchange that are a permanent feature of even the most advanced institutions everywhere. Given the tremendous expansion of Thai educational facilities in the postwar years, the central role in this expansion that was played by the aid agencies, the steep decline in the AID participant numbers, and the relative decline that is certainly underway in the ratio of foreign to domestically educated people in Thailand, the argument that is sometimes made that aid programs create dependency in this respect cannot use Thailand as a case in point.

Another problem concerns the utilization of the skills acquired abroad. In some countries returned trainees have restricted opportunities to apply their new skills or to introduce new ideas. They are still relatively junior and work in bureaucracies where older supervisors retain all decision authority and resent or discourage initiatives by subordinates even if, or perhaps precisely because, their subordinates have better or more up-to-date training. Under these conditions participants' skills can atrophy, and loss of motivation can occur. This problem has been observed often but rarely examined systematically. The few multicounty evaluations of training under various aid program auspices, couducted not long after completion of the training, have focused on the trainees personally and generally have found them benefiting from "enhanced competence" and greater knowledge.[19]

Given Thailand's traditions of bureaucratic behavior, which emphasize deference to superiors, a distaste for confrontation, and a reluctance to delegate authority, one might expect to find a high level of frustration among recently returned participants and limited use of their training. The sudden postwar expansion of overseas education produced a rapid increase in the 1960s in the number of younger Western-educated technocrats working for senior administrators of the old school. However, in some of the institution-building AID projects I have examined through personal interviews with the Thais involved, it is clear that the returned participants (and foundation grantees) were in fact given wide scope to apply their new skills. The experiences of the young officers in the Ministry of Finance, NESDB, the Electricity Generating Authority of Thailand, and the Accelerated Rural Development Department were examples of immediate application of the potential benefits of overseas training.

In these cases the organizations were growing rapidly to cope with mounting responsibilities during the years when the government was turning itself into an engine of development. Quite the contrary to the problem of poor use of participant training, the then young officials of these organizations were often given responsibilities that in retrospect—from the point of view of seniors in these now mature agencies, where new hires now face fully occupied career ladders and moderate, regularized promotion and growth in responsibility—some of them see as having been premature and as marking a unique era in Thailand's institutional development. While participant experience must have varied from agency to agency and from supervisor to supervisor, the years of heavy AID participant training were the years of most rapid growth and transformation of the development functions and organizations of the public sector. It seems a reasonable hypothesis that other units of the public sector, working under conditions similar to those facing the units about which I can speak with some confidence, also had the motivation and need to make good use of the skills learned through participant training.

Besides the general evidence cited above, I will review many individual institution-building projects where a strengthening of Thai professionals' technical qualifications was deemed a necessary condition for achieving the projects' objectives and where the training was accomplished and the project goals attained. I will also review projects that were outright failures, but in no case does it appear that a training failure (inappropriate curriculum, say, or low quality teaching) was among the reasons for the project's lack of success. The literature on overseas training of people from developing countries points to a number of common-sense factors that determine effectiveness—language capability and academic preparation, selection procedures, quality and relevance of training, opportunity to apply newly learned skills, and the incentive structure and institutional environment upon return. As best as can be determined, the AID and other training in the United States and its application on the job seems to have been effective on these counts.

I conclude this review of the program's overseas training with a brief note on the training activities conducted inside Thailand, quite apart from the formal education offered by the universities and the school systems assisted by AID projects discussed below. There were many projects under which American technicians conducted direct on-the-job training. Vastly greater numbers of Thais were trained under projects that provided technical and financial inputs into major RTG programs, especially in public health (thousands of malaria workers and over 150,000 midwives, village health extension staff, and volunteers) and education (in-service training of primary and secondary teachers). In the case of AID, as in any of the development assistance agencies, association with training programs of these types offers opportunities for raising technical capacities on a large scale. At the same time, one needs to avoid making excessive claims where the aid inputs are small or not seminal for the conceptualization or organization of large-scale training, useful as these inputs may be; a scattering of inputs of this character could give a misleading impression of a donor's impact if one merely added up the numbers of people being put through permanent training programs. For this reason I make no attempt to estimate the total domestic training to which the U.S. aid program might be "credited," but do cite some of the important instances below, including the project that introduced to Thailand the concept of in-service training (apart from orientation-type training the Ministry of Interior provided to personnel about to take their first provincial posting). As the first large aid program in Thailand, AID was also in position to break new ground for in-service training (initially in the Ministry of Interior) by providing the substantial supplementary financing (from the counterpart fund) that led to acceptance of the concept by the Thai budget authorities.

FOUR

NATION-BUILDING, 1950–1959

POINT FOUR BEGINNINGS: 1950–1954

Within four months of the signing of the Point Four agreement in September 1950, thirty American experts had arrived in Thailand.[1] In response to the Thai request that the assistance should concentrate on agriculture, health, and communications, the program began with the projects in rice and other crop improvement, irrigation in the Northeast, fisheries technology, and other agricultural activities; malaria control and hospital system expansion; transportation and power; and small activities in education and public health administration. Within the first three to four years some of these projects achieved quick results and were phased out; other activities that initiated more long-term efforts also recorded initial successes.

Agriculture

About 30 percent of the funds in the first three years were allocated to agriculture. Probably the first completed accomplishment in this sector was the conduct of the country's first soil survey. Problems of agricultural productivity figured importantly in the very first year and continued to be important to the aid program thenceforth.

One of the first objectives of the program was to strengthen Thai agricultural research capabilities, focusing on development of high yielding varieties of basic cereal crops, especially rice and corn. While corn was a relatively minor crop in 1950, rice was the most important economic good in Thailand's livelihood and society. For the previous century cultivation practices had remained unchanged, and increases in rice output to feed the growing population and for sale abroad had derived entirely from expansion in cultivated area. In the postwar years, however, virtually all naturally flooded land suitable for rice cultivation had been put into production. The average area harvested in rice in the five-year period 1949–1953 was double the average area in 1923–1927, but remained virtually unchanged in 1954–1958. Meanwhile, yields per unit area had fallen about 30 percent between 1923–1927 and 1949–1953 averages.[2] Thailand had been conducting research on rice varieties since 1921. The Rice Improvement project of 1951–1958 and the related project to develop the Bangkhen research station at Kasetsart University expanded the scale of Thai rice research and strengthened its scientific basis in an effort to reverse the decline in yields. Thousands of rice samples were obtained from other countries, and over 200,000 varieties and samples were tested. Rounds of extensive selection and retesting were conducted at Bangkhen and ten other provincial research stations, which were provided with equipment and technical assistance. Fourteen varieties were chosen for a large-scale multiplication program reportedly involving over 40,000 farmers.

The result of this vast effort was a group of varieties that yielded increases in rice output of up to 20 percent under field conditions. When the U.S. project ended in 1958, the mission estimated that about one-sixth of the farmers was using the improved varieties. Unfortunately, neither this increase nor the yield potentialities of the high yielding varieties developed by the International Rice Research Institute (IRRI) in the Philippines in the 1960s put Thailand on a path of long-term rising rice productivity. In fact, although Thailand is the largest rice exporter in Asia (Thailand and the United States are the two major rice exporting countries of the world), Thailand has lower yields than all of the twelve other major Asian rice-producing countries. Between 1961–1963 and 1979–1981 Thailand's increase in yields per unit of cultivated area (11 percent) was also lower than all twelve other producers.[3]

According to a World Bank analysis, the failure of Thai productivity to match the levels achieved in other countries results from a combination of agronomic and economic factors. Almost everywhere in the country rice is grown in flooded fields without systems for controlling the water level. The irrigation systems in Thailand's Central Plains rice bowl were designed to spread flood water rather than control the height of water in flooded fields. In all the areas where rice is cultivated under rain-fed conditions, there is always a threat from sudden floods, which can wash across fields or bring about a rapid rise in the level of standing water. Under these conditions the ability of any variety to grow rapidly as the water level rises is a more important trait than relative yield; IRRI varieties were developed under controlled irrigation conditions and require application of chemical fertilizers to achieve their yield potentials. Thus, in addition to the need for fast growing varieties, the Thai farmer faces the risk that fertilizer applied early in the growing season may get washed away. Compounding these agronomic obstacles, the Thai government has in most years taxed the agricultural sector through imposition of an export tax on rice that has pressed the domestic rice price structure down in relation to world market prices. As a result, Thailand has also had the highest ratio of fertilizer to rice prices of any of the twelve Asian producers and the lowest fertilizer application rates.[4]

The pros and cons of Thai rice pricing (and other government marketing intervention) policies are complex and have been debated at length. The rice export tax has in fact been eliminated (or more precisely, reduced to zero—the authority remains on the books) as part of a broad package of economic policy adjustments introduced since 1981. I would stress that with the expansion of rice production in the 1950s dependent on large investments in irrigation that were yet to be made, the kind of varietal improvement achieved at that time was probably the most effective intervention that could have been made for quick impact on yields within the conditions and technology available to most Thai rice farmers. Because many of the subsequent agricultural projects of the U.S. aid program had implications for rice production, especially the projects to expand irrigation facilities and strengthen their management, it is worth pausing at this point to reflect on how the passing of time and changing of domestic conditions in the United States have altered U.S. perspectives on this commodity and on Thai rice in particular.

In the 1950s agriculture produced nearly half of Thailand's national income and up to 90 percent of its exports. More than 70 percent of the cultivated area was given over to rice, accounting for about 40 percent of the value of agricultural production. As the World Bank observed, two-thirds of the population earned a living from rice, and it was "difficult to exaggerate the importance of rice in Thailand's past economic development and present economic well-being."[5] In the *Congressional Presentation* for 1956, giving the rationale for the proposed aid budget for the Thai program, the Eisenhower administration highlighted that Thailand was "economically important to the free world as one of the world's principal exporters of rice." It went on to note that Thailand needed external assistance because its economic position had weakened partly due to the depressed state of the world rice market.[6] The World Bank noted the advances in rice yields that Thailand had achieved, but laid great emphasis on the need for major investments in irrigation, cultivation technology, and extension to ensure the country's continuing ability to produce an adequate exportable surplus.[7] In short, rice exports were vital to Thailand's economy and to the rice-importing countries of the free world, and Thailand's economic progress was viewed by the United States as vital to Thailand's security and continuing role as a U.S. ally in a turbulent region.

The aid agency took the rice production problem seriously, recruited top-flight American expertise, and later took justifiable credit for a solid accomplishment.[8] The immediate accomplishment has long since been superseded by much greater change. What is most striking today, in the context of foreign aid, is that if current aid legislation had been in effect in the 1950s, this contribution to Thai economic welfare, and by extension to American security interests, would have been disallowed under Section 521, as noted earlier, for promoting the production of a crop in competition with American exports.

The conflict between a foreign policy objective (or a humanitarian objective for the relatively poor in a developing country) and the interests of specific groups of American producers (or other categories of domestic interest groups) inherent in this and other strictures in the aid legislation is not a unique case of inconsistency between U.S. national and particular interests in aid (or other) matters. The problem of consistency rises here because in 1986 the role of the United States with respect to Thai rice took a turn that had nothing to do with the aid program or the foreign assistance legislation. It created considerable dismay among the Thais and raised a question as to whether the generally supportive economic policy stance and actions of the U.S. government in the past could still be relied upon or whether the United States was moving in opposite directions clearly detrimental to Thai economic welfare.

The new turn was a provision of the U.S. Farm Bill (Food Security Act) of 1985 that increased the effective domestic rice subsidy and changed the subsidy mechanism so that American growers (and mill-

ers and traders) could export their rice rather than sell it for stockpile
by the Commodity Credit Corporation (CCC).

> The intent is to end the piling up of rice stocks by allowing
> both the farmers and the CCC to sell the crops on the world
> market.
> The prospect of large quantities of rice flooding on to the
> market drove down the world price. Indeed, the price de-
> clined in advance of April 15 [1985, the date the program
> went into effect] . . . as customer demand plummeted in
> anticipation of the opportunity to buy at lower prices. The
> presence of government intervention in the Thai market
> slowed down the Baht price decline, but by May Bangkok
> prices had fallen to the lowest level in a decade, inflicting
> great losses on Thai farmers.[9]

These developments strained U.S.–Thai relations and commanded
headline treatment in the Thai media for months. Public discussion
conveyed a general tenor of puzzlement over how the United States,
of all countries, could inflict damage of such symbolic and real impact
aimed precisely at Thailand (this was not a cause of Thailand receiving fallout from a general trade intervention policy) in the face of the
long-standing relationship between the two countries and the apparent long term commitment of the United States to Thai economic
development.

Thais who understood the complexity of U.S. legislative and policy
processes were less puzzled over this apparent inconsistency than
they were concerned over the appearance of a general trend in U.S.
policy formation for protective and special economic interest considerations to dominate foreign policy interests. Meanwhile the rice
problem took another turn as poor 1987 rice crops in many countries
led to a recovery of world rice prices and in early 1988 concern over a
possible shortage of exportable rice in Thailand. In the longer run, the
outcome of the current "Uruguay" round of multilateral negotiations
under the General Agreement on Tariffs and Trade (GATT) will, one
hopes, set liberalizing rules for world agricultural commodity trade.
In this framework, Thailand is a very active participant in a group of
like-minded grain-exporting countries; the position of the United States,
which took the lead in pressing for the inclusion of agricultural commodity trade in a GATT round for the first time, is parallel to Thai
interests as well.

The early aid project on corn yields laid the basis for much more important increases in production and exports before the end of the decade. Since corn had not been an important crop in Thailand (between 1952 and 1957 corn exports averaged under 1 percent of total export earnings, or 2–3 percent of the value of rice exports), no controlled improvement program had been attempted before 1950. Some new varieties had been introduced in the 1920s, and some superior strains had resulted from natural crossing. The varietal development from 1950 is described by Jere Behrman:

> In 1950, the [Thai] Department of Agriculture began to study these strains. One selected strain . . . seemed superior and became the major commercial variety for most of the 1950s.
>
> Also starting in 1950, collections of corn varieties from Indonesia and the United States were introduced by the jointly sponsored agronomic development program. Of these varieties, a Guatemalan seed (via Indonesia) named Teguisate Golden Flint seemed to respond best under Thai conditions. In 1952, one hundred pounds of this seed were multiplied at Bangken and Tha Phra Agricultural Experimental Stations, and in 1953, selected farmers participated in further multiplication. Because the principal corn buyers, the Japanese, preferred a flint and because the Guatemalan flint tended to give greater yields per unit area than did the Pakchong dent, the Guatemalan corn soon replaced the earlier variety as the major Thai commercial corn.[10]

The data on the spread of Guatemalan corn is not clear, but Behrman concludes that "the only available estimates on the national level suggest that Guatemalan flint yields 300 to 350 kg per rai [1 rai is equivalent to 0.4 acres] as compared with 200 to 250 kg per rai from Pakchong dent, and that by the early 1960s, as much as 60 to 85% of total corn production was Guatemalan."

The year 1958 saw the start of a corn boom. From the 1 percent level of 1957, Thai corn exports jumped to 2.8 percent of export earnings in 1958 and 8.6 percent by 1963, while the volume rose nearly twelve-fold. A large fraction of these exports was Guatemalan corn. Besides the development of an acceptable variety, two other factors contributed to Thailand's ability to respond to the growth in Japanese maize demand during these years; improvements in road transport and the reduction in malaria, which opened up previously uncultivated areas that were now put into corn production.[11] Both the principal road in this connection (the Friendship Highway, opened to traffic in 1957–1958) and the malaria control campaign were major components of the U.S. aid program. Corn became and has remained one of Thailand's top export crops, along with rice, rubber, tapioca, and sugar.

Recognizing that much needed to be done to modernize and diversify crop production beyond varietal improvement, USOM also launched activities in irrigation, credit and marketing, and extension and conservation. With the addition of livestock, forestry, fisheries, agricultural statistics, and support to Kasetsart University, the program engaged virtually every unit of the Ministry of Agriculture (and the then separate Ministry of Cooperatives) and almost every institutional and governmental function impinging on the agriculture sector of the economy (including at various times adult education, community development, and other outreach programs concerning agriculture, which were operated by other ministries).

In all of these areas the projects were similar in several striking respects: The American technicians found the numbers of trained Thais to be grossly inadequate to the tasks at hand, the levels of technology far below international standards, the extent of government and institutional services available to the farmers to be marginal, and the levels of institutional development in most cases rudimentary. For example, the extension system was described as follows:

> Because the Ministry of Agriculture has no system nor organization for giving advice and practical assistance directly to farmers, this project was begun in 1951 to help the Ministry establish a successful national agricultural extension service. Seven departments of the Ministry operated field programs of an extension nature, independently and with considerable duplication and overlapping. Comparatively few of the field personnel of these various agencies had sufficient training to give useful assistance to farmers or to furnish leadership in rural activities. The project also undertook to train personnel in extension work and demonstrations and other extension activities in an effort to show the way.

Regarding resource use the mission found:

> The philosophy of conservation is hardly known in Thailand except among a small body of dedicated men. . . .

> Information on land-use capabilities, soil characteristics,
> and plant food needs . . . is fragmentary and facilities for
> gathering it hardly existed a few years ago. . . . Agricultural
> statistics, especially economic information, has been al-
> most lacking for purposes of agricultural planning and de-
> velopment.[12]

Since it appeared that everything needed to be done, each project
typically sent participants to the United States for long-term training
and for short observation tours to see how things were done there,
financed some equipment to enable the technician to demonstrate
new techniques to Thai counterparts, and provided advice and pilot
projects to help set up new functions and try out new institutional
arrangements. Many of these initial efforts helped launch organizations or processes that developed into viable instruments for promoting development in their respective areas. In other cases the project's
initiatives did not gel for various reasons. Thus the mission withdrew
from forestry in 1954 and responsibility for technical assistance in
this area was picked up by the UN Food and Agriculture Organization
(FAO). (Since then, other countries have provided forestry assistance
including Australia, Canada, Denmark and Japan.) In agricultural
statistics there was considerable progress under a 1955–1958 project,
which also laid the basis for a later project of much greater scope and
duration with the same Agriculture Economics Division of the ministry. Some important agriculture data are still unreliable thirty years
later (such as crop forecasting), but for the bulk of planning, research,
and administrative uses for which the Division's data serve as basic
inputs, the coverage and reliability are high by developing country
standards and of well-established utility.

In irrigation the program racked up its first failure in the single
most costly endeavor in the initial years. Under the Tank Irrigation
and Water Conservation project, assistance was given to the Royal
Irrigation Department (RID) to build 121 small earthen-dam reservoirs (called "tanks") between 1951 and 1958 at a cost of $8.3 million
(of which the project provided $7.6 million). All the tanks were lo-
cated in the Northeast; about four-fifths were designed to supply
water for irrigation (supplemental water in sparse rainy seasons and/
or water for a second crop in the dry season), the rest being smaller
reservoirs for domestic usage. The average irrigation tank would be
able to supply roughly 1,000 acres. The project also provided equipment for water diversion and flood control works in the Northeast,
designed to benefit 250,000 acres, and portable pumps for flexible

response to emergency water situations. By the time the project was completed, it was already evident that the tanks were having little impact on agricultural production and were unlikely to do so.[13] The project did send forty-eight engineers and officers to the United States for training, which was probably the major contribution of the project as an input into strengthening the RID.

The history of the tank project is worth pursuing in some detail. It was the first substantial aid investment in the Northeast region, an area that was to become the focus of much U.S. effort. As we shall see below, AID returned to the problems of water in the Northeast again and again over the years, including later attempts to rehabilitate a few of the same tanks and make them work. The tanks represented the first significant project in a continuous and often frustrating endeavor to find solutions to the region's poverty. The tanks never offered a major option for controlling the water regime of the Northeast. Irrigation from all possible sources, including from the Mekong and its Northeast tributaries, is not thought to be feasible for more than 15 percent of the region's arable land, and the tanks represented only a small fraction of even this irrigable potential. Nevertheless, in the search by the Thai government and the donors to do whatever might yield tangible benefits for the region's inhabitants, the tanks appeared to be a reasonable, if economically marginal, proposition. RID first began constructing tanks in the Northeast in 1939. The first postwar survey of Thai agriculture by FAO in 1950 recommended further tank construction. In 1959 the World Bank was still endorsing the tank: "The return in additional rice production, relative to investments, is not so high as on most irrigation projects recommended in other regions. It is, nevertheless, quite sufficient to justify the necessary expenditure. . . . A stepped-up tank irrigation program is urged as a sound means of contributing to the employment and income of the large and relatively poorer population of the Northeast." As late as 1980 the Bank offered to fund the rehabilitation of all the tanks.[14]

There were serious technical flaws and administrative problems hobbling the tank program. The tanks were unlined, and due to the porous nature of Northeast soils lost much of their impounded water through seepage. Most of the tanks lacked adequate water distribution channel systems because of legal and jurisdictional problems over which department of the government had responsibility for main and subsidiary canal construction for these small earthworks. The role of farmers in channel construction or maintenance, and in systems for water release and distribution, were not clarified or adequately established. RID interest in these mini-projects was not high, compared with the major irrigation and engineering works the department was undertaking in other parts of the country. Careers of RID engineers and administrators were not made from assignments to work on Northeast tanks. And organization of farmers on the very difficult business of group arrangements for water sharing, although a well-developed tradition in the old irrigation systems of the northern provinces, was not addressed effectively in the Northeast.

We will return to irrigation and other Northeast projects below, and then attempt to assess the role of the aid program as a whole in the context of dealing with an entire handicapped region. For this first 1950s round, however, it was clear that between the Thai government, FAO, the World Bank and USOM, the measures designed to provide irrigation water through small tanks were technically and administratively defective. The acreage actually irrigated was always quite low, many tanks ended up being used as buffalo wallows, the tanks were not properly maintained and tended to deteriorate, and in general the return on the investment was low, if not nil.

In fisheries the program found a sector where obvious and simple technical improvements could be adopted with ease, leading to quick and significant results. One of the start-up activities of 1951, the fisheries project introduced improved nets which apparently caught on and began to be imported in large numbers by Thai fishermen. The reported 30 percent increase in the fish catch between 1950 and 1955 was attributed (by USOM) largely to the spread of these nets. The project also provided technical inputs for the establishment of Bangkok's first central wholesale fish market in 1953 and for the building of a frozen fish plant. The record on the impact of this project is less clear than for others. Statistics on the fish catch were very unreliable in the 1950s, and there is not much of a paper trail after the project terminated in 1957, AID having returned to fisheries in later years only peripherally in connection with other activities. As in other areas, the long-run contributions may have been in the strengthening of the Department of Fisheries through participant training in the United States, the setting up of a fish technology laboratory, and the work of the fisheries experts. Fish has been basic to the Thai diet for centuries.[15] With plentiful fish resources in a culture where practically every farmer was a part-time fisherman, and a prevailing technology easily upgraded, the accomplishments recorded by the mission's fisheries experts on completion of their assignments appear plausible enough.[16] In the thirty years since this project ended, the Thai commercial fishing industry has become transformed into one of the world's largest and a major source of the country's foreign exchange earnings (averaging 2.1 million tons in 1980–1984, the annual fish catch was ten times the size reported in the mid-50s).[17] After so many years and large injections of new technologies, and a level of fish production that for some important salt-water species, is threatening their viability in Thai waters, the connections between Thailand's first postwar technical assistance in fisheries and the present state, and problems, of this sector would be tenuous if we were to attempt to trace them. The most we can conclude is that the project and its technicians can be credited with some significant and rapid impact on fish production, and for helping to set the Department of Fisheries on a solid development track, two not insignificant accomplishments.

Livestock is an interesting example of a subject that got early and recurrent attention under the aid program, but where the long-run impact is difficult to judge even though the projects produced many of their expected outputs. Livestock had long been a sector of economic importance in Thailand. The buffalo was virtually the only source of traction in Thai agriculture until the 1960s, while livestock on the hoof was an important export to regional markets. Herds had been depleted during World War II and livestock diseases were impeding their recovery. Livestock also appeared to be a possible more lucrative substitute for subsistence agriculture in the Northeast. Faced with problems of rudimentary commercial feed supply, little development of forage crops, little systematic breeding and no artificial insemination, obsolete slaughtering, inefficient cattle transport that resulted in great weight loss during shipment, and so on, the mission framed a project to address "the whole problem . . . of building up a stable, prosperous livestock industry." Under this broad objective, the project had activities addressing every aspect of the industry. Nutritional and diagnostic laboratories were built, serum and vaccine production was expanded, breeding stations improved, breeding stock imported, feed crops were developed on experiment stations, on-farm feed storage techniques were demonstrated, etc. By 1958 the Livestock Division had eradicated rinderpest with U.S. and FAO assistance. In a very early instance of "policy dialogue" under a U.S. aid program, the mission recommended in 1952 that the government rescind the embargo on livestock exports which it had imposed to keep the herds from declining further, a recommendation the government accepted. Although the development of a major commercial livestock industry in the Northeast has yet to be proven feasible, the herds were reconstituted, the supply of buffalo for traction was suffi-

cient for cultivation requirements (but began to be substantially replaced by tractors in the 1970s), and exports of live animals were
restored.

The difficulty of defining the long-run impact of the blizzard of U.S.
initiatives and subprojects in this area arises from the passage of
time, the subsequent involvement of other donors, and the great
changes that have taken place in the intervening years—besides the
economic decline of the buffalo. Livestock raising was a completely
decentralized, small farmer industry in the 1950s. In livestock as in
all other aspects of agriculture, except for some rubber plantations in
the peninsular South, there were few large holdings, and the individual family farm was the universal unit of production. The Livestock
Division and U.S. technical assistance were oriented accordingly.

The one exception in the livestock sector was the Bangkok slaughterhouse and the associated marketing system for all animals brought
into Bangkok, a municipal monopoly tightly controlled by one of the
leading political factions in the government at that time. The operations of this meat monopoly system were widely recognized as a
serious hindrance to the modernization of the livestock industry in
Thailand and the development of a processed meat export industry.
Nevertheless, the political obstacles to livestock marketing reform
remained insuperable for many years. In 1958 USOM attempted to
initiate a reform of the processing system by developing a loan project
to build a modern slaughterhouse under private ownership, but the
project never got off the ground. Twenty-six years later, in 1984, the
Private Enterprise Bureau of AID/W made a second run at a similar
project. By then private slaughtering had become feasible under a
change in RTG policy allowing export-oriented meat processing firms
to sell portions of their output in the local market. Nevertheless, this
second attempt also stalled when the Thai investors involved fell into
financial difficulties. The project was put back on track by a new
Thai-Filipino investment group and has begun to produce processed
meat under a Swift brand name license.

The poultry story is quite different. Private Thai agro-industrial
enterprises have developed in recent years and have built up large-
scale chicken production and exports based on modern technology
(obtained initially from a Connecticut firm) and on a small army of
individual farmers who raise the chicken supply under contractual
and supervisory arrangements. One company (Charoen Pokphand) is
reputed to be the largest agro-industrial operation in Southeast Asia
and has begun to develop subsidiary ventures in other countries. Pork
production has also developed into a thriving sector.

While the future development of livestock in Thailand appears to lie with the agro-industrial corporate sector, small-scale livestock raising and buffalo traction will remain important components of the rural economy and of the responsibilities of the Ministry of Agriculture. As in several other areas, early U.S. technical assistance and training can be credited with having helped the Livestock Division establish a modern basis for carrying out its functions and continuing to evolve as the technical and economic character of its sector changes over time.

In the remaining agricultural areas, credit and marketing and extension and conservation, the program's activities continued for many years in different forms and need to be looked at from a longer perspective later in this account. The one exception was the mission's relatively short-lived project to help strengthen Thailand's cooperative movement. USOM shared the view widely held in Thailand at the time (and still held in some quarters in the Thai government despite overwhelming evidence to the contrary) that the country's farmers were being exploited by a noncompetitive network of merchants to whom farmers sold their surplus produce and cash crops. According to the old conventional wisdom, the merchants deprived the farmers of a fair share of the market value of their produce through a combination of monopsonist purchasing and usurious lending. Cooperatives were expected to raise farmers' returns by capturing the margins being earned by merchants and substituting cooperative marketing in place of the real services the merchants were performing. As in many developing countries, the cooperatives in Thailand had been created by the government, were closely supervised, and usually were actually operated by officials of the Ministry of Agriculture.

When the cooperatives project began in 1952, membership was very small, the cooperatives were all in permanent arrears, farmers had little to say in their operation, and the volume of produce they handled was insignificant (for example, the rice paddy marketing cooperatives handled about .1 percent of national paddy production).[18] The project provided considerable equipment to the Ministry to enable it to expand services it offered the cooperatives and ran courses and demonstrations designed to develop professional and farmer management as substitutes for management by bureaucrats. One or two coops in areas riding the crest of the 1958 corn boom received intensive technical assistance nurturing from USOM's coop experts. The results were disappointing. Cooperative marketing did not then and has not yet developed into a significant alternative to the operations of the private agricultural produce marketing system.

The failure was not a reflection on the design or implementation of the aid project, but resulted from mistaken premises regarding the nature of the market system and the presumed advantages cooperative marketing would offer farmers, if only the coops were managed efficiently, as I have argued elsewhere:

> The fact that cooperative marketing has failed to achieve any importance is partly due to the apparent farmer satisfaction with the returns obtained from dealing with the private market. This is reflected in the frequent complaint that farmers are not "loyal" to their cooperatives, i.e. they weaken the cooperatives' bargaining power and financial condition by selling to private merchants who compete with the societies and who presumably offer a better price. Given the poor level of cooperative management . . . and the fact that they have been organized from the top down, i.e. imposed by government as a paternal measure rather than arising from the inherent needs of the producers, it would be expecting too much to insist that farmers sell through their coops even if they believe it would be to their disadvantage.[19]

Having achieved little, USOM closed the project in 1963. The RTG would not abandon the concept of ministerial control and administration, the Americans saw no utility in cooperatives not controlled by their members, and only a small fraction of the farmers showed any interest. (In 1980, at NESDB's behest, USAID financed a study on how the cooperatives might be "revitalized"; the recommendations were not implemented by the RTG.) The situation remains essentially unchanged today, for the same reasons that rendered the cooperatives marginal in the 1950s. A close study of agricultural marketing in 1980 in one province of the Northeast concluded that the cooperatives' marketing activities were marginal:

> The major constraints faced by the cooperatives are limited operating funds, poor managerial ability, and the lack of members' participation. One other reason which explains the poor marketing performance of the farmer cooperatives is that (they) have been established amid the more efficient private enterprises. The keen competition from private traders offering better market prospects for

the farmers, has, in turn, driven away the farmers' participation in the cooperatives.[20]

The credit and marketing activities of USOM had another component that yielded quite different results. In 1958 USOM focused attention on the volume of funds available to the cooperatives. Following the recommendations of a consultant study, a project was started to create a new institution, a Bank for Agriculture and Agricultural Cooperatives (BAAC). A joint RTG/USOM team set up to design a new agriculture credit system appeared to be making progress. In 1960 another consultant was brought in to help draft new credit and marketing legislation that among other things would establish BAAC as an independent agency. The Minister of Agriculture rejected the concept of an agriculture bank not under his direct control, and the issue remained hung up until USOM withdrew in 1963.

Three years later the politics changed, and BAAC was established along lines recommended by the U.S. advisers and under the initial management of an official who had worked closely with the USOM credit and marketing project. USOM did provide some technical assistance to BAAC, but the agency failed to follow up what was probably one of the most promising options ever open to AID in the agriculture sector in Thailand; USOM's proposal in 1970 to offer capital funds was rejected by AID/W. As J. Alexander Caldwell remarks, in one of the more obtuse differences of opinion between the mission and agency headquarters in the history of the program,

> AID/W . . . apparently unconcerned over the years of effort that it and its predecessor agencies had put into the concept, turned USOM down on the grounds that it was insufficiently security oriented. Incredibly, given the history of the concept that BAAC was fulfilling so well, AID/W said that assistance to it should be preceded by a full blown study of the agriculture sector to assist in "establishing priorities."[21]

The BAAC has since become the largest source of credit to farmers in Thailand and has a strong reputation for efficient management and adherence to sound banking and loan practices. By its tenth year of operation, 1970, BAAC was lending about B4.3 billion (roughly $220 million) to around 1.2 million farm families. By 1985 its annual lending had risen to B17.4 billion ($655 million at 1985 exchange rates), and its clientele to 2.3 million farm families or over 40 percent of all agricultural households. Only 18 percent of the credit BAAC extended in 1985 went to cooperatives; virtually all the rest was loaned to individual farmers.[22]

This may be the leading example in the history of the Thai aid program where technical assistance to help formulate a basic organizational concept (even helping to embody the concept in enabling legislation) succeeded in laying the groundwork for the development of a major institution, with only a marginal follow-up relationship (a $15 million loan in 1974 from counterpart funds generated by PL 480 sales). BAAC has grown, using funds provided by the Bank of Thailand, the Thai commercial banks, the World Bank, the European Economic Community, Japan, and other sources. It has been argued that BAAC could lend to the less credit-worthy, poorer farmers it does not now reach in large numbers if the bank had greater access to more concessionary loans—that is, funds it could borrow at terms similar to those normally applied to AID loans. The bank provides its credit under supervisory procedures that are generally considered to be sound rural lending practice, but these procedures raise the cost of BAAC loan administration relative to the cost of administering commercial bank credit. Since the bank is politically constrained from charging higher interest rates to less credit-worthy borrowers, it would need to borrow at lower, more concessional rates to cover the risks (and probable higher administrative costs) of relending these funds to the least credit-worthy end of the farming community. Neither AID nor the Bank of Thailand believes that interest rate subsidization is sound policy, a position generally supported by the experience of rural credit subsidy programs in many countries. (For one thing, such subsidies often end up reducing the cost of credit to the farmers least in need of cheap credit.) Nonetheless, BAAC has developed into an organization that combines sound credit administration with innovative programs involving both group borrowing arrangements and production systems that link agro-industrial firms with small farm suppliers. BAAC could well have served as a significant cooperant institution in AID's continuous research over the years for effective organizational and marketing arrangements to benefit the small farmer.

Public Health

Projects in public health have figured importantly in the U.S. aid program since its very beginning. As noted earlier, the senior ranks of Thai medical education and public health services are filled with

American-trained participants. Between the Rockefeller Foundation and AID programs, the Thai–U.S. connection in health has been long and extensive. Even as the AID mission in 1987 was phasing out its presumably last formal bilateral health project (Thailand continues to receive assistance from centrally funded AID health projects), the heritage of personal and institutional relations between Thailand and the United States appears to be greater in the health sector than in any other area. Over the years since 1950, health problems have changed in Thailand, new health technologies have opened up new possibilities for health interventions, and international perceptions of health strategies appropriate to developing country conditions have changed drastically. The objectives, strategies, and organization of the Thai Ministry of Public Health (MOPH) have changed accordingly, as have the health activities of the United States and other donors.

The highest priority and largest allocation of U.S. aid health funds have been accorded to malaria control, starting in 1951. For many years malaria had been Thailand's leading killer and most widespread endemic illness. Some areas of the country were uninhabitable because of malaria, and the economic and human welfare costs were very high. Half the Thai population was believed to be living in malarious areas. The first demonstration in Thailand of the feasibility of massive house-spraying with insecticides as the core of a malaria suppressant strategy was carried out in 1950 with help from the World Health Organization (WHO) and the U.N. International Children's Fund (UNICEF). The antimalaria campaign was initiated the following year, and by 1954 the malarial death rate had been brought down by half, and about one-fifth of the population was considered "protected" by recurrent spraying of the walls of their dwellings.*

With WHO confident in the power of this technology for interfering in the life cycle of the mosquito and in the ability of aided ministries of health to manage the vast logistics of the spraying season campaigns (given enough budget and the required technical assistance) as well as individual case identification and treatment procedures, the malaria control projects in a large number of countries, including Thailand, were transformed into eradication campaigns. By the time the malaria project was terminated in 1974, it had been allocated more funds ($52.5 million in dollars and local currency) than most other activities in the history of the Thai aid program.

The malaria campaign was the largest "vertical" (single-disease)

---

*The spraying is termed "residual" because the insecticide is deposited on surfaces in the home, leaving a long-lasting residue. The mosquito is exposed to the residue whenever it alights on the surface and does not have to be sprayed directly.

program ever carried out in Thailand. It involved thousands of sprayers backed by a vast training and logistical operation and supervision structure. The campaign was divided into multiyear phases of attack and surveillance. Eradication was anticipated in about ten years. Permanent antimalaria vigilance was foreseen as needed in border areas if eradication was not achieved in contiguous countries, a possibility that turned out to be significant in Thailand's case in later years.

Implementation of this vast campaign inevitably was beset by all kinds of problems. Especially troublesome was the falsification of reports on the fulfillment of spraying-squads' quotas of households treated. These reports were found to be inflated in some areas, setting back the planned schedule and extending the attack phase. Still, by 1959 USOM wrote with full confidence that

> the homes of over 14 million people had been sprayed— several times each, in most areas—and house spraying had been discontinued in areas of over 7 million population, due to elimination of malaria transmission. In these areas, surveillance will continue for about three years to complete the eradication of malaria. The results of the antimalaria campaign have included the reduction of the nationwide malaria death rate from over 250 to less than 45 per 100,000 population—a reduction exceeding 86 percent in both cases and deaths.
>
> The project has been highly successful thus far in terms of organization, training, antimalaria activities, and reduction of malaria cases and deaths. American assistance is expected to end in 1962, with the Thai Government continuing the terminal phases of the malaria eradication program through 1965.[23]

With all the caution with which mortality data of those years must be treated, and morbidity data even more so, it is clear that the malaria campaign had produced extraordinary benefits for the Thai population by the end of the 1950s. The deep reduction in death and illness was unprecedented in its scope. Thai health statistics show a malarial mortality rate in 1960 of 30.2 per 100,000 population, which by 1984 had dropped further to 4.4, or about 2,900 deaths, compared with the estimated 45,000 annual deaths in the 1940s.[24]

The major impact of the campaign was made in its first few years. Unfortunately, eradication, for which the world public health authorities had such high hopes, proved to be beyond the antimalaria technology of the 1950s (which remains basically the same today). The disease remains an important, if much reduced, public health problem in Thailand as in other countries. There are three principal reasons for the failure to achieve full eradication in Thailand: the predominant malaria-causing parasite in Thailand has become resistant to antimalaria drugs; the most important of the malaria-transmitting mosquitos in Thailand *(anopheles minimus)* has developed partial resistance to DDT after many years of exposure to residual spraying; and the disease has been continuously transmitted between different areas of the country through the extensive seasonal migration of large numbers of people in the Thai labor force. In the mid-1970s the disease actually showed signs of resurgence. As a consequence a second campaign had to be mounted, with a new infusion of funds, to secure the hard-won gains of the earlier project and to reduce the incidence to much lower levels. This was done in 1979 with AID assistance again at about $4.5 million. An evaluation of this second round, carried out in 1985, concluded that the project had been implemented efficiently, had met many of its objectives, and would probably make further progress. Nevertheless, the still complex technology, dependent on cumbersome logistics and many interrelated intervention and treatment activities, held out no hope for eradication but only the prospect of more effective reduction if the program were vigorously and continuously pursued. The evaluation team, therefore, concluded that

> there are a number of serious problems impeding further progress in reducing the incidence of malaria in Thailand. The Team is of the opinion that the overriding need at the present time is to develop a long range plan which will lead to a solution to these problems and thus increase the effectiveness of the program. The Team report contains numerous suggestions for development of such a plan.
>
> The report also reviews resources for meeting further requirements, identifies certain requirements as being suitable for external assistance, identifies some potential donor agencies and suggests exploration of the possibility of multidonor funding to meet the future needs of the program.[25]

Given the great size, cost, and importance of the campaign for the Thai government and for USOM and the extraordinary tenacity that seemed characteristic of the American public health experts assigned to Bangkok to work on the project, the malaria activity was a major source of the elan and sense of consequence and momentum felt by the staff of USOM at the end of the aid program's first decade. The tone of the team's evaluation report, twenty-five years later, is a sober reflection that the only prospect for keeping malaria under control is eternal vigilance, unless and until the (also long-running) research programs to develop a malaria vaccine and/or much more effective curative drugs produce more powerful answers.

An account of U.S. "vertical" health initiatives begun in the early years would not be complete if it omitted a notable cooperative military-civilian project in communicable diseases now in its thirtieth year, known since 1977 as the Armed Forces Research Institute of Medical Sciences (AFRIMS).[26] Cholera had long been endemic in the Asian subcontinent, recurrently spreading to adjacent regions. In 1958 a cholera epidemic swept through East Asia, and in May of that year cholera broke out in Thailand after an apparent absence since 1950. The Thai government asked for U.S. assistance to study the disease. A team was organized quickly by the U.S. Navy's Medical Research Unit No. 2. The team included epidemiologists and other health scientists from the National Institutes of Health, the Walter Reed Army Institute of Research, and Thai medical institutions. In its one-year life the team undertook groundwork research on biochemical characteristics of cholera and isolated and described its pathogens.

By late 1959 the SEATO countries initiated a three-year followup project to set up cholera research laboratories in Bangkok and Dacca, capital of then East Pakistan. By 1961 the cholera epidemic had receded, and it was decided that the Bangkok laboratory should be established on a permanent basis with its work expanded to cover several communicable diseases. (The lab in Dacca was also established as a permanent institution and remains a leading medical research organization in Bangladesh.) The laboratory expanded into new quarters built and donated by the Thai Army. Funding and equipment were provided by the U.S. aid program, the office of the Surgeon General of the U.S. Army, Walter Reed, the U.S. Navy, and other U.S. military units in Japan, the National Institutes of Health, the governments of Australia and the Philippines, and Thai medical institutions.

When SEATO was dissolved in 1977, the project continued as a Thai–U.S. organization. The laboratory was renamed AFRIMS, with the U.S. component being backstopped by Walter Reed and overall command of the joint activity under a Thai officer. AFRIMS is now the only U.S. Army unit stationed on Thai soil. The unit comprises about two dozen army medical research and support staff. The Thai professional and support staff number around 150.

To this day the mission of the U.S. involvement in this project remains defined in military terms—namely, "To conduct field-oriented medical research and development projects directed toward problem definition and ultimately prevention, control and/or treatment of militarily important diseases of Thailand and surrounding areas." Under these terms AFRIMS has undertaken research on malaria, hepatitis, dengue, hemorrhagic fever, Japanese encephalitis, tick viruses, enteric diseases, venereal diseases, rabies, and drug abuse. While the diseases selected for research over the years have been those that would be especially threatening to military units operating in the field in Southeast Asia, the vectors carrying these ills make no distinctions and continue to attack civilian populations. Some of the results of the research include new antimalarial drugs, a vaccine to reduce encephalitis, and numerous advances in the etiologies, transmission routes, vector control methods, patient immunological response, and so on, of these various afflictions.

USOM also provided small amounts of equipment, pharmaceuticals, and technical assistance to the Ministry of Health for its work in nutrition, quarantine, and control of yaws, plague, leprosy, and venereal diseases. Apart from the case of yaws, these early activities appear to fall into the category of minor assists, too scattered and partial to have had significant impact. The more important projects that rounded out the initial array of health aid included medical education and a set of activities aimed at the development of Thailand's rural health delivery system.

Medical education and the expansion of rural health services were seen as closely linked. It was estimated that two-thirds of Thailand's doctors were located in the Bangkok area, with a rural ratio of one doctor to 20,000 people. To help increase the supply of doctors, the program contracted with Washington University of St. Louis to work with the Siriraj and Chulalongkorn University medical schools. This was followed by a more comprehensive institution-building project in 1957, which constructed and launched a new medical school in Chiangmai in North Thailand with technical assistance from the University of Illinois. Parallel rural health services projects also began on a modest scale between 1951 and 53, divided into separate activities that matched the organizational units of the Ministry. These early projects in health education, demonstration models for provincial and district level health offices, environmental sanitation, and in-service training for public health physicians, nurses, and technicians were integrated into a single rural health project in 1957. For both the malaria and rural health activities, lack of field mobility was one of the major problems in the 1950s. Perhaps the most costly single component of the health sector assistance was the provision of jeeps (only four-wheel drive vehicles could negotiate the provincial road system of the time) and the development of the Ministry's automotive maintenance capability, which the mission had to include in the health program to keep the jeeps operational.

The final component rounding out the early health assistance was a project to help the Ministry expand its provincial hospital system. Only twenty of Thailand's seventy-one provinces had hospitals in 1950. By 1955 every provincial seat had a small hospital, with much of the equipment provided by USOM.

In retrospect, these early projects can be seen as having helped the Ministry lay the groundwork for the later emergence of the full-blown primary health care strategy that has guided the planning and resource allocation of the health authorities in recent years. In addition, the extensive advanced training in the health sector and the many individual health projects of AID, the Rockefeller Foundation, and WHO, UNICEF, and other donors must be given credit for their role in helping the Thai Ministry of Health develop its deserved reputation as one of the most effective health ministries in the developing countries. Still, to put these early activities in proper perspective, they appear (like the array of assistance provided to the Ministry of Agriculture) to have resulted from a desire to help every component of the Ministry under an implicit strategy lacking any sense of priority other than the outstanding attack on malaria. Later health assistance, as we shall see below, was more sharply focused.

NATION-BUILDING: 1955–1959

In 1954 (the beginning of fiscal year 1955) the economic aid program jumped nearly sixfold to $46.1 million compared with the average level of $7.9 million in the first four fiscal years of aid, 1951–1954. Between 1955 and 1959 a net total of $190.2 million was obligated. Funding levels fell by nearly half in FY 1960 and did not return to the late 1950s levels until 1966. However, even though Caldwell's "Nation-Building" phase fits the funding history profile and the changing U.S. perceptions about Thai needs, 1959 does not in fact mark a shift in the level of actual expenditure, as explained earlier, or in the activities actually underway. Keeping this qualification in mind,

Caldwell's divisions remain useful for tracing the changing size and character of the program.

The year 1955 also marked the start of eight years in which portions of the aid appropriations took the form of nonproject grants. In six of those eight years nonproject grants were greater than project grants. In 1956 funds were provided in loan form for the first time since the signing of the aid agreement. In some years the nonproject grants were greater than the loans and project grants combined.

These changes in the program's funding structure paralleled the substantive changes taking place in the program's content. After the French withdrawal from Vietnam in 1954 Thai and U.S. apprehension over the rising Communist tide in the region sharpened quite suddenly,* as I have already noted, and resulted in the twin decisions to increase the size of the economic aid program and to launch the OICC military construction program. These decisions were related not only in their derivation as joint responses to security threats facing Thailand. They were also related in their funding (and the systems for programming and managing portions of the funding) and program content.

As far as the funds were concerned, some of the nonproject appropriations conventionally recorded as economic aid to Thailand were designed to help finance OICC construction projects. Thus of the $113.8 million of nonproject aid between 1955 and 1962, about $40.6 million was allocated to OICC. These funds, along with all other nonproject funds, were appropriated to ICA and were used to generate counterpart local currency of equivalent amounts, which was deposited into a special account held by the Bank of Thailand. ICA's documentation system was used to program and "subobligate" the funds for individual OICC projects, and the aid mission transferred funds from the special account into OICC accounts for actual expenditure, as needed. These funds can be considered economic aid in the sense that their initial use was to provide the Thai economy with fuel products (on a grant basis) that were available for general use through the normal domestic fuel distribution network. Of course, the same funds had a military purpose on the second round, so to speak, as their baht equivalent was used to acquire domestic resources for the military projects. As I noted above, however, the military construction program contained substantial civil works components with immediate or subsequent economic value.

---

*Caldwell notes: "Ambassador Max Waldo Bishop told the Congress in 1956, 'I look at Thailand as the cork in the ink bottle, and if you were to pull this cork the red ink would flow to Australia immediately' (*American Economic Aid to Thailand*, p. 42).

Aside from the direct connection with OICC, the economic aid program in this second phase included a number of major projects that were designed to meet specific military contingencies or were intended to contribute to a general build-up of Thailand's infrastructure as a means of accelerating the expansion of the Thai economy and the creation of a larger base of economic strength to cope with either external or internal efforts to undermine Thai security.

The content of the program underwent a drastic change. While technical assistance continued in agriculture, education, and health, new technical projects were started to help strengthen the general administration of the Thai government, especially the "core" agencies involved in finance and planning, and new capital projects were launched in transportation, electric power, and telecommunications. Assistance to promote private industrial development made its first appearance in the aid program in this period. Small amounts were used to begin a technical assistance project with the Thai police, a project that within a few years would grow to become a major activity before police training was phased out by congressional action in 1975.[27]

Transportation

Transportation quickly became the largest sector of the program, and it was allocated nearly half of the funds between 1954 and 1960. Thailand had emerged from World War II with a transportation system woefully inadequate for the country's economic development and probably the single most important constraint on expanded economic activity. The Central Plain was well served by the river system but the rest of the country depended mainly on a skeleton of single rail lines emanating from Bangkok. Wartime bombing to reduce the railroad's usefulness to the Japanese had left the system in very damaged condition. Interregional movement of goods was virtually nonexistent, except to and from Bangkok. Travel by road, where it was possible, was extremely hard on vehicles and exhausting for passengers. As Caldwell writes:

> Highways had always been of low priority. Roads were designed to serve, not compete with, the railway system. ... As of 1949 there were only 845 kilometers of all weather highway in the kingdom. Much of this was virtually unusable due to lack of maintenance and the disrepair or collapse of rickety wooden bridges. As late as 1954, there were

only 1,600 kilometers of usable road, paved or unpaved, outside of Bangkok. It was impossible to travel by road either to Chiang Mai in the North or to the Malaysian border in the South. A traveler to the Northeast in the early fifties noted that he did not see a single car east of Korat. The MSA noted in 1952 that the roads that did exist did not form a connected system, and were "wholly inadequate to the development of the country, or to its defense in case of attack."[28]

Highways. In line with the initial propensity of USOM and the RTG to provide at least some inputs, even if only minor, into many corners of the Thai government, there had been some small technical assistance and equipment for road construction under the first project in this sector, General Highway Improvement, starting in 1951. Through 1954 these inputs were general assists to the Highway Department, not focused on specific routes (except for the first twenty kilometers of a road from Udorn to Loei in the Northeast). In 1955–1956 the project was used to enlarge the Department's construction budget but focused on routes designated as components of the primary highway system. By 1975 it was decided to revamp the approach, apparently to speed up construction progress and strengthen the technical quality of the work. The general improvement project was phased out, and separate projects were set up to manage the construction of the USOM-financed roads.

With transportation suddenly elevated in 1955 to a level of strategic concern and the availability of funds (and the numbers of transport technicians on USOM's staff) suddenly increased, the entire perspective of the aid mission concerning this sector widened accordingly. Major construction projects were begun, the Highway Department as a whole became the focus of technical assistance, and in 1957 the mission and the department jointly developed a master plan for the primary highway system. It soon became apparent that the technical and financial resources needed for rapid expansion of the Thai highway system were much greater than the Thai government and AID could provide. By 1965 AID financing for primary highway construction was phasing out, and the Thai government was turning to the World Bank, with its much greater resources for capital project financing, for major assistance in completing the highway investment program. Between 1963 and 1978 World Bank highway loans amounted to $223 million. Until this phase-out occurred, the aid mission was playing a comprehensive and foundation-laying role in the transport sector comparable in scope to its role with the Ministry of Public Health.

In the ten-year 1955–1965 period AID contributions to the development of the highway network included system planning, strengthening of the Highway Department, introduction of modern construction technology and international standards, development of a private Thai construction contracting sector able to build bridges and roads, the financing of feasibility studies for a number of individual routes, and the actual construction of a number of highways. Some of these highways, being strategically located in relation to actual or potential economic activity and movement of goods and persons, made immediate contributions to Thai economic development. We see here again, in the transport sector, that between the aid program's involvement on the ground floor in Thailand's modern economic development and the program's flexibility in engaging in strategic sectors, Thai economic development got a high payoff.

The first major highway completed under the program, and probably the most well-known project the aid program ever undertook in Thailand, was the Friendship Highway. Built at a cost of about $20.5 million the 148-kilometer paved route was the first, and for many years the only, all-weather road connecting the whole of the Northeast region with the Central Plain and Bangkok.[29] The preexisting laterite road between the southern terminus town of Saraburi and the Northeastern gateway town of Korat traced a circuitous route more than twice as long as the Friendship Highway and was virtually impassible in the rainy season.

The new highway opened up section by section between mid-1957 and mid-1958. The immediate impact of the project came from the opening of previously uncultivated land near the route to the production of upland crops, principally corn in response to the maize boom described above. Daily traffic rose to one thousand vehicles soon after the road opened, making the Friendship Highway the most heavily trafficked road in the country except for some routes in the vicinity of Bangkok. According to Behrman,

> Traffic counts near Saraburi report that the Friendship Highway is one of the most heavily used in the nation, that half of the vehicles passing the check point were trucks, that 60 percent of those passing were destined or originated in Bangkok, and that the opposite end of the journey for the vast majority was either (Korat) or areas along the highway. Wisit estimates that 88% of the 1959 traffic was

not diverted from other routes, but induced by the existence of the highway itself. Chaiyong reports that the cost of corn transportation was reduced 20% in Saraburi and [Korat] by the construction of this highway. Such statistics are far from complete, but they do tend to support the generally accepted hypothesis that the highway induced considerable agricultural production in the area by providing relatively cheap truck transport to Bangkok markets.[30]

The studies of the impact of the highway have not extended to its broad effects on the development of the whole Northeast region, but there can be little doubt that its position as first connecting link among the Northeast, Bangkok, and export markets, vastly expanded its area of economic impact as the Korat terminus became connected with the ever-increasing all-weather road system of the region over succeeding years. For the kenaf boom in the Northeast that followed on the heels of the corn boom, for the later and more long-lasting expansion of cassava production, and for much else that has contributed to economic growth in the Northeast, the Friendship Highway has been a critical stretch in the road transport system.

As construction of the Friendship Highway approached the end, the two American contractors that were building the road, Raymond Construction and the Sverdrup and Parcel Engineering Corporation, began to shift their forces, including heavy equipment and their 1,500 Thai employees, to a second project, known as the East-West Highway. This route had also been selected by the two governments for strategic reasons, although it was hoped that economic benefits would be generated as well. The second highway runs about 130 kilometers between Pitsanuloke and Lomsak in the north-central part of the country, providing the first all-weather paved connection between the northern and northeastern regions of the country, which lacked even direct rail connection. The road traverses a mountainous area that was heavily forested and only sparsely settled and was designed to facilitate east-west movement of Thai military forces, should that become necessary, obviating the need for such forces to make long southern roundabout detours.

According to USOM, the Thai government requested that this second project also be constructed by the American contractors because the terrain posed construction problems beyond the capacity of the Highway Department at that time. The project included the building of a bridge over the Nan River, which runs through the town of Pitsanuloke. As with the OICC construction projects, these two highway projects trained large numbers of Thai engineers and machine operators in modern highway construction methods and the use of heavy equipment. The total cost of the project was $14.6 million.

The East-West Highway was completed in 1960. It was the first stretch of what ultimately became a road from Mae Sod on the Thai-Burma border to Nakhon Phanom on the Mekong River. Unlike the Friendship Highway, however, the East-West Highway has had only local economic impact. As of 1963, Behrman found its effect on agricultural production in the first three years to be "slight." This is not surprising, since the east and westward extensions had yet to be built. The full extent of this route was subsequently completed, but the through traffic still appeared (by 1986 traffic counts) to be less than a quarter of the north-south traffic on the Northeast route. The economic value of long-haul east-west roads in most parts of Thailand cannot be expected to rival the returns to north-south oriented routes, given the geographic configuration of the country and the preponderant north-south movement of commercial traffic. Nearly 90 percent of commercial tonnage movement in Thailand is estimated to move north and south, originating from and destined for Bangkok.[31]

The East-West Highway project story took an unexpected turn in the 1970s, when the mountains in this region became one of the relatively remote areas of Thailand where insurgents concentrated. To avoid ambush in its operations in the area, the army cleared a swath along both sides of the highway. Much more destructive to the forest were the slash and burn practices of hill tribes who were allowed to settle in the area of the highway after they came over to the government side in the mid-1970s. Large stands of virgin forest were destroyed by uncontrolled burning initiated by the settlers to clear relatively small fields for cultivation.

In sum, the highway facilitated military penetration of an area that became a security problem (different from and long after the threat in response to which the road was originally built); opened up land for migrant settlers who in return ceased insurgent activity; resulted in local deforestation; and led to some minor increases in agricultural production and interregional traffic. The security contingency for which the road was originally built has not arisen, while internal security in the region has been restored. The economic effects have been minor, and the environmental impact detrimental. I should be clear on this latter point. The road itself appears to have had no environmental impact beyond its area of construction; the forest access it created enabled subsequent events to unfold in a manner completely unforeseen and unintended. Since most of the highway runs through areas designated as reserved forest, the government is considering a reforestation program rather than any further development of the highway's contiguous land.

In 1957 two new projects were started to complete the entire route from Bangkok to Nongkai.The Bangkok-Saraburi project reconstructed the existing highway from Bangkok to the southern end of the Friendship Highway, while the Korat-Nongkai project carried the paved route all the way up to the Mekong, where traffic could then ferry across to Vientiane, the capital of Laos. The Bangkok-Saraburi section, the main artery leading from Bangkok to both the northern and northeastern regions, was the most important roadway in the country. The 107-kilometer highway was reconstructed between 1957 and 1961 at a cost of $12.9 million. I know of no studies of the economic impact of this reconstruction comparable to the studies of the Friendship Highway's effects, but given the economic primacy of this route in the country's entire road network, it is likely that the project generated benefits greater than most infrastructure projects of that era, although its history as a U.S.–assisted project is much less well-known than the story of the Friendship Highway. In any case an effort to separate the impact of these individual projects would be artificial since together they make up one integrated main stem of the interconnected primary system.

The most unique aspect of the Bangkok-Saraburi and Korat-Nongkai projects was the method of construction. The engineering design work was done by an American contractor, but the construction was performed by Thai contractors. Since this was the first time local private construction firms had ever been engaged to build roads, with the Highway Department acting as supervisor rather than direct builder, USOM had to tailor the implementation to make the work feasible for the fledgling contractors. The highway was divided into a number of subprojects so that the firms could bid for lengths of road commensurate with their construction management capacities. In a second innovation, USOM set up a Highway Equipment Pool project that procured heavy road-building equipment from U.S. military surplus for rental to the local contractors, who by and large had never invested in such equipment since highway construction had always been done directly by the Highway Department. The pool was managed by the Highway Department with the help of a U.S. engineering firm, Charles M. Upham Associates.

The policy of using local contractors had actually been introduced two years earlier by USOM on a road bridge project that itself must have had very widespread economic impact, but for which there are no studies or evidence. Even more crippling to the usefulness of the highway system than the terrible condition of the road surfaces was the dilapidated and collapsed condition of the country's road bridges, which in effect broke the highways into small segments. Depending on the season, a portion of any long trip in the 1950s was spent scouting out and driving through streams, either because the bridge was unusable or fording the stream looked a safer bet. Under the $6.2 million Highway Bridge Replacement Program over 1,000 bridges and culverts were built throughout the country, opening up 4,000 kilometers of road that were previously unusable by heavy vehicles. Small bridge construction, which could use standard designs, lent itself to private contracting. When the project began, in the face of RTG skepticism over the ability of the local firms to carry out the work, there were only seven firms in the country that were able to undertake the contracts. By the time the project ended, there were seventy-six such firms. At first the contractors could build only the standard design structures. They fell into financial difficulties because they tended to underestimate costs when putting in their bids. While the bridge project experience helped the contractors to overcome these problems, they experienced a new set of difficulties when they took on the small road segments of the highway construction projects. Managerial weaknesses in work scheduling and financial planning posed greater problems than the engineering aspects of the road work. After two or three years these new problems had been largely overcome and construction was proceeding at a satisfactory rate. Local contractors then performed most of the work on AID-financed roads until the program phased out of highway construction.

It is interesting to note, parenthetically, that the bridge and culvert project was the first example of "privatization" in Thailand. In the 1980s, privatization (the turning over of a public sector activity for private sector operation or ownership) became an important policy objective of many developing country governments, cheered on by the World Bank and USAID among others, as the economic drag of inefficient state management grew to be generally acknowledged as unacceptable. USOM's privatization of civil works in Thailand thirty years earlier stemmed from the belief of American engineers that private contracting would be a more efficient and expeditious way to get the job done, even though the aid agency had no particular policies on the subject. Although this experience represented a significant contribution of the aid program (and then OICC) to the development of the private Thai construction industry, it was an incidental benefit stemming from the manner in which the mission (and OICC) preferred to implement a set of projects with entirely unrelated purposes.[32]

The two remaining major highways funded in part with U.S. aid were the Korat-Nongkhai and Bangkok–Nakhon Pathom routes. The former was the extension from the northern terminus of the Friendship Highway up to the Mekong, reconstructing the preexisting 414 kilometers of laterite road. The work was done by Thai contractors, as I have noted, under the supervision of the Highways Department and with technical assistance from U.S. consultants. The route was built between 1959 and 1961 at a cost of $12.6 million, mostly in local currency. The full strategic route from Bangkok to the Mekong was now in place as a hard-surface, all-weather road, one of the major routes of the national system. Through its connections with subsequently built and improved arteries and feeder roads reaching into all corners of the Northeast, this highway was of prime importance in the economic development of the whole region.

The Bangkok–Nakhon Pathom project reconstructed the main road leading from Bangkok westward, connecting the capital with the peninsular south transport system. Second only to the Bangkok-Saraburi stretch in terms of traffic load, this 50-kilometer project was built in 1964–65 at a cost of $5.8 million, again largely in local currency, and by local contractors. I know of no evaluation of the economic impact of the reconstruction of this route, but its central role in the country's road transport system is also self-evident. The two roads formed part of the core of the highway system within a radius of 150 kilometers of Bangkok, which in 1984 was carrying 50 percent of all Thailand's motorized traffic (excluding motorcycles). Finally, mention should be made of feasibility studies that were made for other routes (such as the Lomsak–Chumpae stretch of the extended East-West route and the Chumporn–Nakhon Srithammarat highway in the peninsula) and the $5.8 million project (all local currency) to build some major streets in Bangkok between 1957 and 1961.

The story of Bangkok transportation is grim. As has been the case with many urban areas, vehicular traffic has continuously expanded in Bangkok to fill up expanded street capacity. The streets constructed at that time under this project centered in a section of the city undergoing rapid growth and expanded traffic capacity at the time, including opening up for housing and commercial development a long strip of land (from Pratunam eastward along the Petchburi road extension) that had remained relatively undeveloped until then. The project represented one chapter in the continuing effort of the Thai government to cope with the largely haphazard growth of the country's one predominant metropolitan area.

AID shifted from the primary highway system to the network of secondary provincial roads in the early 1960s and then phased out of transportation altogether by 1974. (The provincial roads will be discussed in chapter 5.) Extensive additional investment has taken place with major funding from the World Bank and some bilateral donors. The contribution of AID's earlier years of transport assistance continues as a permanent one in terms of the role of the Highways Department, the continued use of the roads AID helped to construct, the development of the first comprehensive plans for the road network, and in general the continuing accumulated growth of the economy as a whole in which the transport sector has played a central role. By 1984 total road length comprised 48,000 kilometers of mostly all-weather surfaces and 100,000 kilometers of gravel and earth rural roads. According to an IBRD study,

> Since the mid-1960s, the Thai economy, as a result of a strong showing of the agriculture sector, grew at a rapid pace and generated a high demand for transport. Roughly some 75% of total demand in 1981 was for bulk or semi-processed agricultural produce.
>
> To accommodate the growing demand, the Government undertook large transport investments (in particular for road infrastructure) and created a policy environment in which, with some exceptions, a competitive transport industry developed. Today [1984] all [provinces] are interlinked with a good interregional network, and transport services have penetrated the majority of previously remote rural areas. In comparison with other similarly situated countries, the transport system is, by and large, good. There are, on the whole, no significant physical or administrative impediments to meeting current transport demand.
>
> The country's various transport modes have developed soundly and impressively over the past quarter century, with appropriate balance among the modes to serve different transport functions. As a proportion of total public investment, the share of transport is likely to decline somewhat from past levels.[33]

One of the enduring questions posed by critics of foreign aid concerns the character of the technologies taught or otherwise transferred. The observation that many industrial projects in particular used technologies that were capital-intensive in economies that were capital-short and relatively well supplied with low-cost labor led to considerable criticism of the technology decision process and the actors involved, whether aid agencies, foreign industrial enterprises, or developing country officials and engineers. These projects often operated far below capacity, were unable to achieve the economies of scale that make capital-intensive processes profitable, and contributed to further distortions when protectionist infant industry policies forced domestic enterprises to buy the higher cost product of the protected firm rather than import a cheaper alternative. Analogous criticisms were made of civil works technologies employed in developing countries where large numbers of otherwise underemployed laborers could be applied to labor-intensive construction instead of using heavy machinery.

There is no direct study of the technically feasible alternatives available for the terrain and expected traffic loads of the roads built under the aid program that would address this particular point. Given the steep grades of sections of both the Friendship and East-West highways, which traverse hilly and mountainous areas (in some very steep sections of the East-West Highway too sloping for the operation of heavy equipment, the initial clearing of forest cover was done with elephants) and the extensive rock cuts that had to be made, a more labor-using alternative was probably not feasible. The specifications for compaction, surfacing, and so on, were, if anything, of a standard somewhat below what would have been justified if it had been possible to foresee the enormous traffic growth and persistent violation of axle-load limits by truckers, as far as the Friendship Highway and the other sections of the whole Bangkok–Nongkai route are concerned. Some regrading and repaving had to be done on the Friendship Highway within the first year after its opening. Given the heavy use of much of the Thai highway system, the fact that Thailand did not then and does not now have the large-scale rural underemployment conditions under which labor-using engineering alternatives become both feasible and socially desirable and that the later necessity to rebuild important routes to much higher engineering standards in order to accommodate the growth in road transport did not arise, labor-intensive road-building does not appear to have ever been considered a relevant option in Thailand.

Air Transport. The 1955–1959 period saw an expansion of U.S. aid activities into virtually every mode of the country's transportation system in addition to the highway network. I have already referred to the airport construction projects undertaken for military and civilian purposes and implemented jointly by USOM and OICC. A small civil aviation project begun in 1951 provided a basis for a much more ambitious USOM program starting in 1955 and comprising eight separate projects. Military considerations aside, it was apparent to the RTG, to U.S. civil aviation authorities (then the Civil Aviation Administration [CAA], now the Federal Aviation Administration [FAA]), and to the U.N.'s International Civil Aviation Organization (ICAO) that Bangkok's geographic position was certain to make it a major traffic hub. The air traffic capabilities at Bangkok's Don Muang International Airport were rapidly becoming overloaded. The domestic air system also needed strengthening and expansion.

The first phase of the program in aviation lasted about ten years. It included the financing and installation of navigational aids at Don Muang and thirteen other civil airports, various communication systems, airport improvements (control towers, runways, aprons, power plants), and an instrument landing system at Don Muang. About one hundred participants were trained in the operation and maintenance of these facilities. Plans were developed for a local aircraft overhaul and maintenance facility. The main implementing agency on the U.S. side was the CAA, working closely with the Thai Civil Aviation Administration and the Thai military aviation authorities. The United States also played a role in the reorganization of the Thai civil aviation agencies in 1963.[34]

By 1965 Thailand had a system of domestic airfields for daylight operations as well as the basic navigational aids, communications systems, and technical capabilities to operate Don Muang and control much expanded traffic at an internationally acceptable level of efficiency and safety. The CAA staff was down to one last technician, and the principal project (Aeronautical Ground Services Improvement) was slated to phase out. As a result of the growth of the Vietnam conflict, however, the decision was made in early 1965 to extend the Ground Services project into a second phase, which turned out to be much larger, in terms of both equipment and technical assistance, than the first ten years. The prime reason for this second phase was the realization that the build-up in military air traffic was going to place greatly increased demands on Thailand's civil aviation structure for handling the military traffic and mixing it safely with the expanding civil traffic. The objectives of the second phase included development of Thai flight equipment inspection capability, installation of additional navigational equipment, improvement of aeronautical communications, installation of lighting so that seven additional airports could operate at night, and a second round of training, especially for air traffic controllers.

When the project finally phased out in 1974, Bangkok had become one of the major hubs of the world, as expected. Only eleven other airports in the world had more scheduled carriers operating. Tourism was already the fifth largest earner of foreign exchange, and 80 percent of all visitors to Thailand were coming by air. Cargo traffic was also growing rapidly (over 25 percent a year due to the Vietnam conflict). While there were clearly many organizations involved in the complex and costly development of the aviation infrastructure and operational capabilities (including the airlines, ICAO, and others), the U.S. civil and military inputs were predominant among the external sources. The Thai government's inputs were of course very substantial.

It is not an exaggeration to conclude that the two decades of U.S. assistance in airport construction and the development of Thailand's aeronautical ground services facilities and capabilities were fundamental for the growth of this transport subsector into one of major importance for the country's economic development, quite apart from its importance for the role of the Royal Thai Airforce in the country's defense posture. Bangkok has become one of the major centers of air transport in Asia, besides serving as the main point of entry for the majority of Thailand's enormous flow of tourists. In 1988 the main issue confronting Thai air transport planning was where to locate the new international airport capacity the country's growing air traffic will need in the 1990s. Needless to say, Thailand has had to make substantial additional investment and continuous technical upgrading to meet the economy's needs for growing international and domestic passenger and commodity traffic. While Japanese economic aid has helped to finance some of this investment, American aid has not played a significant role since 1974. Thus, although the subsequent expansions and modernization of the Thai aeronautical system have been changing the physical and technical inheritance of the preceding years, this important component of the country's infrastructure rests on an initial physical and institutional foundation to which the U.S. aid program made a major contribution.

Finally, mention should be made of a $1.6 million project under which Pan American World Airways was contracted to give technical assistance to Thai Airways, then the country's one national airline. Thailand now has a highly competitive and profitable international airline and a domestic airline (recently combined), both offering vastly greater air service than was available from the ailing parent company when this project began in 1956. Unlike the case of the airport and aeronautical services, however, credit for the later development of Thai airline services cannot be attributed to the early U.S. aid project. After a promising start the project ran into a series of difficulties and was terminated when the first contract ran out in 1959. Thai Airways then entered into a successful relationship with Scandinavian Airlines.

Rail Transport. Rehabilitation of the war-damaged railway system was an obvious need in the very first year of the aid program. The maintenance shops in Bangkok had been bombed repeatedly and were badly in need of equipment, electric power generators, and rolling stock parts. The Railways Improvement project met these needs and sent thirty-seven technicians of the State Railways of Thailand (SRT) to the United States for training in railroad administration and operation. Under a second project begun in 1955 the SRT received additional rolling stock for the Northeast line and a traffic control and communication system, all for improvement of service on the Northeast lines. An additional 125 boxcars and 40 tank undercarriages were given to SRT to enable the railway to handle the transshipment of goods bound for Laos. Two other projects assisted the State Railways to extend the Northeast line 60 kilometers from Udorn to Nongkai and to build a ferry landing and connecting rail spur to complete the transport network from Bangkok to Vientiane. These last two projects were designed to benefit Laos primarily, since the bulk of Lao imports had to be shipped through the port of Bangkok and up the Northeast rail line.

After 1958 the United States provided no further aid to the railways. As with all the capital projects of these years, the financing of this tranche of equipment and construction to meet immediate, if not emergency, needs was not seen by the aid agency as the beginning of a long-term investment relationship. The World Bank became the main source of external funding for SRT through a series of loans every several years, amounting to about $60 million by 1981. In the process of designing and negotiating these loans, the Bank also recurrently analyzed the rail system's operations and problems and negotiated for policy and operational changes the Bank thought were required for the efficiency and by the financial condition of SRT. The U.S. aid program's involvement in the rail system did not extend to this level of institutional concern or continuing commitment to the growth of rail transport.

Water Transport. Last (and least) place in the transport sector belongs to one of the very first American aid projects in Thailand and the only foray into water transport other than the Nongkai ferry landing (leaving aside, of course, the OICC construction of the Sattahip naval base). I refer to the purchase of the second-hand dredge *Manhattan* in 1951 from the U.S. Corps of Engineers. The task of the *Manhattan* was to keep open the channel up the Chao Phya River leading to the port of Bangkok. Unfortunately, as it was towed from Philadelphia, through the Panama Canal, and across the Pacific, the dredge was damaged by the arduous journey, and it had to be repaired before it could be put to work. After several years of service it was replaced in 1959 by a new dredge financed under a $1.75 million AID loan. The *Manhattan* was saved from sinking into complete obscurity, however, by an accident of Thai political history. Since the dredge was an early and conspicuous symbol of American assistance to Thailand, its rededication as the *Sandon II* was the occasion of a formal ceremony, attended by many Bangkok luminaries, during which the U.S. Ambassador formally presented the vessel to Prime Minister Pilbulsonggram. In the middle of the proceedings the Royal Thai Navy suddenly launched a coup. The Prime Minister was taken from the *Manhattan* to a nearby naval vessel. When the Thai Air Force then sent this vessel to the bottom of the Chao Phya, Pibul swam to safety and another six years as the head of the government.

Power

Second only to transportation in the infrastructure phase of the aid program were the projects to help develop Thailand's electric power sector. As with transportation, the build-up in power activities was based on a minor component of the initial 1951 array of technical assistance. One was a project that assisted the Royal Department of Mines to do the first exploratory drilling at lignite deposits at Mae Moh in the northern province of Lampang and in Krabi province in the South. When the Mae Moh deposit proved large, a follow-up project financed heavy equipment to begin mining operations in 1954. The output of high-grade material rose to over 100,000 tons by 1958, all consumed by power stations in Bangkok. At that time proven reserves at Mae Moh were 30 million tons and total expected reserves 120 million tons.[35] Proven reserves have since risen to 650 million tons, possible reserves to 1,434 million.[36]

To generate power for use in the North, in 1957 Thailand borrowed

$5.5 million from the U.S. Export-Import Bank to help finance the construction of a 12.5-megawatt lignite-fired thermal power station at the Mae Moh site. This plant was an important addition to the meager power supply then available in the North. Development of the smaller Krabi deposit was not feasible until the oil price "shocks" of the 1970s made lignite a competitive domestic alternative to imported petroleum. With funding from World Bank loans in 1980 and 1985, Thailand expanded the share of electric power generation using lignite (measured in tons of oil equivalent) to about 25 percent, the bulk of which used Mae Moh lignite.[37] Thus, while Mae Moh lignite was an important contribution to the development of the local economy in North Thailand when it came on line in 1960 (and was a source of fuel for the cement industry), its national economic potential (and the smaller contribution of Krabi) as a domestic power source reducing the country's dependence on imported petroleum came two decades later, after completely unforseen changes in the structure of world energy prices.

More important than Mae Moh, even though not measurable in its impact, was a second early project for Power Services and Training that became the vehicle for USOM's across-the-board role in helping to put Thailand's power sector on a modern footing. The centerpiece of this effort was four years of technical assistance provided by a U.S. contractor, the Rogers Engineering Company, to the National Energy Authority and other RTG agencies concerned with the power sector. As in the transport sector, the need for a broad and sustained program of investment in power generation and distribution facilities and for development of the technical and institutional infrastructure to install and operate a modern power system was patently evident—as was the fact that Thailand had barely entered the age of electricity. There was no national power distribution grid and no village electrification. The provincial or district seats that had small municipal generators usually had power only a few hours a day, subject to frequent outages. Electric light was prevalent only in Bangkok, and even the railway system still used wood as its principal fuel. The World Bank noted that Thailand was one of the lowest power consuming countries in the world in the mid-1950s. The Bank described the electric power situation in the following terms:

> [The] emphasis on power development finds ample justification in the present and prospective needs of the economy for electricity. . . . Throughout the post-war period, the expansion of generation and distribution facilities has lagged

far behind the growth in demand for power. . . . About half
[of total generating capacity] is in Bangkok. But both in
Bangkok and in the provinces, only half of existing capacity is in the public utility systems. The rest is in private
establishments which have found it necessary to install
generating facilities to meet their own needs. . . . Practically all the private capacity consists of small, high-cost
diesel units. The facilities of the public system also have
comparatively high operating costs. . . . A severe power
shortage existed in Bangkok as early as 1950, and since
then it has been getting worse. . . . There is little doubt that
this shortage has been a significant deterrent to the development of commercial and industrial activity in the Bangkok area during recent years[38]

The U.S. program's role in this situation was to help the energy
authorities create the institutional and technical basis for the development of the public power system and to help finance the most
urgently required increases in power generation and distribution facilities before leaving the field to the World Bank and a series of large
hydroelectric projects. Not surprisingly, the technical and organizational capabilities in the electric power sector were in as rudimentary
a state as the physical endowment. Under these conditions, Rogers
Engineering established close relationships with the small cadre of
senior Thai power officials and found itself in a position to provide
fundamental training, institution-building, and system design services, including preparation of the first master transmission and distribution plan for the country as a whole, a plan the Thai authorities
followed for many years. Rogers also did the engineering and design
work for the Mae Moh and Bangkok projects. Without technical assistance of this scope it would have been impossible for the Thai power
authorities to carry out the investment program of those years or to
have built up the institutional capacity, now very substantial, to
manage the development of a major economic sector.

As far as the infrastructure itself is concerned, besides the Mae Moh
power plant, the U.S. projects in the late 1950s included a 75 MW
thermal power plant in Bangkok and related improvements in the
city's power distribution system (utilizing a loan of $5.4 million from
the U.S. Export Import Bank); 25 megawatts of diesel generating
units for Bangkok and 2.7 megawatts for ten provincial towns; and a
loan of $19.8 million towards the construction of the distribution
system that would bring to Bangkok the power from the first IRBD

and West German–financed hydro project, the Yanhee (later renamed the Bhumibol), which had an ultimate installed capacity of 535 megawatts.

Since then the power sector in Thailand has grown at more than 15 percent a year, around twice the rate of growth of the GDP. Installed capacity has risen from 176 megawatts in 1960 to 6,155 megawatts in 1985.[39] Natural gas production has been developed from offshore deposits in the Gulf of Thailand, and major changes have occurred in the structure of power demand and supply in response to the rise in oil prices. The Electricity Generating Authority of Thailand has become one of the country's largest and most efficiently managed enterprises with all of its key staff having been trained overseas. The energy sector now contains an array of institutions and operating enterprises that in most cases did not exist in the 1950s. While the U.S.–financed installed capacity represented no less than 65 percent of the total capacity of Thailand's power system in 1960, the investment has long since paled in comparison to the expansion subsequent to the infrastructure phase of the aid program and to the external financing provided for that expansion by the World Bank, the Asian Development Bank (ADB), and bilateral donors such as West Germany, Japan, Canada, Australia, New Zealand, and Finland.

In the power sector, as in other sectors, it was clear that the aid program itself (and the Export-Import Bank) could not continue as significant sources of external funding in relation to the country's requirements and compared with the funds the World Bank and other sources could make available. The technical assistance contract, however, had the scope to help the power authorities establish their capacity to absorb large-scale external resources and to plan and manage the long-term expansion of the power sector. Once these foundation-building activities were phased out, AID did not return to the power sector for years, and then only for more narrowly focused projects in small-scale generation and rural electrification.

Mining

Tin mining has been important in southern Thailand and a significant export for centuries. Thailand has long produced from 5 to 15 percent of world tin output, making it the third or fourth ranking world supplier. However, except for the lignite deposit and one northern tin mine, there was no mining of any significance in the rest of the country or in other minerals well into the postwar years. There were two reasons for this. One was a law prohibiting private mining north of a line drawn just above the tin areas of the peninsula, reserving the exploration and development of mineral resources in the rest of the country to the state. The second reason was the paucity of information on Thailand's geology. USOM's initial institution-building project with the Royal Thai Department of Mines financed participant training for the Department's geologists, engineers, and other personnel, plus laboratory and library facilities and surveying and exploring equipment. The project was carried out by the U.S. Geological Survey (USGS) under an interagency agreement with ICA.

The USGS technicians addressed the legal constraint on private mining and persuaded their Thai counterparts that the law should be changed and that the Thai geological survey operation should serve a private mining industry in a manner similar to the system employed in the United States. The Thais accepted the advice, the law was changed, and the project went on to help the development of the first private mines north of the old line, a manganese mine at Chieng Khan in Loey province and a gypsum mine at Tapan Hin in Pichit province. In addition to financing Thailand's first airborne geophysical survey over portions of the Northeast and providing training and demonstrations in underground mining techniques, the mining projects equipped an experimentation center to upgrade the efficiency of ore beneficiation and introduce modern metallurgy technology.

At this writing, nearly thirty years later, the extractive sector is much changed.[40] Over one thousand mines were operating in 1985, nearly half producing minerals other than tin. Thailand now produces more than thirty minerals, including zinc, fluorite, gypsum, lead, barite, columbite-tantalite, and antimony. It is the world's largest producer of tantalum ore, a strategic mineral. The value of mineral exports can fluctuate widely with cycles in world commodity prices. In the peak year of 1980 mineral export earnings were second only to those of rice. In 1985, by contrast, Thai tin export tonnage was down sharply under restrictions imposed by the International Tin Council, and values were further depressed by the collapse of the London tin market in October. As a result mineral exports fell to sixth place that year.

The uncertainties of tin aside, the long-term outlook for growth of Thai mineral exports is promising. In addition, the availability of some of these minerals has induced investment in manufacturing based on the domestic materials. In sum, the mining sector has grown substantially and has added to the country's export diversity and domestic manufacturing potential. The legal framework has evolved to support private sector development of these resources. A new mineral resource assessment was started in 1984, and it included a countrywide airborne geophysical survey, assisted by the Asian Development Bank and the Canadian International Development Agency.

Needless to say, the proliferation of mines has also created new problems. Conflicts have arisen between mining interests on the one hand and competing economic interests (such as tourism) and environmental groups on the other. The legal framework and government policy processes needed to rationalize and mediate these conflicts are inadequate. Illegal mining and smuggling of ore to avoid royalty payments also occur.

In the nearly three decades since the U.S. aid program assisted the initial diversification and technical development of the mining sector, the U.S. government has played no further role in the subsequent evolution of these benefits and problems (except for the impact on the world tin market of alternating U.S. stockpile accumulation and reduction policies). (American corporations have had a significant role mainly in the development of offshore gas and in oil exploration.) AID may now be coming back to this sector, however, in the context of a broad natural resources and environmental project the mission was developing in 1987, this time to help the RTG cope with the environmental and resource-use conflicts that the mineral sector's success is causing.

During this period another large USOM project assisted the Royal Department of Mines in conducting the first major exploratory drilling program in the Northeast, which was designed to evaluate the groundwater potential of the region rather than mineral resources. The project financed four drilling rigs and technical assistance from an American engineering contractor. Of the 680 wells drilled under the project, about two-thirds yielded potable water. With very few exceptions, the producing wells tapped aquifers that could supply water in quantities adequate only for drinking, not for irrigation. The project trained departmental staff who have continued ground water studies and well development since and have gathered substantial information about the geology of the Northeast through a number of stratigraphic analyses. Although groundwater resources in the Northeast have proven inconsequential for irrigation and remain insufficient for domestic water requirements in large parts of the region (well drilling continues to be an important activity in rural development programs in the Northeast), the groundwater project succeeded in its institution-building objective of helping the mining department develop the technical ability to conduct groundwater assessment itself.

Education

The second phase of the aid program was not limited to the infrastructure. As Caldwell's phrase "Nation-Building" suggests, USOM's projects extended into basic institution-building in many areas of fundamental importance to the development process. In addition to the health and agriculture activities described above, there were new initiatives in education and public administration based on small beginnings in these areas in 1951–1952.

Caldwell describes the issues in Thai education:

> As the decade of the fifties opened there were three key problems facing education in Thailand: the insufficient number and low quality of teachers; the inefficiency of the elementary, grades 1–4, schools; and the paucity of teaching materials ... 77% of all teachers had no certificates of any kind. ... while three-fourths of Thai children attended school at some point, only 13% ever completed fourth grade. In 1950, 59% of pupils entering grade one had to repeat it. ... two-thirds of the population could neither read nor write. ... only 39% of the districts had schools above the first four grades.[41]

In the face of these daunting problems, USOM launched a number of small projects financing participant training, U.S. technicians, and miscellaneous equipment for demonstration schools, curriculum improvement, education plant improvement, and so on, in virtually every segment of the educational system as it was then structured. The projects covered teacher training, primary and secondary education, vocational agricultural schools, vocational technical education, and adult education, all feeding into a reform plan that had been based on UNESCO norms.

In higher education the first large activity was a project under which the University of Texas helped to strengthen the undergraduate engineering school of Chulalongkorn University. Under a second project, begun in 1952, USOM provided equipment to help Kasetsart University improve its physical plant. This project was expanded in

1955 through a contract with Oregon State College that sent about sixty Kasetsart faculty to the United States for training while U.S. professors assisted in research, curriculum development, and the like. A third project began in 1959 in response to a proposal by the Thai government to establish a regional graduate engineering school as a SEATO institution. With major financing from the United States and additional contributions from the various SEATO members, the institution was created by making use of faculty and technical assistance from Colorado State University. The school was first set up as part of Chulalongkorn University. In 1958 it became an independent institution, the Asian Institute of Technology (AIT) and had developed into an international class institution of higher learning. While U.S. aid support for AIT has declined since the years when AID was providing major resources for its establishment, funding has continued for scholarships and special programs.

The primary and secondary level objectives were ambitious if not unrealistic. The Americans hoped that a combination of training in the United States and the creation of model demonstration schools in Thailand would have enough leverage to bring about thorough-going reform of curriculum, educational methods, and the quality of teaching.

For elementary education reform, Chachoengsao province, southeast of Bangkok, was selected for development of an elementary level center for demonstrating new approaches. Supervisors and teachers were brought from other parts of the country for in-service training once the center was a going concern. At the secondary level four schools in Bangkok were selected for development as demonstration centers where large numbers of teachers received in-service training. Other projects worked at the supervisory levels of the primary and secondary systems. In technical education Wayne State University was contracted for seven years to help the Ministry establish the country's first Technical Institute, which was located in Bangkok and had branches in Chiengmai, Korat and Songkhla. Another project assisted the sixteen vocational agriculture schools, focusing on the schools in Mae Joh and Surin as demonstrations. Under a third project, also financed from regional SEATO funds, the University of Hawaii was contracted between 1959 and 1965 to help the Vocational Education Department strengthen trade schools.

In retrospect senior Ministry of Education officials describe their early relationship with Wayne State University as seminal for the formation of the ministry's capabilities and educational philosophy in the vocational and technical fields. The first participants in these areas went to Wayne State in 1954 and brought back new educational approaches and methods that were accepted and implemented by the ministry. Except for the single technical institute in Bangkok, established in 1952, technical education in the rest of the country consisted only of carpentry and home economics. Under the Wayne State project, teacher training was introduced at the Bangkok institute, the three regional institutes were set up, the curriculum was expanded, and the training equipment and materials required for the new curriculum were installed. Under the SEATO/Hawaii University project, fifteen of the provincial carpentry schools were converted to vocational schools offering automotive, electrical, and mechanical training. Under a later project with the Department of Vocational Education, the program helped the Ministry expand a rural vocational training scheme conducted by mobile units.

With the expansion of the program's resources in FY 1955, the mission rationalized its scattered primary and secondary educational efforts and launched a few larger-scale attempts that were expected to be more commensurate with the reform and expansion needs faced by the Ministry. In terms of sheer size, given the rapid growth then taking place in the school age population, one of the most strategic requirements was to expand the teacher training institutions. In 1958 these institutions were graduating 5,400 teachers a year, compared with a need that was estimated at 10,000 a year. The level of training, both academic and in teaching skills, of the 100,000 teachers already in the system at that time was very low. Only 4 percent of the secondary teachers had a college degree, and one-third had no teacher training or no schooling beyond the tenth grade.

Two major projects were started in the mid-1950s to help the Ministry address these problems on a more ambitious level. One project financed a contract with Indiana University to develop the Prasarn Mitr College of Education in Bangkok into a first class apex institution of the teacher-training system. The second was a General Education Development project that helped set up in-service teacher-training centers in each of the country's twelve education regions. Each center had a teacher-training institution, schools at the primary, secondary, and vocational levels, a supervisory unit, and a resident American advisor. A number of the earlier projects working on different aspects of in-service training were folded into this project.

The Indiana University/Prasarn Mitr project ran for eight years. The cost of the project as a whole, including the Ministry's outlays for construction and other elements, amounted to around $13.8 million, of which USOM provided dollar support of $2.8 million. It is worth quoting Caldwell for the insight his account gives into the nature of a "soft" institution-building project and the reasons for its success:

> The purposes of the College were set out in a memorandum written in 1954 after three months' joint study of educational conditions in Thailand. . . . [it] envisaged the creation of an "outstanding institution dedicated to preparing educational leaders for the country." . . . The teaching program was to be "radically different from that which is typical of the training of teachers in Thailand" and the College was to have an impact on the entire educational system. . . .
>
> A total of 34 foreign advisors were eventually to serve 44 man years under the program. Thirty of the advisors were directly from the staff of Indiana University. They ranked high by American professional standards. . . . advisors were not to spend more than 20% of their time in the classroom. This restriction helped ensure their continued understanding that their prime responsibility was to assist the Thai staff to gain confidence and competence and not to teach future Thai teachers themselves. . . .
>
> The participant training program in the United States was particularly successful. One hundred and fifty Thai were sent; fifteen earned doctorates, and ninety master's degrees. All returned to serve with the College, and as of 1967, only six had left it—all for positions of greater responsibility within the government. (Pp. 98–99)

After describing the substantial increases achieved in the size of the student body, the numbers of graduates, books in the library, and the like, Caldwell concludes:

> A number of "firsts" could be attributed to the joint program: it had resulted in the first four-year degree-granting program designed to prepare teachers and educational leaders; the first foreign assistance program carefully to define staff training needs prior to study abroad; the first system of student counselling by trained professional counsellors (at Indiana); the first summer session; the first systematic educational extension program; and the first air-conditioned library in Thailand. (P. 101)

It is clear from this experience that among the Thai Government, USOM, and Indiana University, enough had been learned by the mid-1950s (presumably ICA and Indiana were also profiting from aid experience in other countries) to assemble the components for successful institution-building, including such things as basic mutual understanding of the policy objectives and professional norms that would govern the institution, high-level support and sustained commitment within the Ministry, careful meshing of the institution's outputs and programs with the realities of the environment it was supposed to affect, a variety of conditions to ensure the commitment and enthusiasm of returning participants, special arrangements on the U.S. campus to cope with participants' adjustment problems, and the creation of strong bonds and confidence between the assisted institution and the American contractor.

This latter point is especially interesting in terms of a curious difficulty Caldwell describes that arose in 1958 as a result of a change in ICA policy toward institutional contracts as an instrument of technical assistance. Apparently the new ICA administrator, James Hollister, wished to reverse the previous reliance on contracts (presumably in favor of reliance on ICA's own "direct-hire" technical staff and on the so-called Participating Agency Service Agreement [PASA] arrangements under which ICA drew on technical staffs of other departments of the U.S. government) and sharply cut back on the freedom of operation of existing contracts, or so at least the policy was interpreted by USOM. "Contract personnel were not to visit the Ministry of Education or discuss matters with Ministry personnel without prior approval from the chief of USOM's Education Division. Scheduled visits by contract personnel to provincial teacher training institutions were cancelled, and attendance at Thai-sponsored professional conferences was forbidden" (p. 100). The Ministry itself strongly supported Indiana's role, these problems were overcome, the contract was extended, and USOM's "resistance" gave way. In the light of the aid program's subsequent history, this episode now looks bizarre. AID's relations with and utilization of American universities through contractual arrangements have been very extensive and fruitful (although not always successful, of course), and the agency has for many years used its field staff as project managers rather than as operating technicians and staffed its projects under contractual arrangements.

It is more difficult to see the results or to form judgments about the effects, especially the long-run impact, of some of the other education projects of the 1950s and 1960s. USOM became dissatisfied with the contract with Oregon State at Kasetsart University and terminated

that project in 1959 after four years. Although the project had provided Kasetsart with large quantities of equipment and teaching aids,
buildings (constructed with counterpart funds), graduate training in
the United States for faculty, and technical assistance on curricula,
teaching methods, and research, four years of institutional assistance
was not a long enough period for major change in an institution as
complex as a university. As illustrated by the AIT, Prasarn Mitr, and
other major university institution-building projects (of both AID and
the Rockefeller Foundation) discussed below, an assistance program
lasting anything short of a decade cannot be expected to make a
substantial impact. Several years of training are required to bring
entire faculties to staffing levels with an adequate mix of master's and
doctoral degrees. Several additional years are then needed before the
faculty can shape matured curricula and courses and gain enough
research experience to be able to guide the research work of future
students. The development of the physical plant, the libraries, and
professional networks through which schools maintain their currency
with the state of the art in their subjects are also time-consuming
tasks.

Writing in 1959 about the condition of Kasetsart, the World Bank
noted the importance for Thailand of university research and instruc-
tion in agriculture and the expansion in student body and curriculum
that had occurred with the U.S. financial and technical assistance,
but was severely critical of its quality:

> [Its] standards of education are unimpressive and the em-
> phasis of curriculum is misplaced. The staff includes well-
> qualified members in their particular fields, but they are
> few in number and the attempt to make up for deficiencies
> . . . by numerous part-time appointments is unsatisfactory.
> Possibly the greatest short-coming is the lack of sufficient
> instruction and experience in the practical application of
> scientific and technical knowledge to the particular cir-
> cumstances of Thai agriculture. Few of the Kasetsart teach-
> ing staff have field experience; there is no commercial
> training farm at or near the university. . . . Discussion of
> field problems with an agricultural officer trained at Kaset-
> sart is usually disappointing.[42]

Kasetsart is a very different institution today, thanks in no small part
to a major assistance program of the Rockefeller Foundation that
began four years later, continued for over a decade, provided graduate

training in the United States for large numbers of the faculty, and posted Rockefeller agricultural science staff to Kasetsart to hold teaching and other assignments during the years the senior Thai faculty members were studying in the United States. AID also funded a second round of institutional support through the University of Hawaii from 1962 to 1968. The World Bank, Japan, and other donors have extended additional assistance to the university. Lacking close follow-up studies of the specific areas in which the AID projects worked, I am unable twenty years later to disentangle the many inputs into Kasetsart's development.

While senior Thai education administrators have (in personal conversations) attributed basic accomplishments of education doctrine and technique (apart from participant training) to the AID projects in general education, these activities predated the introduction of systematic evaluation by AID so that their effects are not readily tracked or documented. In addition the educational system has been restructured and now boasts new institutions as well as new problems of meshing with a rapidly changing economy and concomitant changes in the demands for education and for specific skills. In any case, it is much easier to evaluate projects and outcomes in terms of cost-effectiveness rather than cost-benefit relationships. Gains in efficiency can be measured through analysis of the costs of producing one graduating student at a given level, comparisons of student achievement over time or between schools of one type or another, analysis of drop-out and repeater rates, and so on. Gains in benefits are more ambiguous and difficult to measure and have been the subject of much controversy. The private benefits to graduates at different levels have been measured in many countries where income differentials can be explained, at least in part, by differences in educational attainment.[43] But the social benefits have been shown to follow different patterns from the private benefits and are not captured in income differences. The noneconomic benefits societies gain from the first few years of schooling are normally thought to be of great importance, although such factors as citizenship, national cohesion, and socialization are beyond the scope of the project evaluator's art.

Unfortunately, we lack objective and systematic evaluations of most of these projects. The difficulties can best be illustrated in the field of vocational education. Although the Wayne State and Hawaii University projects, along with their Thai colleagues responsible for vocational and technical education, did creditable work to produce a larger supply of better-trained, skilled graduates, the effectiveness of formal vocational education has remained a very controversial issue in the education community. It was clear already in 1960 that the growth in the supply of skilled technical manpower was more than sufficient to meet the country's needs. In a survey of manpower needs and availabilities for projects under the Mekong Basin program, a manpower expert concluded that Thailand had "no current national shortages of professional, technical, skilled and semi-skilled workers" and that in a few years the country "would be in a position to supply manpower to the other countries and to alleviate any shortage of manpower they may still experience at that time in carrying out construction projects in relation to the Mekong Basin development plan."[44] The large-scale training of Thai technicians and machinery operators under the USOM and OICC construction projects have been already noted. There was in addition a steady flow of workers moving from the small family enterprise sector, where they trained on the job as apprentices, into the formal sector. On-the-job training in formal sector manufacturing enterprises is also a very important form of technical education in Thailand. When the question of employment impact arose during one of the reviews of the Technical Institutes project, it was found to be unanswerable because the institutes had no system for keeping in touch with graduates. Although AID phased out of technical and vocational education around 1975, the RTG and many international development agencies continued to give high priority to this field; in 1975 there were twelve aid agencies assisting twenty-five separate projects.

The vocational training issue remains unresolved (even as the growth surge of 1987–1988 has created shortages of industrial skills). In a 1980 policy paper on education in developing countries the World Bank indicates the continuing uncertainties:

> If diversified secondary schools are inappropriate for train-ing middle-level skilled manpower, can technical and vo-cational schools do any better? Twenty-five years of expe-rience has not solved the controversy about the formation of skills within the formal system, called by its opponents "the vocational school fallacy." Part of the problem lies in the difficulty of forecasting accurately the requirements for specific skills in the economy. For that reason, full-time pre-employment vocational training should, of necessity, impart general skills. . . .
> The viability of the vocational and technical school model for training within reasonable costs, depends to a large

extent, like the rest of the education system, on the degree
of its efficiency and quality.[45]

In short, the Bank maintains its belief that formal training at the
vocational and technical levels has an important role to play in meeting the skilled manpower requirements of a developing country, but
sees that the effectiveness of such training hangs on the appropriate-
ness of its content and the efficiency with which it is taught. The AID
projects in this field aimed to help make the course content more
appropriate to the economy's needs, as best the Ministry could dis-
cern them at the time, and to increase the efficiency of the schooling
by providing advanced training to the faculties and more relevant
inventories of machinery and other training aids. Further financial
assistance for the expansion of the vocational system came from other
donors, including the World Bank, although AID did provide another
round of technical assistance during 1968–1972 in conjunction with
an IBRD loan. In the late 1970s the demand for vocational training
increased substantially, and vocational schools in Bangkok had seven
applicants for every student place.[46] By the 1980s the general public,
at least, would seem to have had little doubt as to the usefulness of
formal vocational system education as preparation for entry into the
labor market.

As the teacher-training and primary and secondary education projects phased down in the 1960s, AID turned its attention to informal
education in rural areas and technical training in conjunction with
the World Bank loan in vocational education and to meet the specific
manpower needs of the so-called Accelerated Rural Development Program (ARD), which became the largest activity under the aid program
in the later 1960s, as described below. Once one gets beyond the
projects that were assisting individual educational institutions and
tries to develop the evidence for impact of the projects in general
primary and secondary education, the uncertainties become even
greater than those with respect to vocational and technical education.
The educational system in Thailand in the early 1950s was a bare
skeleton of the system the country would need to support economic
growth. Thai educational planning then was strongly influenced by
international educational norms developed by UNESCO, which, as
reflected in the Karachi plan of 1959, put great emphasis on expansion of capacity, especially for early achievement of universal primary
enrollment.

Thailand has put substantial resources into the development of the
public educational system over the years, periodically changing its

targets, restructuring the system and the curriculum, and instituting critical reappraisals. The expansion has clearly been accomplished. In 1980 adult literacy was estimated at 85 percent compared with perhaps 33 percent in 1950. Public expenditure per student in the primary grades had risen over forty times. Primary enrollment stood at 97 percent of the seven-to-twelve age group. The government was allocating 20 percent of its budget to education, putting Thailand among the top quartile of developing countries by this measure of public effort. One brief observation by Cornell historian David K. Wyatt sums up the expansion and its implications for the structure of Thai society:

> During the last twenty years, the proportion of high school graduates to primary school graduates has increased four-fold. While there were twenty-six primary schools graduates to each secondary school graduate by 1960, there were only seven to one by 1980. The increase in the proportion of students gaining higher education has been just as dramatic. The increase in the relative proportion of youths continuing on to secondary and higher education certainly is important, for it reflects increased educational opportunities and changing economic and social aspirations. Just as significant, however, are the absolute numbers of such persons, which include men and women in almost equal proportions. The tenfold increase in the number of university graduates over the past two decades, from less than a hundred thousand to nearly a million, coupled with a similar rise in the number of secondary school graduates, has given Thailand's middle class a critical mass.[47]

While the system did expand very rapidly, there have been serious problems of educational quality, high drop-out rates, imbalances between rural and urban completion rates and university student ratios, questionable policies governing the private secondary system, and so on. I refer only to the transformation that has taken place in the educational system and the complex of problems it still faces to make a simple and obvious point—namely, that compared with the continuous life of the individual institutions, where their present status and functioning can be traced back to the founding years and their early external assistance, the evolution of the education system as a whole defies neat tracing and attribution of strengths and weaknesses to particular assistance interventions (among the many such interventions).

In personal conversations with a few senior Thai education officials, I have heard that in their own eyes the AID projects and their own training in the United States in their respective educational specialties had major impact on the educational philosophies of the different divisions of the Ministry and on the long-term development of their educational sectors. Harking back to my earlier observation of the Thai view that participant training was the most important contribution the U.S. program has made, I can cite some figures the mission collected in a briefing paper in 1969.

Between 1952, when the first 7 education participants went off to the U.S., and 1969 when the number was 174, the total number of education participants had cumulated to 1,512. Two-thirds (1,011) had gone for advanced degrees. Two or three decades have passed since these educators and the large numbers trained under the American foundations' programs returned to their career ladders in the Ministry of Education and the various institutions. I could not begin to untangle the factors and influences (of budget, politics, external ideas and funds, labor market conditions, and so on) that have shaped the present Thai education system. For whatever consequences it has had, the U.S. aid connection in this sector has been among the more important.

Public Administration

Public administration was the last remaining area in which the aid program raised its ambitions and resource inputs during the mid-1950s. Weaknesses of planning and administration in each sector of government and of institutional infrastructure of the 1950s were at the heart of virtually every project in the aid program. But it was the Public Administration Division of USOM, more than any other part of the mission, that worked with the "core" agencies and functions of the Thai government—finance, budget, development planning, civil service—and that was responsible for activities that addressed the problems of general efficiency in the workings of the bureaucracy.

Two studies of the early 1950s set the stage for USOM's entry into general public administration. One was an analysis of the public service done by the dean of the Chulalongkorn Faculty of Political Science, Kasem Udyanin, and Rufus B. Smith, a former chancellor of New York University, who was being financed under a Fulbright grant. The second was a study of public administration in Thailand by one of USOM's first contractors, the Public Administration Service (PAS) of Chicago.[48] These papers set out some of the technical deficiencies of administration and made recommendations for overhauling the training facilities and programs available to civil servants. USOM had already started a project in 1952 to send civil servants to the United States for training in core areas such as tax administration, customs, general management, and economics. While this provided an immediate response to the need to upgrade economic management skills (training seventy-two officers through 1957), it was evident that Thailand had to have a domestic institution that could give in-service training and higher academic education in public management skills. A government request for U.S. assistance led to a contract beginning in 1955 under which Indiana University would assist Thammsat University in establishing a new Institute of Public Administration.

A second major contract, which began earlier in 1952, provided the RTG with several years of fiscal management expertise from the PAS. Other projects financed a study of tax administration, technical assistance for the government's statistical services, and the advisory services of an American economist to work with the Ministry of Finance. While some of the recommendations of the tax study were adopted, this project appears to have had only minor impact. Much more important was the PAS contract, cited by Thais and Americans alike who are familiar with this period as one of the outstanding and seminal projects for the budget and financial system reforms it introduced and for the first working experience it provided for a number of the small cadre of postwar trained economists and administrators. Between 1956 and 1964 PAS worked with the Comptroller General's Department of the Ministry of Finance and with the National Audit Council. The establishment of the Bureau of the Budget as an independent office under the Prime Minister was done at PAS' recommendation and greatly raised the power of the Bureau compared with its previous status as a division within the Comptroller General's Department.

PAS was deeply involved in the development of reformed budgeting procedures and systems and in the drafting and presentation to Parliament of the enabling legislation. After some delays, its recommendations for modernizing the government's accounting and financial audit system were accepted and implemented. PAS also helped set up in the Budget Bureau the government's first organization and methods unit and designed reorganizations of the agriculture and education ministries and the highways department. The training PAS conducted was entirely on the job and thereby introduced the RTG to the concept of in-service training. The half-dozen team members developed excellent personal relationships with their counterparts and dealt effectively with senior Thai officials, leaving a legacy of mutual respect and goodwill towards the aid program generally—feelings that remain strong to this day among the now senior administrators who worked with PAS as junior officials. The Thai "alumni" of the PAS project include people who later became heads of many departments and agencies, including Revenue, Customs, Comptroller General, Budget Bureau, Government Savings Bank, National Economic and Social Development Board, Thai Oil Co., and ministerial level positions in Commerce, Communications, and Finance.

The Indiana University contract with the Institute of Public Administration (IPA) presents an entirely different experience, with results more difficult to evaluate than those of the PAS project or Indiana's other project at the Prasarn Mitr College of Education, which was running at the same time. The Indiana/IPA project was the first of the aid program's institution-building efforts for which an extensive evaluation is available. The author is Professor William Siffin, a member of the Indiana Team. His evaluation is remarkably frank and reveals many of the problems a team of foreign experts can encounter when assisting in the creation of a new organization with political overtones in an unfamiliar cultural and institutional environment. Some of the project's problems fell into the category of what might be termed the "technical" aspects of institution-building. For example, virtually all the Prasarn Mitr participants returned to the College and remained on its staff; many of the IPA participants either were not employed by the Institute when they returned (due to inadequate budget) or left the faculty after a short spell. Prasarn Mitr succeeded in expanding its production of graduating teachers; in the first nine years at IPA, only about 12 percent of the students got their degrees.

Siffin (and Caldwell, who reviewed a number of papers on both projects) saw Indiana's Prasarn Mitr project as a clear winner, Indiana's IPA project a "mixed" outcome. Now, nearly twenty years later, Prasarn Mitr remains a strong institution, but the much-expanded teacher-training college system faces a crisis of purpose as the declining numbers in the young age groups translates into a declining need for newly trained teachers; the IPA has been absorbed into the National Institute of Development Administration (NIDA), and this successor institution has become one of Thailand's leading institutions of higher learning. (NIDA was established in 1966. It now has a teaching staff of about 150, an all-graduate student body of about 1,100, and faculties of business administration, economic development, and statistics in addition to the original public administration faculty of IPA. NIDA also offers continuing education, in-service training, and consultation and research services.) Clearly, the fact that the same U.S. institution in both projects, in the same country, and under the same aid mission sponsorship was attempting to achieve institution-building objectives in both cases was not enough to ensure similar results. Prasarn Mitr was a going institution with a clear mandate and objective and an established budget. The IPA had no history, no explicit mission similarly understood by the institution and the Indiana team, and no assured plan for budget growth and staff configuration as a framework for the training and curriculum development work of the contract. The project's ambitious plan for creating a network of ministerial in-service training units that would be serviced by IPA never got off the ground.

Nevertheless, the IPA was a going institution when the project ended. It had faculty and students, it was accumulating a body of masters' theses, and regularly publishing a journal of public administration. The basic reason for Siffin's discontent with the outcome, however, is not to be found in his list of academic and organizational shortcomings. Rather, it was the failure of the IPA to function as a catalytic agent promoting fundamental change throughout the Thai bureaucracy.

> In the minds of the Westerners associated with the IPA, the Institute was implicitly dedicated to "rationality, efficiency and purposiveness." In fact, however, it was from the start subject to "substantial bureaucratic value penetration" from the rest of the Thai society and bureaucratization.
>
> [The dean] saw the IPA not as an instrument of radical reform but as a useful service enterprise, a bureaucratic adjunct that would help produce officials . . . who would be more literate and articulate and useful. . . . He felt too that desirable adjustments and developments within the Thai bureaucracy could be promoted through the IPA without any sharp discrepancy between established bureaucratic values and those manifested by and promoted within the IPA. (Quoted in Caldwell, p. 104)

Indiana (and USOM) saw the basic objective of the project as normative, not technical. The Thai side, or at least the dean uncontested, saw the objective as technical and incremental. Siffin interviewed a number of IPA graduates in his effort to uncover the impact of IPA training. He concluded that

> they do not emerge from the IPA program disenchanted, or imbued with reformist zeal. They see themselves as some-what more able to function and thrive in the bureaucratic milieu—somewhat more skilled, more perceptive, and perhaps more critical. (Quoted in Caldwell, p. 106)

The experience of Public Administration Service gives some additional perspectives on the role of foreign technical assistance in administrative reform. In 1980 PAS returned for a third round with some of the same RTG units the organization had worked with during these units' formative years in the 1950s, including the Budget Bureau, Comptroller General's office, the Auditor General, and NESDB. The objective of this new three-year project was to help "improve and integrate planning, budgeting, accounting and evaluation processes in the government." An evaluation near the end of the project found:

> The results are mixed with both strengths and weaknesses apparent. Many of the weaknesses are serious and stem from the broad, general and overly ambitious terms of reference in the "scope of work." . . . Taken literally, the terms of reference could not be satisfied by a contract twice the amount of the PAS contract. And they were not. When the contract terminates . . . no proposed system will be fully operational. Yet most of the projects are promising and are at the threshold of implementation.
>
> The contract provided for the development of horizontal (government-wide) as well as vertical (operating ministries) systems. . . . So far the systems that have been designed are horizontal and affect primarily the central staff agencies . . . systems development at the ministerial and provincial levels has been negligible. The main thrust of the scope of work was the integration of the management systems. In practice integration was spotty and fragmentary on the part of both PAS and the central staff agencies.[49]

The mixed results of this return engagement can be attributed to two major differences from the PAS project in the 1950s. First, the institutional experience PAS had gained in its earlier work did not translate into real institutional continuity; besides misreading the potential for systems reforms in Thailand (echoing the earlier Indiana/ IPA misreading), the PAS team (in part) had deficiencies in its working relations with Thai officials. Some members developed counterpart relationships as effective as those of the 1950s PAS groups; others lacked the necessary interpersonal skills. Second, the core agencies of the RTG had developed substantially in the interim. It was one thing to design major systems in the 1950s, starting from scratch so to speak, when the thin ranks of young technocrats were eager to install modernizing reforms with outside help. It was quite another to attempt subsequent system overhaul when powerful agencies had been operating for years under experienced administrators. The project produced some useful results in NESDB and Budget Bureau planning and operating processes, although these results were apparently of little use in the Auditor-General's office. But these results were very limited compared with the project's broad objectives.

The distinction between incremental and technical improvement on the one hand and fundamental change in the norms and workings of the Thai bureaucracy on the other lies at the heart of much of what the U.S. aid program tried to accomplish over its entire history. I will come back to this subject below when I attempt, from the perspective of 1988, to review the major themes and objectives of the aid program over time and their present results. But at this point an introduction to the role of the bureaucracy in Thai society will be useful for an understanding of the milieu in which the program was operating and for an appreciation of some of the central characteristics of the Thai polity, and of its perception by American scholars.

The study of Thai society was very much an American academic enterprise in the 1950s and 1960s. Even as a Thai social science community, especially anthropologists and political scientists, emerged in the 1960s and 1970s as the naturally dominant and more numerous body of researchers on Thailand's society and polity, the basic paradigms and concepts developed by the earliest of the American social science researchers continued to frame the scholarly picture of Thai society and the way it worked. The early paradigms have since been superseded by more complex analyses. Thai scholars have now eclipsed the foreign social scientists in many areas, developing new paradigms in the study of the military, the Buddhist monkhood, Sino-Thai integration, and other subjects of Thai history and political science. Still, the social science literature on Thailand continues to build on the initial constructs and their adjusted later forms. (I might also note that most of the leading Thai social scientists learned their trade at American universities and retain close personal and professional relations with the now older generation of American counterparts.)

The relevance of this academic work for the administration of modern economic development and for the aid program in particular (apart from the insights the anthropologists have been able to provide for the designing of individual projects in rural areas) arises from the central role the government bureaucracy has long played in Thai society. Thailand has a long independent history, uninterrupted by the imposition of foreign colonial ruling and administrative structures, during which absolute monarchs developed an indigenous governing structure, the staff of which was at once the feudal power structure, the officials of the administrative system, and the holders of all secular social prestige. The rest of the population appeared (according to the first paradigm) to be "loosely structured," that is, to have few forms of social organization and to relate to these forms and to each other in nonbinding and shifting allegiances. The central organizing principle of Thai society was seen as the "patron-client" relationship. Ordinary people associated themselves with local patrons, people of some local power and influence. Low-level patrons in turn were linked with higher patrons in a system linked to the most powerful people of the court and the royal family, including finally the king.

In 1932 a small group of military officers and intellectuals forced a substitution of a constitutional monarchy system in place of the old absolute monarchy. The patron-client system for ordering the society was changed only at its apex, which subsequently comprised a group of individuals and their factions. Beneath the apex was the bureaucracy, which, primarily through the Ministry of Interior, extended down from Bangkok into the lowest local jurisdictions, with policy, administrative, and financial power highly concentrated in the capital, the country's one massive urban area.

When the foreign social scientists began to study this system in the 1950s, they found villagers politically inert, no meaningful political party system—there were only labels for factions surrounding individual personalities—and a bureaucracy (and army) many of whose leading officers were aligned with one member or another of the apex "coup group" through complex lines of patron-client cliques.

The one significant new element in the postwar period was the private sector. Prior to World War II, commerce and the incipient industrial sector (mostly very small enterprises engaged in rice milling, food processing, ice plants, and other light consumer product activities) were almost entirely in the hands of the Chinese community. From 1932 until the late 1950s, the government pursued a dual policy towards this minority community. On one hand it set up a range of state enterprises that was intended to replace private Chinese enterprises in the same lines of business or to preempt the manufacture of other commodities the private sector had not yet invested in. At the same time the leading political faction patrons (all military or police in the 1950s) offered protection and accommodation to the leading members of the Chinese business and financial interests, thereby extending a modern form of the traditional clientele system into the emerging postwar manufacturing and banking sectors.*

While ultimate power was in the hands of the military, only the bureaucracy had the training, legitimacy, and structure for actual administration of the country. The private sector had few structures or institutions to which an aid program could relate directly. Farmer organizations were also very weak (and the "disloyalty" the USOM cooperative experts found among the farmers who were members of marketing coops was commonly attributed to the "loose structuring" characteristic the mission's professionals had picked up from the anthropologists). Thus, the bureaucracy appeared as the principal agent of change, the only intermediary between external development assistance and the mass of economic actors in the Thai economy, the farmers and the private sector. It was only natural then that the essential orientation and behavioral mores of the bureaucracy emerged as factors equally important for Thai economic development as the more technical determinants of government efficiency and technical aspects of economic policy. But in the eyes of the American students of the "culture" of the Thai elite and of technicians in various fields who encountered the workings of a bureaucracy so different from that of the United States, much of the orientation and mores were counterproductive for efficiency and development, if not absolutely anti-development.

At this point a brief indication of some of the conditions facing aid workers will be useful for the unfamiliar reader's understanding of what it was that Siffin thought needed to be radically reformed— views with which most of the U.S. mission then would have con-

---

*The American social science studies of Thailand, before they receded after the Vietnam War, concentrated heavily on rural village society. Many of these rural studies focused on hill tribe communities, members of ethnic minorities who are important in the areas where they are concentrated (mainly North Thailand), but whose culture is not the culture of the majority of Thailand's rural inhabitants. American researchers also carried out what are now classic studies of the urban Chinese community and of Thai politics. Some of the important works in this literature are listed in the bibliography.

curred. I can do no better than quote a few passages from one of the most recent and authoritative works on modern Thai politics by two authorities, David Morell and Chai-anan Samudavanija, from Princeton and Chulalongkorn universities respectively.[50] The reader should appreciate that the view of the sociopolitical elite system here, as of 1981, revises and enriches the paradigm of the 1950s and 1960s; it is also more complex and complete than the average aid technician would have understood at the time, but fairly represents the reality as seen from the perspective of USOM.

In American society the bureaucracies, federal and state, are generally viewed as only one set among many varied and powerful institutional structures. In the eyes of many Americans the word "bureaucracy" has pejorative connotations. The contrast with Thailand is striking in this respect:

> Thailand is basically a bureaucratic society. Each [Thai] has his place, of which he is cognizant. . . . In a sense the polity *is* the executive branch of government, represented by a school teacher, a policeman, a district officer, or a community development worker, all of whom are employees of the national bureaucracy. . . .
>
> Through his direct and indirect contact with the political system, every Thai learns of the overwhelming power of the bureaucracy and its direct influence over his daily life. He also observes that the bureaucrat has high social status. It is therefore preferable to become a bureaucrat if at all possible. . . .
>
> The 1932 coup changed the men who employed power at the top, but the people still had no way to participate in politics. To them, officials were innately superior; the officials agreed. There was no concept on either side of bureaucrats as public servants, except in the most paternalistic sense. (Pp. 18–19)

How does this bureaucracy, the very spine of the society and polity, actually work and behave? What is the nature of the bureaucratic culture with which foreign technicians must work on a daily basis? What is the style of the interpersonal relations governing ordinary business? How does the bureaucracy make its decisions? Foreigners must have answers to these essential questions if their programs to promote change are to have any hope of succeeding.

Morell and Chai-anan describe the key characteristics of Thai cultural and social norms:

> One key to understanding Thai politics is to be found in the phrase *greng jai*. The best brief translation perhaps is deference, but this deference extends in many directions, including down . . . a person does not correct a friend's error because he feels *greng jai* and does not wish to hurt the friend's feelings. . . . In many ways this concept determines social intercourse, family relations, business associations, and the process of government. A man is reluctant to criticize his boss, friend, father or prime minister. In return, the superior is responsible for taking care of the subordinate in various ways, protecting his interest through paternalistic reciprocity.
>
> Orders flow from superior to subordinate for implementation, policies are made at the top, and subordinates are reluctant to report truthfully to their superiors on developments which seem unlikely to please.
>
> Thais dislike people who are loud, unruly or make trouble. Such attributes are considered lower class. Even speaking in a loud voice is a negative comment on one's background.
>
> *Woon wai* describes a state of nuisance and confusion that may lead to instability and, to many Thais anarchy. . . . Students . . . were called *woon wai* when they demonstrated against the government. . . . military officers and civil bureaucrats may intervene to dissolve the parliament, saying that because the assembly was so *woon wai* it caused government administration to be *yung yak* (extremely difficult). . . . The proper behavior mode is to be quiet, calm, and submissive. In contrast, *woon wai* and its confusion upset peace and order in society, the most un-Thai action of all.
>
> Graduation from the same school, and especially membership in the same class, is inordinately important in Thai politics, more so than in many other more differentiated political systems. . . . *Roon diew kan* [old-boy network] provides an essential mechanism for effective patron-client relationships. (Pp. 27–30)

The authors then describe the bureaucratic consequences of these mores: concentration of decision-making at the top; factionalism and personalism; favoritism and nepotism; work performance that is "ego-oriented" rather than "task-oriented"; overlapping responsibilities (which also arise from the loose enabling language of much of Thai legislation); poor coordination. I would add three other characteristics especially frustrating for American aid technicians anxious to "get on with the job": excessive use of large committees for coordination; opaque decision-making processes; and a preference for eliding disputes rather than confronting them in adversarial circumstances. For the foreigner schooled to think of government bureaucracy in functional, Weberian, legal-rational terms, the Thai polity-bureaucracy was an exotic institution that had to be reformed if the Thais were to be able to achieve their own goals of economic development and expanded public sector services.

Morell and Chai-anan conclude that these characteristics added up to a bureaucracy of considerable inefficiency:

> factionalism, personalism, the tendency to pass the buck, and top-down development practices, along with inadequate coordination at all levels, have contributed to the institution's inefficiency. The dominant bureaucratic values, so incongruent with legal-rational norms, prevent the bureaucracy from attaining full effectiveness in providing human resource services. All these traits are characteristic of a polity in which there exists an imbalance of power between the bureaucracy and other political institutions. (P. 49)

And yet, this was not the whole story. They note, as of 1981, that despite these characteristics, the bureaucracy's flexibility and the capabilities of individual officials have enabled the system to achieve "a number of successes while maintaining a high level of support for national economic growth." As I noted also by way of introduction, all the themes, projects, and problems of the postwar period must be seen against the background of one of the most successful development performances among Third World economies. The fact is that with this rapid economic growth and change, the Thai polity and the bureaucracy have also been changing, even in the few years since the Morell and Chai-anan's book. By the 1980s, less than twenty years after the end of the Indiana/IPA project, the private sector was undergoing rapid transformation into a modern mode, the Chinese community was fast assimilating into a new urban culture, an entirely new relationship between government and the private sector was emerging, and the balance of professional capability, economic power, and social prestige was shifting away from its historic concentration on the side of the bureaucracy. Rather than trying to form some conclusions as to the role of the aid program on the evolution of the Thai bureaucracy on a project by project basis as I go along, it will be better to postpone such an attempt until later, when these projects have been fully described.

I will add only one footnote at this point on what the passages quoted above may say for the proposition that participant training was the salient contribution of the U.S. aid program. The most effective strategy for reorienting a bureaucracy of factions and personalized processes and raising its long-run efficiency may well be to saturate its decision-making levels with people who are better trained and have been exposed to a "task-oriented" environment. They can make the system run better no matter what shape its formal institutions take. In this view, USOM was on the right track in its large-scale training, even as it hoped, like Archimedes, that it might find (in the IPA or other later bureaucracy-change projects) the place to stand from which the whole system could be levered. The more narrow and technical objectives of the IPA dean were being served and could be judged dysfunctional only against the larger reform objectives, which were probably unrealistic for the time.

To round out this account of technical assistance in public administration, two last subjects deserve to be noted. One of the most important technical deficiencies of public administration in the postwar years was in the area of economic statistics. As in most developing countries, the systems for collecting basic data for monitoring the economy's performance, for conducting research on economic problems, or for formulating economic policy were very weak. The capacity of the statistical services to process and publish statistical series on a timely basis was also very inadequate. For twelve years starting in 1957, USOM financed the training of 120 participants from the RTG National Statistics Office (NSO) and the services of outstanding technical advisors from the U.S. Bureau of the Census. Working on the preparations for the 1970 census and on wage, price, and household expenditure surveys, the project trained NSO staff in the use of computers, the conduct of sample surveys, and other statistical functions. The NSO also benefited from technical assistance in later years from the U.N. Statistical Office and other sources. Between this $1.7 million project and the long activity assisting the Office of Agriculture Economics develop its statistical capabilities, the program made substantial contributions to the creation of Thailand's present strong statistical services.

Finally I should note the Civil Service Improvement project undertaken between 1965 and 1971. The objective of the project was to "modernize" the administration of Thailand's civil service. The project was carried out by the California State Personnel Board. The principal outputs of the project were a new classification system covering 60,000 positions in the bureaucracy, the drafting of new laws and regulations for installing the new job classification system, and the training of the core staff of the Civil Service Commission in various personnel management functions.

REGIONAL DEVELOPMENT

The infrastructure phase of the aid program saw the introduction of some major programs under a new concept: regional development. At the same time that Thailand, the United States, and other SEATO member states were moving to create regional security arrangements and military capabilities in the wake of the Geneva accords, international efforts were also developed to seal the peace in Southeast Asia by building up economic strength in the area, especially in the form of regional projects that would create infrastructures and institutions shared by the nations comprising the region's new political configuration.

The Lower Mekong River Basin Program

For about twenty years between the mid-1950s and mid-1970s the United States was a major contributor to a far-sighted international effort to lay the basis for development of the water resources of the Mekong River. The Mekong is one of the world's great rivers, flowing 2,750 miles, or 400 miles longer than the Mississippi. It rises in Tibet and flows through China until it reaches and marks the border between Burma and Laos and then between Thailand and Laos for a short distance. After turning east and then south through Laos, the river forms the border again between Laos and Thailand along the northern and eastern rims of Thailand's Northeast region. Leaving the Thai border just below the point where it is joined by the tributary Nam Chi from the Thai side, the Mekong flows south through

Laos, Cambodia, and into southern Vietnam, forming a vast delta in its lower reaches. The lower basin of the river, starting at the Burma-Lao-Thai common border area and including its tributaries in the four riparian countries, covers an area of over 600,000 square kilometers with a population of around 42 million. The river system as a whole has a large potential for hydroelectric power, irrigation and flood control, and navigational development that could bring substantial benefits to the region's population and economies.

In 1957 the riparian countries—Thailand, Laos, (later, the Lao People's Democratic Republic), Cambodia (later, Kampuchea), and (then South) Vietnam—established a Committee for Coordination of Investigations of the Lower Mekong Basin. The Committee was created under the sponsorship of the U.N. regional organization for Asia, then named the Economic Commission for Asia and the Far East (ECAFE) and known since 1974 as the Economic and Social Commission for Asia and the Pacific (ESCAP). The Mekong Committee set up offices in Bangkok and launched an ambitious program of potentially vast investment dimensions. It drew strong support from donor countries and international agencies, with financial contributions to activities managed or sponsored by the Committee cumulating to $563 million by 1986 (see table A.16).[51]

The enthusiasm of the United States and other donors was based not only on the boldness of the concept and the technical realization that much of the river system's potential could be developed only through riparian cooperation. The enthusiasm also stemmed from the hope that joint development of the riverine spine of Southeast Asia would create strong common interests among the four countries and thereby promote, under international auspices and a U.N. framework, more harmonious relations following the French withdrawal from Indochina. The same political hope inspired the creation in 1955 of the Regional Economic Development program of the United States, which was administered in Bangkok out of a separate office from the bilateral aid mission. The regional projects were designed to bring together officials, educators, and professionals from Southeast Asian countries (but not limited to the riparian nations) in development activities that would also create mutual interests and bonds.

These technical and development activities and the vision of the Mekong as a vast binding program proved no match for the divisive forces at work in the region. In the face of the second Vietnam War and its consequences for Cambodia and Laos, the regional development programs did not thrive as such. The regional U.S. office was closed around 1975. After contributing $46.4 million to the work of the Mekong Committee from its inception to 1975, the United States withdrew when the Vietnamese membership passed into the hands of the now unified Socialist Republic of Vietnam. Under the Khmer Rouge regime, Cambodia withdrew from the Committee, which then renamed itself the Interim Committee for Coordination of Investigations of the Lower Mekong Basin, "interim" implying the expectation that Cambodia one day would rejoin.

It is remarkable that despite the terrible upheavals in the region, the data-gathering and analytic work the Committee initiated in the mid-1950s (essential first-order business because of the paucity of hydrological data gathered before the Committee was established) has continued all through the turmoil, interrupted only in part by the failure of Cambodia to report information from its territory since its departure. In addition, while the information base has continued to accumulate, the Committee has sponsored the development of numerous tributary projects, which have been financed either through the mechanism of the Committee or bilaterally through country development programs.

The core of the data-gathering effort is a daily record that has been accumulating from a network of 431 hydrology stations and 339 meteorological stations installed and maintained by the Committee. The Committee has also used satellite imagery for mapping the region's physical characteristics and has conducted research on soils, irrigated farm management, irrigated fish farming, water-borne diseases, environmental management, and navigation improvement. A sizable number of development projects have been implemented, mainly in tributary irrigation, hydropower, and flood control schemes, but also in river ports, navigation, and river boat construction.

Thailand has been the senior of the riparian countries in terms of its financial contributions to the work of the Committee, its much greater stock of relevant expertise, and its ability to share data and experience. Nine tributary projects have been constructed in the Northeast (see table A.17), of which three provide power and irrigation, five irrigation only, and one power only. Four of these projects were financed with U.S. assistance, the others with assistance from the U.N. Development Programme (UNDP), Germany, and the international banks. Numerous other projects are in various stages of planning, fund-raising, and construction. Projects in or involving Thailand to a significant extent, which were financed by the United States prior to its withdrawal from the Mekong Committee framework, are shown in table A.18. The total U.S. contribution to these projects was $36.3 million.

The largest tributary project thus far implemented is the Nam Ngum in Laos north of Vientiane, a 150-megawatt hydroelectric facility that sells its substantial surplus power to Thailand through an interconnected power grid. The large-scale main stem projects dependent on international cooperation have not gotten off the drawing boards. The proposed Pa Mong project in particular, the would-be giant of the Mekong system, absorbed a good half of the U.S. financial input in the early years of the Committee and remains doubtful to this day. The first feasibility study of the Pa Mong was carried out by the U.S. Bureau of Reclamation over a ten-year period. The project was deemed feasible, although cost, estimated in 1975 at around $2 billion, and the potential scale of reservoir inundation in Thailand posed serious difficulties. The main high dam would be sited twenty kilometers upstream from Vientiane, spanning the Mekong from the Thai to the Lao sides of the river. As the water rose behind the dam, it would flood a reservoir area of over 3,700 square kilometers. The installed power generating capacity was projected at 4,800 megawatts (compared with the 535 megawatts of the Bhumibol Dam). The potential irrigated area was put at 700,000 hectares (280,000 acres) in Northeast Thailand alone, with a much larger ultimate potential if ancillary pumping were installed. Later studies, however, concluded that Pa Mong's physical and economic potential would be considerably lower. Various configurations have been studied involving different heights for the main dam, which would impound different volumes of water, produce different levels of power and irrigated area, and drown lesser areas under the reservoir. The reservoir size has been a key problem for the Thai side since large numbers of people would be forced to relocate. Flooding of some of the potential reservoir areas could be avoided by construction of saddle dams across the heads of exposed valleys; these are technically feasible options that would reduce the numbers of displaced persons from 400,000 to a possible 100,000 but lower the irrigation and power benefits.

Under the first major project the United States helped finance, apart from the Pa Mong studies, an American engineering firm laid the basis for the collection and analysis of the hydrological data necessary for understanding the river. The project set up water stage recording gauges at thirty-seven places on the main stem and tributaries and rainfall and evaporation recording stations at seventy-nine locations in the basin. The contractor also collected engineering data on the river's configurations from the mouth to the Burmese border. A channel improvement project financed a study by the Asian Institute of Technology of the potential effects of blasting away rock formations that were obstructing river traffic, formations that were subsequently removed. Another small project studied Mekong ports and cargo handling facilities. The heaviest traffic on the Lao/Thai stretches of the Mekong occurs between Vientiane/Nongkai and Savannakhet/Mukdahan, including both internal and cross-border commerce. Projects to improve navigation and port facilities have figured importantly in the development plans of the Committee, which continues to envisage the river playing a more significant role in the future as a commercial artery for Indochina trade. For the entire lower basin to serve as a route for international trade it would be necessary to submerge the Khone Falls at the Lao/Cambodia border by constructing a dam for that purpose.

The Mun and Chi rivers are the main Mekong tributaries in Northeast Thailand. In 1961 the Royal Irrigation Department, the U.S. Bureau of Reclamation, and the American contractor working on the data network project joined forces in a five-year study of the irrigation and flood control potential of the Mun and Chi basins, including the Nam Yang, a tributary of the Chi. The Yang reconnaissance report concluded that development of the Yang project was not feasible. The Mun and Chi studies laid the groundwork for subsequent pump irrigation projects (in which the United States did not participate). Three of the U.S.–assisted projects shown in table A.18—Lam Pao, Lam Takong, and Lam Phra Plerng—are situated on upper reaches of the Mun basin but were initiated prior to the Mun and Chi basins study project.

It is not easy to form a judgment of the upshot of all this work as far as Thailand is concerned (or of the basin as a whole). Most of the U.S.–funded projects in the early years of the Mekong Committee were designed to generate information on which later investment decisions would be based. Most of the Northeast tributary projects were decided upon and built when the broad system data-gathering and analytic base work of the Committee were just getting underway. The Pa Mong studies, as I have said, have come to nothing thus far, and the future of the scheme remains problematical if not dubious. The Huai Mong and Mun-Chi projects and the many additional Northeast projects being studied and discussed with potential donors do rest solidly on the work of the Committee. Investment in irrigation in the Northeast has generally yielded low returns. The Mun-Chi project has just recently been completed however, and as with all irrigation projects the production benefits can be expected to develop only over a period of many years. According to the U.N. Development Programme, field surveys have shown increased production of subsistence and cash crops and a 40 percent increase in cropping intensity. Per capita income in the area was said to have risen $60 already (or about 15 percent) as a result of the project. The navigational and port projects have been useful, and the Committee has undertaken a fair amount of technical assistance and experimental work.

The Mekong program has faced a number of problems in recent years. Since 1967 development of mainstream projects (above the Vietnam delta area) has been at a standstill. While the data-gathering effort has proceeded, investment in irrigation and other capital projects has been confined to the tributaries. (The loss of recording station data from Cambodia can be largely compensated for by inference from the system data upstream and downstream from the Cambodian stretch of the river.) The focus on tributary projects has led to some tension over the orientation of the Mekong Secretariat and the content of the program. The active riparian member governments have wanted to press ahead with tributary projects even if these "national" projects appeared to the donors to be deflecting attention away from "regional" activities. Despite the political difficulties hindering further work on mainstream projects, at least some of the donors (including UNDP) preferred that high priority should continue to be given to the investigation and planning work that forms the core of the Secretariat's "regional" responsibility and of the very concept of the Mekong as a resource for integrated regional development. In the last couple of years this tension appears to have been resolved, with the updating of the 1970 Basin Plan now accepted as a prime subject on the Secretariat's work agenda, along with the strengthening of the hydrological and meteorological information systems.

The Secretariat also went through a period of administrative problems, including an effort to "riparianize" the staff by replacing members from countries outside the region with professionals from the riparian states, an objective that was only partially attained. The Secretariat was reorganized in 1985 and appears to be gathering strength as it has returned to its original regional purpose.

One must assume that sooner or later a settlement will be reached in Southeast Asia under which Cambodian independence will be restored, the refugees will return home, Vietnamese armed forces retire, and normal relations resume among the riparian states. When this occurs, the Mekong's development potential will reemerge as a major factor for the future of the region. The riparian governments, donor countries, and international agencies with an abiding interest in Southeast Asian stability and development are likely to return to the original concept for a second try at creating regional mutual interests through development of the Mekong system. If the future of the region does evolve in this way, the three decades of donor input would finally begin to yield the stabilizing dividends hoped for at the start. Even under an optimistic scenario, however, the benefits for Thailand's economic future from further development of the system's water resources are likely to be relatively modest compared to the potentials for the other riparian states. The most significant project for Thailand now being studied would be the Nam Theun hydroelectric scheme in Laos. This project would generate between 400 and 1,200 megawatts for transmission and sale to Thailand. The really substantial benefits for Thailand would flow from the general framework of peace and normalized economic relationships that the integrated development of the Lower Basin could help to cement.

Regional Telecommunications

Telecommunications was the second major area where it was hoped that a common infrastructure would foster regional political ties. Here again motivation was both economic and military. The objective was to install a modern telecommunication system within Thailand, with connections to new systems to be installed in Vietnam, Laos, and Cambodia. The U.S. contribution ($17.8 million) to the Thai portion of the entire system was financed in part with a MAP grant of $3 million, the rest coming from so-called regional aid appropriations. Once this large project was finished in 1963, AID left the telecommunications sector (except for the Northeast radio component of the counterinsurgency assistance program). While there is no doubt that the project increased the capacity of Thailand's communication system at that time, it is less clear what lasting impact the aid involvement may have had in this sector. The project did not attempt to address the problems of administration of Thailand's telecommunications, problems that have continued to plague the system. As the RTG recognizes, telecommunications remains the weakest component of the country's economic infrastructure.

> Since the period of the First Plan, the first twenty years placed little importance on communication development. In particular, public communications grew slowly. . . . The telephone service continues to face a serious shortage problem and users remain dissatisfied with service quality. . . . The major causes of the problems in the telephone service

are poor management and operations in the service organization, lack of good coordination within the service organization itself and with related agencies and lack of the flexibility of commercially oriented operations.[52]

One might conclude that even if the telecommunications project were a cost-effective answer to the communications expansion needs of the time (there is no postproject evaluation that attempts such a measurement, but the history of rejections of engineering designs and recontracting for alternative systems for this project reflects close engineering scrutiny by USOM's project manager and implies careful professional oversight), the investment has long since been depreciated and superseded, and any institutional impact (if any) was neither very great nor long-lasting.

CONCLUSION

From the perspective of thirty years later, these early years had several remarkable characteristics. As a young economist in USOM's planning office at the time, I shared the occasional discomfort of the planners and budget makers in the late 1950s over an aid strategy that was more encyclopedic than shaped by priorities. The program seemed to be driven by bureaucratic forces from Washington that pressed the field mission to develop projects in every subject for which headquarters had an organizational unit. To be fair to the agency, of course, it must be recognized that some of these pressures emanated from congressional or other sources convinced of the importance of some subsector or other in the development process and anxious to be represented in as many country programs as possible. On the other hand, the remarkable thing about this proliferation of activities in so many subjects and areas of governmental and institutional responsibility was that we seldom questioned the ability of the United States and of the aid agency to deliver the goods, whatever they might be. Individual technicians and occasional major university or commercial contractors created problems through mediocre or unacceptable performance, but the capability of the United States to meet virtually any need Thailand might have for which foreign aid was a relevant vehicle was seldom if ever questioned.

This overwhelming confidence in the technical and economic prowess of the United States was shared by the Thais. The disparities between the two countries were apparent in every field, and virtually every unit of government and every technical and educational institution wanted to partake of the training and other benefits that could be obtained by having a project with USOM and a technical office in one's own subject in the mission. The aid coordinating office that was set up in the Thai government in the early 1950s primarily to deal with USOM had no capability or mandate to impose priorities, nor did the government as a whole have a development plan before 1961. Even by 1961 the development assistance available to Thailand from other governments and from the U.N. system (apart from loans for capital projects from the World Bank) amounted to only 11 percent of the AID program.

Some special credit for this confidence in the role of USOM and in the bona fides and technical competence of the aid program must be given to the public administrators, especially to the PAS contract members and to the economic advisor, Dr. John Loftus. This small group worked closely with the handful of senior Thai policy officials (and their first cohort of junior officials) who held the reins of financial and economic policy. It would be difficult for anyone coming on the Thai governmental and business scene in the 1980s to imagine the collegial atmosphere in which the advisors became almost a part of the machinery or to imagine the small scale of the circle responsible for the analysis of overall Thai economic problems on a day-to-day basis and for the shaping of policy responses and long-run development strategies. Some of this handful of Thai officials was of a prewar vintage, conservative, courtly, and carrying on the old traditions of *noblesse oblige*. The advisers had to develop working relations appropriate to separate generations—the senior old guard and the new postwar and better-trained younger technocrats. For a number of years the older generation recognized its dependence on the young and on the foreigners for coping with the transformed circumstances of the postwar world, while the younger Thais realistically saw their own need for the foreigners as they, the "new men," were gaining experience.

The work of Loftus from 1956 to 1961 was invaluable. Thailand had had long experience using the services of foreign economic and financial advisors, partly for their technical contributions and partly flowing out of the nineteenth-century practice of balancing the presence and influences of the major Western powers with interests in the region. Loftus worked in a dim cavernous office in the old Ministry of Finance building, which sits on the exotic grounds of the Grand Palace and temple compound. Surrounded by dusty mounds of files more suited to an archaeological laboratory than to the daily business of government finance, Loftus served as both general advisor and, in effect, exofficio member of the Ministry. One of his most significant assignments concerned the National Economic Development Corporation (NEDCOL), one of the last enterprises of the era of government direct investment in manufacturing. The corporation owned sugar, paper, and gunny bag plants and had fallen into bankruptcy. The exact character of the enterprise—whether state, private, or some hybrid—was unclear, and one alternative put forward in the Ministry was for the RTG to just walk away from its guarantees. Loftus argued that the foreign creditors of the company would see this as a government default and that Thailand's unblemished century-old record for credit-worthiness would be seriously impaired. The Minister accepted his recommendations that the government take responsibility and sent him to Europe and the United States to negotiate refinancing while seeking to put NEDCOL's management on a businesslike basis along lines Loftus had proposed. NEDCOL has long since faded into obscurity, while Thailand's credit-worthiness has remained among the strongest in the Third World. Loftus was the last in a line of American advisors in Thailand going back to 1903.* While the mission then moved on to financing the planning and advisory services of other Americans attached to the National Economic and Social Development Board as well as other individuals and teams (in planning exercises for Northeast Thailand and Bangkok, for example), the aid mission itself did not then, or since, engage in direct "policy dialogue" over Thai macroeconomic or financial policies, a point I will elaborate on below.

USOM played one last role during this period that is worth recalling in the context of public administration. During those years a number of senior political and administrative personalities were notorious for their intervention into processes of granting contracts for large public sector construction projects in order to extract bribes and rents through various devices. The best way for technocrats of probity to insulate a project from these corrupt practices was to engage USOM (or the World Bank or other international donors) every step of the way in the feasibility studies and engineering, bidding, and supervision activities. Projects thereby caught up in the

---

*The first American "General Adviser to the Government" was Edward H. Strobel, a Harvard University law professor. The Thai Minister of Foreign Affairs in 1903, H. R. H. Prince Devawongse believed that "In our dealings with America there is absolutely no danger of territorial problems." Strobel served mainly as advisor in foreign affairs and developed a close personal relationship with King Chulalongkorn. The foreign affairs advisors continued to be American until the role ended at the start of World War II. See Vimol Bhongbhibhat et al., eds., *The Eagle and the Elephant*, pp. 56–60.

procedures and oversight of the external agencies were relatively transparent in their development and implementation and impervious to shady practice. The savings to the Thai exchequer from this rather obscure "external economy" created by aid program red tape must have been far from trivial.

FIVE

COUNTERINSURGENCY AND DEVELOPMENT, 1960–1974

PHASEDOWN: 1960–1964

During the third period of the program's history, the completion of a number of the large-scale projects of the 1950s was not offset by new starts of a similar size. As a result, the level of obligation fell from the 1959 high of $45.5 million to an average of $26.0 million in 1960–1963 and then to $12.2 million in fiscal 1964. The level of activity remained higher than the actual obligation level as the "pipeline" of funds obligated in the late 1950s continued to be drawn down to finance the completion of the earlier project surge.

In the politics of aid, the amount of new money committed and publicly announced as the year's "aid level" has a high profile; the actual size of the resource flow (the funds actually disbursed on goods and services), which represents the real level of aid activity, is obscure, known only after the fact, when the accounting system catches up with the flow of vouchers and actual transactions. Thus, while Caldwell is correct to characterize this period as a phasedown in terms of new obligations and the U.S. policy intent, it did not see a diminution in terms of current activity as reflected in the flow of funds or the size of the mission. In fact, these were years of high activity as the transportation, health, agriculture, and other projects begun in the 1950s were carried to completion.

As Caldwell rightly describes, this was a short transitional period during which the U.S. administration apparently saw declining economic and security need for U.S. aid in Thailand, but during which the security situation was starting to move in the opposite direction and would soon, when recognized, result in a recovery in the aid level and increases to volumes much greater than those of the 1950s.

> The key reason for the lower aid level [was] the official optimism on matters Southeast Asian that prevailed in the United States in the late fifties and early sixties. The lack of overt communist military activity in Vietnam and the apparent settlement of the Laotian crisis at the 1962 Geneva Conference gave the impression to those not closely familiar with the local situation that the region was not likely to become a source of major problems.
>
> ... in June 1961, Henry R. Labouisse, first Administrator of the new Agency for International Development, announced that supporting assistance to Thailand would end as of fiscal 1962. Such aid as Thailand needed would be provided in the form of development loans, probably in much smaller amount than had until then been given.
>
> Aid Administrator David Bell testified ... in June of 1963, "We expect our economic assistance should be diminishing there, and it should not be too long before we can close out our economic assistance program altogether."[1]

I well remember the conflict of views in the American official community in the early 1960s over the seriousness of the incipient insurgency activities of the Communist Party of Thailand. As USOM's member of the small Embassy-USOM-USIA (U.S. Information Agency) task force that was formed to think about the insurgency and develop ideas for possible responses, I agreed with those who argued against overreaction to what was a mere scattering of isolated incidents, compared with the level of activity (and theoretical debate about counterinsurgency) in Vietnam. There was a strong sense among those who saw greater menace in the Northeast that one of the most important tasks the Americans faced was raising the level of concern, creating a feeling of urgency, among Thai officials. The very first activity proposed and carried out jointly with the RTG, with U.S. funding support (mainly USIA), was a pilot project to send a mobile "hearts and minds" vehicle on trips through remote areas of the Northeast. The vehicle was equipped with audiovisual gear and medicine and other handouts and carried a small team of Thai officials, including the district officer (nai amphur) of each district it traversed, plus one USIA observer. The idea was to test out a method for improving the image of the government, especially of its local officials, in the eyes of the villagers in order to lower the potentialities for Communist propaganda penetration, based as that was on the general image in the region of government officials who were distant and seldom visible most of the time, who provided little or no benefit, and who were more likely to insult and exploit villagers if they did appear than to provide any useful service.

As the Thais readily admit, civil servants historically avoided being posted to the Northeast if they possibly could, while Bangkok routinely posted to this region the least effective officials. Some members of the insurgency working group questioned whether it was a good idea to increase the mobility and opportunities for direct dealings with villagers of officials whose behavior might well confirm what the insurgents were saying. The results of the first couple of forays of this little project were in fact mixed in this respect, but the lessons learned formed the initial experience of U.S. officials in Thailand in this problem and were soon reflected in major programs. My skepticism was heightened by the results of this pilot endeavor, but then tempered when, on a trip through a very remote area of the Northeast, in Loei province, my group came upon a large burned-out bridge. According to the provincial officials at the site, the bridge had been destroyed by the CPT only hours before we came on the scene. It would be three more years before the weight of opinion in the United States came down firmly on the side of those arguing that the internal threat in Thailand required a larger-scale U.S. assistance response. By 1965, as pointed out earlier, conditions in Vietnam had deteriorated sufficiently to cause a major change in both Thai and U.S. perceptions and a major increase in economic and military aid.

COUNTERINSURGENCY: 1965–1974

The fourth period of the U.S. aid program in Thailand was marked by a sharp rise in the level of economic and military resources the United States provided to Thailand. This increase to the highest levels of resource transfer reached at any time in the program's history before or since was driven by the concern of both governments over the escalating military conflict in Vietnam and the rising domestic insurgency inside Thailand.

Although the focus of this study is on the developmental effects of U.S. aid to Thailand, the security aspects must be examined for three reasons. First, there is the simple point that the security-oriented projects got the lion's share of the funds during this period, and, as stressed here several times, security in one form or another had been a, if not the, basic rationale and justification to the Congress since the start of the program. Second, an absence of domestic security can be a more powerful constraint on economic development than any other single problem. People are not likely to risk investing in illiquid forms in areas where the safety of their capital would be in doubt. Insurgencies of the "national liberation" type have also commonly (as was the case in Thailand) attempted to reduce the effective reach and reputation of the central government in the areas of insurgent operations by intimidating or assassinating local officials, including teachers, police, and village headmen. Such tactics weaken the local institutional structures that, among other things, support the development process. The failure or inability of a central government to sustain law and order or to prevent the supplanting of local authority in "liberated villages" can easily lead to a breakdown in the commercial and local financial systems that articulate with production activities, especially if the insurgency operates under an ideology (as has been the case with most Southeast Asian insurgencies) that asserts that the existing economic structure is exploiting the mass of rural inhabitants.

As noted earlier, in the years just before and after World War II economic policy had been based on erroneous convictions regarding the nature of commodity market operations in rural areas and that all empirical studies have demonstrated that the commercial system is highly competitive, operates on small margins, and generates farm-gate prices that give farmers "fair" returns in relation to the final prices of their produce. The argument of the CPT insurgents was based more on the conditions of backwardness in the areas where they were operating, especially in the Northeast; on the small-scale corruption and arrogance villagers faced in their occasional encounters with local officials; and on the traditional cultural barriers between the Northeasterners (largely Lao culturally but also composed of other ethnic groups more or less differentiated from the Central Plain and Bangkok Thai) and the rest of the country. These latter cultural differences included dialect, language, and customs and were the basis of resentment in the Northeast over the condescending attitude of the Central Plain Thai, who tended to view their country cousins as backward and unrefined. The cultural differences and the sense that the relative poverty and underdevelopment of the Northeast's infrastructure were due partly to deliberate neglect of the Northeast, and not solely to the general underdeveloped state of the country as a whole, were reflected in the relatively radical and combative behavior of Northeastern representatives in the Thai legislature during the Phibul government years (1947–1957) and in the heavy Northeast represention among CPT leaders.

This points to the third and most important reason for emphasizing the developmental importance of the security problems that drove the aid program in this period—namely, Northeast regionalism. The location of the Northeast (contiguous to Laos and Cambodia), the potentialities for separatism, and the area's relative isolation and poverty combined to draw the attention of Vietnam and the PRC and to make the Northeast the focus of American development and counterinsurgency support. One of the main themes of Thai history has been the gradual consolidation of the country in a modern nation-state form through the extension of Central Plain Thai control over parts of the country with which the Thai rulers in earlier historical periods had only rather loose suzerainty relationships. While Thailand has a much greater cultural homogeneity than many third world countries, it nevertheless has considerable regional diversity. To the Central Plain Thai, Northern Thai, Korat Thai, Northeasterner Lao, and numerous related but differentiated smaller groups and so-called Hill Tribes (not to mention the distinctive Moslem Malay minority in the South), the differences within Thailand's relative homogeneity are quite perceptible and in many cases highly significant.

We need not go into the roots of Northeast regionalism any further than to note that many of the Northeastern political leaders were drawn into sympathy with the postwar anticolonial national liberation drives in Southeast Asia through the alliances they formed with the left wing of Bangkok's turbulent postwar politics, but more importantly through their conviction that their region faced systematic economic neglect. The rise of Northeastern (or "Isan") regionalism as a modern political phenomenon dates only from the postwar years, despite the long history of the differentiation I have noted. According to Charles Keyes,

> The pattern of increasing temporary migration of north-
> eastern villagers to Bangkok beginning in the post-war pe-

riod greatly spurred the development of "we-they" attitudes among Northeasterners. Moreover, the "we" was beginning to assume a more regional character.

During [Prime Minister] Phibun's second period in power between 1947 and 1957, many representatives from the Isan area played upon a growing sense of regionalism to put pressure on the central government to direct more attention towards the Northeast. The objective which these MPs promoted on behalf of their regional constituency was the reduction or elimination of alleged discrimination of the national government towards the Northeast. These representatives claimed that there was ample evidence that the central government ignored, and even suppressed ... Isan political leadership and overemphasized bureaucratic centralization to the detriment of the Northeastern region. They also claimed that the government was not doing enough to stimulate development in the Northeast so that the region could attain the same economic level as the rest of the country. Finally, they maintained that the central government, and the Central Thai in general, treated Northeasterners as cultural or class inferiors.[2]

While it was true that most of the political Left in Thailand in the 1950s was Northeastern—a fact that lent support to the view among some government leaders that the opposition MPs from the Northeast were involved in conspiratorial arrangements with the Laotian Communist party (the Pathet Lao), the Viet Minh, and the PRC—not all the Northeastern politicians were on the Left. Further, the Northeastern peasantry was still unsophisticated and relatively isolated and probably not very engaged with international issues in Southeast Asia. Nevertheless, given regional resentment, the outspoken Northeastern opposition in the Parliament (until Premier Sarit, himself a Northeasterner, closed the assembly in 1958), the strength of the Northeastern "left," and the rising Communist tide in Laos and Vietnam in the early 1960s, events were drawing together in a way that appeared to threaten the integrity of the Thai state. The RTG began to round up alleged Communist agents in the Northeast in 1961. With the build-up of the Northeastern airbases under the OICC program, one more factor was added to this regional configuration—namely, the suspicion that Thai insurgents were being activated from outside

to threaten the security of the bases and to weaken Thai support for
U.S. military activities in Vietnam.*

To meet these problems, the RTG developed a policy with three
components: suppression of Northeastern political opposition, promotion of the economic development of the region, and promotion of
the integration of the inhabitants of the Northeast into the Thai state
as a whole. William Klausner, an American anthropologist with intimate knowledge of Northeast Thailand, has noted that Northeastern
cultural orientation toward Laos did not carry over into the political
realm, where identification was directed toward the Thai monarch.
Keyes thought that Isan regionalism was never conceived by Northeasterners in separatist terms (or as Lao irredentism). Still, it is un-
derstandable that the Thai government would want to take measures
to ensure that such a possibility did not emerge from a further drift
toward a sense of fundamental regional conflict of interest and that
the U.S. government would support such measures. Continuing regional division, whether it evolved into separatism or not, would have
major negative consequences for the economic development of the
country.

The deterioration of security in Thailand and in Indochina during
this period had several effects on the role of U.S. aid in Thailand. The
size of the program roughly doubled. The economic development of
the Northeast assumed great urgency, especially in the form of activities that would improve both the perceptions and substance of the
government's relationship with the Isan population. Nonmilitary security forces in the Northeast became major recipients of assistance
under AID appropriations and administration. While the political and
security objectives of AID's Northeast activities imparted a sense of
urgency for quick impact, the projects included much that was developmental in character, especially investment in physical infrastructure. Thus, in addition to asking whether or not the program was

---

* The *New York Times* reported in 1966:

> During the past month, clashes between Communist guerillas and Thai security
> forces in border areas along the Mekong River have become more frequent and
> bloodier. The change, United States sources believe, is attributed both to more
> aggressive counter-measures and to Communist measures to spread terrorism.
> North Vietnam and Communist China, it is believed, have ordered the 18-month
> Thailand United Patriotic Front to launch a major effort now—for tactical
> reasons tied to the Vietnamese war. Although opinions vary, some specialists
> believe that the current terrorist activity is aimed primarily at forcing Bangkok
> to limit its support for the United States effort in Vietnam. It is also believed
> Hanoi and Peking want to discourage Thailand from providing bases for any
> ground thrust aimed at cutting the vital Ho Chi Minh trail through neighboring
> Laos. (June 26, 1966)

effective in terms of its security objectives, the program's development substance should also be examined.

At this point a brief history of the insurgency will be useful for putting the U.S. assistance in context. Thai governments have adopted a strong stance against Communist political activity ever since the 1932 coup. The first anti-Communist legislation was passed in 1933. In 1946, in order to secure Soviet agreement to Thailand's membership in the United Nations, the Thai government abolished the anti-Communist laws. A year later the new Phibul government cracked down on the Communist Party of Thailand and in 1952 outlawed the party again. By the late 1950s the CPT began to receive support and training from Vietnam and the PRC. In 1961 the CPT formally adopted a strategy of Maoist rural insurgency at its Third National Congress. The following year a radio station calling itself the Voice of the People of Thailand began broadcasting from China, while the CPT began to develop its infrastructure and supporting organizations. In January 1965 the Chinese Foreign Minister, Chen Yi, announced that a war of "national liberation" was being launched in Thailand.

The first guerrilla attack on Thai security forces took place on August 7, 1965, in the Na Kae district of Nakhon Phanom province in the Northeast. The government's initial response was to meet the insurgency with force alone, but these tactics were unable to prevent the gradual spread of CPT organization and of armed attacks on government forces and officials to other parts of the country. In 1968 General Saiyud Kerdphol, one of the leading strategists of the counterinsurgency effort, estimated that there were perhaps 2,000 CPT combatants operating in 80 groups in the Northeast, especially in two districts along the Mekong, opposite Lao territory, supported by 10,000 village sympathizers and part-time fighters. In the rest of the country there were an estimated 600 CPT insurgents concentrated in certain districts in the North and in the central-western and midsouthern areas. Assassinations in 1967 were running about ten a month, armed clashes about one a day.[3]

According to General Saiyud's account, the government's strategy for coping with the insurgency evolved through several stages. Following the first response in force, the RTG recognized that it faced an unconventional challenge that called for a combination of civilian, police, and military responsibilities. By the end of 1965 a new coordinating organization was set up to develop an integrated strategy, the Communist Suppression Operations Command (CSOC), later (and still) called the Internal Security Operations Command. The strategy formed by CSOC combined military action against the insurgents with civic

action by military and paramilitary forces, which included development and propaganda programs to counter the political efforts of the
insurgents in the villages and to improve the relations between villagers and local officials. The CSOC approah appeared to be working
well in the limited areas where the CPT had begun its operations.
When the CPT responded by initiating armed activity in other areas
of the country, responsibility for counterinsurgency was shifted to the
Thai Army, which reverted to a policy of forcible suppression and
disregard of CSOC's programs to secure villager loyalties. In the North
in particular, the suppression campaign caused innocent deaths and
created animosities and refugee problems among the Hill Tribes that
took years to overcome. When it became apparent that the military
campaigns were counterproductive and that the numbers of insurgents by 1970 had risen to five or six thousand while the number of
"Communist-influenced" villages had risen to four or five thousand,
the army fell back on the CSOC strategy.

Between 1970 and 1973 the CPT appeared to make little progress
in the Northeast and Central Plain, but did succeed in expanding its
numbers in the North and peninsular South. In 1972 the number of
armed clashes rose to nearly two a day, causing 2,100 casualties
among government military and civil personnel. Insurgent casualties
were about 400, while over 1,100 were taken into custody. In the
implementation of the counterinsurgency strategy, the regional army
commanders actually had wide authority over the tactics they wished
to employ to fit the circumstances of their areas as they saw fit. This
diversity of strategy was a sensible approach, given the socioeconomic differences among the northern Hill Tribes, the settled societies of the Northeast and the Central Plain, and the Thai and Moslem
areas of the southern peninsula. But it also meant that the strategies
were not equally effective in conception or implementation in different parts of the country. Still, compared with the scale of organization
and operations of the Communist parties in Malaysia in earlier years,
and then in Laos and Vietnam, and with the level of violent struggle
in Vietnam in particular, the insurgency in Thailand had not succeeded by the early 1970s in developing into a threat to national
security that might get beyond the control of the Thai government.

Then in October 1973 events took an unexpected turn. A student
uprising in Bangkok launched a chain of events that resulted in the
resignation of the military government and ushered in three extraordinary years of democratic civilian rule. In a heady atmosphere of
open politics and widespread strikes, farmer protests and continuous
student agitation over public policies they viewed as inadequately

addressing the problems of poverty and social inequities, Thailand went through five governments in three years of unprecedented instability and tension in public life. As the students lost the support of the middle class in Bangkok, who saw the agitation and indiscipline as having gone too far, a right-wing reaction developed that accused the students of aligning with the CPT. In a well-planned campaign the reaction infiltrated student, labor, and farmer organizations and brought about their destruction. The reaction culminated in an attack by the leading right-wing youth organization, largely comprising vocational students, against the university students based at the Thammasat campus. In a few hours of fighting a number of students were killed with brutality seldom witnessed by Thai society. The ferocity of the attack on these youths and the unleashing of such deep antagonisms made October 6, 1976, a watershed in modern Thai history.

The immediate consequences of the right-wing resurgence were a repressive military takeover of the government to restore law and order; a year of more repressive and strident rule than Thailand had ever experienced under the civilian Thanin Kraivichien, whom the military had installed in October 1976 as Prime Minister; the loss of faith of thousands of students and intellectuals in the possibilities for social progress through democratic politics or through the workings of the established bureaucratic polity; and the movement of two to three thousand people, mostly students "into the jungle" to join the CPT-led insurgency. The severity of the government's anticommunism resulted in an immediate increase in CPT strength and a sharp rise in the level of insurgent activity. By October 1977 the military recognized the divisive implications of these policies and brought in General Kriangsak Chomanand to replace Thanin. Many in Bangkok reported that they had breathed a sigh of relief that "the Dark Ages of modern Thai politics" had ended.[4]

The infusion of middle-class students and intellectuals appeared at first to change the whole complexion of the insurgency. Before October 1976 the CPT appeared to be retreating, its rural support eroding in many parts of the country and its operations confined to relatively remote areas. The students brought a sharp rise in the numbers of adherents, a sense of outrage, a dedication to social progress and reform, and a level of talent and education that the CPT had never found in the villages. The students also strengthened the Thai image of a party that had been viewed as an alien instrument of a foreign power (the PRC). For several reasons, however, the CPT was unable to capitalize on this surprising windfall, even though it did intensify its armed activity over the next two years, new adherents having brought the insurgent forces up to an estimated 12,000. To the contrary, the year 1979 saw the beginning of the end for the insurgency.

The Vietnamese invasion of Cambodia and overthrow of the Pol Pot regime caused a split in the insurgency into antagonistic pro-Vietnamese and pro-Chinese factions. The sight of neighboring Communist regimes at war with each other, the dogmatism of the pro-PRC faction, and the revelations of the atrocities of the Khmer Rouge gave the dissident students a new perspective on the Thai Communists, whom many defectors described as equally domineering and authoritarian in their treatment of the rank and file as the military regime in Bangkok. In 1975, in the wake of President Nixon's reopening of U.S. relations with China, Thailand also had moved to repair relations. As China's relations with Vietnam deteriorated over the Cambodian takeover, China and Thailand found common interest in a policy of sustaining the Cambodian resistance to the government Vietnam had installed in Pnom Penh. One result of this rapprochement was the cessation of PRC financial support for the Communist Party of Thailand and the closure of the radio station that had been beaming antigovernment messages to Thailand from China.

Defections from the insurgency rose in response to a new RTG amnesty policy in 1978–1979 aimed at the students. Several leading personalities surrendered to the government in 1980–81, followed by mass defections from 1982 on. The effectiveness of the military operations increased. By October 1983 the government was able to claim "total victory" and the destruction of all major CPT bases. In 1984 the number of insurgents was estimated to have fallen to one or two thousand. In 1987 the government extended its amnesty and settlement program to the remnants of the Malaysian Communist insurgency, which had been holed out in jungle areas on the Thai side of the Thai-Malaysia border for many years. In the face of Malaysian refusal to offer a similar amnesty to the Malaysian insurgents, the RTG accepted a series of group surrenders in a program to finally eliminate the insurgent presence from southern Thai soil by allowing the aging rebels to settle and integrate into the southern Thai scene.

There has been much debate over the reasons for Thailand's success in this thirty–year story. Many factors were involved, some entirely outside Thailand's control, some entirely Thailand's doing, and some in which the U.S. aid program played a significant part. To recap, the important factors contributing to the decline of the CPT and the insurgency included the following: (a) the effects on the CPT leadership, the insurgent membership, and ordinary villagers of the influx of Cambodian refugees with their accounts of the Pol Pot regime, the influx of Laotian refugees fleeing Communist rule, and the Vietnamese invasion of Cambodia; (b) the withdrawal of Chinese financial and propaganda support; (c) Vietnamese expulsion of pro-Chinese members of the CPT from their sanctuaries in Laos and Cambodia; (d) the failure of the Thai villagers to respond to the appeal of the CPT; (e) the gradual substitution by the RTG of programs of amnesty, rural services and village development, Hill Tribe and other resettlement, and reabsorption of the students into the mainstream in place of earlier search-and-destroy tactics of force; (f) the introduction in the 1960s of in-service training for the nai amphur (district officer) and of a policy of sending the best officials to work in the Northeast in place of the traditional treatment of that region as a bureaucratic Siberia; (g) the programs to provide transportation, power, water, and government health and other services to areas previously neglected and most exposed to insurgent activity; (h) the failure of the CPT leadership (largely uneducated) to develop a coherent vision of an alternative society and a program relevant to the specific characteristics of Thai society; and (i) the CPT's inability to develop an effectively binding relationship with the students who had fled autocratic government in Bangkok only to be disillusional and repulsed by the rigid, autocratic behavior of the CPT cadre.

To attempt to reach some judgment as to the role of the U.S. program among these complexities, it is necessary first to describe the counterinsurgency-oriented projects and see what can be said about the effectiveness of their implementation and the specific outputs they were intended to, and actually did, produce.

As pointed out before, the separation between security and nonsecurity aspects of the aid program cannot be sharply drawn since the rationale for the emphasis on the Northeast was at once its relative poverty and its location and exposure in the context of the security problems of the Southeast Asia region. Still, it is possible to make meaningful distinctions even if one cannot be very exact about the numbers. Table A.10 lists the projects of the mid-1960s and mid-1970s that were designed as direct responses to the insurgency. The projects are divided between those concerning counterinsurgency operations per se and those intended to improve socioeconomic conditions and villager-government relations. AID and counterpart fund expenditures for security projects per se totaled $131.3 million. Expenditures for the socioeconomic and administrative projects was $223.8 million.

In one sense the entire aid program in this period can be called security-oriented since its overall justification to the Congress was to help the RTG cope with related internal and external threats to the country's security. Taking individual project narratives of the congressional presentations at face value, Caldwell came up with a figure of 55 percent ($141 million) of the total gross obligations from 1965 to 1970 ($257 million) as devoted "specifically for counter-insurgency purposes."[5] This appears to overstate the proportion somewhat because it includes some activities (such as family planning) that would have been undertaken even in the absence of insurgency, and where a counterinsurgency rationale looks perfunctory, if not facetious. Projects that were basically security in their content (police, village defense units, village radios, and the like) amounted to $69 million in this period (1965–1970), or 27 percent of total obligations, but this figure overstates the content that was of a technical security nature since the police project included $6.9 million (these numbers exclude counterpart), which was allocated to the civic action activities. Apart from the border police portion, the project with the National Police Department was designed to help expand police manpower in the provinces, increase their communication and transport capabilities, and raise the quality of their performance through strengthening the police training institutions as well as through participant training. The focus of the project was on the technical aspects of police work in coping with the insurgency and on improving traditional law and order activities, but some attention was also given to behavior and relations with villagers.

The Thai government's first ideas on civil programs in the Northeast to counter the CPT were formed in 1962 in a Northeast Development Committee chaired by Prime Minister Sarit. The Committee's program up to that time had been based on a growth pole concept. Infrastructure investments of certain types (such as the first Northeast university) would be concentrated in the town of Khon Kaen. It was hoped that the impetus to Khon Kaen's urban development would be more effective in promoting general development of the region than the continued spread of such investments evenly throughout the area.* The Prime Minister's personal concern over how fast such an approach could be expected to reach the villages led to the development of a new program for direct village development activities.

Two activities were launched, both of which received substantial U.S. assistance. The first was a Mobile Development Unit (MDU)

---

*Some of the initial thinking about a Northeast growth pole town was done in the AID mission at the behest of Ambassador Kenneth T. Young, Jr., who thought that the agroville concept in Vietnam (the fortified agricultural village) might be applied in Thailand. USOM staff doubted that the scale or nature of Northeast insurgency warranted the agroville concept and proposed a growth pole approach instead. A proposal for a feasibility study was submitted to AID/W, but no study or project involving USOM eventuated.

project, which was relatively easy to launch in a short period of time.* The MDUs were civic action teams of up to 120 military and civilian officials. They were designed to demonstrate RTG interest in rural areas where insurgent violence made normal government activity dangerous and to have immediate impact on village attitudes toward the central government. After an initial year of U.S. support through the military assistance program, USOM took over the provision of aid inputs. The MDU project gradually withered because no regular RTG agencies were willing to absorb the activity and because the Royal Thai Army's attention was diverted by its manpower needs for its participation in the Vietnam War.[6] At its peak, the project fielded twenty-nine units and over a very wide area, built small roads, bridges, libraries, and schools, village wells, small dams, and the like, and provided training and services in health and other subjects.

The MDU concept was ephemeral in nature and could not have left behind any outputs other than the miniprojects it was designed for. According to Caldwell, the MDUs were criticized for being ad hoc and contributing nothing permanent to the strengthening of local government operations. On the other hand, he noted that two studies found benefits in terms of lessons learned by the Ministry of Defense about rural problems and the complexities of counterinsurgency and in the form of positive impact on villagers and lessons for the promotion of community development. While the MDU project did not survive in the face of its character as a bureaucratic anomaly, there is some evidence, described below, that it deserves a passing grade.

The second of Sarit's Northeast initiatives was the Accelerated Rural Development (ARD) program. The U.S. project to assist ARD became the largest single development activity in the history of the Thai aid program. It began as a small RTG Program in the six Northeast changwats considered at greatest risk to insurgent activity (Loei, Nongkai, Udorn, Nakhon Phanom, Sakon Nakhon, and Ubon). The objective of ARD was also to demonstrate government concern for village welfare and development in these areas through the provision of local infrastructure such as village access roads, wells, and so forth. However, in order to achieve rapid implementation and to demonstrate to villagers that these benefits were being created by the provincial and district officials (in their capacity as central government civil servants), the work was to be carried out by the provincial authorities directly and not by administrative units located in Bangkok or by ad hoc mobile units. The initial equipment budget was very

---

*The USIA Mobile Information Teams mentioned above may have been precursors to the MDUs.

modest (a mere $250,000), and the scope of the program was severely constrained by a shortage of engineers. The program was established under a new organizational unit in Bangkok reporting to the Northeast Development Committee, rather than being added to the responsibilities of any of the existing units in the RTG. The Prime Minister accepted the argument that none of the existing units that might be appropriate for managing ARD had the administrative flexibility required for the speed of implementation that was considered essential.

After the program had been operating a few months, USOM offered to help, attracted by the local level orientation of ARD. The result was a $75.3 million, thirteen-year project (1964–1977; the last year in which new funds were put into the ARD project was FY 1975) that was the centerpiece of the RTG effort on the civilian side to preempt rural loyalties for the government and wean away villager support the CPT had already gained. The AID project financed the bulk of ARD's construction equipment, provided participant training to meet ARD's engineering requirements (ARD operated in its first year with virtually no engineers), and helped in the planning and management of the program by stationing engineers and advisors in Bangkok and in each of the changwats. As the U.S. inputs expanded the scope of the program, the bureaucratic position of the ARD unit had to be regularized to give it the needed status and administrative connections. Thus ARD was established as an office within the Ministry of Interior. From a starting staff of 65, ARD grew to a 10,000 person organization. USOM trained 101 of the core staff, virtually all of whom received masters degrees in the United States, largely in engineering. Over the life of the USOM project, the RTG provided 60 percent of ARD's budget, the United States 40 percent.

While the U.S. advisors played an important role in the implementation of ARD, the concept of the project and its basic operational modes were developed by the RTG. This can be seen from two differences that arose immediately between the ARD director, Prasong Sukhum, and the aid mission. Consistent with its experience under the bridge- and road-building projects, USOM argued that ARD should contract out the construction activities to private firms. Prasong argued that private contracting would not meet the political demonstration objectives of ARD; contracting would have the appearance of a USOM activity (so widespread and well-known was the mission), thereby reducing the RTG to a marginal role. USOM also argued that the substance of the program should follow the Indian community development model, emphasizing village self-help and a "software" role for the RTG rather than having the provincial authorities descend on the villages with benefits distributed from above. Prasong insisted that the political purposes of the program again favored a top-down approach in which the equipment and the palpable actions of officials were essential. On both counts, USOM acceded to the Thai view.

As one would expect when any new program is getting underway with a rapid expansion in budget and equipment, shortages of skilled staff, far-flung field organization, and an operating program confined to areas dangerous to government personnel, ARD encountered many implementation problems. When the evaluation unit of the Thai Bureau of the Budget conducted a field study of ARD in its third year of operation, it found many weaknesses of staffing, equipment maintenance, inventory management, and the like, and expressed doubts over the psychological effects all this activity was having on villagers. The doubts over ARD's political efficacy arose especially from the heavy emphasis ARD was giving to building roads instead of working on agriculture. The Thai evaluators in effect repeated the argument USOM had made that software activities would be more effective for achieving the program's ultimate objectives than the equipment-oriented construction work.

Over time the operational problems of ARD were overcome. Its maintenance program, for example, has managed to keep some of the USOM-financed equipment in operation in 1988. In the beginning those provincial governors able to manage a fast start-up were able to monopolize ARD's resources, leaving little equipment and other inputs for the changwats with less capable governors. The resulting imbalances were corrected through a systematic programming and mapping system that ARD set up with the help of James Dalton, who served for many years as the principal USOM advisor to ARD.

The creation of ARD as a rival to the Community Development and Public Works departments (which might have hosted the program otherwise) generated resentments within the Ministry of Interior. Some officials still argue that it might have been a better choice to put the ARD program into one of these two established departments and make the changes in leadership that would have been necessary for either of these units to be able to implement the program at the time. The program would certainly have gotten off to a much slower start if it had been lodged in one of these units, but ARD could then have served to strengthen that unit rather than leaving them both behind and drawing off (as it did) some of the best staff of the Department of Local Administration. Agriculture and other old-line ministries also resented the disproportionate aid allocated to ARD and cooperated with the new Interior unit only with great reluctance. This was not the only instance in Thailand when the aid program was party to the creation of a new organizational unit to get around administrative bottlenecks rather than resolve them within the table of organization and established rules of bureaucratic procedure. (In this case the new unit was created by the RTG; in another important case examined below, the ad hoc bureaucratic "solution" was dreamed up by the aid mission.) Development assistance organizations, including the World Bank and others, have often been drawn to creating special organizational units outside the established structures of the government in the interest of getting the job done and avoiding entanglement in an inefficient existing bureaucracy. There have been famous cases where the damage done to the ignored establishment appeared in the long run to offset some considerable portion of the benefits gained from faster implementation. But that does not appear to have been the case here.

The role and organization of ARD became established, and it remains a permanent unit within the Ministry of Interior. In one significant organizational respect, however, USAID's reform hopes were not realized, as F. J. Moore and his associates note:

> It [ARD] has retreated somewhat from the pattern of United States country organization which was A.I.D.'s guiding concept. The organization especially with respect to financial planning and management has become more centralized because of its dependence on the central budget, once direct grant funding of provincial activities stopped. However, it is evident that ARD has maintained a field orientation. Its provincial staff is trained and committed to promote rural development; and the central ARD organization not only tolerates but encourages local initiative, especially where it takes the lead in coordinating the services of other RTG agencies at the district and provincial level to promote village welfare.[7]

This is an interesting example of the recurrent efforts (under successive mission directors and project frameworks) to promote decentralization of government functions. When the U.S. project was in full swing, the devolution of operational control to the changwat governors was integral to the Thais' own ARD management concept. Thus ARD became a powerful and conspicuous demonstration of the advantages and feasibility of decentralizing an important program. It is arguable whether the retreat was due to the cessation of outside funding directly to the provinces, or whether it was an inevitable reversion to standard operating procedures once the counterinsurgency goals were evidently achieved and the functions of ARD became routine rather than extraordinary. In any case, while the mission did not achieve permanent change in the distribution of control between Bangkok and the field in this largest single project in the program's history, the orientation of ARD and its staff has remained a significant exception to the traditional mode of the bureaucracy, and the provincial level continues to have some scope for local initiative.

ARD has racked up an impressive record of physical accomplishments. The principal measured output was the building of some 20,000 kilometers of rural roads of which 12,000 kilometers were built during the period of the AID project. Large numbers of wells, bridges, small reservoirs, and spillways were constructed as well. ARD also fielded teams that traveled through remote areas providing primary health care and potable water to villages never reached before by government services. Smaller ARD activities included agriculture extension, vocational training, the organization of youth and women's groups, and the formation of village cooperative stores.

In an associated project the Northeast Technical Institute in Korat was strengthened so that it could produce the equipment operators and other technicians ARD needed on a large scale. This was a big project by itself, involving twenty-one American advisors over five years at a cost of $5.8 million. At this time at least, it was unlikely the Korat institute would have gotten an infusion of equipment and technical assistance anywhere near this scale or achieved the level of institutional capability it did if it were not for the ARD project. The project also used private consultants on contract as trainers, probably for the first time in an RTG activity, and this practice led to a general acceptance by the government of the idea of contracting for consultant services from local, as distinct from foreign, firms.

The outstanding accomplishment of ARD, in terms of physical output, was its road-building. While any set of roads of such size, including many in areas that are mountainous and remote, will have heterogeneous effects (some roads will have minor traffic and economic impact, while others will be so located that heavy traffic soon turns the analyst's attention to the problem of maintenance), the overwhelming impression from studies of the ARD roads (and additions to the rural road network financed under World Bank, Australian, and other auspices)—and of rural change in Thailand generally —is that improvement in ground transportation has been the most powerful factor promoting change in provincial Thailand in the past four decades.

Some of the evidence for the transforming effects of building secondary and tertiary roads was collected by USOM within two or three years of construction. (In order to get early feedback on the effects of ARD and other Northeast projects, the mission set up a research division in 1965. Staffed with social scientists, the division produced a number of field studies that were carefully done and apparently objective, given their often critical conclusions.) Other evidence has accumulated since, based on economic studies and village opinion surveys. While the measurable impact varied from road to road, as I have noted, and depended also on the weather and the general economic climate prevailing at the time of the individual studies, the market widening and the sudden spread of mobility (the penetration and frequency of bus and truck traffic) were observed in the zone of influence of every route studied. Northeast villagers continued into 1987 to report road penetration (and electrification) as having made the greatest impact on village life.

An evaluation in 1980 of the impact of ARD roads contains many details and observations of the penetration of government services, a fall in the cost of goods, daily commuting of children to nearby town schools, opening of new land to cultivation, spread of commercial crop production in areas that had been subsistence in character before, increasing nonfarm enterprise activity, the extension of power lines into areas previously without electricity, and so on. One significant negative effect was the acceleration of deforestation in sloping countryside opened by some of the ARD roads in the North. But overall, the economic and social effects of the road program were found to be powerful and favorable, as F. J. Moore and his coworkers report:

> Our report, on the whole, paints a positive picture. The contribution of the A.I.D. project far exceeds the expectations suggested in the formal documentation over the years. We come away impressed with the lasting impact of the rural roads component of the ARD program. It has helped to establish the permanent institutional capacity of the RTG to sustain an ongoing rural development effort, and it has improved the welfare of rural people by tying villages and towns into the mainstream of village life.
>
> The rapid economic transformation, so evidently related to the extension of roads into formerly isolated areas of

north and northeast Thailand, is fully compatible with the
social and cultural traditions of the people. There is no
sudden break in established patterns of behavior and relationships; but roads clearly quicken the pace and increase
and widen the channels of communications open both for
traditional and new messages. (P. 15)

On the impact on poverty (the main subject of chapter 6) and on the
relative distribution of gains from the road program, the same evaluation has this to say:

In the first instance then, the welfare curve merely shifts to
a higher level without any essential change in shape. The
poor remain relatively poor, although a whole range of new
services and new experiences to which the roads provide
access enhances their potential for economic and social
mobility. Starting from a higher base, the more affluent
can take advantage more quickly of new opportunities which
the roads create in the short run. However, nobody loses
because everyone shares, at least to some extent in a rapidly expanding pool of production and ideas. . . . Our hur-
ried travel in the North and Northeast has given us a feel
for the pervasive and lasting excitement inherent in the
promise of better things to come in the wake of the roads.
We have been struck by the sense of confidence in the
future brought about by fuller participation in the opportunities of the nation at large. (P. 16)

The impressions here of the distribution of benefits are borne out by
the analyses of income change described in the next chapter. These
impressions are worth repeating, even if they are anecdotal observations; the economists seldom convey excitement.

An interesting technical controversy arose between ARD and the
Thai Highway Department. To avoid the expense and time required
to buy new right of way, ARD built its roads over old bullock trails.
Highway Department engineers criticized this practice, arguing that
new right of way should be chosen to ensure that future upgrading
could be done with proper alignments and road widths. While ARD's
choice was made mainly on political timing grounds, an AID study
later concluded that the right choice had been made judged on economic criteria (that the present value of the set of roads was likely to
be higher if the decision to invest in upgrading was delayed until it

became clear where the traffic demands it, rather than building every road to high specifications in advance). ARD did the right thing but not for economic reasons, as the study indicates: "Intermediate-technology choices were made in the ARD program . . . not because they emerged from a cost-benefit analysis. Rather, the choices were forced by circumstances, and the organizational site of the choices was away from the influence of equipment-intensive road designers."[8] Although the specification issue is only a footnote to the present interest, it is interesting as an early example of "appropriate technology," a subject that rose in importance in AID (and the development community generally) in the 1970s as part of the general emphasis in that decade on employment, poverty, and the participation of the rural poor in the development process.

After the MDU and ARD programs had been in operation only three years (along with health, potable water, and other ongoing programs in the Northeast that were redirected to sharpen their contribution to the overall counterinsurgency effort), the aid mission conducted an intensive evaluation in two changwats.[9] This micro research is worth describing in a little detail for what it reveals about the care with which these programs were monitored, the physical and psychological conditions the programs were intended to affect, and the impact and mistakes of the programs in their initial years of operation. The research was conducted by USOM's resident anthropologist, three Thai members of the mission's research division staff, and seven Thai associates who were social scientists, researchers, and officials of the Community Development Department and the National Research Council. The study consisted of formal attitude surveys in the villages, intensive interviews and resident observation in some of the villages, and interviews with changwat and amphur officials. The staff divided into two teams and spent three and a half months in the field.

Two changwats were chosen for comparative study. Sakon Nakhon, which is mountainous in areas and not far from the Mekong, was chosen because of its relatively high level of insurgent operations. Mahasarakam, in the center of the Northeast plateau, was free of CPT activity. The study describes the ethnic differences between the two provinces. While all the villages share basic cultural identity, there is considerable subcultural difference from one village to another in Sakon Nakhon (between the majority Thai Lao of the Northeast and such ethnic subgroups as Thai Yaw, Thai Yoi, Phu Thai, Kalerng, and so on). The Sakon Nakhon ethnic villages were observed to have a strong sense of their separate identities and to feel superior to the Thai Lao. While basically conservative in outlook and preferring to live most of their lives in their villages, the people were found to admire modernism and to aspire to improving their circumstances. Their experience with government had been generally negative, and they recounted the familiar stories about the arrogance and insensitivity of local officials who demanded to be fed the most expensive foods during their very occasional visits and about the corruption of the provincial police who seldom caught cattle thieves and other criminals and who could be bribed to release those criminals who were apprehended.

One might conclude, in the light of what is noted above concerning traditional Northeast attitudes toward Bangkok and the central government, that the attitudes and conditions in Sakon Nakhon contained promising elements for a campaign of deliberate subversion. On the other hand, there is also evidence that the CPT had managed thus far to poison the waters in which they would have to swim by alienating the villagers with their seemingly random and pointless violence. The villagers in Sakon Nakhon were "terrified" of the CPT and resentful of the government's failure to provide them with adequate protection. They were confident of the government's ability to suppress the insurgents, but "mystified" by the RTG's failure to employ bombing and other strong measures. Some of the villagers complained of helplessness and spoke of apprehension over their being forced to cooperate with the insurgents.

The researchers were especially interested in whether the rural development programs were enhancing local security and the wellbeing of the village people. In the amphur with the highest level of insurgent activity, there were seven main RTG activities all receiving direct or indirect U.S. aid support: an MDU unit had been operating four years; Community Development officers had been working there three years; health centers had been established; one main road had been completed (a USOM-financed "security road") and a local ARD road was under construction; a village council program had been operating for a few years, and village leader training was being conducted. U.S. aid projects were involved in all these activities (with the exception of the local council activity). The MDU unit was found to have made a substantial impact, although (as noted above) the scale of MDU operations had been cut back, in this case from a 124-person operation in the beginning to 24 at the time of the study. The MDU had installed a wide range of local infrastructure facilities, often built with voluntary assistance from villagers, including roads, wells, latrines, electricity, health centers, temples, playgrounds, dams, and the like. The local economy was found to be "rejuvenated" thanks to the new access to nearby market towns and the major access opened up by the "security road." There were all the typical signs of rural change—corrugated metal roofs replacing thatch, radios and bicycles, a shift from homemade to store-bought clothing, regular bus service to the amphur seat, rising pace of village self-help projects, and so on. The other activities appeared to have mixed performance, effective in some villages, ineffective in others, with the individual personalities and competence of the responsible workers and officials the main determinant of program performance.

What was the upshot in this third or fourth year, taking the whole set of interventions together? Weighed against the top problems reported by the villagers themselves, the projects had made some clear responses to village needs, especially in infrastructure for water and transportation. Protection against the CPT and banditry had improved in the areas where the RTG had strengthened its relevant presence (through MDUs, for example), but not in others. Some of the installations (such as water pumps) broke down quickly and became indications of RTG interest but misguided or incompetent follow-up, a "mixed" outcome. Structural problems like land titling and land-use permits had not been addressed (and remain serious problems today). Corruption was still a problem, but changes in officials' behavior toward villagers was occurring as the new RTG policy toward Northeast assignments was beginning to spread its effects. While market access had improved greatly, the much larger set of changes needed in marketing and agricultural inputs had not begun to appear, and production had not changed. (It should be noted that Sakon Nakhon is one of the Northeast changwats most removed from Bangkok and was likely to be only slowly drawn into changes in agricultural production occurring elsewhere in the region.) In general, the study found substantial effect and favorable villager reactions to the programs in the areas close to and affected by project sites (and road locations) and to activities being conducted by officials who developed positive personal relationships. A principal conclusion seemed to be the need for just getting on with the job—that is, spreading the projects over a wider geographic area but with more dense coverage and attending to the many details that made a difference to villager perception of government. The study concluded that it was "of the utmost importance that the officials treat the villagers with respect and dignity and on a plane of equality, if they expect to gain the confidence and loyalty of the people."

It is remarkable how strongly these themes of pragmatic small-scale benefits and of the nature of interpersonal relations between villagers and officials emerge in studies of this period, including those by American anthropologists like Keyes:

> An essential point . . . is that a rapid program of develop-
> ment could bring many Central Thai to the Northeast who
> might know little or even care little about local culture.
> The resultant contact which the Isan people have with
> Central Thai officials could exacerbate rather than alle-
> viate traditional regional sentiments of distrust of the Cen-
> tral Thai.
>
> Further, economic development rapidly implemented is
> bound to include many mistakes and partial failures which
> also could create further questions in the minds of the
> northeastern populace as to the effectiveness of the Central
> Government. In the case of the Mobile Development Units,
> for example, selection of a particular village for the appli-
> cation of development schemes has caused resentment in
> neighboring villages which were not chosen as sites for
> development.[10]

Similar warnings about the potentialities for negative and exacerbat-ing effects from putting corrupt and overbearing officials on wheels were made by David Morell and Chai-anan Samudavanija (writing twelve or thirteen years after Keyes), who thought that the net effect of U.S. aid to MDU and ARD activities was negative.* Viewed from the perspective of 1988, these observations are remarkable for two reasons: first, because the political paradigm these writers see as making the difference (through the accumulation of rural microlevel irritants) between stability or the spread of subversion to a level of general crisis has so little to do with the Marxist or other Western paradigms that comprised the intellectual baggage of the CPT (and some Western students of Thai politics); and second, because these fears were apparently recognized by the RTG and acted upon. Mis-takes and exacerbations were the unavoidable price that had to be paid while an effective constellation of programs was being developed

---

*"In general, U.S. assistance programs worsened rather than improved this situation. By supporting a series of corrupt, self-serving military governments, U.S. aid allowed even more extension of government into the countryside, and therefore directly stimulated negative interaction between officials and villagers. U.S. aid built ARD roads into the villages, into which the police could now drive in their USOM-provided jeeps, carrying their U.S. weapons" (Morell and Chai-anan, *Political Conflict in Thailand*, p. 91).

out of a miscellany of experiments.* In the noisy midst of this experience, an objective observer might well conclude that the negative and counterproductive were the main drift of events. In fact, things were moving the other way.

One of the major keys to the decline of the insurgency must have been the reforms the RTG introduced to raise the technical competence of Northeast officials and change their orientation toward the populace. I have already noted the change in assignment policy under which the best rather than the least able officials were assigned to the Northeast. Credit must also go to extensive in-service training programs and to the Nai Amphur Academy in particular, an institution set up by the Department of Local Administration in 1963 to train the senior district administrators, focusing first on the Northeast. These training programs received substantial financial and technical assistance from AID.

The Department of Local Administration (DOLA) in the Ministry of Interior is the core of the administrative system through which the Thai government governs the country. While the various technical officials stationed at the changwat and amphur levels (such as officers in agriculture extension, medical officers) report directly to their own ministries in Bangkok, the changwat governors report to the Permanent Secretary of the Ministry of Interior while the amphur officers are responsible to the Department of Local Administration (DOLA). The Department is responsible for coordinating administrative and development activities in the provincial jurisdictions and (along with the provincial police) for maintaining law and order. (The administrative and order functions that characterized DOLA's role entirely until recent years are reflected in the Thai name for the Department, in which the word *pokrong* is more accurately translated as "control" rather than as "administration.")

Caldwell describes the two USOM projects for helping to strengthen DOLA as among the most successful of the program's institution-building efforts. It is worth quoting from his account in detail.

> The Local Government Administration and Local Government In-Service Training projects were begun in 1963, in conjunction with the establishment of a Training Division in [DOLA]. Their goal, as stated by USOM in 1967, was to

---

*For example, Caldwell records the observation of an ARD field advisor: " 'as I have observed at Mobile Development Unit No. III, it is quite possible to improve (a person's) economic status and furnish him with the best services while his loyalty to the government is actually reduced because of a lack of understanding or consideration by its employees' " (*American Economic Aid to Thailand*, p. 136).

"improve the relationship between the central government
and the people at the village level." . . . the training program for Nai Amphoe which by the late sixties was considered to have special relevance to counterinsurgency, when
initially discussed in the early sixties, was seen purely as a
method of improving government administration.

In the same year [1963], the Nai Amphoe Academy was
set up, offering a nine-month training course for forty DOLA
officials who had been selected to future appointment as
Nai Amphoe. . . . The Academy's objectives were to increase the administrative and technical skills of future Nai
Amphoe, to develop in them democratic views, to motivate
changes in behavior away from traditionally authoritarian
attitudes of the Thai bureaucracy.

The Academy had two American advisors who made some significant
inputs into the orientation of the training. The advisors

were asked to help establish a rating system for applicants,
which in fact was followed closely in making decisions on
acceptance. (Indeed, in a rare demonstration of mutual
trust and respect, the American advisors were asked to
serve on the selection panel and thus had a role, for several
years, in picking a proportion of the incumbents of the
most important post in rural Thailand.) Thus, a heavy dose
of systematic, merit-based considerations was injected into
what had previously been a highly personalistic and unstructured process.

The Academy quickly began to seed the Northeast with its graduates:

As of 1970, six classes totaling 267 persons had graduated
from the Academy. Every new Nai Amphoe since 1966 is a
graduate. Graduates have been assigned in disproportionate share to the Northeast and other difficult and remote
areas, thus reversing the long-standing tradition that saw
posting to such places as a form of punishment. In fact,
there has been competition among the students to be assigned to difficult areas.

The reinforcing connections between the training program and the
ARD project, noted by Caldwell, were particularly interesting as an
example of how separate insurgency-driven initiatives came together:

> As of May 1968, 49% of graduates had been sent to the ARD provinces—which at that time represented only 20% of all provinces. . . . The ARD program has for the first time placed in the hands of the provincial and district bureaucracy resources permitting tangible signs of achievement. While it will be argued . . . that development projects are less important in the eyes of Thai villagers than is efficient and honest administration, the fact remains that energetic officials seem to be drawn to the ARD provinces in part because work there allows an opportunity that is not available elsewhere to demonstrate managerial competence to one's superiors.

An RTG evaluation in 1969 came to several favorable conclusions, as Caldwell relates:

> The director of the Academy was found to be very highly respected for his grasp of substance and technique, for his personality, and for his managerial ability. . . . Fifty percent of graduates said that the most important things they gained from the experience were "new attitudes and conduct."[11]

Under USOM's In-Service Training Project, DOLA's Training Division expanded its capacities. The number of officials trained rose from around 1,800 in the Division's first year to nearly 18,000 in 1970. An evaluation of the program in 1971 also reached very favorable conclusions on the quality of its training. Caldwell notes that the quality of the three American advisors was "unusually high."

Several of the points I have made are illustrated in a routine bit of USOM staff work done in November 1967. In an unpublished nine-page trip report, the American ARD advisor stationed in Ubol province and a member of the USOM research division describe their findings after four days of discussions with officials, villagers, and several local farmers who had joined the CPT and then recently defected back to the government. Altogether about forty persons in this amphur (Leong Nok Tha) had returned to the government side and to active cooperation with local officials. The six men interviewed reported they had joined the CPT in response to propaganda appeals over government neglect of the poor and the offer of "study abroad," which turned out to be indoctrination and guerilla warfare training at Hoa Binh in North Vietnam.

The interpretation by the authors of the psychology of going over to the cause of insurgency is a simple statement of an insight that echoes the more elaborate analyses of the published social scientists:

> On the surface, it would appear that relatively simple persuasion was required to get men to join. However, [the] threshold of the man's resistance was overcome by the little persuasion on top of a relatively ambivalent loyalty-attitude which has been widely recognized and discussed in other research papers. Or, perhaps it would be fair to say that little persuasion was needed to draw the man away from a status quo that had too little positive appeal, based in the man's experience.
> . . . the men cited that conditions were better in their home areas than before. "Before" meant arrests for timber cutting and fines paid without receipts with an admonishment by the officers that a report to the Amphoe was not necessary . . . losing several rai of land . . . even though he held the initial permit . . . "The land officer refused to see me" . . . lack of medical facilities . . . fear of officials . . . [i.e.] circumstances that failed to elicit a strong attachment to the local Thai situation.[12]

After they returned to Thailand, the men said their morale began to erode because of the difficulties of insurgent life in the jungle and the realization that years of hardship lay ahead. The decision to defect was apparently triggered by their learning that the Nai Amphur had an open-arms amnesty policy under which they could return without punishment and work with the government. The returnees cited the improvements they found in their district in terms of activities in the villages and the "changed nature of personal relations" with the officials involved.

Describing these village development activities, the report notes the conviction of the officials that "the villager must be involved in meaningful activities with officials, and in a fashion that permits the villager to relate favorably to the government officials." In short, the nature of the interpersonal relations between villagers and officials is seen as the key to the problem; but at the same time, those relations must have content that is meaningful to the circumstances of village life. The authors reach the obvious conclusion that "to extend this program successfully over a large area will require very large resources in the form of motivated and well-trained Thai officials, and in the form of material" (p. 8). Given the components of USOM's various projects to help train the key officials, expand the capacity of the police to provide village-level protection, and provide major financing and material for "meaningful" activities in village access, water, and community development and health, agricultural, and other services, the aid program appears to have been guided by a coherent approach that related fairly directly to the village realities that were the context of the insurgency problem.

With so many novel things being attempted within an administrative framework that itself was recognized as part of the problem, it was inevitable that there would be many problems of counterproductive execution (as many observers expected). There were also outright project failures, which is also hardly surprising given the nature of the circumstances. A project that supported the creation of villager defense units collapsed after USOM financing ended because the police would not concur in an informal security program that put weapons in village hands.[13] Another project that would have set up ten-man teams in villages in sensitive areas to organize, democratize, and propagandize their villages, was conceived in the U.S. Embassy and then aborted by the Embassy, after it became clear that DOLA and the police would participate only under duress.[14]

Caldwell criticizes the USOM efforts for things omitted and misconstrued. I need not review his positions on psychological or tactical aspects of the RTG counterinsurgency effort and the U.S. role in it; in the event, as could not be known then, none of the inadequacies in his (and other critics') judgement proved decisive. His basic criticism is that the USOM program was wrongly conceived because it assumed there was a direct relationship between development and villager loyalty and therefore wrongly focused on development activities. On the other hand he views the emphasis on village access as well placed because it facilitated greater villager-official contact, which for him was the critical point in the contest with the CPT. The argument seems inconsistent: if the objective was increased and improved RTG-rural relationships, what would all this government contact have been about, if it were not a socially and economically relevant activity (apart from suppression of banditry and protection against CPT violence)? His argument also ignores the history of Northeast political discontent during the early years of open politics, touched on above, in which the economic disparity between the Northeasterners and the Central Thai was the main issue. In any event, both the RTG programs and the USOM project inputs attempted to address all the aspects of the insurgency problem that appeared significant, a reasonable approach when the stakes are high and the uncertainties are great.

It would take more extensive analysis of the complexities of this experience than is possible in this study to arrive at conclusions that could be called definitive on the relative importance and interactions of the factors listed earlier in bringing about the decline and disappearance of insurgency and the CPT in Thailand. In the late 1980s the "red tide" that was expected or feared in Southeast Asia twenty years ago now looks like past history. The years of warfare and the economic rules of the game imposed in the successor Indochina states have left them exhausted. The market economies have outperformed the region's varieties of socialist economies and brought greater benefits to the poor. As far as Thailand is concerned, those social scientists who opined in the 1960s and 1970s that neither Marxist rhetoric nor any adapted form of Marxist materialism would take root in Thai society appear to have been vindicated by circumstances. Those writers who emphasized the set of grievances and of weaknesses in the Thai polity as setting the stage for potential revolutionary change appear to have been proven wrong.

The debate among the social scientists holding these contrasting views had an unsatisfactory looseness and impressionistic quality. Both sides, looking ahead at impenetrable futures, sketched possible scenarios that seemed intelligently argued and plausible. It was impossible, of course, to put probabilities on the alternative scenarios and consider them more than personal judgements. And, most pertinent for an attempt to weigh the effects of individual factors and program interventions over time, there is no way of knowing what would have happened, what minor factors (such as the number of Thai villagers prepared to make the step from passive resentment to active opposition in extralegal forms) might have grown into numerically weighty factors, if the Thai government's multifarious responses had been different in content, magnitude, or execution.

These are not merely academic questions. If the pessimists had been right and the government's response inadequate, the recent history of the whole of Southeast Asia would have been altered profoundly, with possible implications for the current strategic positions of the United States and the Soviet Union in East Asia that could have been much less favorable for Thai and for U.S. interests than is now the case. It helps to give proper perspective to these questions to recall that some of the closest students of Thai political affairs could lay out plausible pessimistic scenarios and treat the Communist Party of Thailand as a serious factor as recently as eight years ago. The ink was barely dry on their analyses around 1980 when the insurgency went into sudden collapse.

The writers who said that Thai culture was too tough and hostile to appeals for subversion or revolutionary change stressed the non-combative and nonmaterialistic character of Buddhism and the individualism and disinterest in disciplined organization that the religion tends to create amongst its adherents.* They also stressed deeply rooted behavior patterns resistant to confrontation as a method of conflict resolution. The country is an old polity, never colonized, and is strongly attached to the symbols of monarchy and nation. Loyalty to the present King has probably been a factor of greater psychological importance than was recognized in the 1960s, a factor enormously strengthened by the King's frequent travel to the villages, his seasonal residence in different parts of the country, and his role (partly as a hydraulic engineer) in rural development in some of the most insecure areas through the hundreds of projects he has initiated.[15] Finally, for all the problems of poverty and isolation, landlessness was not a problem during the insurgency years, and there was no landlord class to speak of (except in certain parts of the Central Plain) such as has served as a primary target for rural-based insurrections in many countries.

In the end there is the simple fact that the insurgency has faded away, despite the turbulence of the 1973–1976 period and the year of repressive government that followed. The withdrawal of support from the PRC and the catastrophes in Vietnam and Cambodia may well have been major factors in the collapse of the CPT. But equal if not greater importance cannot be denied to the fact that the RTG recognized the village-level problems that the insurgency could have turned to its purposes, gradually blanketed the insurgent areas with development programs and benefits, and restaffed and retrained the cadre of district officers. The government began with strong assets in villager predispositions and attachments to the symbols of monarchy, religion, and country. Whatever it did was apparently sufficient to deny the CPT the social and economic "asset" potential (of discontent and deprivation) on which a successful insurgency could have been built. Given the important role the U.S. aid program played in this

---

*The occasional insurgent activity in the four Moslem provinces of the South is a separate problem, having more to do with Malay identification and feelings of cultural discrimination than with the political or economy-based issues of the CPT or of the disaffected students. The number of Moslem insurgents remaining after the government's amnesty program of 1980–1981 is believed to be very low. This local antigovernment violence is apparently still capable of occasional revival. A rash of incidents in the first few months of 1988 is described in *Asiaweek*, April 15, 1988, p. 27.

denial process, it appears to deserve the credit accorded to it by those Thais who believe USOM made signal contributions to the restoration of stability and the country's subsequent ability to get back to the business of economic development.

POPULATION

Although counterinsurgency was the dominant theme of the aid program during this period, there were many other development projects underway, working on problems some of which rivaled counterinsurgency in their long-run import. One of the most significant of these other subjects was population. The Thai population had been growing slowly for decades, rising from around 8 million when the first census was taken in 1911 to perhaps 18 million in 1942, when Prime Minister Pibul stated that the country needed to reach 100 million people as a basis for national power. Before 1960 Thai governments had been pronatalist and had tried to promote large families and early marriage.

Mortality fell rapidly after World War II, from 30 deaths per thousand to less than 15 by the mid-1960s. The population growth rate rose from the prewar rate of 1.9 percent to 3.3 percent around 1960. The first suggestion that this explosive population growth was detrimental to the country's development came from the World Bank's economic study mission in 1959. The mission noted that the "already fairly high" population growth rate would rise further, causing economic "pressures," and recommended the promotion of family planning.[16] By 1962 the government had begun formal reconsideration of its population policies, a process that led to Cabinet adoption in 1970 of a policy of reducing the country's population growth rate.

The policy change process was marked by a series of seminars, official studies, and pilot projects that tested the potential public interest in family planning and possible political repercussions. The New York–based Population Council played an important role in this process, financing the first national seminar held on population policy, in 1963, and further technical and financial support for subsequent seminars and pilot family-planning projects. Although there was some opinion in the RTG, especially in the Ministry of Interior, that Thailand still had empty land needing to be settled and that population growth should not be discouraged, all the formal studies by the National Research Council, the Ministry of Public Health, and NESDB concluded that the adverse effects of population growth (on the education system, employment, demands on the health system, pressure on marginal lands, and so on) were substantial.

The policy reexamination decade culminated in a report to the Thai Cabinet in February 1970, prepared by NESDB's Population Unit (which had been set up two years before with Population Council assistance) in collaboration with the Health Ministry and the Institute of Population Studies (located at Chulalongkorn University, and established also with assistance from the Population Council and the University of North Carolina). Noting that the growth rate would climb even higher if nothing were done to offset the continuing fall in mortality rates, the report stressed that detrimental effects of population growth fell largely on the rural poor. Five years of pilot projects had shown a strong interest in family planning among virtually all segments of the population and a demand so strong, in fact, that it could be met only by the kind of large-scale program that could be developed by government, complemented by the activities of the private voluntary agencies and commercial distribution of contraceptives. The report recommended a formal population growth reduction policy, family-planning programs, supporting research, and formal machinery to coordinate the efforts of the agencies involved. Although the Cabinet resolution adopting an antinatalist policy was "so vaguely worded that the government's intentions remained unclear," the Ministry of Public Health took the decision as a mandate for full-scale program development.[17]

From the first pilot family-planning projects, through the years of rapid program expansion after the formal adoption of a population policy, family planning in Thailand has been remarkable for innovation and pragmatism. The Thais have experimented with a wide variety of contraceptive techniques and delivery systems. The authorization for trained paramedics and/or traditional midwife practitioners to provide contraceptive services (IUD insertion, pill distribution, Depo-Provera injection, and the like) greatly expanded the availability of the means for family planning. Postpartum programs in hospitals, educational and distribution schemes run by private voluntary agencies, and community-based distribution systems were among the panoply of promotional and service programs introduced in the 1960s and 1970s. While some of these ideas were proposed to the Thais from the outside (and implemented with assistance from agencies such as the Population Council, AID, the U.N. Fund for Population Activities (UNFPA), UNICEF, WHO, International Planned Parenthood Federation, and the World Bank), many novel approaches were developed by the Thais themselves. Some of these innovations (including the minilap female sterilization procedure, which can be performed as an outpatient procedure without general anesthetic, developed by Thai physicians in 1972) were adopted in family-planning programs throughout the world.[18]

The national program that emerged during the first few years had the following characteristics: 1) family planning was integrated into the existing health services, not offered as a separately administered program; 2) a number of elements thought to be important in programs in other countries, such as incentive payments to health workers or acceptors and employment of full-time family-planning workers were not adopted; 3) accessibility was greatly expanded by liberalizing the rules governing what kinds of health personnel could perform specific family planning services; 4) the program had solid support from Thailand's strong medical profession, providing good technical leadership; 5) in-service training programs reached throughout the delivery system; 6) there was good coordination between the health ministry and other governmental and nongovernmental agencies (especially the very innovative Thai Population and Community Development Association) providing family planning and related services; and 7) the communications and mobility required to manage the logistics of the system were facilitated by the infrastructure systems that were expanding during this period. Needless to say, no program of this magnitude, with all its innovations and sudden changes in norms, could have been implemented without many problems of management, logistics, coordination, monitoring, and so on. Perhaps most fundamental to its success was the early attention to building up institutional capacity to conduct research and evaluation and the willingness of the health authorities to take research findings into account and adjust their programs accordingly.[19]

In the first decade under the antinatal policy, the Thais achieved striking results. Contraceptive use among married women fifteen to forty-four years of age rose from 14 percent in 1969–1970 to 58 percent in 1981. So-called continuation rates (measuring the extent to which women who adopt a contraceptive method continue to use it) "are among the highest reported in the developing world."[20] The demographic impact was immediate and powerful, as Allen Rosenfeld and his coresearchers found:

> The total fertility rate in Thailand dropped from 6.5 births per woman in 1962–1963 to 4.0 in 1974–1975, the annual rate of population increase fell from three percent in the late 1960s to less than two percent by 1982, and is pro-

jected to fall to 1.5 percent by the end of 1986. While it is true that the decline started before the NFPP [National Family Planning Program] was organized, it only began to gain momentum in 1968, the year after the forerunner of the national program was established. The fertility decline has taken place in all regions of the country (although northern and central Thailand have experienced the most rapid declines), among women in urban and rural areas, and among the less educated as well as the better educated. Northeastern Thailand, which is both the most populous and the poorest region, has experienced the greatest fertility decline in recent years, while southern Thailand, which has a large Islamic population, still lags behind the other regions.[21]

In 1965, with a birth rate of 41 per thousand population and a death rate of 10 per thousand, Thailand's population growth rate was 3.1 percent. By 1985 (with female contraceptive use estimated at 65 percent) the birth rate had dropped to 26 per thousand, the death rate to 8, and the growth rate to 1.6 percent. The birth rate had been cut 37 percent, and the total fertility rate (the number of children that would be born to a woman who, over her productive span, had children at the rates [for each age] prevailing in that year) had fallen to 3.2. The World Bank has projected that Thailand could reach a net reproduction rate of one (that is, the "replacement level") by the year 2000, at which time the country would have about 66 million people, compared with the present population of about 55 million. (Due to the young age structure, the population would continue to grow for many years after the reproductive rate of the child-bearing population is down to replacement level and is projected by the Bank to top out at around 100 million.)[22]

The extraordinary character of this demographic transformation can be appreciated by comparing the Thai experience with other countries, as J. Knodel, Aphichat Chamratrithirong, and Nibhon Debavalya do in their study:

> The place of Thailand within this list of [fifteen largest third world] countries is of considerable interest to those concerned with changing patterns of childbearing. The fertility decline in Thailand is the third largest decline behind only South Korea and China. If the dominating case of China is excluded, the average fertility decline for the re-

maining lesser developed countries collectively is only slightly over half the magnitude in Thailand (24 percent compared to 44 percent). Thailand's total fertility rate of 6.4 during the first half of the 1960s was quite typical of large Third World countries, if anything, slightly above average. By the first half of the 1980s, total fertility in Thailand had fallen to 3.6 and was the third lowest rate of all 15 countries.[23]

The 64 percent contraceptive prevalence of 1984 was close to the estimated average prevalence of 68 percent for the developed countries. According to these same authors, "The relatively high level of recent prevalence in Thailand is particularly remarkable given the very low levels that characterized Thailand less than two decades ago" (p. 6). Quite apart from the significance of this demographic change for Thailand, it appears to be an experience of unusual potential for the general understanding of population change, perhaps challenging some of the basic concepts that have been drawn from historical demography, principally the idea of the mechanics of demographic "transition," in which populations experience first a period of rapid growth as mortality rates fall and then a lagged fall in fertility as a gradual response to the broad process of socioeconomic development (and the educational, urbanizing, and other changes that comprise such development). The same study notes:

> Although Thailand is not among the least developed of the Third World countries, neither does it rank particularly high with regard to many conventional indices of socioeconomic development. Most striking, perhaps, is that the fertility transition is taking place while the Thai population is still largely rural and agricultural. There seems to be a general receptivity among broad segments of the population, including those with little or modest education and living in rural areas, to the changes in reproductive patterns that are now taking place. An examination of the Thai demographic transition, and particularly the fertility decline, is important not only in terms of the heightened policy concerns about rapid population growth that have developed over the last few decades but also in terms of understanding the determinants of fertility transition, one of the central problems of modern population science.
> The transformation in reproductive attitudes and behav-

ior that has been taking place in Thailand over the last
decades is so far-sweeping and profound that it can aptly
be called a reproductive revolution. (P. 8)

There is no doubt that the international agencies assisting Thailand's health and development policy authorities made important
contributions to these achievements. In the very earliest years, when
public response, medical acceptability, administrative mechanisms,
and monitoring and research techniques had to be tested without
benefit of a government policy or budget, the technical inputs and
financial aid from the outside were of prime importance to the Thais
who were in the vanguard of population policy concern. The role of
the experts provided by the Population Council in particular, starting
in 1963, in the development of the first research and policy analysis
and in the creation of some of the key institutional capacities, along
with the participant training the Council financed for medical and
demographic cadre, is readily and graciously acknowledged by Thais
who were involved.[24] For most of the 1960s the Council's work in
Thailand was funded largely by the Rockefeller and Ford foundations.

AID's direct assistance to the population program began in 1968.
The AID project was particularly important as a source of funds to
supplement the RTG budget for the National Family Planning Program (NFPP). In the years 1972–1981 AID funding amounted to about
37 percent of the total expenditures on NFPP, with UNFPA providing
about 17 percent and the RTG funding most of the remainder (with
smaller UNICEF, Japanese, and other contributions). A second AID
population project followed in 1982 and was completed in 1989. The
total AID direct input amounted to about $32 million. These projects
financed commodities, local training for NFPP field staff, research
and evaluation, and participant training in the United States. Additional resources were provided through centrally funded AID projects
with the Population Council, the Association for Voluntary Sterilization, Family Planning International Assistance, the Research Triangle
Institute, the Program for International Training in Health, International Planned Parenthood Federation, and the Program for International Education in Gynecology and Obstetrics. The AID projects were
recurrently evaluated by outside experts and appear to have been
implemented and monitored with care.

The whole demographic and family-planning experience thus far
stands out as an exemplary case of effective external support in one of
the major component processes of modern development. Many of the
individual foreigners involved were unusually competent in their field

and adept at crosscultural professional collaboration. The leading Thais involved in this process were also people of high competence, who understood how to bring about basic policy change in their society. They were also within the tradition of Thai receptivity to working with and adapting to the ideas of foreigners, and they knew how to make good use of outside expertise. In the judgment of one of the principal Americans contributing to this experience,[25] the Thais would have arrived at the same policy and programmatic position by themselves, but the foreigners enabled them to get there faster and more effectively by supplementing their technical and financial resources at the right time. The widespread preference for smaller families among the Thai population, the flexibility and pragmatism of the health authorities and their willingness to try reasonable proposals put forward by respected experts, the refusal to be bound by ideological approaches to their problems, the absence of any theological basis in Buddhism for opposing family planning—these were the necessary conditions behind the experience. The external aid (and the international sanction provided by the antinatal stance of the U.N. system agencies) provided some of the sufficient conditions for moving the whole process along at a faster pace. The cumulative gains in time, from a slowing of the growth in school-age population, to slower growth in the requirements for employment generation in the 1990s, and the whole complex of implications of a lower population growth curve and ultimate stabilization at population levels substantially below what they would have been otherwise will be of profound significance for the future development of the country.

SIX

FOCUS ON POVERTY, 1975–1984

For nine years between 1965 and 1974 the basic rationale for the Thai aid program was to help the RTG cope with internal and external security threats. During this decade supporting assistance (SA), which was the appropriation category for grant funds the Congress provided for security-oriented assistance (in contrast to Technical Assistance and Development Loans), came to be the major appropriation source for funding the Thai program. The FY 1974 *Congressional Presentation* section on Thailand begins with the familiar restatement of the rationale of the preceding years:

> The basic U.S. assistance objective is to help improve Thai capacity for dealing with threats to its internal and external security. Supporting Assistance strengthens the ability of the government to maintain economic growth and internal stability over the long term.[1]

A year later the program's objectives had changed quite fundamentally. The basic reasoning is summed up in the FY 1975 submission to Congress:

> The objective of U.S. assistance is to help Thailand become a stronger and more modern nation, particularly by helping her to mobilize her natural and human resources in an

effective manner while reducing the economic disparities that exist among certain segments of the population and among various sections of the country.

Given the fact that the United States has accomplished about all that can be accomplished by an external donor in assisting in the development of the Thai counterinsurgency capability, and taking into account the emergence of a new civilian-dominated government in Thailand with which a more conventional aid relationship appears to be called for, it is appropriate and feasible to shift from Supporting Assistance to an emphasis on economic and social development for the purpose of improving the welfare of that segment of Thai society that has not heretofore shared the benefits of economic growth.

A.I.D. assistance will be concentrated primarily on those sectors in which progress would contribute directly to the well-being of the rural poor.[2]

The *Presentation* narrative also notes that assistance to the Thai police was ending "in accordance with foreign assistance legislation" and that FY 1975 would be the last year of funding for the ARD project. The return to a development focus was reflected in the funding shift from SA to the new Development Assistance (DA) "Functional Account" categories of Education and Human Resources Development, Population Planning and Health, and Food Production and Nutrition, which were introduced into the so-called "New Directions" aid legislation in 1973.

As shown in table A.1, the U.S. aid level (excluding PL 480) had been declining every year since the peak in 1967. The reduction in funding requirements of the ARD and police programs was the main reason for this decline. The FY 75 *Congressional Presentation* notes the change in funding composition but does not explain that the cessation of ARD funding would bring the aid level down to its lowest volume in twenty years. In addition to the termination of the big counterinsurgency projects, other factors and arguments came together at this time to reduce the size of the overall program. The decline of the need for insurgency assistance coincided with the U.S. withdrawal from Vietnam and the subsequent closing down of the U.S. airbases in Thailand and withdrawal of U.S. forces. With the elimination (temporary as it turned out, given the Vietnamese occupation of Cambodia in 1979) of the regional security rationale, there was a revival in administration and congressional quarters of the argument (first made in the 1952 *Congressional Presentation,* it will be recalled) that Thailand had less of an economic need than many other aid recipients. To accommodate to this view, AID began in FY 1974 to "harden" the aid terms by providing some portion of the annual program in the form of loans rather than all grants. There was also some consideration of closing down the aid mission altogether, leaving residual activities under the management of the Embassy. While the idea of complete closure never became policy, the Bangkok mission staff was reduced very sharply (partly in response to general congressional pressure on AID to lower its overhead costs). In fact both the American and Thai employee complement of the mission already had been declining from the peak numbers of 1969, when the U.S. staff (including contract personnel) stood at 423 and the Thai staff at 527, for a total of 950. Sharp cuts were made between 1973 and 1976, bringing the American staff down from 141 to 33, and the Thai staff from 418 to 77, levels that have remained almost constant in the years since.

Except for the dropping of ARD and aid to the police, the line between the "Counterinsurgency" period and the "Focus on Poverty" was not very sharp in practice. The agriculture and health projects, continuing activities that had grown directly out of the projects of the 1950s and 1960s, were focused on the rural population, in the Northeast in particular, and were appropriate to both counterinsurgency and poverty-oriented programs, as I noted above. The rural poor comprised the major fraction of the population to whom family-planning services were being extended. The general participant-training projects of the period fed the basic institutional capacity-building that was seen as underlying all RTG and U.S. program objectives.* (The last remaining project of the transitional year provided continued funding for a narcotics control activity described below.)

Under the 1973 legislation AID began to build up its centrally funded activities. These comprised a broad span of projects managed by the central technical bureau in AID/W, most of which could make available to interested field missions technical assistance additional to the programs the missions were running with country-allocated funds. While some of the centrally funded projects dovetailed closely with mission-funded projects (as in aspects of family-planning research that were more effectively developed first by American university or other contracts), other projects offered assistance in subjects

---

*The importance of strengthening the institutional capacities to deal with poverty was apparently not universally understood. Some New Directions advocates sought to eliminate all "general" participant training projects on the grounds that they did not directly benefit the poor.

(such as specific crops) that were not integral to the programs of many individual missions. The centrally funded program was also increasingly poverty-oriented.

This phase of the aid program also saw a rise in mission funding of private voluntary organizations (PVOs) as intermediaries working directly with the poor and underprivileged; a small-scale hydroelectric project to introduce a new energy technology as part of the RTG's programs to cope with the effects of the second "oil shock" in 1979; and housing investment guarantees aimed at lower-income shelter.

In the FY 1983 *Congressional Presentation*, the poverty orientation of the program was for the first time complemented by new themes of assistance to the private business sector and of the need to reorient the program in light of the preceding decades of development. In FY 1984 this recognition of Thailand's increasing institutional maturation and of the transformation and modernization processes at work in the economy appears explicitly in a reference to Thailand having moved "into the ranks of the emerging middle income countries" and the move of AID "adapting its approach to reflect this transition" by addressing both "efficiency and equity."[3] While the focus on poverty continues to be a strong theme into 1988, the current program is in a transitional period again, as the projects developed to be pertinent to Thailand's middle-income status have moved in quite different directions. Since the shift to a middle income status orientation for the Thai aid program was formally adopted by AID in February 1985, I date the poverty focus period of the program from 1975 to 1984.

INCOME AND POVERTY IN THAILAND IN THE MID-1970S

The attention given to poverty alleviation in the Foreign Assistance Act of 1973 reflected a dissatisfaction in the international development community and in many developing countries over the course of third world development in the postwar period.* Developing coun-

---

* A few sentences from Section 102, Development Assistance policy, are worth quoting here because they refer to many of the features of the AID projects discussed below:

> The Congress declares that the principal purpose of United Stated bilateral development assistance is to help the poor majority of people in developing countries to participate in a process of equitable growth through productive work and to influence decisions that shape their lives, with the goal of increasing their incomes and their access to public services which will enable them to satisfy their basic needs and lead lives of decency, dignity and hope. Activities shall be emphasized that effectively involve the poor in development by expand-

tries as a whole had been expanding at rates that had exceeded the pace of growth ever experienced by the rich countries during their earlier decades of industrialization. The developing countries appeared to be benefiting from the catch-up opportunities available through transfers of technology from the more advanced economies. Those developing countries able to participate in the growth of world trade (itself the result of European and North American economic expansion combined with the continuing process of trade liberalization) were also hooked up to a powerful engine of growth that only began to run into trouble after the first oil price "shock" in 1973. The ranks of the developing countries had grown rapidly as decolonization brought independence to large areas. Although growth rates varied widely among the developing countries and major differences (of institutional capacity, economic structure, social stability, and economic prospects) were already evident in the 1960s, there was broad satisfaction that development was generally on track, even if for many countries the achievement of acceptable standards of living was still a good way off.

To be sure, there were disagreements on the future. The mainstream of development economics had concluded that the Latin American effort to push growth harder, through a combination of high protective barriers for domestic import-substituting industrial development and inflationary financing of public sector investment, had been taken to counterproductive lengths and that the correct formula for sustainable growth was a combination of more conservative fiscal policies, more open and competitive markets, and greater encouragement of foreign investment. Many developing country intellectuals had a very different perspective; they viewed the international economic system as governed by a set of rules that favored the rich countries and deprived the poorer countries of their rightful share of the system's growing wealth.

Especially for those who had been satisfied with the course of development, the end of the 1960s brought disturbing evidence (from census data, household surveys, and other sources) that the benefits of the aggregate growth many developing countries had been enjoying were distributed very unevenly among their populations. The income

---

ing their access to the economy through services and institutions at the local level, increasing their participation in the making of decisions that affect their lives, increasing labor-intensive production and the use of appropriate technology, expanding productive investment and services out from major cities to small towns and rural areas, and otherwise providing opportunities for the poor to improve their lives through their own efforts. (U.S. Senate, U.S. House of Representatives, *Legislation on Foreign Relations Through 1986*, Current Legislation and Related Executive Orders, 1:18)

differentials between higher- and lower-income groups were widening in many countries. In some cases (Brazil was one of the key countries over which this was fiercely debated) the evidence appeared to show that the absolute level of poverty of the lowest 10 to 20 percent of households (the lowest one or two deciles of the income distribution) had actually deepened. In the terms in which the problem was discussed, growth was not "trickling down," and GNP had to be "dethroned" as the object and measurement of the purposes and pace of economic development.

The finding that economic growth was not distributed evenly was not surprising. In his pioneering work on the historical development of the industrial countries, Professor Simon Kuznets first observed the apparently general experience over several decades in which income distribution became more skewed in the early years of industrial transformation and then returned to a more even pattern as these economies had matured. (Simon Kuznets, *Six Lecturer on Economic Growth;* The Free Press of Glenco, Ill., 1959.) Taiwan and Korea in particular stand as examples of how much more quickly the distribution can be turned around in a fast-growing economy depending on the economic policy framework imposed by government (and on the initial social and economic conditions—such as the land ownership patterns—that constrained or facilitated the emergence of equitable distribution). In sharp contrast, various forms of "socialist" economic models appeared to offer more direct policy routes for achieving greater economic equity.

Out of this complex debate, the international development "establishment" (including the World Bank, pieces of the U.N. system, and some of the development research faculties and institutions) shaped a revision in its consensus strategy for developing countries. Instead of pressing solely or mainly for growth maximization, symbolized by the focus on the expansion of measured aggregate output, or GNP, development policies and programs were to be adjusted so that the relatively poor segments of the population could "participate" in the growth process directly, mainly through policies that would promote employment and the growth of the agriculture sector and programs and projects that would directly and quickly meet the "basic needs" of the poor. "Participation" meant direct involvement of the poor in the (usually local) processes through which projects (for their benefit or their vicinity) were chosen and formulated and direct receipt by the poor of the benefits of development. "Basic needs" referred to health care, literacy, shelter, nutritional status, and other things of obvious primacy for the notion of a minimally acceptable standard of living, even if it was very modest. The reader not familiar with these terms or the issues they raise will appreciate that the terms are loose, that societies and governments (and aid agencies) have different ideas about the political and economic content of participation, and that basic needs depend on the conditions in any society, the political processes through which resources are allocated, and how the interests of contending groups are harmonized or conflict.

The primacy accorded to participation and basic needs gave rise to extensive research on poverty—how it should be defined and measured and what could be done to reduce it—and to a whole new generation of development projects. As we have seen in the Thai case, much of the content of development programs had been directed at things that affected the living conditions of the poor directly from the very beginning of the post–World War II push for development. The new concern for faster impact on the poor resulted in some reorientation of these ongoing activities (as in health, as described below) and in some new approaches altogether.

What was the condition of the poor, the nature of the poverty problem in Thailand, as the AID program changed its focus? I shall spell out the framework of the problem, even if only briefly, in order to be able to evaluate the objectives and results of the aid program's efforts in this regard.

Once the Thai economy overcame the initial problems of postwar adjustment, including the reestablishment of a sound exchange rate and fiscal policies in the first half of the 1950s, economic growth got off to a good start. In the 1960s the pace accelerated, with growth reaching over 9 percent in real terms in the second half of the decade, or over 6 percent per capita. Different factors were prominent at different times during these two decades as spurs to the country's economic expansion—export prices, new export markets for nontraditional crops, rising domestic savings and investment levels, increasing foreign assistance, and (in the mid-1960s especially) the high levels of U.S. military expenditures in Thailand. The latter in particular contributed to the country's ability to increase its foreign exchange reserves and avoid inflation despite the rapid growth in economic activity.

Although agricultural output grew at a very respectable 5 percent a year in the 1960s, the faster growth of the GNP as a whole reflected the higher rates of expansion in manufacturing, construction and other sectors, which were beginning to change the country's economic structure. Agriculture's share in total output fell from 40 percent in 1960 to around 32 percent by the end of the decade; nevertheless, 80 percent of the labor force was counted as agricultural. The disparities between labor productivity in agriculture and productivity in other sectors and the concentration of manufacturing, banking, and government in the Bangkok region meant that Thailand's rapid overall growth was unevenly distributed geographically and between urban and rural households. Already in the late 1960s, the problem of distribution was recognized as arising out of the structural characteristics of Thai growth, aggravated by the regional aspects discussed above and the economic dimensions of the insurgency. The position as of 1970 was described by the World Bank as follows:

> Thailand's economic growth over the past decade has largely resulted from the activities of a dynamic private sector, assisted by external capital and operating in an environment of stable economic policies. These policies have been implemented principally by indirect means, in monetary and fiscal affairs as well as regarding the promotion of investment and saving. The activities of the public sector have, with few exceptions, been aimed to preserve stability and security and to improve the country's infrastructure.
>
> The rapid growth of the economy and the need to maintain security have resulted in growing attention to existing disparities of income within the country. The relatively slow growth of agriculture and the concentration of new economic activities in Bangkok have widened the gap between urban and rural incomes which was already substantial at the outset. Insurgencies in the Northeast, North and South have led to increased security spending in these areas, but have also brought to the fore the need for regional planning aimed at the improvement of living conditions and economic opportunities in the provinces.[4]

The turbulent years between 1970 and 1975 (when the focus of the AID program shifted from security to poverty) were marked by the first oil shock, sharp swings in the prices of Thailand's main export commodities, and the dramatic political events initiated by the student demonstrations of 1973. The continuity and stability of development planning of the previous years was interrupted. Still, in late 1974 the World Bank recorded continued progress at the macroeconomic level:

> The good performance of the Thai economy continued during the first three years of the Third Plan [1972–1974]. Real GDP expanded rapidly; investment and saving have been high for a country with $230 per capita income; the external accounts have been kept well under control; and domestic prices were stable until driven upward by massive external forces.[5]

I need not recount the details of those years. The important conclusion as far as the purposes of the aid program were concerned was the impact of these events for raising the importance of lagging rural incomes. While the rise of poverty to the top agenda of national economic issues has not been even or continuous, it did become a major dimension of Thai development planning and of political concern.

The great majority of Thailand's poor live in rural areas. It is important to note, parenthetically, that while virtually everyone living in rural Thailand in the 1950s was poor, the poverty in this land-abundant country seldom was as deep as in the Indian subcontinent, the Brazilian Northeast, or others of the Third World's most disadvantaged regions. Thai rural poverty tends to be concentrated in the Northeast and other areas where the agricultural natural resource endowment is itself poor. With average urban (mostly Bangkok) incomes roughly two and a half times rural income levels in 1969, the salient characteristic of poverty in Thailand was its geographic association and derivation. At a local level within poor rural areas, there were income differences among villages. Those villages that had better soil conditions, were closer to roads, or were higher on the queue for government services (such as MDU units or small-scale irrigation works) tended to get on an income growth track earlier than less favored villages. Within a single village, however, income disparities normally were not great. Land holdings did not vary much in size (there was nothing comparable to the vast differences between mini-smallholders and large plantation owners that marks economies in Latin America or the Philippines), and tenancy and landlessness were not significant problems, except in some local areas of the North and the Central Plain.

The typical poor farm family put much of its labor and land into producing the rice that would comprise its staple diet for the year. With the transportation and marketing infrastructure quite limited in the Northeast, the most rational survival strategy, tested through generations, precluded the high risks of relying on the production and sale of nonstaples, even if their value, if successfully marketed, would exceed that of rice (in terms of the net return to the land and labor involved). The farmer relied on cattle and buffalo traction for working the soil. The family's human capital assets were limited, constraining their upward mobility. There were only rudimentary health or welfare services to serve as a safety net for families that ran into trouble.

There were important social assets, however, that offered some mitigation of these circumstances. Families would typically send one son into the Buddhist monkhood. The village monks, residing in the local *wat* (temple), performed important social and psychological support functions for the villagers, who in turn, according to long tradition, provided the monks with the daily food and the few robes and articles the Buddhist monks are allowed to possess. Any food the monks did not consume each day was available for destitute villagers for the taking. Geographic labor mobility emerged during the 1960s as an increasingly important economic trend. Seasonal movement of the young to take temporary harvesting work in other parts of the country or jobs in Bangkok began to be important as supplementary sources of income for previously subsistent families. In the 1970s employment on construction projects in the Middle East began to draw large numbers of young Northeasterners. There were no caste or class barriers to serve as additional constraints on the poor as in many other societies.

The constraints on income growth in the Northeast were more severe than in other parts of the country. Even subsistence was not easily wrung out of its poor soil and its irregular rainfall. The soils respond poorly to chemical fertilizers. Rainfall is often heavy in the monsoon months between June and October, causing lowland floods. In many areas the soil is sandy and does not hold water. The dry season is long and hot, and seasonal shortage of potable water is common. Between late arrival and inadequate volume of rainfall, Northeast crops tend to fail one year out of three. Rain-fed rice cultivation has long been the main agricultural occupation. The principal varieties of rice grown in the Northeast are glutinous, or sticky. Glutinous rice is the preferred staple of the Northeast diet, although there is virtually no international trade in glutinous varieties and they fetch lower prices than nonglutinous rice in the domestic market.

The pressure against diminishing forested areas in the Northeast was rising rapidly during the postwar years. In the twenty years before the war, the population of the Northeast had been increasing by about one million persons a decade. Between 1950 and 1960 the population rose an estimated 2 million, and by 1970 another 3 million. Compared with the region's population of 3 million in 1920, with a density of 19 per square kilometer, the population in 1970 was 11.7 million and the density 73 per square kilometer. Over the whole period, the Northeast population remained about one-third of the country's total inhabitants.

With water one of the principal factors in the relative poverty of the Northeast, water projects have figured importantly among RTG and donor programs to improve conditions in the region. Unfortunately, only about 15 percent of the arable land of the Northeast is potentially irrigable, given the topographic and water-flow limitations on reservoir impoundment and river water pumping. By 1987 only about 7 percent of the region's cultivated area was being irrigated. As noted earlier, the tank irrigation program USOM had helped finance from the early 1950s had produced very disappointing results.

By the early 1970s agricultural research in the Northeast had developed very little in the way of improved technology. The occasional "boom" in a new crop had taken place quite apart from any government programs. Except for the kenaf boom of the late 1950s (which had faded in the mid-1960s when export prices fell) and the boom in cassava exports to Europe for animal feed (cassava production spread rapidly to the Northeast in the early seventies, and has continued on), diversification has taken hold more slowly than in other parts of the country. Industrial development apart from milling was minimal, limited to small-scale manufacturing of food products, small farm implements, and other items for local markets in the region. Manufacturing on a larger scale would be dependent on the development of larger output of agricultural products needing to be processed into exportable forms. This would require the integrated development of production, processing, and marketing networks, based on small farm suppliers and institutional and economic innovations that were not evident in the 1970s.

THE USAID POVERTY PROGRAM

Three approaches were open to the mission. The first was to work at the level of the individual village by linking up with the Peace Corps and giving grants to private voluntary organizations that work directly with the poor. The second option was the site-specific, typically multisectoral, or "integrated," area development project, involving many villages that formed a coherent grouping by virtue of location in an irrigation command area or within some administrative structure. The third option involved activities at a more general systemic or regional level, specifically helping to develop breakthroughs in technologies that could be applied by large numbers of poor farmers or strengthening the institutional structures or administrative systems that had development-promoting responsibilities pertinent to problems of poverty (preferably with direct contact and involvement of the target groups). The fourth possible approach—continued investment in infrastructure—was ruled out by the limited resources available to the program, the availability of substantial investment funds from the World Bank and other donors, and by the prevailing AID philosophy against projects that appeared to be only indirectly, if not questionably, related to the economic position of the poor. (Although there was occasional debate within AID/W over distinctions between the "poor majority" in general and the "poorest of the poor" and over whether AID projects should be required or pressed to "reach" the very poorest, this further distinction was not adopted as a planning criterion.)

The first two options had the great advantage, as far as AID/W and Congress were concerned (and domestic supporters of AID who were motivated by a feeling of responsibility to make sure that aid from a rich country actually benefited identifiable poor people), that one could "see the whites of the eyes" of the poor. The beneficiaries could be identified and counted. Compared with the unstructured and uncertain flow of benefits that would—that might—"trickle down" from a major highway or an addition to power generating capacity or the strengthening of a university to the people in the lower deciles of the income distribution, these projects offered the prospects of fine-tuning the flow of benefits. In countries governed by regimes indifferent to poverty, such projects offered a way around government altogether, a way to promote long-term growth and carry out morally justifiable resource transfers despite a hostile environment. Although governmental or elite hostility to policies or resource allocations favoring the poor was not a characteristic of many aid recipients, including Thailand, the implementation (and chief constituencies) of the New Directions legislation did not distinguish between equitable and inequitable policy environments and called for whites-of-the-eyes projects as a general requirement. Area concentration would enable AID to apply relatively substantial resources in relation to the numbers of beneficiaries, albeit at the cost of severely limiting the beneficiaries to small fractions of a country's poor.

The third option had the appeal of leverage. If one could identify weaknesses of concept and implementation in the systems and institutions that were working to alleviate aspects of a country's poverty, relatively small investments to correct such problems might have large-scale benefits by raising the efficiency and impact of poverty-oriented programs. Of course, many weaknesses of public administration in Thailand had been addressed by technical assistance projects for years before the poverty focus of the mid-1970s. Still, the reform and strengthening of institutional processes is a long-term proposition; with the perspective of poverty alleviation in mind, specific characteristics of the institutional structure could be identified as most pertinent and most likely, if strengthened, to yield the desired results for the low-income beneficiaries.

In the remainder of this chapter I will review the experience of AID's projects under the three options. The projects identified by AID as poverty-oriented during this period are listed in table A.12, grouped under the option categories described above.

Option One: Hands-On

USAID has had two programs in recent years in which the beneficiaries were unambiguously known to be among the poor, even among the "poorest of the poor." One of these, the Accelerated Impact Program, provided small grants for individual village projects undertaken by Peace Corps volunteers. The idea was to give the villagers ready access to small amounts of money needed to implement volunteer-assisted activities, but not readily obtainable from the normal procedures of the government bureaucracy. The average size of a grant was $580. The projects covered the usual range of village activities (water storage, weaving, fish ponds, livestock, and the like) and were supposed to be replicable and set up as revolving funds. The project has been operating since 1983, at a level of about $50,000 a year from AID central funds. An evaluation in 1984 gave the project high marks.[6]

This "impact" project has been a relatively minor activity in the aid program. It is worth some reflection, nevertheless, because it comes closest to meeting the criteria and objectives of an ideal poverty-oriented activity as conceived in much of the literature on basic needs development strategies. All the individual subprojects took place in villages. The AID grants went directly into the village project funding mechanisms—that is, neither the funds nor the activities were "trickle-down" in character. The activities were chosen and implemented by the "participating" beneficiaries, who provided both their own funds and labor, in a form of "self-help". The technologies involved were simple and labor-intensive—"appropriate," in other words. Each subproject required only a few hundred dollars of supplementary external aid. The activities appeared sensible and useful and were administered hands-on by Americans living close to the local life-style.

Despite these merits, the Impact village project approach cannot be a model for an aid program that is designed to make as widespread and substantial a dent on poverty as is possible for the amount of funds available to the program as a whole. One subproject of this nature in a village is unlikely to have a major impact on the income level or entire range of basic needs that must be met even in that village; yet, if every poor village so defined were to get one such grant a year from AID, it would take roughly between $7 and $17 million,* a substantial fraction of the total funds available. An even greater constraint on the feasibility of this approach is its management intensity. The evaluation noted that "Successful supervision of this project was extremely time-consuming." It would also take a small army of Peace Corps volunteers. The Peace Corps program in Thailand has been running at a level of about 175 volunteers for a total cost (including supervision and support) of around $2 million a year. Thus the total cost to the United States of a large-scale Impact type program would be considerably greater than the village grant levels themselves.

Finally, and perhaps most important, are the questions of substance raised by attempting to assist development at the village level through a direct, or "retail," program. The Peace Corps unquestionably does useful work in Thailand and is a popular program among the Thais. But the basic rationale and purpose of all the volunteer programs (there are several from other donor countries as well as a U.N.-sponsored volunteer program) lies in their symbolic and psychological value as demonstrations of concern among the people of donor countries, in contrast with their governments, for the welfare of people in disadvantaged countries. The contributions of the volunteers to the advancement of the families and villagers with whom they work are certainly real, but they are not presumed to have the element of

*A classification system currently used by NESDB puts villages into three categories depending on the extent to which they have various amenities, social capital, production activities, and so forth. Of the 52,908 villages in 1986, 20 percent were considered "progressive," 25 percent "backward", and 55 percent "middle." The low figure of $7 million is based on the "backward" 13,000 villages; the $17 million, on the backward plus the 29,000 middle. Figures are taken from NESDB, "A Profile of Rural Development Conditions in Thailand in 1986," the Rural Development Monitoring/Evaluation Project, August 1987.

magnitude or leverage that is needed for helping to move massive numbers of people forward. In addition, a program that hangs on the successful interaction of individual foreigners with villagers of a strikingly different culture requires particular skills of personality beyond mere technical skills. As an AID study notes, besides a willingness to live for a couple of years in often difficult conditions, "success at the village level required careful planning and cross-cultural sensitivity together with flexibility and ability to learn through one's mistakes. Cross-cultural sensitivity includes patient understanding, compromise, cooperation, careful listening and explanation."[7] In sum, the heavily administered, sensitively guided, hands-on projects at the micro level have much to be said for them as a *complement* to activities that work at institutional, technical, policy, and infrastructure dimensions of the development process and that are inherently more widespread and leveraged in their impact.

The second activity that has had most of the features of hands-on work directly with the poor is the Private and Voluntary Organization Co-financing Project. Financed from central funds between 1976 and 1979, then as a mission project from 1980 until the present, this project extends grants to nongovernmental organizations working in Thailand. By 1983 (when the mission did its first evaluation) grants had been provided to forty PVOs, most of which were American organizations or local affiliates. Very few were indigenous Thai PVOs. The project activities supported by the AID grants were classified mainly as general community development, training/education, and agricultural development. Some of the recipient organizations included Catholic Relief Services, the National 4-H Council, the Overseas Education Fund (of the League of Women Voters), the Thai Hill-Crafts Foundation, World Education, and the YMCA.

These grants put the AID mission at one step remove, so to speak, compared with the Peace Corps project, since the PVOs generally are conducting programs with the villagers and do not place their AID grants into village funds to be used directly by the villagers themselves. Nevertheless, the PVOs are viewed—and see themselves—as working directly with the disadvantaged in a participatory manner and with the appropriate technologies, in contrast to the paternalistic if not more remote forms in which government deals with villagers. The 1983 evaluation found the project generally effective and worth continuing, with the PVOs having succeeded in reaching even the poorest of the poor and having managed the funds in an acceptable manner. Since this project itself deals with organizations rather than beneficiaries, the mission expected the PVOs to conduct more monitoring and evaluation than had been the practice. Three problems we cited: the lack of sufficiently detailed project designs made it hard to measure the outcomes; there was little replication of activities beyond what was actually financed by AID, so that lessons learned were not disseminated; and the project had failed to develop much support for indigenous Thai PVOs, as compared with the American organizations that continued to get the lion's share of the funds.

These were interesting lessons that were similar to the conclusions of general studies of the roles and limitations of PVOs in the development process.[8] PVOs have the ability to "retail" development assistance in a way an aid mission cannot, but they also have constraints that have limited their coverage. Indigenous PVOs can mobilize devoted talent that cannot or does not want to work within the framework of government and can supplement the work of bureaucracies at low cost and with greater flexibility than is usually possible for government officials. These strengths are not automatic however. Few of the Thai PVOs had the management or accounting staffs necessary to meet AID's requirements for ensuring that the activities are good and the management is sound. According to M. Anderson and N. Tannenbaum's evaluation,

> The Thai people . . . uniformly indicated that the USAID proposal process and required reports are a barrier to their seeking and acquiring AID support. In some cases the Thai PVOs had used an American PVO as a front to handle these aspects of AID relations for them. . . . When the overhead costs of the U.S. PVO are reasonable, this may be a sensible use of U.S. PVO expertise and access. On the other hand, when these costs are high . . . the actual project benefits relative to costs are greatly reduced. Also, if USAID emphasizes the development and strengthening of indigenous PVOs, then continued reliance on U.S. PVOs to "front" in this way postpones the goal. To encourage more Thai PVOs to apply for USAID funds, AID may either 1) provide support through its own staff to these PVOs for proposal writing, and subsequent reporting (including financial reports), or 2) undertake activities to develop the capacity of these PVOs to perform the functions themselves.[9]

In response to this evaluation, the mission introduced the objective of channeling at least 40 percent of the Co-financing funds to the indigenous PVOs, although there is no agency-wide AID policy in this respect. In doing so, the mission appears to have taken seriously the caution expressed in the evaluation that "there is a sensitive balance to be achieved between assuring that the quality of project design is adequate to warrant AID support and giving AID too much involvement in or control over PVO activities." To help raise the ability of Thai PVOs to qualify for Co-financing funds and to carry out projects effectively, the mission has allocated about 10 percent of the annual funding to training and strengthening activities for the local organizations. In 1987 six out of the seven grantee PVOs were Thai. The main themes of their projects were working with the disadvantaged and microenterprises; with narcotics abuse prevention; and on environmental problems. Nevertheless, the limited impact of hands-on projects remains a key problem. The mission found the Cofinancing project to be its most management-intensive activity per dollar of USAID funding. And the number of people benefiting directly from the individual PVO activities financed in the past four years has reached only about 11,000.

As in the case of the Peace Corps–managed project, the evaluators (appropriately in my view) raised the issue of replication, of extent of impact. How can a donor help local PVOs to mount substantial programs without injurious effect on their independence and their special voluntaristic character? The institution-building aspect of the Cofinancing project has become its most important contribution; in a reversion to the standard search of AID projects for development leverage, the project is now attempting to strengthen PVO institutional structures and widen their potential contribution. By reverting from retailing to wholesaling, the Cofinancing project may be able greatly to increase its impact on the poorest of the poor.

The Thai PVO sector is important for reasons other than the specific content of its activities. The PVOs represent an "alternative development" movement. There are well over a hundred working in the provinces. While some of them are squarely placed inside the Thai "establishment," run by well-known members of Bangkok's social elite, others are outside and serve as channels for the energies of students and prominent social critics who prefer to remain independent of the establishment, who are skeptical of the government's commitment to reducing poverty and promoting social justice, and who, according to David Richards,

> reject the use of power conflicts and violence as a way of solving problems. They associate such methods with dictatorships and feel that their use can only lead to further

misery. [Thai PVOs] feel that developing people's con-
sciousness and carrying out small-scale, peaceful, practical
activities is a more appropriate and secure path to social
change in Thai contexts.[10]

While thus far AID funds have gone mainly to PVOs that are engaged
in development work, one PVO working in the largest of Bangkok's
slums is also active in human rights issues. The Cofinancing project,
as an instrument through which AID can assist in the growth of this
voluntaristic sector, is acceptable to the Thai government.

Option Two: Site Specific

Virtually all the major development assistance agencies working in
Thailand have had water projects in the Northeast, including the
World Bank, the Asian Development Bank, and the German, Japanese, Australian, and New Zealand bilateral programs. The poverty
focus of the U.S. aid program led to renewed attention to irrigation—
and another round of effort with the tanks and the larger scale Lam
Nam Oon project in Sakon Nakhon changwat. Lam Nam Oon is a
large project by Northeast irrigation standards, but small compared
with the irrigation systems of the Central Plain. The project consists
of a 3.5-kilometer earthen dam to impound sufficient water to irrigate
about 74,000 acres (185,000 rai), including supplementary water for
the main wet season crop in years of inadequate rainfall and natural
flooding and water for cultivation of a second, dry season crop. When
construction began in 1967, there were about 10,000 families farming
in the project area, or roughly 65,000 potential beneficiaries, around
.5 percent of the population of the Northeast at that time. AID provided funds in 1967 to help finance the construction and a second
infusion of funds in 1977 for the construction of the canal system and
for technical assistance in management of the water system, farmer
training, research, and so on. In keeping with the interest AID shared
with the international development community in area development,
the 1977 project added on as a second objective a locally based integrated rural development component. By 1977 AID's total input was
planned at $8 million (actual expenditures ended up at $6.7 million),
or $640 per family (the number of families having risen to 12,500 by
the last years of AID's involvement).

In 1982, fifteen years after the project began, a joint RTG/USAID
team evaluated the status of Lam Nam Oon, including the still on-

going technical assistance, the physical condition of the irrigation system, and the impact on the putative beneficiaries. The findings were unsatisfactory.

> The construction of the irrigation system is virtually complete, although for most of the project the final on-farm distribution channels remain to be built. Between the limited development of the on-farm distribution network, and the non-functioning of a large fraction of the canal outlets ... only about 20 percent of the area intended for dry season irrigation has actually received water after four seasons of system operation.[11]

It was found that the farmers were cultivating less area than they could have if they had used all the water the system was able to deliver in the dry season. In fact, this underutilization of dry season water supply and the very low rate of return on the investment to create the system were not unique to Lam Nam Oon. Other similar projects in the Northeast and elsewhere, financed by the RTG and other donors, suffered similar underuse. The evaluation found three explanations: 1) the farmers lacked confidence in the promises of the project officials that they could actually deliver the water even where the canal system was operational; 2) even if they did successfully irrigate and cultivate a dry season crop, the farmers had no confidence that the underdeveloped local marketing system would buy up their produce at profitable prices; 3) in the dry season farm families typically sent some members to other parts of the country where they knew from experience that employment was available.

On the other hand, the evaluation also found that the integrated rural development aspect of the project was going surprisingly well. In the face of the endemic problems of coordination, let alone integration, of field activities of different ministries and departments, the officers assigned to Lam Nam Oon had developed a high degree of cooperation and joint programming. Although their activities were not yet paying off in terms of numbers of farmers making use of the irrigation system, their teamwork appeared to hold significant lessons for RTG field operations. In one aspect of the group's work in particular there seemed to be a possible answer to the problem of system underuse. With inspiration and technical support from the resident AID contract assistance team (one of them had been a Peace Corps volunteer in a nearby changwat and spoke fluent Northeast Thai), the RTG technical group (which was led by the Royal Irrigation Department [RID] engineer, who served as project chief, and by the official representing the Community Development Department) was beginning to experiment with ways of drawing private agribusiness entrepreneurs into purchasing arrangements with the farmers that would reduce, if not eliminate, the marketing risks that had stood as barriers to greater dry season cultivation. The RTG officials group served as intermediaries, trying to fashion arrangements to ensure that the firms would receive the planned production and that the farmers would get a reasonable and reliable guarantee of sale at no lower than an agreed-upon floor price. The outcome of these efforts was still uncertain at the time. It was clear enough, however, as of 1982, that about $60 million altogether (RTG and U.S. funds; around $5,000 per beneficiary family) would go into this long-gestating project and that only very modest returns had been forthcoming for the country and the farmers.

Some five years later the AID project at Lam Nam Oon had phased out and another evaluation team descended on the irrigation site for a retrospective look. The team found that the technical recommendations of the previous evaluation had been largely adopted and that the physical condition, maintenance, and so on, were now satisfactory. The channel system and land-shaping work had been completed, and water delivery research had been conducted. The team suggested that the negative conclusions of the earlier evaluation had been "premature" in light of the efficiency of current operations and the specific advances that were being made.

> The physical facilities are in generally satisfactory condition and are able to supply irrigation water at designed quantities. A computerized water management system has been developed and is being tested ... [This is] a major innovation in irrigation systems in Thailand.
>
> A core group of agencies—RID, the Community Development Department, the Office of Land Consolidation, the Department of Fisheries and the Department of Agriculture —continue to cooperate closely in operations and planning.
>
> As a result of this project, RID has come to realize that it can no longer focus solely on the infrastructure aspects of its irrigation projects, but must also take the initiative in inducing the cooperation of other agencies needed to ensure that the infrastructure is used productively. To this end, RID is in process of establishing an internal unit to

promote such cooperation and to manage four model irrigation projects to demonstrate the necessity of integrated
or policy coordinated approaches to agricultural development.[12]

The fact that the Permanent Secretary of the Ministry of Agriculture picked up on the system for public-private sector cooperation at
Lam Nam Oon for the integrated development of the production and
marketing processes (these activities have continued to be assisted
under the Agriculture Technology Transfer project [discussed below]
since the termination of the overall Lam Nam Oon project) and initiated policies and organizational arrangements in the Ministry to build
on the Lam Nam Oon experience is likely to be the project's most
important long-run contribution since it holds out the promise of
benefiting farmers in underutilized irrigation systems in many parts
of the country. Contract farming, or managed production, as these
arrangements between small-farmer suppliers and agribusiness firm
buyers are commonly labeled, has emerged as a major advance in
production and marketing systems in Thailand in recent years. The
work at Lam Nam Oon actually built on an earlier successful commercial venture in which a progressive patriarch of a family agribusiness enterprise hired two ex-Peace Corps volunteers who were adept
at working with small farmers. Other enterprises in Thailand, both
domestic and foreign, some quite large, have developed such arrangements on their own. The Lam Nam Oon project has been unique for
its development of such arrangements within the framework of a
government-administered irrigation system and for its demonstration
of the potential for a promotional role for government field technicians in bringing the producers and processors together.

As for Lam Nam Oon itself, the jury is still out, although there are
signs that the project has turned the corner. The dry season cultivated
area is still worked at only a fraction of its potential, but it appears
that the labor-intensive character of the production that has begun to
develop, even if still in an experimental stage, may make it more
appropriate to reevaluate the project based on employment days generated and value of output. Eight private firms are now engaged in
the proving stages of managed production arrangements to raise seed
crops (fruits and vegetables) and baby corn and tomatoes for processing. The cultivation is being undertaken by 2,500 of Lam Nam Oon's
family farms, which are employing, besides their own family members, the labor of people from another 2,500 of the project's families.
There is no denying that the return to the now twenty years of invest-

ment and institutional development at Lam Nam Oon and ten years of technical assistance remains low. If the need for integrating the private sector into the project had been recognized at the outset, the returns would have been greater and sooner in coming. Nevertheless, the reader should be aware of the fact that extensive review of irrigation project experience in Thailand and other developing countries (no matter who has financed the project or implemented it) has shown an almost universal pattern of unrealistic expectations during the planning phase and very long periods before the projects mature, the farmers adapt their technologies effectively, and the resulting production begins to approach the original targets.[13] In 1988, at a time when export-driven agricultural diversification has become one of the most dynamic factors in the Thai economy, it is plausible to suggest that a third evaluation of Lam Nam Oon five years hence might describe the project as one that moved from near collapse to a role as a pioneer model in a long search for viable irrigated diversification.

After the second round of AID financing for Lam Nam Oon in 1977, the mission turned once again to the small-scale irrigation "tanks" in its continued search for workable water projects. The approach this time was to select a few of the larger tanks with the best prospects from an engineering point of view and see if a low-cost solution to successful operation might be found, modifying their design where necessary and applying some of the on-farm development and organizational ideas being tried at Lam Nam Oon. The project started in 1980, but it took three years of design and redesign before the mission was satisfied that it had viable plans (mainly for rehabilitation of the deteriorated tanks and creation of an on-farm water distribution system). The funds allocated would be enough for three tanks out of the 133 built under the tank project back in the 1950s. Construction work finally started in 1984, having been delayed by the mission's tougher approach to the problems of tank design, borne of its earlier irrigation experience.

By late 1987 the rehabilitation of the three tanks was complete and one was operational, having gone through a round of farmer training. Farmer water-user associations had been organized and were functioning successfully. Dry season cropping in the operational system covered 40 percent of its area. The RID was said to be satisfied that the project had demonstrated a feasible low-cost method for putting the potentially viable tanks into operation with an acceptable rate of return. If a proper evaluation after a few years of operation shows this to be the case, it would be a happy outcome for one of the longest stories of project failure in the history of the program.

Two other area-specific projects in the Northeast are interesting for what they reveal about the difficulties of promoting development in a poorly endowed region. These two efforts (Land Settlement, 1979–1984, and Sericulture, 1976–1980) were designed to raise productivity and income among farmers living in eight to ten "land settlement" projects. Under the jurisdiction of the Department of Public Welfare, settlements are areas that provide a structured framework for legal landsite occupation by landless or otherwise qualifying families. Some of the sites are associated with Northeast irrigation projects. The Land Settlement project was a general area development activity that included road and water development and technical assistance in agriculture extension and research. The objective was to demonstrate improved methods of soil conservation and crop diversification in a "bottom-up" approach that stressed farmer "self-help" and that would be replicable elsewhere in the region. The Sericulture project operated in some of the same settlements; the project's goal was to raise the incomes of 1,000 farmers by 50 percent through silkworm cultivation.

Both settlement projects had yielded modest and uncertain results by the time AID assistance came to an end. A basic problem was simply that the projects were terminated after only a few years, in contrast with the mission's persistence with Lam Nam Oon and the tanks. Despite the planned expenditure level of $1,800 per farmer under the sericulture project, the number of farmers who had taken up silkworm cultivation was less than half of the original target, and their cocoon sales and net earnings were lower than what had been planned and expected. On the other hand, the incomes of the participants had risen significantly, and the institutional structure for further expansion was in place.[14] In the case of the general settlement project however, the end-of-project evaluation concluded that the activity was beginning to build up momentum just as it ended. The evaluators found that the project had contributed to the "sustainability" of agriculture in the settlements and a "marginal" improvement in living standards during the three years the project was active. While almost all the farmers did adopt improved rice varieties, the future of their diversified cropping was uncertain since most of the farmers still depended heavily on rainfall. Although the settlement project was supposed to demonstrate replicable bottom-up approaches, the project itself was very administration-intensive. And even though it was implemented through the single administrative framework of the Public Welfare Department, the benefits of the research component were "seriously reduced" because of poor communication between the researchers and the extension agents.[15]

It should be clear from these brief accounts of area-specific projects how formidable have been the problems of raising farm productivity in the Northeast, even when the assistance effort takes the form of small, local projects that work with small numbers of identified beneficiaries, that can fine-tune their activities to fit local conditions, that work within coherent administrative frameworks, and that apply relatively large external resources for the numbers of beneficiaries involved. (Other projects I need not describe here, such as a fish pond project in selected Northeast villages, had similar "mixed" results.)

The last major area development project is mentioned only in passing because at this writing it is still in its final stages of operation. The Mae Chaem Watershed Development project covers an area in Chiangmai province in the North, which has a large Hill Tribe population. Their traditional shifting cultivation practices have led to substantial deforestation, degrading the environment of the watershed. The project was started in 1980 and has been allocated more than $9 million of AID grant funds. The objective is to develop stabilized agricultural alternatives to the shifting cultivation by a primary target group of 3,400 Hill Tribe families, and thereby reduce the opium production which has been a major source of hill tribe income in the past. As with all area development projects, Mae Chaem has included the financing of local infrastructure and expansion of government services as part of the package of interventions designed to support the changes being promoted in the inhabitants' economic activities. The project also includes a local opium detoxification activity. After a mid-course evaluation and restructuring of management, the implementation of the project appears to have been put on solid ground. While the number of primary beneficiaries in this case is small in relation to the funds provided, the project has larger implications, both for the inhabitants of the watershed and downstream areas and for the reduction achieved in drug supply.

Option Three: Systemic and Northeast Region-Wide Projects

A third set of projects addresses research, ways to get research results to farmers, and the whole rural development system. In practice vertical, individual activity approaches overlap with horizontal approaches to the full range of public sector functions that interact with the totality of village life. The shift from vertical, or sectoral perspectives was at the heart of development thinking in the 1970s, and was proposed as a better way to involve the farmers in the processes affecting their welfare. It was also expected to be more effective because horizontal, or integrated rural development programs (and donor projects) would address the whole range of factors that interact at a micro level and that jointly determine village conditions from health to farm productivity. As a result we find in the AID portfolio since the early 1970s multifaceted projects in agriculture, health, rural development, and in the planning and operating practices of the governmental machinery as a whole in the field, both in its dealings with Bangkok and its developmental functions at the amphur and changwat levels. It will help to clarify the contrasts among these heterogeneous projects if we move from the more narrow and conceptually sharper activities to the more general, i.e., from seed research to the integrated operation of all field services; from single-disease interventions (malaria) to integrated primary health care.

Agricultural research in Thailand, and AID's role in Thai research development, has a complex history that has both striking successes and long frustrations. Research to raise the productivity of farmers in developing countries has been of fundamental importance in international development efforts for several decades, reflecting the large role agriculture plays in determining the economic condition of the poor majority of Third World populations and the macroeconomic importance of agriculture in developing countries. Third world agriculture has been a major subject for bilateral aid programs of virtually every donor country and international development bank. Research has been central to these development programs, and has been addressed through country programs to build up local scientific research capabilities and through the creation of a network of international research institutes (like the International Rice Research Institute in the Philippines) that focus on specific crops or (like the International Crops Research Institute for the Semi-Arid Tropics in India) on agriculture in a specific environment. For many countries the interaction between an international center and the domestic adaptive research capabilities has proven to be a successful formula for achieving significant gains in locally applicable production technologies. All this scientific work is a necessary, but not sufficient condition for achieving the final objective of on-farm production increases. The actual adoption of these technologies by large numbers of farmers is a process that is also shaped by such factors as the effectiveness of the country's extension services, the availability and pricing of inputs (the improved seed, water, fertilizer, etc.), the educational level of farmers, the size of holdings and the conditions of ownership or tenancy, and the perceived product prices, risks and marketing opportunities. The economist's notion of "expected rate of return" captures the upshot of all these factors for a farmer who has to judge the risk of departing from his known traditional technology, with its established survival and subsistence record, for the higher net income promised, or offered, by the purveyors of the new technologies.

For most third world countries, agricultural research is basically a postwar (WW II) development. The research carried on by colonial administrations generally was limited to major export crops that were organized in plantation systems (like the work of the Rubber Research Institute in colonial Malaya) or the problems of areas occupied by the foreign settlers (as in the so-called White Highlands in Kenya). I noted above the fact that agricultural research in Thailand had its beginnings in the 1920s, but that its scale was very modest and confined to rice and maize. The early postwar work done under USOM and Rockefeller Foundation auspices, while important, was focused on these two crops, as was donor support of development of the research functions of Kasetsart University and of the field stations of the Ministry of Agriculture. In a sense, these first steps were both obviously essential and relatively easy to carry off successfully. The end product of the research was to raise the productivity of two crops already grown on a wide scale. The focus was on varieties, on genetic improvement through varietal selection, not on large changes in technology or crop patterns. While the research work itself was arduous and required a build-up of Thai scientific capacity, the adoption of its results did not require massive reeducation of farmers, or creation of new marketing systems or export market penetration.

The AID program in the poverty-orientation period has had an excellent example of the potential impact of a project that channels a specific technological improvement into the existing production and marketing system. Although the program had provided participant training and other inputs for seed improvement even apart from the early work on rice and corn, the systematic work to develop a full-fledged modern seed system began only in 1972 with the establishment of a seed production program by the Department of Agricultural Extension. In 1977 the department set up a formal Seed Division. USAID-supported technical assistance to the Department from Mississippi State University led to a contract in the same year which lasted for a full decade. Mississippi State's strength in seed technology and strong dedication to this project (the chief of party for the contract resided in Thailand for ten years until the very completion of the project) merits substantial credit for the development of the seed industry in Thailand, although the end-of-project report stresses the many contributions made by the UN Food and Agriculture Organization (FAO) and other bilateral aid agencies, by the extension department and by Thai and foreign private companies that have gone into commercial seed production. Only 173 tons of seed of major crops were produced in Thailand in 1976 (apart from farmer use of own seed); in 1987 the figure was over 23,000 tons. The value of the increase in annual production that can be attributed to the use of this improved seed was roughly estimated at $450 million.[16] A seed division had been established with a trained staff of about 420. A nationwide network of seed production and distribution stations was in operation as part of a well-structured system that included seed coordination machinery in the government and the involvement of many organizations and private companies. One expert judgment summed up the results of all these efforts:

> within the projected completion date of the Seed Development project, Thailand has made more progress in establishing a seed program/industry than any other developing country, many of which were assisted by much higher levels of funding and more concentrated technical assistance. The RTG and AID should be pleased with the Project's accomplishments. Given even the same rate of progress in the next few years, Thailand will have the outstanding seed program/industry in the region. FAO and others are already looking at Thailand as a base for regional training and workshops in seed program/industry development.[17]

The seed improvement project by its nature was a technology input activity, not a poverty-focused one. Nonetheless, since the seed has been mainly for crops which, under Thai agricultural conditions, are neutral in their technologies with respect to farm size and do not require a shift to more capital intensive methods merely because of the change in seed,* poor farmers are among the beneficiaries. These

---

*Buffalo traction for land preparation has proved too slow in double-cropping areas, leading to substantial replacement by small tractors, especially in the Central Plain. However, contract plowing has developed very widely, enabling smaller farmers to switch from animal to machine traction without investing in the machinery.

include not only rice and maize but also sorghum, peanuts, lentils, and a number of horticultural crops. More directly, the extension department has integrated the distribution of the improved seed into its regular programs to reach small farmers, and a large fraction of the seed produced by the Seed Division's own system is allocated to poor farmers hit by drought or flood in a relief measure to replace the planted seed they have lost. The division has also supported the development of a private seed industry.

In 1984 the mission started another agriculture technology project that has been financing a diverse set of subprojects. The Agriculture Technology Transfer (ATT) project, managed with the assistance of an American adviser working in the Ministry of Agriculture, operates in effect as a fund for production and processing research and technology transfer that might be of interest to any of the departments of the Ministry. The subprojects have worked on such things as control of aflatoxin contamination of maize,* fungi contamination of mungbean, maintenance of postharvest quality of fresh fruits and vegetables, animal diseases, drying systems, and prawn culture. Like the Lam Nam Oon project (where one of the ATT subprojects is located), ATT is promoting joint efforts among the Ministry, the universities, and private enterprises interested in the specific commodities or problems being studied. The potential economic impact of these activities can be very significant. For example, corn contamination by aflatoxin has occasionally reached levels that have led Japanese authorities to ban corn imports from Thailand, and that caused Thai corn exports to sell at $5–10 per ton discounts in world markets. Applied research under the ATT project has solved this problem by developing changes in cultural practices and demonstrating the use of mechanical dryers. Some of the other activities under ATT have included the introduction of new animal disease vaccines, the reduction of certain aquaculture diseases, the development of a sanitary method of home processing of fermented fish (widely eaten in the Northeast and a transmitter of parasites if improperly prepared), and help in the penetration of fresh fruit and vegetable markets in Europe and Japan and the establishment of seaweed processing. An activity currently underway, assisted by Cornell University, has successfully demonstrated the use of a vaccine to overcome a papaya ringspot virus that has been decimating this fruit. Papaya is an important staple food in rural Thailand. Mass innoculation of papaya seedlings is planned to start in 1990.

---

* Aflatoxin is a moldy grain fungus suspected of being carcinogenic.

ATT lacks the appearance of a hands-on poverty project and is not confined to the Northeast or billed as a poverty project (and therefore is omitted from table A.12). Nevertheless, ATT activities like those described are likely to generate important dietary and diversification and marketing opportunities for poor farmers as well as for larger producers and commercial operators. The yield increases obtained under the improved seed project have been of the order of 15 to 20 percent. As important as this one-input advance has been (its major future contribution may well be in providing the seed basis for large commercial production of now relatively minor crops), neither the seeds nor ATT projects by themselves constitute powerful instruments for the general alleviation of Northeast poverty, due to the interaction of unfavorable resource conditions in the region's predominantly rainfed agriculture. Dissatisfied with the lack of integration among the agriculture ministry's functionally compartmentalized research efforts in the Northeast, the ministry and USAID decided to develop a Northeast center for concentrating interdisciplinary research for the region. The Tha Phra research station near the town of Khon Kaen was chosen as the site. For several years and through research activities under different agricultural subprojects, the mission concentrated much training, institutional development and field research at the Tha Phra station. Support was provided through a contract with the University of Kentucky under which more than 125 ministry scientists received advanced degrees in the United States. After this first round of AID support ended in 1975, research at Tha Phra declined rapidly and the original institutional concept for the center had to be abandoned. Partly because Tha Phra never got the legal status needed to offer a scientific career ladder, large numbers of the returning participants found work elsewhere in the ministry, many since then having risen to leading scientific positions.

By the time AID returned for a second round of assistance to Tha Phra in 1981, the role of the center had been changed. It was now to serve as a training facility and to help coordinate field activities of the different departments within the Ministry of Agriculture. The continuing anomalous bureaucratic position of the center has not made accomplishment of the coordination task easy either. Nevertheless, although the Tha Phra experience stands thus far as an example of the difficulties facing aid efforts to solve problems by creating new institutions outside long-established bureaucratic systems, the ministry's policy in recent years of assigning to the center the coordinating responsibilities for some aid-funded agricultural projects in the

Northeast has given Tha Phra some financial leverage and resulted in some significant accomplishments.

AID's second round at Tha Phra consisted of one of these projects cited at the center, the Northeast Rainfed Agricultural Development Project (NERAD). The NERAD project was the latest in the program's long pursuit of ways to break the constraints on agricultural productivity in the Northeast. Instead of searching for single crop breakthroughs however, NERAD attempted a more decentralized approach, looking for integrated farm system improvements that would be specific to the conditions in nine different representative subdistrict (tambon) locations. This systemic approach would be accomplished through improved field coordination among nine departments of the ministry. In the mission's view, as described in the NERAD project documentation, the effectiveness of agriculture research in the Northeast as of 1981 had not advanced much since the 1950s:

> Programs of the Thai government's Ministry of Agriculture and Cooperatives have not focused, or focused effectively, on the needs of these (Northeast subsistence) farmers. Technology development has been either commodity-oriented or discipline-oriented under relatively protected experiment-station conditions, and links between research and extension have been minimal. . . . The project purpose is to develop a replicable agricultural development program for increasing farm productivity and farm incomes, particularly among lower income farmers in the rainfed agricultural zones. . . . The intent is to establish adaptive research and extension programs. . . . AID funds provide technical assistance, training for farmers and extension personnel, intensified Cooperating Country support in target areas; construction and equipment purchase; and water resources development, land/soil modifications, surveys, mapping, research and demonstration.[18]

The total cost of the project has been about $16 million, of which AID provided $10 million.

A midcourse evaluation in 1985 found the project in serious difficulty. The evaluators believed that the underlying objective was sound for the Northeast—that is, the development of farming systems research closely linked with extension—but that the design of the project was flawed. Between the geographic (and ethnographic) spread and the large number of components and departments involved, "the people responsible for implementing the project do not have a clear understanding of what the project is supposed to accomplish. This lack of mutual understanding has manifested itself at all levels of the cooperating departments and agencies." The NERAD project was apparently stumbling over the same endemic coordination problems that had thwarted the first Tha Phra effort. Surprisingly, given the project's objectives and the general agency concern for "participation" of beneficiaries (thoroughly adopted in some of the projects described above), NERAD was also criticized for not involving farmers adequately. "In many cases the villagers have no role in the management of the project-sponsored activities but are only onlookers wondering what is going to happen to these activities." To be fair, it would have been surprising if NERAD itself had been able, in effect incidentally, to break powerful traditions of bureaucratic paternalism, a subject to be discussed later.

Despite these criticisms, the evaluation recommended that (with suitable corrections) the project continue because its objectives were important, the integrated approach held some potential, and the project had succeeded in some significant respects.

In the meantime the mission had in 1983 started a second integrated farming systems project centered in the Research and Development Institute of Khon Kaen University (KKU). The Institute had been operating only one year and had received substantial support from the Ford Foundation as well as Canadian, Japanese, and other assistance. The functions of the Institute included some similar in concept to the objectives of the NERAD project: farm system research, training field workers, and coordinating rural organizations. But unlike NERAD the Institute had the advantage of including these functions within a single organizational frame, rather than trying to achieve integration by roping together many departmental fiefdoms. The KKU project was also evaluated midcourse in 1985 and found to be well designed and managed. The multidisciplinary research was viewed as a model for the university. The ultimate significance and applicability of the research findings remain to be seen as of this writing. The links created between NERAD and KKU appear to have been especially effective, and the NERAD project has turned around, having produced twenty-one technological improvements and some new dissemination approaches that have been taken up by the Department of Agricultural Extension. An independent completion report in 1989 recorded some positive conclusions:

> NERAD can be described as a project that had a slow and shaky beginning and a strong and successful finish. The shaky beginning was in part caused by what most people concede was a poorly written Project Paper. . . . The strong finish occurred because in the last three years of the project, the project team focused on identifying, consolidating, replicating, and disseminating their findings. The project produced an impressive set of well-documented analyses, reports, handbooks, and other useful final products.[19]

While the completion report found that NERAD had identified many promising innovations, it also noted that few had yet been proven. Thus NERAD's impact on agricultural productivity in the Northeast can only be seen over time, perhaps by the mid-1990s. On the institutional objectives of the project, the report found that the long-sought improvements in coordination among the departments in the agricultural ministry continued to elude AID's efforts.

As an institution-building project, KKU appears to be developing successfully. The Institute is rapidly becoming an important intellectual and research center in the Northeast, although five years of activity is too short a period for reaching a conclusion over the likely long-run role of an institution of this kind.[20]

It will be recalled that the aid program's activities in health in the 1950s and 1960s addressed specific diseases (malaria having been much the most important), helped build up the hospital system, and contributed to Ministry of Health programs across the board. AID continued to support rural health services development into the 1970s. Under the Village Health and Sanitation, Comprehensive Rural Health and Potable Water projects, the quality of the Ministry's staff continued to be strengthened, health education and services continued to expand, and rural areas were assisted in a steady accretion of village and household water and sanitary facilities. These projects led to a major effort starting in 1978 to support the Thai government's primary health care (PHC) program.

The concept of primary health care was formally adopted by the World Health Organization (WHO) and its member states in 1977. In contrast with the disease-oriented, or "vertical" strategies represented by the malaria, smallpox and similar health campaigns, the PHC concept stressed the creation of delivery systems, or "horizontal" facilities that would shift resources from urban-based, hospital-based curative medical services to a widespread system of preventive and primary care. The PHC concept would have the bonus of helping to get more out of limited health budgets through the emphasis the PHC philosophy put on community participation and the devolving of health functions onto village workers supported by semiprofessional or paramedical personnel. Highly trained medical staff could be reserved for higher levels of supervision and treatment. In many countries the PHC concept was no less than a minor social revolution. It shifted resources from the urban middle class to the rural poor, developed community-based organizations to take local initiative, and loosened the monopoly (and mystique) of the medical professionals on many health functions and medical procedures.

The adoption by the RTG of the formal title of Primary Health Care (and the associated and rather imprecise WHO target of "health for all by 2000") did not in fact represent a major shift in Thailand's health strategy. By 1977 the Ministry of Public Health (MOPH) had accumulated considerable experience in rural health delivery systems through its established public health system and a number of pilot and research studies dating back to the 1950s. As noted above with respect to the country's family-planning history, the Thai medical authorities were above all pragmatic and willing to test the viability of various schemes and delivery system configurations as they sought models that would work under Thai rural and bureaucratic conditions. The early AID rural health projects were important contributors to this process of evolving a suitable PHC strategy.

Twenty-six precursor research and pilot projects leading up to the Thai PHC strategy are described in a paper of the Health Ministry.[21] The earliest of these, conducted in 1956–1959 with USOM support, was a village sanitation project that provided the first demonstration of community organization techniques for building wells and latrines. The largest comprehensive pilot project of the group was also supported by AID and ran for eight years between 1974 and 1981. This project was designed to test methods for providing primary and curative care for an entire province (Lampang). The Lampang project strengthened the provincial and district-level hospitals as referral and supervisory medical units linked to the primary level health centers and services. At the primary level the project defined the roles of and trained paramedics and village health workers and volunteers. It also set up coordination mechanisms at each level to round out the operational system that brought together the health structure and the key general administrative officials. Many lessons came out of the Lampang and other projects among these twenty-six, some of which were conducted by Buddhist monks, others with aid from WHO and other outside organizations. By 1976 the MOPH concluded that enough experience by trial and error had accumulated to give Thailand a basis for designing a PHC strategy for implementation as a national program.

Two lessons the MOPH drew from its review of this experience are of general interest for this study: the demonstration of how pilot projects, including "failures" that show what won't work, can lead to successful working models that can then be replicated over large areas (the attention the MOPH paid to administrative details was critical in this respect since replicability depends as much on the feasibility of scaling up the management of a program as it does on mobilizing the necessary financial resources); and the importance of time and continuity for the evolution of workable large-scale systems. "At the beginning, the concepts were narrow with specific activities such as sanitation or malaria control. Later on the development model has been extended to be an 'integrated model' with various village cooperatives or funds. At present [1984], these are in the process of evolving into the integrated rural development model, [the] widest system ever [in Thailand]" (ibid., p. 59). It would appear that public health was an early, perhaps the first, sector where concepts of self-help and villager participation in government-sponsored development activities were developed and successfully applied in Thailand.

The primary health care concept received strong AID support worldwide. In Thailand the Rural Primary Health Care Expansion project carried on for eight years (1978–1986) at a total cost of $27.2 million, of which USAID provided $6.5 million and the RTG $20.7 million in counterpart funds. In its first phase the project was implemented in twenty changwats in conjunction with a population project assisted by World Bank funds. The second phase expanded to thirty-seven changwats (half the changwats in the country) and included community nutrition activities in 1,800 villages and sanitation and drinking water supplies in 1,000 villages, which were aimed at the control of diarrheal disease. The project had many elements of training, monitoring and evaluation, and operation of services. No less than 150,000 people received training under the project, including courses for a few months to a year for professional staff and short training sessions for nearly 115,000 village health workers. The capacity and activity of the field system expanded substantially as measured by the administrative data on the outreach work at the village level. While the primary system and its use were growing, the health authorities were not satisfied with the extent to which the basic concept of entry at the primary level was being adopted by people seeking medical care. The lowest level health center entry points of the system remained underutilized as the populace preferred to enter the referral system at the district health center and hospital levels. In general, progress in water and sanitation, nutrition, and diarrheal control was recorded by the end-of-project evaluation in 1986, but in each area the Thai-American team also found shortfalls and uncertainties over impact.[22] The uncertainties were attributed partly to the fact that more time would be required before impact on health status would become measurable and partly to the fact that neither the service data nor the evaluation and research were considered adequate to give strong support to the favorable conclusions some had already drawn.

It is difficult for a layperson to sort through the complex issues of detail, alternative system configurations, and impact measurement that remain unresolved among the health professionals who have worked in and studied the Thai primary health experience thus far. On the one hand, there is the expansion in the field system, the investment to upgrade its professional caliber, the widespread availability and use of modern drugs and other health interventions, and the continuing increase in the use of health services by the population. On the other hand is the rising life expectancy and improving health status of the population and the changing profile of morbidity and causes of mortality (the decline of the traditional diseases). Yet the demonstration of substantial causal connection between the health system interface with the population and the health status of that population remains in dispute.

In view of the very large contributions made by the aid program and the American foundations, and, of course, by the World Bank and other international and bilateral sources, to the development of Thailand's medical and public health capabilities, it is worth reproducing here a recent summary of the country's health status, taken from a study of Thailand's human resources by the Thailand Development Research Institute:

> Available indicators of health status are crude death rates, life expectancy at birth, infant mortality rates, nutrition status of infants and children under five, and leading causes of death and illness.
>
> The crude death rate per thousand has dropped steadily partly because of overall development and public health services, and partly because of changes in the age compo-

sition of the population—now numerically biased toward the younger and healthier age groups.

Life expectancy at birth has increased by five years since 1965—male expectancy in 1980–1985 was 60 years and female 66. Life expectancy is projected to increase another five years for the generation that will be born after the year 2000.

Infant mortality rates have dropped by half or more since 1965 to a national average of 45 per 1,000. But regional disparities persist . . overall rural rates [are] 25 percent higher than urban rates.

MOPH surveys show a significant improvement in nutritional status of preschool children between 1981 and 1984 . . . similar regional variations persist.

Leading causes of death were [in 1983] accidents, heart disease and cancer—conditions which will increase demand for curative services and hospitalization. Twenty years ago, the leading causes of death were diarrheal disease, tuberculosis and pneumonia. Leading causes of illness (among children and the elderly in 1982) were diarrheal disease, malaria, dysentery and dengue hemorrhagic fever —conditions which are reducible by environmental sanitation and vector control and perhaps eventually preventible by vaccines.

Overall, these indicators of health status . . . compare favorably with countries at the same and higher levels of per capita income. But a consequence is that Thailand must simultaneously respond to illnesses which are characteristic of high income countries and to persisting conditions related, in part, to poverty and the environment.[23]

The indications of progress against nutritional and environmentally related disease in recent years coincides with the years of the major expansion in the field services of the MOPH. The availability of village-level health services has reached virtually 100 percent coverage, "making Thailand one of the few countries to introduce primary health care . . . on a national scale," according to UNICEF.[24] Service data on immunizations, village visits, and educational activities, child weight monitoring, village drug funds, distribution of oral rehydration packets (a simple technology for home treatment of the dehydration that accompanies severe diarrhea), and so on, all show a massive increase in health interventions within a short period of time. Between 1981 and 1985 MOPH allocations to PHC doubled, while budget allocated to Bangkok declined.[25]

Despite these substantial improvements in health status and the apparently related public health interventions, the evaluation of impact of the PHC expansion activities in the areas where the AID project was operating was hesitant (if not skeptical) to accept the evidence of causal connection between program activities and health status change. This hesitation is based on the particular strengths and weaknesses of the program service data and research findings developed under the project and addressing its specific functions. But the preference among health evaluators to question demonstrations of causal relations between health interventions and health status outcomes is a general characteristic of such analyses, not peculiar to Thailand or to this project. The basic analytic problem is that the older vertical programs (like malaria eradication) attacked diseases clearly attributable to specific causes (or vectors), while the new services-oriented programs focus on diseases (and deprivation conditions like child malnutrition) that have multiple causation. The etiology of diseases (like diarrhea) that can be caused by combinations of vector, environmental, and personal hygienic behavior and are also affected by family economic status and social, dietary, and other factors is much more complex. The measurement and demonstration of causal relationships between changes in specific elements among these complexes of factors and health status are difficult to achieve at acceptable standards for scientific inquiry.[26]

Programs must proceed nevertheless, and what the evaluations contribute is the identification of questions needing to be better understood and of aspects of operational programs that appear to be working below their potential or that should be questioned altogether as to their utility. The Thai PHC program will no doubt continue to evolve as health research in Thailand and practical experience demonstrate the need for adjustments. As the TDRI analysis points out, health status is changing in fundamental ways in Thailand as a result of the interaction between the broad process of economic development and the interventions of the health system. Thai pragmatism will probably lead the PHC paradigm to a balanced mix of vertical and horizontal services. The gradual overcoming of the health problems of poverty, a process still in midcourse, is being followed by the rise of health problems more typical of a middle-income society. In international health circles the medical and public health systems in Thailand are considered among the strongest in the Third World, containing many lessons and technical assistance capabilities for other

developing countries. The Ministry of Public Health has a reputation
for being among the most efficiently managed in developing countries. The Ministry also has a reputation as one of the best administered among the ministries of the Thai government. It is much less
bedeviled by the problems of interdepartmental coordination, having
integrated all line functions under the office of the permanent secretary. Health was the first ministry to rotate department heads and to
install integrated ministerial planning. Senior ministry officials attribute many of the ideas behind the reorganization that established
the planning system and recast the ministry in its present form to a
training experience these officials had as a group in 1970 at the Johns
Hopkins School of Public Health, sponsored by WHO. The strength of
the medical teaching and research institutions was noted above. With
all the necessary qualifications over important details of the system,
aspects that still need strengthening or reform, and the difficulties of
unequivocal demonstration of causal chains, the health sector performance in Thailand appears outstanding, and the credit that senior
Thai health administrators have given to the role of American intellectual and financial assistance in this performance appears deserved.

Rural Development

The last two poverty-oriented projects of this period that fall into the
multifaceted, integrated mold are the Decentralized Development
Management Project (DDMP) and Rural Development Monitoring and
Evaluation (RDME). DDMP was the latest in a long line of mission
projects since the early 1950s to address fundamental problems of
public administration in Thailand. In this renewed foray into the
operations of the RTG bureaucracy in the provinces the mission was
working within the context of two RTG provincial programs, the
National Rural Development Program (NRDP) and the Rural Employment Generation Program (REGP).

The basic administrative and social unit in Thai society is the
village; a group of villages form a subdistrict, known as a tambon.
The tambon council and its head, the *kamnan*, are elected by the
villagers. The council serves in a dual capacity as a representative
governing entity and as the lowest unit in the administrative hierarchy in the Ministry of the Interior. The REGP and NRDP programs
are two of the more recent instruments among many the RTG has
experimented with to strengthen the role of the local governing institutions. Although the programmatic objectives of both these schemes

are cast in terms of poverty alleviation, they also have the common institution-building objective of giving the tambon councils some degree of responsibility over the allocation of program funds and the implementation of scheme projects. The NRDP program has allocated regular budget resources of a number of participating ministries to a large set of villages identified as relatively disadvantaged; allocation is made through an elaborate planning and administrative system involving the tambon and each layer of the hierarchy up to Bangkok. The REGP program bypasses much of the Ministry of the Interior's bureaucracy, financing grants to the rural tambon for local employment-intensive public works projects during the slack periods of the annual agriculture production cycle. Begun in 1975, the REGP went through several changes before settling in 1980 into the administrative form it has maintained since.

The NRDP began in 1981 as one of the centerpieces of the Fifth National Economic and Social Development Plan. The program was designed to identify the relatively poor villages of the country and to focus on them a number of activities of different RTG departments under which communities could obtain health, educational, agricultural, and other benefits. The eligible villages were in effect at the head of the queue for those programs. Through them a village could accumulate a range of common facilities, such as fish ponds, potable water holding systems, and so on. The number of participating villages was around 12,600 (out of the country's total of 52,900 villages), identified through a data-gathering and research system that attempted to categorize communities by relative endowments of social capital and general state of welfare. After the program got underway the World Bank signed on with a loan of $50 million. Between the World Bank funds and the RTG budget for NRDP, the program was very large and was in position to offer significant incremental resources to the participating villages.

Given the enormous village coverage of NRDP and the complexity of the system under which it was administered, it was not surprising that implementation was uneven from one local jurisdiction to another, from one departmental program to another, and up and down the elaborate planning, budgeting, and expenditure processes. In several respects NRDP was an attractive option for AID. It separated the more from the less disadvantaged. The fact that poverty in the Northeast in particular tended to be a function of location rather that differential household characteristics meant that a program providing benefits to a village as a whole was broadly equitable; it was not likely to favor higher-decile households in the income distribution because the differences between richer and poorer households were much narrower than was the case in towns or in Bangkok. The villagers were brought into the planning and decision processes that determined the mix of projects each village would have each year. One did not have to be a perfectionist to find flaws at many points in the system, but over the years the data accumulated by the elaborate monitoring system (required, incidentally, in order to be able to meet reporting requirements of the World Bank loan) have recorded a large accretion of social capital at the village level.* Under the NRDP system the allocation of resources and village activities was determined through a flow of documentation from the grass roots through the provincial administration to the coordinating committee structure in Bangkok, then back down again after technical and budget reviews in the capital.

AID undertook the Rural Development Monitoring and Evaluation project at the behest of the RTG and the World Bank as a technical complement to the Bank's Rural Development loan (UNDP was a third party to these arrangements with an additional technical input). The RDME project was to provide computer hardware and technical assistance and training to strengthen the NRDP information, analysis, and evaluation systems. Several Thais received training from the U.S. Bureau of the Census, but the technical assistance component was not fully or well utilized by NESDB and was cut back after a midcourse evaluation of the project. In this case the disappointing results had little to do with the larger issues of rural development, apart from the assumption in the project plan that a greater degree of interagency coordination would be possible than turned out in the event. (The main problem had to do with the administrative and tax status of the U.S. technicians. RDME was a loan-funded project, and neither the Thai nor the U.S. side realized during the planning of the project that Thai legal and administrative practices for the looa-funded technical assistance were more restrictive and cumbersome than the procedures for grant-funded assistance. Another loan-funded project, to provide technical assistance to the Provincial Water Works Authority foundered at about the same time for similar reasons.) The RDME project has provided microcomputers and has helped develop soft-

---

*Examples include: "288 district hospitals were constructed and subdistrict health offices established in all target areas; primary health care was developed and disease prevention carried out in over 80 percent of the target areas; over 60,000 rural households were trained in modern agricultural techniques; 2,655 additional village fish ponds were constructed, thus increasing the sources of protein-rich food for village consumption; cattle and buffalo banks were established for 20,000 households; and the number of illiterate people in rural areas was reduced by 300,000" (NESBD, *The Sixth National Economic and Social Development Plan [1987–1991]*, program 2, ch. 2, para. 2).

ware for provincial, departmental, and national management information systems. The ultimate effectiveness and impact of this work
remain to be seen.

The REGP program has racked up some significant accomplishments. It has channeled funds directly into rural areas; generated
sizable off-season employment; created local water, transport, and
other public works facilities; and strengthened the technical and administrative capacities of the tambon councils and their self-confi-
dence as instruments of local development. These accomplishments
are not uniform of course. The program has worked better in some
areas than other; the allocation system has lacked flexibility and has
led to some substitution of project contracting for direct management
by the tambon based on local villager employment; contracting has
in turn opened the door to charges of favoritism and corruption; and
while technical standards have improved, many of the weirs and
other structures built in the first years of REGP deteriorated rapidly.
Finally, the institution-building fell short of expectations in the view
of a Thai social scientist who concluded, in 1987, that despite "genu-
ine effort by the Central Government to help rural self-government,
the influence and control of the state machinery is still very much
apparent."

> To conclude, despite the fact that the original thinking
> behind Tambon Counils includes the noble concepts of lo-
> cal participation, self-government, democratic practices,
> and so on, the present role of Tambon Councils . . . does not
> fit with expectations. . . . If institutionalization is defined
> as an ability of an organ to survive and to perform effi-
> ciently as well as to be recognized as indispensable, then
> after 30 years, the intended institutionalization of the Tam-
> bon Council has yet to be realized. Nevertheless, the ad-
> ministrative development . . . in the form of rural public
> programs [has] shed a different light upon the role and
> function of Tambon Councils as important institutions of
> rural development. These programs actually give a new
> lease on life for Tambon Councils as the Central Govern-
> ment channels the funds and basic authority to use them
> more or less directly from the top to the bottom of admin-
> istrative echelons, essentially bypassing the usual admin-
> istrative and financial control of the Provincial Administra-
> tion. Thus, the "bottom-up" approach to rural development
> has been given an effective boost.[27]

The AID mission developed the Decentralized Development Management Project to field a number of teams that would work at the provincial level and below to strengthen the REGP planning and implementation processes. After about four years of operation, AID had this to say about DDMP:

> A candid evaluation of the [DDMP] project . . . revealed differences among implementing agencies as to the project's ultimate goal. From AID's perspective, DDMP was designed primarily to foster local autonomy. . . . others viewed the project more as a mechanism for realizing efficiency and effectiveness within the existing administrative system. Despite differences in perception, the evaluation team concluded that the project is beginning to produce results in helping small townships plan and implement rural infrastructure projects.[28]

The reader may well have a sense of *dèja vu* from this passage, recalling the comments of Siffin quoted earlier (in chapter 4) on the Institute of Public Administration project back in the 1950's, when the Americans saw the Institute as a catalyst for fundamental bureaucratic change while the Thais viewed the Institute as contributing to incremental improvements in efficiency. On the other hand, the DDMP project succeeded in developing training and planning materials and innovations that appear useful for improving the ability of local officials to use REGP resources effectively. Whether or not the Department of Local Administration adopts these pilot level innovations for general implementation remains to be seen.

Both the REGP and NRDP programs can be fairly credited with having added significantly to the social assets and services of an important fraction of the rural populace in a manner that was somewhat less paternalistic and more participatory than previous government programs. While they did succeed (especially REGP) in decentralizing implementation, the attempt to decentralize decision-making made only modest progress in the face of the powerful forces that have long sustained the country's highly centralized governmental processes.

THE DECLINE IN POVERTY

The account of AID's main activities aimed at the alleviation of rural poverty in Thailand has now been virtually brought up to the present.

What has happened with poverty in Thailand, especially in the Northeast, and what conclusions can be drawn as to the overall impact of
the AID program?

Before an answer to these questions can be given, a review is
needed of the observations made above that for one rationale or
another, the AID program has focused much of its activity since the
beginning on the reduction of poverty. I refer to projects (in agriculture or transportation, for example) that addressed constraints to the
growth of production and income and projects (as in health) that
addressed living conditions associated with or caused by poverty.
Many of these activities "reached" the poor (like household spraying
under the malaria project or ARD roads to end village isolation), and
much of the focus on the Northeast has been, perforce, poverty-oriented. The distinction intended since the New Directions legislation
has concerned partly the manner in which the poor were to be drawn
into projects as active "participants" and partly the intent to target
the most disadvantaged (or relatively disadvantaged) among populations whose members are mostly very poor by American standards.
Thus, although the "Focus on Poverty" period, along with the particular style of projects developed during this time, dates formally from
the early 1970s, the more appropriate perspective for examining the
record on poverty impact would include the full thirty-eight years of
U.S. assistance.

It is possible to sketch out the main lines of Thailand's income
growth and progress towards reduction of poverty by drawing on a
few summary studies.* Of fundamental importance has been the vig-
orous overall growth of the Thai economy. All regions of the country
participated in this growth, although at different rates. Bangkok and
its surrounding areas grew faster than other regions. Based on a
comparison of household surveys carried out in 1962–1963, 1968–
1969 and 1975–1976, a World Bank study reached conclusions worth
repeating in part:

> The reduction in the incidence of poverty recorded in these
> surveys is quite striking and is a commendable achieve-
> ment for Thailand. Remarkably income disparities have

* The reader will appreciate that there are many problems of definition and measurement
respecting income and poverty that make quantitative estimates very imprecise, especially in
developing countries (because of problems with raw data and because of the importance at
low-income levels of real income that does not get counted, including nonmonetized benefits
of social capital, which have figured largely under ARD, the NRDP program, and the like). The
broad lines of what has happened are clear enough for this account, however, which will not
be burdened with all the qualifications the interested reader will find in the references cited.

not increased for those groups covered by the surveys, and there have been some interregional reductions in these disparities. . . .

According to the measures used, [poverty] has been cut approximately in half from 57% to 31% of the population between 1962 and 1975. Real per capita income throughout the period has grown steadily at about 3% per year and a wide cross section of Thais has enjoyed substantial real income growth throughout the period.[29]

Nor surprisingly, the study also found that some areas enjoyed no increase and saw little alleviation of poverty. Nevertheless, the survey data indicated that interregional and rural/urban income differentials had declined. Nearly half the country's poverty was located in the Northeast, but this region saw a decline in incidence along with the country as a whole. In 1962–1963 the incidence in the Northeast was 74 percent. By 1975–1976 the proportion of the Northeast population below the poverty line had dropped to 44 percent.

The driving forces behind income growth in the Northeast are easily specified. According to the same World Bank study:

Growth of rural income in the Northeast has been associated with increased access to markets through the extension of the road system and with the diversification into upland crops—maize, kenaf, and cassava. Further analysis shows that the diversification and income growth depend not only on the access to markets, but also on suitability of the land available for the crops grown. Maize areas are the most affluent. Cassava and kenaf are poor people's crops; but where they have been introduced they have raised a large number of the poor marginally above the poverty line. Those who grow little besides rice have remained predominantly poor. Growth has been evenly distributed within wide areas of similar land use, and per capita household income distribution within both the better-off and the poor rural areas of the region is remarkably equitable. Systematic pauperization of large segments of the population has not accompanied rapid growth.

The studies identified a number of areas where government programs in the past have had significant and positive effects on poverty alleviation, even though that was not their principal objective. These include the provision of economic infrastructure, communications, roads, power, etc., the maintenance of political stability that allowed market structures to develop widely throughout the country, and the establishment of an open economy providing access to foreign markets for selling surplus agricultural output and acquiring modern inputs and consumption items.

The evidence does not indicate that inadequate and poor distribution of certain basic services such as education and health services has been a major impediment to income growth in Thailand, so far. Basic levels of education and health services have been provided in the past, and these have been sufficient for the needs of the agriculture expansion based primarily on traditional practices, which has been the principal source of most rural income growth and the prime factor in the reduction in poverty. (p. iii)

More recent analyses that carry the picture forward to 1981 (based on the 1981 Socio-Economic Survey) have shown further declines in the proportion of the population below the poverty line (under varying definitions of this concept).[30]

Several additional points should be noted to put this experience in proper perspective. First, the early 1980s saw deep and sustained declines in the prices of Thai export commodities. The decline probably caused many rural areas to lose some of the income gains of previous years. These prices generally began to recover in 1987. Second, recent studies (see, for example, Medhi Krongkaew 1986) have suggested that the *distribution* of income among households has been growing more unequal even as the whole income range has been rising absolutely. In the Northeast relative income distribution became more unequal between 1963 and 1981, but among the rural population it remains considerably less skewed than in the rest of the country. Third, while the proportion of the Thai population at poverty income levels has declined substantially, the absolute number of people living at these income levels has not fallen very much—a fact that reflects the rise in population size over this period among all groups.

Fourth, besides the sources of growth for the Northeast noted in the World Bank passage quoted above, income in this region has benefited from infusions from outside—from the U.S. military expenditures incident to the construction and operation of the air bases from the mid-1960s to the mid-1970s and from remittances sent home by Northeastern workers employed in Middle East construction projects since the mid-1970s. Fifth, off-farm and nonagricultural employment has been rising as sources of income for rural families. Northeast farm families have diversified themselves as individual members move seasonally or permanently to supplement family income with off-farm wage labor, often out of the agriculture sector and out of the region.

Summing up, we see a long and uneven rise in income in the Northeast and a reduction in poverty in most areas (the Northeast and elsewhere). While the population has increased substantially, the ranks of the poverty stricken have not grown. Those in poverty have fallen moderately in absolute numbers, substantially as a fraction of the population. The main sources of increased money incomes in the Northeast besides exogenous military expenditure and remittance receipts, have been expansions in upland crops (chiefly maize and cassava) and in off-farm employment. The main contributions of government programs have been the building of the infrastructure that allowed the private marketing system to gain low-cost access to Northeast farmers and the restoration and maintenance of domestic security. Maize and rice have benefited from RTG varietal research and seed distribution. The RTG has actually tried to discourage cassava production, fearful of its long-run effect on soil fertility. (The European Economic Community [EEC] has been helping the RTG search for alternatives to cassava production. The boom in Thai cassava exports to Europe stems from the EEC agriculture policy that has created an artificially high price structure in the Community's animal feed market.) The expansion of agricultural output in the Northeast has been largely extensive in character, based on expanding the area under cultivation, while yields either have not been rising much, or have been declining (as in the case of cassava areas in the southern changwats of the Northeast). Irrigation investment has made a modest contribution. The growth in agricultural production in the Northeast (and therefore income) has been uneven, reflecting the wide variation in production potential of locale-specific ecosystems, even within the broadly poor resource endowment of the region as a whole.[31]

Finally, real income—or perhaps what I should describe with that elusive phrase "quality of life"—has improved in poor villages in ways that are not reflected in measured income—ways that include the effects of the plethora of REGP and NRDP projects since 1981, the expansion of educational and health services, and all the transformations inherent in the bringing of the Northeast out of its long isolation. The NRDP is driven by a concept of poverty, or of deprivation, that owes as much to Buddhist strands of thought as it does to standard economic ideas about income. The principal architect of NRDP (which was the central poverty program of the Fifth Plan) has argued that the true character of poverty involves the conditions of hunger, disease, and ignorance.[32] Income alone is inadequate as a measure of one's status with respect to these conditions, and, I might add, it is not a sufficient condition for their elimination. Given the strong association between living standards and location (in rural areas), it was a natural step to define poverty (and NRDP project eligibility) by village rather than by household income status. To classify villages more or less characterized by hunger, disease, and ignorance, NESDB developed the system of indicators of village status mentioned above.[33] Thai economists have yet to bring these two approaches to poverty together into one conceptual framework, but it is likely that deprivation—that is, life in conditions judged to be substandard and unacceptable according to Thai ethical norms—is declining at a faster rate than is implied by the changes captured in the concept of the single, measured poverty income line.

What can be said in conclusion about the role of the U.S. program? First, the substantial progress in raising incomes and alleviating the effects of poverty was greatly facilitated by the creation of the transport and other infrastructures that ended the isolation of the poor regions of the country. The program's early years as a major financier of highways and bridges and other facilities and as an institution-builder for the government agencies responsible for the subsequent proliferation of infrastructure can be seen as having laid much of the basis for this essential component of poverty reduction in Thailand. It goes without saying that the major credit belongs to the Thai government's development planners for establishing the priorities for the allocation of public sector resources. Other donors also played very important roles, especially Australia and the World Bank in road construction. Second, AID's large technical and financial contributions to the RTG's programs to restore domestic security, especially in the relatively backward and poor areas of the country, were important to the success of these programs. A climate of security and stability was important, probably the sine qua non, for the extension of the marketing system into the remote reaches of the Northeast, and it enabled the region's farmers to respond to the cassava and other crop opportunities that have figured in the area's income growth.

Third, the seed, research, irrigation, extension, and other agricultural projects, in their accumulation over many years, have made contributions to income growth among the poor. (For the most part, however, these contributions remain modest for the Northeast, if not disappointing.) The research and extension systems in Thailand have been reconfigured from time to time as the RTG and the donors have searched for answers to their low effectiveness (respecting the poor in particular, but also in general for farmers throughout the country).* It appears that all donor programs have been in the same boat in this regard. Some important breakthroughs may be emerging from the farming systems activities and from the managed production approach in the underutilized irrigation projects.

Fourth, the assistance AID has provided for the Thai government's policy of upgrading and reorienting the civil service structure of the Northeast region, especially for the selection and training of the district officials, was substantial and helped raise the general performance of the administrative system. Fifth, the long involvement of the program in the evolution of the public health system and the projects in malaria, water, and sanitation and in population services has contributed importantly to these public service functions. Their impact on health status and on the ability of the poor to determine preferred family size have contributed to raising living conditions. Sixth, some relatively small groups among the poor have been helped by individual area development projects and by village-level projects conducted by PVOs and the Peace Corps utilizing small AID grants. Some of these activities have generated models and lessons that could be useful for wide application in programs addressing poverty.

Altogether it would be fair to say that despite some suboptimizing approaches, some projects that had disappointingly low returns, and some apparent outright failures (and some activities where the results are not yet in), the U.S. program has made creditable contributions to a creditable Thai record in poverty reduction. In the Northeast these programs have worked against formidable difficulties in the region with the greater concentration of poverty and will have to continue to find better solutions if the gains made thus far are to be sustained and built upon.

---

*In 1980 the World Bank wrote that "Until recently the extension service has not been very effective, but most of its deficiencies are being addressed under Bank-assisted extension projects . . . steps are being taken to eliminate duplication. . . . there is inadequate coordination and cooperation between the Department of Agriculture and the Department of Agricultural Extension. . . . the increase in research activities and development of new technology has been slow" (National Agricultural Research Project, *Staff Appraisal Report*, pp. 13–14). By 1987 it appeared that one of the major innovations the Bank introduced for agriculture extension (the "training and visit" system) was proving ineffective and that further reconfiguration of the extension system would be needed. See Hawaiian Agronomics (International), Inc., *Development Impact in the Northeast*, p. 26.

URBAN POVERTY

The poverty focus of the AID program in this period was not entirely rural and agricultural. Through AID's Housing Guarantee (HG) program and the centrally funded Integrated Improvement Program for the Urban Poor (IIPUP), the mission attempted to address some of the problems of slum-dwellers in Bangkok and selected regional cities. The IIPUP project was a small three-year effort (1980–1983). It was intended to help the government's National Housing Authority (NHA) develop a capacity to carry out projects that combined community services with shelter construction. In fact, IIPUP had little impact. The NHA had no commitment to expand its responsibilities into allied services and was even being urged by the World Bank and AID to improve cost-recovery on its housing investments, an objective incompatible with adding on social services. The Authority also had overriding management problems that precluded attention to IIPUP's purposes. Under these circumstances the relatively tiny IIPUP inputs were in no position to affect the very much larger shelter investment program to which IIPUP was attached.[34]

AID's major urban assistance efforts were made through its Housing Guarantee authority program. Under the HG authority AID facilitates a flow of investment funds from American savings and loan institutions into housing projects in developing countries by extending guarantees to these institutions. The HG program also finances technical assistance. (The HG office in the Bangkok mission administers all HG projects in the region in addition to its work in the rest of Thailand.) As a mechanism for moving funds into shelter investment in Thailand, the HG program has had only modest success. Out of $15 million authorized in 1979, only $10 million has been utilized. The funds were loaned to the National Housing Authority for low-income housing; according to the HG criteria for eligibility, the occupants must have an income that is below the fiftieth percentile in a country's income distribution. Most of the units financed were located in Bangkok, although five other cities were also authorized.

A second HG allocation for Thailand, for $25 million, was extended in 1984 but was subsequently rescinded because no mutually acceptable agreement could be reached with NHA. By 1984 AID's policy was stressing the placement of HG projects in rural towns and smaller cities; the second authorization had a stipulation that three-fourths of the funds had to be used outside Bangkok. NHA focused on Bangkok, partly because the organization's work on low-income shelter centered on slum upgrading (for which it took World Bank funding) and the preponderance of the country's slum population is located in Bangkok. In addition, NHA was under no pressure from the RTG to use the $25 million, since HG terms at the time were less attractive than the terms Thailand could obtain from commercial financing. Other possible borrowers (the Government Housing Bank, Bangkok or other city administrations, or private organizations) were either not ready or not interested in using the funds at the time.

Technical assistance provided by the HG program has made some interesting contributions to the development of shelter policy and planning in Thailand (including work on a major RTG housing policy statement, on the Bangkok region development program of the Sixth National Development Plan, and with the Bangkok administration and the government Housing Bank), also stressing low-income housing and ways to encourage private developers to build for lower-income occupancy. Finally, as noted earlier, some of the PVOs receiving AID support are working on problems of urban poverty, especially in Bangkok's large Khlong Toey slum area.

SEVEN

THAILAND IN TRANSITION: NEW ROLES FOR FOREIGN ASSISTANCE

AID began in 1983 to inform Congress that the evolution of the Thai economy was changing Thai needs for external aid and was opening up new problems and opportunities for a continuing U.S. assistance role in the country's development. Several things had come together by then to set the stage for a reappraisal of how American aid might best contribute to Thailand's future economic development. The turmoil in the international economy in the years following the 1979 oil price rise had forced macroeconomic policy issues back to the center of RTG policy attention. Thai economic planners agreed with the World Bank view, shared by AID, that the best route for future development of the Thai economy was to strengthen the country's long commitment to a competitive, open trading strategy. The ASEAN group generally was seen as a major component of an East Asian subregion and a larger Pacific Rim region, a dynamic area that would be propelling future global economic activity. In the context of the Fifth Five-Year Plan and so-called structural adjustment loans from the World Bank, the RTG embarked on a complex program of institutional strengthening and policy reform. The broad objective of this restructuring was to raise the efficiency of the Thai economy while correcting the macroeconomic imbalances (essentially the deficits in Thailand's external accounts and public sector finances) that were threatening to exceed prudent levels (although nowhere near the levels that were crippling a large number of developing countries).

The sense that Thailand was approaching a different kind of watershed also contributed a strong impetus to the broad notion that efficiency could no longer be taken for granted. In this case the watershed involved the country's natural resources and environment. The warning signs that Thailand's reliance on extensive agricultural expansion was degrading its natural resource base, raised back in the 1950s by FAO, USOM, and the World Bank, could no longer be treated as a long-run issue of no current urgency. The single greatest shock to Thai complacency about natural resources came when remote sensing data from the Landsat satellite revealed that the country's forest cover was diminishing at an alarming rate.*

Other elements in the changing picture were the new emphases on the private sector and on development policy brought to AID by the change in U.S. administration in 1981. The Bangkok mission found both of these changes easy to accommodate. The same fifth development plan that emphasized poverty alleviation also gave high priority to adjustment of the economic policy framework, the problems of economic efficiency, and the responsibility of the public sector for promotion of the private sector as the principal engine of development. At the same time the idea began to form among the Thais that their rapidly transforming economy might in the foreseeable future be entering the ranks of the Third World vanguard, the newly industrializing countries.

The beginning of the transition of the AID program—of the search for a new program strategy more attuned to Thailand's emerging needs and the comparative advantages of aid from the United States as compared with other countries or the U.N. system—can be marked by a study of future options for the program commissioned by Mission Director Robert Halligan in 1983. The principal raw materials for this study were the views of forty to fifty prominent Thais who were interviewed at length. Many suggestions were made by those respondents, but the most commonly held views saw the most useful roles for USAID in education and manpower development, science and technology, management, public-private cooperation, and agriculture. These choices partly reflected the traditional areas associated with USAID's past activities in Thailand, such as the participant-training program (under which many of the interviewees themselves

---

*According to TDRI, "Thailand's forests continue to disappear at a considerable rate. The pace of deforestation has been accelerating since the early years of the century, but it has moved into a higher gear since the 1960s. In 1961, for example, some 53 percent of the country was still covered with forest, a proportion of which declined dramatically to the 1986 figure of 29 percent. In other words, Thailand lost about 45 percent of her forests over this 25-year period" (Thailand Natural Resources Profile, p. 74).

had obtained U.S. degrees). But, as N. W. Temple notes, they also seemed to indicate general perceptions about the comparative advantages of assistance from the United States:

> The U.S. is regarded as a leading source of advanced technology and one which is more favorably disposed than other countries to sharing and transferring technology.
>
> Especially in a period when Japan's commercial and aid presence is large and growing rapidly, Thais believe it will be in their national interest to maintain access to other technological reservoirs as well.
>
> Thais see the U.S. and its private sector as an important market for Thai goods and a valuable source of technology, management and capital inputs for Thailand's development. U.S. firms are world leaders in agribusiness and hydrocarbon technologies, which are Thailand's two principal areas of industrial interest given its natural resource endowments.[1]

One of the most significant insights of this study was the author's sense that the Thais saw poverty as a problem that by the 1980s had been contained; it was no longer a problem of which U.S. aid held particular relevance or leverage.

> It was interesting to find that very few Thais interviewed explicitly associated poverty and "basic human needs" concerns with their image of USAID's future contribution to Thailand's development. This focus was not excluded by them, and it did sometimes creep into the discussion indirectly. By and large, however, Thais did not seem to perceive helping the poor as the central justification for USAID's presence in the same way that it is perceived by USAID staff. While this is partly a function of the sample of people interviewed, it also bespeaks other factors. "Basic human needs" are now increasingly regarded in Bangkok circles as the special problems of disadvantaged sub-groups in society, rather than as a systemic condition justifying top priority. Many basic services are already in place on a fairly comprehensive scale. The remaining large-scale or high-cost infrastructure, training, and relief needs in basic services are increasingly being met by other multilateral donors (IBRD, ADB, WHO, UNICEF) and the RTG itself, so

the absolute need for USAID's comparatively small monetary input is lessening.[2]

One might take issue with the perception of the status of poverty implied here (in fact, five years later, with macroeconomic adjustment well in hand, there are signs that the focus of development planning may be shifting back to the "lagging sectors" of the economy), but this would not affect the views this study recorded about the relative usefulness of American aid at this stage of Thailand's development.

In 1970 Caldwell had observed how changes in aid direction take several years to accomplish and how the program at any time contains a mix of projects, some working on the planning agenda of previous years, some addressing what are anticipated to be the "emerging" problems of the foreseeable future. The present transitional period illustrates the point again. Under Halligan's successor, John R. Eriksson, a new set of projects has been launched over the past several years alongside the poverty-oriented projects still being implemented. Some of the new activities follow lines suggested by the 1983 study. While some of the new activities are still pertinent to problems of poverty, others, in the jargon of the 1970s, can be labeled "trickle-down." The basic data on these projects is shown in table A.2.

POLICY ANALYSIS

It is the Emerging Problems of Development project that best captures a sense of shift in the U.S.–Thai aid relationship. The idea behind this project is to identify problem areas where significant future policy decisions will be required and to help the policy processes deal with these problems based on high-quality research and analysis. The concept is broad enough to include some funds for midcareer professionals in NESDB and DTEC to obtain advanced degrees in the United States. The largest single allocation has gone to support policy research undertaken by the Thai Development Research Institute, the country's first independent think tank (set up in 1984 with a founding grant from Canada). Funds were also provided for a number of studies contributing to the formulation of the current sixth development plan's sections on urban transport and financial management, science and technology, family planning, and natural resources management. Through a process that solicits the policy concerns of government agencies, the Emerging Problems project identifies significant policy issues needing examination. After review of proposals by NESDB, DTEC, and the mission and revision of research methodology where necessary, funds are granted for the policy studies without further review by AID/W. The process had developed bugs from time to time, but policy problems are being studied and experience is being gained on how a mutually acceptable, jointly administered Thai–U.S. mechanism that routinely helps to promote examination of significant policy problems can be operated. Studies and pilot activities supported by EPD have helped pave the way for major new projects in science and technology and in natural resources and environment.

DEVELOPMENT OF THE BUSINESS SECTOR

The emphasis AID management of the 1980s has put on the role of the private sector in developing countries and on private sector projects in the aid program represents a sharp turn from the agency's central concern for basic needs and poverty during the previous decade. For the Thai aid program, however, it meant a return to an area that had been well represented during the first twenty-five years of its history. The impact the road- and bridge-building projects had on the development of the Thai construction contracting sector, an important side effect of the methods USOM preferred for implementing these activities, has already been described. There was also a series of projects (listed in table A.14) designed to help the RTG develop some of the relevant institutional infrastructure. The major activities are described in this section.

The Board of Investment (BOI) is the RTG agency responsible for promoting foreign investment in Thailand and for administering the system under which domestic as well as foreign private firms obtain investment incentives if they meet BOI criteria. AID has provided technical assistance to BOI several times since its establishment in its present form in 1965, including help in drafting the legislation that set up BOI to replace a previously ineffective investment promotion system. Under a follow-on contract with the technical advisers (Checchi and Company), BOI was assisted in implementing the new legislation and getting its new organization functioning. USOM's Private

Enterprise Office also worked with the BOI in the 1960s to develop promotional missions to the United States and contacts with potential American investors.

Other institutional activities included advisory assistance and training for the Ministry of Industry (industrial surveys, publications, establishment of an advisory service center, degree training in the United States, and the like); technical and capital assistance contributing to the establishment of the Industrial Finance Corporation of Thailand and to its policy and organizational development; advisory assistance to the Ministry of Commerce and the central bank, the Bank of Thailand; and technical assistance to some individual Thai firms provided by the volunteer International Executive Service Corps (240 volunteers between 1965 and 1984).

In the 1980s' round of private sector projects, the principal activities have been the Private Sector in Development Project, a $3.5 million effort that began in 1983, and a new follow-on project, Rural Industries and Employment. The first project had three components: technical assistance to BOI to identify business opportunities and attract private investment interest in them; "establishment of means for effective policy analysis by the private sector to analyze important issues . . . affecting private sector development and to recommend appropriate policies to the RTG . . . by financing staff and studies for the Joint Standing Committee for Commerce, Industry and Banking"; and "establishment of linkages between private sector associations with counterpart associations in the U.S. to encourage mutual cooperation, transfer of technology and future business relations through staff support for the Thai counterpart of the U.S. Joint Agricultural Consultative Corporation."[3] A separate project set up an Institute for Management Education for Thailand (IMET) to provide short-term training for Thai entrepreneurs, with emphasis on businessmen from the provinces. Other activities (developed by AID's private enterprise bureau in Washington rather than by the field mission) included a small loan and a guarantee facility with two Thai banks to promote loans to provincial (largely agribusiness) firms.

It is difficult to evaluate the ultimate usefulness of many of these activities, especially the odds and ends of advisory assistance in the earlier years of the program. The difficulty arises from the fact that these inputs were only a few among many from various sources, and that detailed evaluative records are not available that would enable one to trace the course of specific inputs and their probable effects. In 1982 an AID evaluation team reviewed the program's past assistance to the set of institutions and agencies charged with private sector promotion and regulation:

> It is difficult to assess the impact of AID's private sector programs so long after their conclusion. As with all other assistance, some projects were more successful than others. There is general agreement that the capabilities of the institutions to which assistance was directed needed to be upgraded, and that their inadequate functioning was a constraint to private sector development. It can only be assumed that AID assistance resulted in some improvement. There is room for much more.[4]

Chapter 1 noted the difficulty of evaluating the relationships between aid inputs and final outcomes. The problem of identifying these relationships is even greater in the case of "the private sector" than in the case of primary health care or other areas discussed earlier. Even if more detailed records were available on the immediate "outputs" of these activities, as in fact is the case with the projects of the 1980s, judgment about impact would remain difficult because of the large disjuncture between the specific inputs of these projects and the objectives AID defined for itself in the documentation, including the materials prepared for its *Congressional Presentations*. The mission's summary description of the Private Sector in Development Project illustrates the point:

> The goal was to contribute to the RTG's Fifth Development Plan structural adjustment objectives of improving Thailand's balance of trade and reducing unemployment problems, particularly in areas outside Bangkok.
> It was expected that a number of new investments and other business arrangements would be made in export oriented, labor intensive and natural resource based industries as a direct result of the surveys, promotional program, policy dialogue and U.S./Thai agribusiness linkages benefitting from assistance under the project. In addition, the relationships established between the private sectors in Thailand and the U.S. were expected to stimulate a steady flow of information on markets and new technology between the two countries. The improved policy analysis and planning capability established under the project to

address private sector related issues were expected to result in realistic policies and regulations that would steadily
improve the investment climate for industries particularly
in priority development areas.[5]

The disjuncture arises from the simple fact that investment decisions by American business, whether an investment pattern in any
period is export-oriented or not, whether such investments are labor-
intensive or not, or are located in the greater Bangkok area or outside,
are all economic outcomes that are powerfully affected by many things
quite beyond the scope of this project, indeed in policy realms that
may not be affected by foreign aid in general or by any outside view.
I need only mention the question of a country's exchange rate to
illustrate this point. The devaluation of the baht in late 1984, for
example, has been the single most important factor behind the export-oriented boom of the last two years and the enormous increase
in the interest of Japanese investors in locating plants in Thailand.
The BOI is the key agency that serves as the door through which these
investments are entering the country (by virtue of its function as
setting the conditions and privileges for firms that want to take advantage of tax and other concessions). To the extent that AID's project
(and other donor assistance) is helping to improve BOI's performance
in carrying out these functions, the assistance can be properly said to
be contributing to the rising investment inflow. But it would be a
great overstatement to attribute much causation to an improvement
in BOI's efficiency as compared to the impact of exchange rate relations and of all the other basic economic and political factors that
make Thailand, at this time, the most attractive investment location
for many Japanese and other foreign enterprises.

The problem with respect to aid to the BOI can be taken one step
further. The investment patterns promoted by the BOI—which of
course is following the general industrialization policies of the Ministry of Industry and of the RTG's development policy as a whole—
have changed over time and have during some periods been subject
to much criticism. There have been issues of the wisdom of the import-substitution industrialization policies prior to the structural adjustment of the early 1980s (the structural adjustment represented a
reshaping of policy, even if incomplete, away from import-substitution), of the promotion of some specific industries that involved an
inefficient use of resources (such as automotive assembly), of the
ineffectiveness of BOI preferences for location of investment outside
of Bangkok, and so on. Perhaps the best way of summing up this

complex experience is to note that the BOI has been the agency through which a large fraction of the modern corporate sector has trooped on its way to making new ventures and that the expansion of this sector has been a major factor in Thailand's development, but that the policy package BOI implemented could have been better, although its promotional outreach efforts probably did facilitate (maybe even increased) the inflow of private investment, especially when the basic economic factors have been markedly favorable. This is an unavoidable simplification of a subject too complex to cover properly in this study. But it does lead me to think that in the case of the AID assistance to BOI, including that for its initial formulation, a more positive conclusion is probably justified than the 1982 evaluators' view that some improvement "can only be assumed."

The disjuncture is much greater in the 1980s than it would have been for a project with similarly stated objectives in the 1950s or even 1960s. When USOM's private enterprise office was first set up and when the first investment potential surveys were carried out by U.S. technical advisors, the mission's activities in this field were pioneer efforts. As in so many of the subjects I have touched upon, the program's early private sector activities had the prospect of much long-term leverage because the state of institutional development and of Thai experience was so limited. Even more fundamental was the underdeveloped state of the private sector. Most enterprises in Thailand were small family operations. The thin ranks of more modern banking and manufacturing enterprises, largely located in Bangkok, were also mainly family operations. Manufacturing was very limited in terms of level of technology, scale of output, backward linkages to the manufacture of intermediate outputs, and access to nonfamily capital. The business sector was not well organized. For the most part the interests of business in government policies and functions that affected their investment opportunities and market positions were pursued through individual arrangements and accommodations between entrepreneurs and powerful persons in government. Commerce and industry were largely in the hands of the ethnic Chinese minority.

A recent analysis by Anek Laothamatas of the evolution of the business community puts its experience in the postwar period in the context of the Thai bureaucratic polity paradigm:

> Between 1932, the year the absolute monarchy was overthrown, and 1973, when the country's longest-ruling military regime was toppled, Thailand was in a sense a bureaucratic polity. ... Unlike the bureaucratic-authoritarian

regimes of Latin America, however, the Thai bureaucratic polity operated among docile, politically inert social groups or classes, leaving decision-making authority in the hands of a small elite of bureaucrats. Autonomous, organized political activities of nonbureaucratic groups—student, worker, peasant, business—were minimal and affected the policy of the state mainly in an informal, particularistic, and often clientistic manner.

The state-business political relationship was by no means an exception to this. Ethnically Chinese, poorly educated, and often confronted by the nationalistic policy of the government, the "pariah entrepreneurs" could only keep a low political profile. They affected policy only defensively and in a covert, particularistic manner—mostly in the implementation rather than the formulation stage of policy making. The prevailing forms of business influence were outright bribery or creation of patron-client relationships with military-bureaucratic leaders, mainly by inviting the latter to join executive boards or to hold stock in companies at no cost.[6]

The emergence of a new private sector and a new business-government relationship paradigm in the last fifteen years has been remarkable, one of the most important and still understudied aspects of Thailand's postwar development. The corporate sector is taking on many of the characteristics of the business sectors of modern, internationally oriented, more highly developed economies. The integration of the Chinese into Thai society has been one of the most rapid and important changes contributing to this modernization process. The larger family concerns especially are becoming professionalized, hiring engineering and management talent from the growing pool of such skills rather than limiting themselves to their own kin, and are gradually going public in order to tap outside capital. The business community has grown enormously in its membership, product diversity, sophistication, and organization. It has also begun to enter the political arena. Individual businessmen have joined political parties and run for parliamentary seats from which they have sought to protect or advance business interests. More and more businessmen are to be found in Thai cabinets. And a network of business associations has grown up, through which groups of producers or the business sector generally attempt to promote their interests through negotiation with government and lobbying in different forms (p. 451).

In this much enlarged and developed business sector, individual aid projects are unlikely to find scope for major impact on the sector's evolution or on macro-level outcomes. Nevertheless, the latest round of AID's private sector activities appears to have found a niche for a meaningful contribution. The focus of this activity has been a Joint Public Private Sector Consultative Committee (JPPCC) established in 1981. The JPPCC is the latest and first really successful formal arrangement for policy dialogue between the RTG and the business community as a whole. While the Committee had precursors that had fallen into disuse, this current version appears to have taken root and been formulated in a way that gives the operations of the Committee the publicity, high-level attention, and quality of staff work that its predecessors lacked. Membership on the private sector side is composed of representatives of the leading business organizations, with arrangements for including the foreign chambers of commerce. The Thai side is headed by senior officials who attend all the meetings and formally by the Prime Minister who attends occasional major meetings. More than forty JPPCCs have been set up in the provinces where there has been a growth in recent years of business groups asserting local interests often at variance with the interests of Bangkok business.

The JPPCC has been serving mainly as a forum in which the private sector can exchange views directly with leading officials of the key departments and agencies with which business has most of its governmental relationships. The exchange process has gradually improved in substance as the private side has begun to present its problems and views in a systematic manner through well-staffed papers. The format of the meetings call for the senior officials responsible for individual items to respond on the spot and for specific issues to be assigned for further discussions and taken up again at subsequent meetings if the parties are not satisfied. The issues raised by the private side have ranged from policy to red tape. Numerous RTG responses and accommodations have emerged from this deliberative process.

The Thai government and the local business community have not been adverse to involvement of American organizations in this institutional evolution in the private sector. As Anek points out:

> Interestingly, several American agencies, governmental and non-governmental, have played a considerable role in assisting various Thai public and private efforts to develop business associations and government-business sectoral consultation. [USAID] in Thailand, after extensive discussion with the Thai NESDB began a four-year $4 million

"Private Sector in Development" project in 1982. Funds in this project financed, in part, NESDB training programs for secretaries of provincial JPPCCs. The Thai Chamber, the Association of Industries, and the Banker Association—the three most established business organizations in the country—also have commissioned many sophisticated research projects on their internal problems as well as on their public laws, regulations, and policies unfavorable to business operations, all with generous grants from USAID. Another American agency that has been crucial to the development of business associations in Thailand is the Center for International Private Enterprise (CIPE), an affiliate of the U.S. Chamber of Commerce. CIPE was created and funded by the National Endowment for Democracy which in turn receives annual appropriations approved by the U.S. Congress. It has provided financial assistance for . . . regular seminars and short course training programs to upgrade the business and management capability of up-country businessmen. . . . Finally, the Asia Foundation has contributed to the improvement of the publications program of some associations, such as the Songkhla Provincial Chamber. (p. 460–61)

The Private Sector in Development project has made very useful contributions to the professionalization of the JPPCC dialogue by financing the staff and research work. While leading Thai corporations have become well staffed with modern trained professionals and have supported the development of a relatively elaborate business-sector organizational structure, the apex business organizations had no experience in dealing with the technocrats of government on the plane of general policy and in a format that mobilizes portions of the business community as a coherent community of interest. A few Thai planners, who see the process of the evolution of business organization and behavior vis-à-vis the government in its larger socioeconomic context, recognized the timing was finally right in the 1980s for fixing a JPPCC arrangement that could help to further the evolution of Thai business and accelerate the solution of regulatory and other problems impeding international competitive efficiency. In the event, the JPPCC has been making significant contributions along these lines.

To put the JPPCC experience thus far into proper perspective, however, it must be stressed that the institutional structure of the private sector does not yet represent all the varied segments of that sector. It still lacks organizational components or processes that can canvass and express the different and often conflicting interests within the sector. The private side representatives in the JPPCC process are leading Bangkok-based financial and industrial businessmen. Besides the provincial interests, which are only starting to organize as such, there are some industrial product groups that have opted to remain outside the coordinating organizations. More importantly, the industrial sector has a very large base of small enterprises that lack any organizational cohesion. While the private side's agenda in the JPPCC has included much that is consistent with the interests of small business, it has not yet addressed the institutional and policy problems that concern mainly the base of the business pyramid.

The Private Sector project shares a certain diffuseness with some of its companion projects of the same ilk. Some components will not fare as well as the JPPCC. If this project is seen in terms of impact on large-scale macroeconomic trends in the economy, a future evaluation will find it difficult again to establish impact. It would be naive to expect that such institutional arrangements by themselves might offset powerful economic forces, such as those that have led to Thailand's high concentration of manufacturing in the greater Bangkok area. But if seen in terms of an instrumental objective—the development of open, regular, and professional dialogue between business and government—the project seems likely to be making very useful contributions. The character of communication between government and the investment community of a country is not a trivial factor in the development process.

AID's latest private sector activity is the Rural Industries and Employment project. Initiated in 1986 for a planned cost of $14.8 million, this project is intended to promote the expansion of small- and medium-scale enterprise outside metropolitan Bangkok. Like several of the earlier investment oriented projects, this again takes on the more difficult dimensions of private sector development. (I mention only in passing the objectives AID proposed to Congress in the FY 1986 *Presentation*, "to absorb underemployed rural labor and increase rural wages." The project is likely to generate some provincial employment. It would take extraordinary success and leverage, however, for the project to create enough incremental demand for labor that it would emerge as a measureable force for pushing up wages. The agency's enthusiasm for a private sector project that also might help alleviate poverty is understandable, but the evaluators who eventually get around to this project will almost certainly find fault if they take these objectives literally.) The project does contain some innovative ideas that probably would not have been tried in the forms proposed, if the mission had not persisted in the lengthy planning and negotiation process that led to final agreement with the cooperating RTG agencies. These initiatives include both new approaches to technical assistance and training for small entrepreneurs and a guarantee fund to draw Thai commercial banks into making loans (and developing the experience of handling such loans) to enterprises based in provincial towns that have good projects but inadequate collateral (Thai banks have a narrower and more conservative definition than American banks as to what constitutes eligible collateral). This project will also fund continuing support for the provincial JPPCC network begun under the Private Sector in Development project as well as for the expansion of provincial chambers of commerce and branches of the Federation of Thai Industries. In addition, the project is supporting studies of the constraints on growth of "up-country" enterprise.

There have been many efforts to provide technical and financial assistance to entrepreneurs who are located outside the greater Bangkok area and whose businesses are small or medium by Thai standards. For many years the Ministry of Industry has had programs aimed at this group, with apparently one major success involving handicraft manufacturers in the Chiangmai area and an effective pilot industrial extension project in the Northeast conducted by the Ministry of Industry with UNIDO assistance. Previous funds specially established for smaller enterprises have had little impact. This is also a field that has attracted other external development agencies, including a guarantee scheme operated by the Industrial Finance Corporation of Thailand with funds from Japanese aid. Still AID's Rural Industries project contains some new twists that might prove more effective than past efforts. The designing of this project (in which I had a small role) was able to profit from the findings of considerable prior research (including an off-farm employment research project AID financed in 1979–1980) and by the experience gained under the previous programs.

SCIENCE AND TECHNOLOGY

A major project in the Mission's current portfolio is designed to help put the application of science and technology (S&T) to production processes in Thailand onto a modern and established basis. Thailand has accumulated a significant scientific capability that is underutilized in terms of application to economic activity. Information about the country's scientific and technological status, in terms of manpower, institutional capabilities, the problems of private industry's acquisition and utilization of technology, the generation of local adaptive technology, etc., has been insufficient for policy analysis and planning in this area. There has not been a very clear or operationally useful concept of either the role of science and technology in the country's future development; or of what needs to be done to tap into the areas of rapid world technological change that are relevant to the Thai economy. The resources devoted to research in particular, especially by the private manufacturing sector, have been very low when measured by the typical international criteria of research-and-development (R&D) activity levels (0.3 percent of GDP in 1985, compared to over 3 percent in the U.S. and 1.6 percent in Korea). There has been a substantial gap between the levels of Thai capacities and application of science and technology (there are exceptions of course, medical science being the outstanding one) and the levels found in Korea and other countries that are members of the NIC group to which Thais aspire.

The AID project is planned for a total U.S. input of $35 million and a Thai input of about $15 million. The funds are to be used for local research and for strengthening the mechanism for S&T acquisition and application. A new semiautonomous organization (the Science and Technology Development Board, or STDB) under the Ministry of Science, Technology, and Energy has been created to administer the funds. The board has representatives of the private sector and the government and academic communities, including businessmen, officials, and scientists. The objective is to promote R&D activity that has practical and commercial applications potential as well as to enhance Thai standards, testing, and quality control capabilities, to improve access to international technological information, and to support studies of policy constraints in these areas. The research funding represents the largest single dedication of monies for S&T that Thailand has ever had available. Technical assistance under the project and links to American scientists is being provided by the U.S. National Academy of Sciences.

In a very real sense the transfer of scientific and technical knowledge and the development of Thai scientific human resources and institutional capabilities have been at the heart of the aid program right from the start. The program has even dealt with "high tech" before, a prominent example being several projects in remote sensing (the reception, processing, and interpretation of terrestrial data recorded by satellite). Beginning in 1972, when Thailand began to acquire Landsat imagery data, AID (and other sources) trained Thai scientists in remote sensing technology. Further training and equipment were provided through 1982 to the RTG agency responsible for remote sensing (which by 1981 had established a station near Bangkok for direct reception from Landsat and other satellites). The AID input into these projects was about $500,000. In a much larger $5.6 million project begun in 1979, AID was the major donor in the establishment of a regional Center for Asian Remote Sensing Training at the Asian Institute of Technology, located north of Bangkok. Technical assistance to the Center was provided by NASA and American universities. An evaluation in 1983 found teething problems in the RTG's utilization of this technology, functions that could be more effective if additional peripheral hardware were acquired, areas of application in agriculture that could be more extensively developed, and so on. The overall judgment was that the technology was well on its way towards adoption and effective utilization and that in many specific respects further Thai access to American institutions strong in remote sensing technology would continue to be important and useful.[7]

What distinguishes the S&T project as a new conception is its focus on applications in the private sector, its concern for S&T policy as a broad developmental issue, and its objective to help fix deliberate attention to S&T in effective institutional settings. Like the Emerging Problems project and the Agriculture Technology Transfer project (which provided a model for some aspects of the S&T project), the S&T project is another case where the aid mission and the RTG have set up a mechanism (the STDB) for promoting a general area. The Board is intended to have the flexibility to finance relatively small individual research efforts and to respond more quickly to opportunities than would be possible under the usual planning and financial obligation processes of both governments. The S&T project is also interesting as an example of how a U.S. aid program much diminished in size, relative to RTG and other donor resources, can still stake out ground where U.S. assistance can gain leverage for contributing to future Thai development. The keys to this capability appear to be the selection of an area where the Thai governmental and professional communities see a strong comparative advantage for the aid relationship with the United States and the concentration of aid funds in sufficient magnitude to make a "critical mass." (In mid-project, as of this writing, the STDB has not yet developed the administrative style and flexibility envisaged. Its ultimate effectiveness remains to be seen.)

Thailand has also been one of the major participating countries under three centrally funded AID programs in science and technology (see table A.1.2) administered by the Board on Science and Technology for International Development (BOSTID) of the National Academy of Science. The Program in Science and Technology Cooperation initiated in 1982 offers research grants to individual scientists in developing countries based on selection from competitive applications. In the first five years of this program Thai scientists had garnered about one-quarter (over $6 million) of the grants, the largest fraction won by scientists from any of the eligible countries; the Thai awards were mainly in health and medical science. The other two programs provide grants for cooperative research with Israeli scientists and for investigation in selected subjects chosen by BOSTID, such as fast-growing tropical trees, malaria transmission, and rapid diagnosis of children's acute respiratory infections. The strong Thai participation in these programs reflects both the scientific and institutional strengths Thailand has attained in recent years and the effort the aid mission has been making to publicize these opportunities in the Thai scientific community and to help applicants frame their proposals.

RESPONSES TO OTHER CURRENT PROBLEMS

I conclude this section bringing the program up to date with brief notes on three activities that address problems outside the boundaries of the main program objectives during this period—namely, narcotics production and addiction; a modest contribution toward reducing the country's energy dependence on imported petroleum; and problems of Thai border villages created by armed incursions from Cambodia and Laos and by the presence of large refugee populations.

Narcotics

The northernmost provinces of Thailand are part of the Golden Triangle area, which includes part of Burma and Laos and is well known for opium cultivation and narcotics production and export. The RTG has been carrying out narcotics suppression programs for some years, including development of alternative crops for the communities that were earning their livelihood from opium cultivation; integrated settlement projects to reestablish such communities in a completely new and structured environment; treatment of addiction; and during the last four years destruction of poppy fields and illegal drug production facilities. For the most part these programs are administered by the RTG's Office of the Narcotics Control Board (ONCB). These programs have gotten considerable support from separate funds being provided by the U.S. State Department's Narcotics Assistance Program and the U.S. Drug Enforcement Agency (DEA), as well as by the U.N. Fund for Drug Abuse Control and several other bilateral donors (Australia, Germany, Norway). An AID project in 1974 financed equipment for the Thai customs authorities to help strengthen their traffic interdiction capabilities. AID's more recent projects in this area include the Mae Chaem project cited in chapter 6, with its Hill Tribe settlement focus, and the grants to PVOs working on narcotics education and treatment (table A.15).* U.S. contributions to the ONCB programs for narcotic crop destruction and for assisting cultivating communities to shift to other commercial crops have been made through the State Department and DEA. The impact of the RTG's traffic interdiction is as problematical as interdiction efforts elsewhere, including in the United States. On the production side, however, the RTG programs have chalked up considerable success. Production is reliably estimated to have been cut by 75 percent in Thailand's Golden Triangle area from the levels of several years ago.

Energy

After having been a major player in the early postwar development of the energy sector in Thailand, the aid program has had a return engagement on a small scale, prompted by the oil price rise of 1979. The objective of the Micro-Mini Hydro project is to develop a few small hydroelectric power sites as models that can then be replicated by the National Energy Authority (NEA). The project is providing NEA with a model for site selection and analysis and for construction

---

*The Mae Chaem project includes a Land Use Certification program which gives legal title to farmers for cultivation of public land. The grant is conditional: if a farmer produces, uses, or traffics in drugs, he loses title. The project also includes a detoxification program that has treated hundreds of addicts and has elicited self-help activities by the villages, such as drug-watch committees and support systems for former addicts. The PVO projects are being carried out by CARE and by two Thai organizations, the Population and Community Development Association and the Duang Pratheep Foundation.

of hydro sites that are economical to develop despite their small size (less than 6,000 kilowatts) because they serve remote communities. The project itself is financing up to twelve sites. NEA was planning to develop 175 sites over ten years. Although the total power generation capacity that would be added by these sites is small in terms of contribution to the country's overall power needs, the technology was a cost-effective method of providing electric power to the communities involved when the project was launched. In the meantime, however, oil prices have declined, and the economics of these sites has been adversely affected. Overtaken by events, the technology the Thais acquired under this project is unlikely to be applied as planned unless oil prices rise substantially again.

Indochina Impact: Affected Thai Villages

Thailand has been the major haven for refugees fleeing from Cambodia and Laos as a result of the Indochina conflict and Vietnamese occupation of Cambodia in 1979. In 1980 the number of refugees housed in Thailand reached 300,000. The existence of these camps has created security, political, and other disruptions in these areas. In addition, Thai villages along the Cambodian and Laotian borders have been subject to periodic hostile crossborder incursions—military patrols and, along the Cambodian border, shelling. To help the RTG cope with these problems, the aid program has included a grant of Economic Support Funds averaging $5 million a year since 1980. The total ESF contribution through 1989 is likely to be around $42 million. The funds have been used for local development projects in 412 border villages with a population of about 300,000 altogether. About a third of the U.S. contribution has gone for irrigation and domestic water projects, another third for local roads, and the rest for education, health, and other activities. The Affected Thai Village program is thus similar to the National Rural Development Program with its miscellany of local investments and services implemented by various RTG departments. In effect, the border village grants are financing another area-specific development program for relatively disadvantaged populations. Villages along the Cambodian and Laotian borders tend to be relatively disadvantaged in general socioeconomic terms (the bulk of them are in the Northeast), and they also suffer from additional disadvantages arising from the security problems imposed by external conditions.

This program also receives substantial support from the U.N. Border Relief Organization (UNBRO) and the Japanese and German governments and smaller amounts from several other countries. The total U.S. contribution as of this writing has been $42 million, other donors $62.3 million, and the RTG $35.2 million. The program is implemented by some thirty-five RTG civilian and military agencies and is coordinated by the Thai Supreme Command.

EIGHT

THE AID EXPERIENCE IN PERSPECTIVE

In the preceding chapters I have tried to assemble enough evidence to identify the main activities and objectives of the U.S. aid programs in Thailand and their effects. In many instances projects have failed completely or partially to achieve their objectives. Others may yet prove useful and cannot be judged until more time has passed. There have also been many cases where individual projects or sustained efforts over many years through various related activities appear to have achieved substantial results, or at least to have been associated with specific Thai development objectives that were being achieved and where the program's involvement can reasonably be assumed to have made material contributions. Overall, I have described American development assistance activities that a) made salient contributions to removing development bottlenecks and laying the basis for one of the more successful growth performances in the third world, b) provided significant help to a security-cum-development campaign to eliminate a Communist insurgency, and c) declined in recent years in its relative importance, focusing first on poverty alleviation and currently on a set of issues most relevant to a transition to the higher ranks of middle-income country status. This last chapter summarizes the program's contributions before concluding with some observations about the broad social and political ramifications of the aid relationship.

HUMAN RESOURCES AND INSTITUTIONAL DEVELOPMENT

Beginning with a look at the participant-training component, noting the common-sense view among the Thais that education and training in the United States were the most important contribution the program had made to their country's development, I also noted the prominence many of the participants have achieved. This Thai judgment is correct, but it needs to be enriched in a more complex formulation that embraces the institutions in and through which people with modern skills are enabled to put these skills to work. The reader has probably already encountered many institutions and organizations assisted by the aid program and the American foundations. The development of this complex of institutional capabilities—that is, the trained individuals and the organizations in which these people mobilize themselves and achieve their effectuation—can best be grasped and appreciated if all the (successful) institution-building scattered over the whole period and over many sectors of the economy and areas of intellectual endeavor are encapsulated. The institution-building and associated training, in my view, emerge as the primary development contributions of the aid program. Many of the specific accomplishments and the ability of the Thai institutions to promote economic development and to cope with the attendant problems have rested on this cumulation of institution-building.

Institutional Development

Economic development is characterized by an increase in the importance of human resources in relation to other factors that together produce technological advance and rising productivity and income—namely, land, natural resources and physical capital. Some of the richest and most productive economies, such as those of Japan, Switzerland, and Singapore, owe relatively little of their wealth to natural resources and land. Even in the United States, where land, natural resources, and physical capital are all abundant, studies of the sources of economic growth have attributed significant shares to improvements in the efficiency or performance of the stock of human capital.*

* There are many problems of theory and measurement in the literature on the sources of economic growth. The general conclusion, however, is not doubted by critics or economic

Like the proliferation of forms of physical capital (buildings, equipment, and so forth), human capital is also highly differentiated. Human capital is divided by subjects, specialities, and individual differences in capabilities and preferences. Just as the division of production functions (Adam Smith's division of labor) must be brought together and articulated to form a production process, so the intellectual functionings of differentiated human capital must be brought together in systematic relationships—in institutions and organizations—for a very broad range of activities (though not for all, quite obviously, as illustrated by the individuality of artistic creation and much invention). It is remarkable that the literature on economic growth has considerable guidance on the "how to" of creating a particular institution but contains little effort to develop a systematic treatment or framework of analysis for the role of institutional development as a whole. The analyses of the contributions of human capital to economic growth implicitly assume that the institutional arrangements within which humans operate are not independent factors affecting the efficiency of human capital, let alone the ability of the humans involved simply to make their skills functional. This failure to incorporate the institutional dimensions of economic development in any systematic manner may account for the subordinate role technical assistance has played in the literature.

In fact, it appears fundamental to the conditions of underdevelopment that Third World countries typically lack the thick network of institutions one finds in advanced economies that serve to create new knowledge and human capital and to mobilize much of the human capital stock for application to the society's functioning. The creation

---

historians. A recent paper conveys an idea of the approaches used and some of the conflicting results.

> Analysis of the role of human resources or human capital in the growth process has a long history in the post World War II literature . . . the definitive work remains that of Denison [whose] latest estimates show that less than 60% of the growth in GNP (1929–1973) in the United States can be attributed to the growth of traditional factors, mainly capital and labor inputs. The remaining growth is a result of economies of scale, improvements in resource allocation, and other factors, plus a large residual which is labelled as "advances in knowledge." Education is considered by Denison to be a factor input, and alone accounts for 14% of the growth in GNP . . . If education were to be combined with the residual "advances in knowledge," then the human capital component would be about 38%. . . . Kreuger found that differences in human capital explained about half of the differences in per capita GNP between the United States and a sample of developing countries. . . . On the other hand, H. Correa found that while health and nutrition factors were important, education advances appeared unrelated to output growth for a group of Latin American countries (Norman Hicks, *Economic Growth and Human Resources*, pp. 3–4)

of local capabilities, including the institutions that store, adapt, create, and apply knowledge, is the central task of technical assistance. Of course, economic aid to augment financial and physical resources available to poor countries is also critical for the growth process and plays an important role in institutional development as well.

Noted earlier was the short supply of skills and professions Thailand needed in the immediate postwar years, and the important contribution participant training made in helping to build the country's human capital stock. A parallel observation can be made about Thailand's stock of institutions relevant to economic development. We have seen a large number of projects that centered on the creation or strengthening of institutional capacities. To give some perspective on the cumulative stock after three decades of such activities, I have listed in table 8.1 all the institutions to which the U.S. program and the American foundations have made significant contributions, with a rough categorization of contributions of major or minor importance to the development of each one. Institutions that received only marginal assistance have been omitted. The major/minor judgment in each case is based on the extent to which the aid activity contributed to an institution's initial conception and design, staff development, policy or management development, and/or the resources helping to determine the scope of operations. The category "institution" is broadly conceived; it includes educational institutions, free-standing organizations, and government departments and public sector agencies. In the case of some ministries that have reorganized since the time when AID projects were operating (especially health and education) the institution-building is lodged in their staff and their capabilities and only to a lesser extent in their current formal organizational structures. To round out the picture, tables 8.2–8.4 list the major American institutions, government agencies, and corporations that have implemented institution-building projects in Thailand under AID contracts.

If one had the information to map Thailand's institutional position in 1950 and today, taking into account both the institutional needs then and now, and some measure of the effectiveness of the existing institutions at both times, it would be possible to convey a more systematic idea of the extent of Thailand's institutional development over this period and the role the U.S. aid program and the foundations have had in that development. The list in table 8.1 includes organizations (and their functions) that did not exist in 1950, and many public-sector entities whose capabilities then were minimal. Many of these institutions have gotten significant assistance from other international and bilateral aid sources; other important insti-

TABLE 8.1.

Institutional Capacity-Building in Thailand

Institution/Organization	AID Contribution	
	Major	Minor
Educational Institutions		
Chiang Mai University Medical School	x	
Chulalongkorn University[a]		
Engineering	x	
Medical		x
Kasetsart University[a]	x	
Khon Kaen University Development Research		
Institute[a]	x	
Lampang Yonok College	x	
Maejo Institute of Agricultural Technology		
Mahidol University[a]		x
National Institute of Development		
Administration[a]	x	
Payap College	x	
Prasarnmitr College of Education	x	
Surin Agricultural Campus	x	
Technical Institutes	x	
Asian Institute of Technology	x	
Thammasat University	x[b]	
Institute for Management Education for Thailand	x	
Office of the Prime Minister		
Board of Investment	x	
Bureau of the Budget	x	
Civil Service Commission		x
Department of Technology & Economic		
Cooperation	x	
Electricity Generating Authority of Thailand	x	
National Economic & Social Development Board	x	
National Statistical Office	x	
National Education Commission[a]	x	
Ministry of Agriculture and Cooperatives		
Department of Agriculture	x	
Department of Agricultural Extension	x	
Department of Agricultural Economics	x	
Department of Cooperation Promotion		x
Department of Fisheries		x
Department of Land Settlements		x
Department of Livestock Development	x	

TABLE 8.1. (continued)

Institutional Capacity-Building in Thailand

Institution/Organization	AID Contribution	
	Major	Minor
Royal Forestry Department		x
Royal Irrigation Department		x
Ministry of Communications		
Airports Authority	x	
Communications Authority	x	
Department of Highways	x	
Meteorological Department	x	
State Railways		x
Telephone Organization		x
Ministry of Defense		
AFRIMS	x	
Ministry of Education		
Department of General Education	x	
Department of Nonformal Education	x	
Department of Teacher Education	x	
Department of Vocational Education	x	
Ministry of Finance		
Bank for Agriculture and Cooperatives		x
Comptroller General's Department	x	
Revenue Department		x
Ministry of Industry		
Department of Mineral Resources	x	
Department of Industrial Promotion		x
Ministry of Interior		
Accelerated Rural Development Office	x	
Community Development Department	x	
Department of Local Administration	x	
Metropolitan Electric Authority	x	
Provincial Electric Authority		x
Department of Public Welfare		x
Town and Country Planning		x
Department of Labor		x
Ministry of Public Health	x	

TABLE 8.1. (continued)

Institutional Capacity-Building in Thailand

Institution/Organization	AID Contribution	
	Major	*Minor*
Ministry of Science, Technology, & Energy		
Remote Sensing Division	x	
Science and Technology Development Board	x[c]	
Other organizations		
Office of the Auditor-General	x	
Industrial Finance Corporation of Thailand	x	
Thailand Development Research Institution[a]	x[d]	
Institute of Management Education & Training	x[d]	
Labor Unions		x
Joint Public-Private Sector Coordinating		
Committee	x	
Various Private Voluntary Organizations[a]		x
Social Science Association of Thailand[a]	x[b]	
Institute of Population Studies	x[e]	
Seventh Day Adventist Hospital	x	
Association of Thai Industries		x
Provincial Chambers of Commerce;		
Interprovincial Chamber of Commerce	x	
Bangkok Metropolitan Administration		x

NOTE: In addition to some of the institutions listed, the Asia Foundation has provided grants to a number of Thai organizations not shown: the Institute for Security and International Studies, the Southern Thailand Social Science Group, the Institute of Asian Studies at Chulalongkorn University, the Tribal Research Center at Chiang Mai University, and Muslim educational institutions in southern Thailand. These institutions have not been listed because of the difficulty of getting a sense of the relative size and importance of the Asia Foundation grants to each recipient organization.
[a] Also received foundation assistance.
[b] Rockefeller and/or Ford Foundation programs.
[c] Semiautonomous under umbrella of Ministry of Science, Technology, and Energy.
[d] Major financial assistance. Technical institution-building assistance would be rated minor as noted in the text.
[e] Ford Foundation and Population Council.

tutions developed over this period do not appear in the list because they have not figured in American assistance programs (or were marginal recipients). The institutions on the list are still evolving, and they vary in their current effectiveness and scope. Much additional institutional capacity will have to be developed over the coming years.

TABLE 8.2.

American Institutional Contractors

Institution	Counterpart Thai Institution
California Polytechnic College	Agricultural Teachers College
Colorado State University	Asian Institute of Technology
Cooperative League of the U.S.A.	Ministry of Agriculture and Cooperatives
Harvard Institute of International Development	Thailand Development Research Institute
University of Hawaii	Department of Vocational Education, Kasetsart University
University of Illinois	Chiang Mai Medical School
Indiana University	National Institute of Development Administration
	Prasarnmitr College
Iowa State University	Department of Agricultural Economics
University of Kentucky	Ministry of Agriculture and Cooperatives
Michigan State University	Ministry of Education
Mississippi State University	Department of Agriculture
University of North Carolina	Institute of Population Studies
Oklahoma State University	Department of Vocational Education
Oregon State College	Kasetsart University
University of Texas	Chulalongkorn University
Washington University of St. Louis	Siriraj and Chulalongkorn medical schools
Wayne State University	Technical Institutes
National Academy of Sciences	S&T Development Board
Scripps Oceanographic Institute	———

Given these obvious qualifications and referring back to the individual projects and institutional development activities discussed above in the text, it is clear that the U.S. programs have been present at the birth and have provided important assistance in the growth of Thailand's institutionalized capacities for modern economic development.*

*In the face of the institution-building experience that looms so large throughout this account, it is puzzling to read a recent assertion, by Herbert P. Phillips, a writer familiar with Thailand, that these institution-building efforts largely failed. I quote this contrary view in full because it appears as an essay in one of the few books available on Thai–U.S. relations, *United States–Thailand Relations*, which is a collection of papers written for a forum sponsored on the

TABLE 8.3.

U.S. Governmental Agencies That Have Implemented USAID/T Projects

Organization	*Program Activity*
Army Corps of Engineers	Mekong Basin surveys
Bureau of the Census	Statistics
Bureau of Reclamation	Mekong Basin surveys
California State Civil Service Commission	Civil service
Center for International Private Enterprise[a]	Provincial business organization
Department of Agriculture	various
Department of Labor	Labor legislation, administration
Federal Aviation Agency	Telecommunications
Geological Survey	Minerals survey
National Parks Service	Natural resources
Navy, Bureau of Yards and Docks, Officer in Charge of Construction (OICC)	Telecommunications
Public Health Service	Health education
Weather Bureau	Meteorology

[a]CIPE is an affiliate of the U.S. Chamber of Commerce, funded by Congress through the National Endowment for Democracy.

What, then, constitutes the difference between aid giver and receiver insofar as institutionalized capabilities are concerned? While the technical aid providers also depend on imports of technology, they do not need an international system of development assistance agencies to help them identify their institutional and knowledge development requirements or to help plan and administer programs to

---

U.S. side by one of the leading American university institutes of East Asian studies.

we must judge the "Americanization of Thailand" not primarily in terms of the cultural impact of the Americans who were there or the "institutions" they may have tried—but for the most part, failed—to build, but rather in terms of the infrastructure they constructed (roads, airfields, ports) and the consumables they delivered (gasoline, helicopters, carbines). The failure of American "institution building" derives simply from the fact that the institutions and practices that were already there had their own inherent integrity, an integrity based on 700 years of indigenous historical development. Too, the nature of the "host-guest" that characterized the American presence, particularly the short-term tenure of the American impact. ("Some Observations on the Americanization of Thailand and the Thaification of the United States," p. 54)

Since this text contains no discussion of specific institutions or projects nor any reference to evaluations of literature on USAID/T projects a reader is given no basis for this sweeping, and in my view untenable, judgment.

TABLE 8.4.

Major U.S. Private Contractors for USAID/T

Organization	Activity
A.D. Little Associates	Industrial development
Charles Upham Associates	Highway engineering
Checchi & Co.	Board of Investment
Collins Radio	Telecommunications
Daniel, Mann, Johnson, Mendenhall	Groundwater
Harza Engineering	Mekong
Litchfield, Whiting, Bowne	City planning
Louis Berger Inc.	Planning, irrigation
Morrison-Knudson	Telecommunications
Pan American	Thai Airways
Public Administration Service of Chicago	Public administration
Raymond International	Highway construction
Rogers Engineering	Electric power
Sverdrup & Parcell	Highway engineering
Tippets-Abbott-McCarthy & Stratton	Potable water systems
Transportation Consultants, Inc.	Highway engineering
U.S. Consultants Overseas, Inc.	Don Muang Airport Control Tower
Vinnell-Christiani & Nielson	Airport facilities
Vinnell Corporation; Philco-Ford	Korat Technical Institute

meet these requirements. The domestic professionals and institutions of the providers are fully capable of defining their own development needs, deciding whether to develop local capabilities in specific disciplines or to continue relying on capabilities found in other countries, and of finding and adapting the most suitable foreign options. Most importantly, institutional self-reliance is attained when related sets or networks of domestic institutions—educational, financial, technical, commercial, and governmental—no longer rely on outside infusions of funds or foreign professionals to sustain them over time as each generation of institutional leadership turns its responsibilities over to its successors.

Over a relatively short interval in Thai history, perhaps twenty-five years, Thailand moved through a transition from an institutional and knowledge base that was grossly inadequate for a modern economy to a position of self-reliance in many disciplines and institutional capabilities, a position of growing domestic capability to spawn new capacities with only selected reliance on increasingly specialized technical assistance from outside. There are many indications of this fundamental transition. One is the rising standards Thais are insisting on before accepting foreign experts or their advice, already noted by Caldwell in 1971.[1] The recent institution-building experience of the Thailand Development Research Institution illustrates the country's ability to create new capacities by mobilizing Thai expertise, hiring recent graduates of Thai universities, and launching the whole venture under Thai administrators. The technical assistance needed by TDRI in its first five years has been limited and specialized (the Harvard Institute of International Development has provided one resident economist in one area of analysis, supplemented by short-term consultancies) compared to the large foreign inputs (several man-years of resident advisory work) in the start-up years of the first economic think tank, the NESDB.

A comparison of the TDRI experience with the Rockefeller Foundation approach to institution-building requirements of the 1960s is particularly striking, even taking account, in the case of Mahidol University, of the large differences between a policy analysis institution and a medical school. Although the formal institutional project with Mahidol lasted about twelve years, the Foundation continued its support for research and special activities for about twenty years. Six life-science departments of the university were created from scratch with Foundation assistance. Twenty-two Foundation scientists were posted in Bangkok for varying periods for over a decade, averaging four-year assignments. Most of them served in senior capacities as part of the Mahidol staff while their Thai counterparts were obtaining advanced degrees in the United States; five acted as department heads for up to nine years. While the Mahidol experience was not free of criticism and debate (such as over the relevance of Mahidol research to major Thai medical problems and the higher priority, at least in earlier years, assigned to curative medical training rather than preventive primary public health), Mahidol is clearly an international-class teaching and scientific institution and a good example of what can be accomplished through what might be termed a "high density" institution-building relationship.

In the 1950s and 1960s Thailand was heavily dependent on foreign expertise across the board. During that one-time transition period, foreign aid had an opportunity for powerful leverage to hasten change. Although Thailand has become a technical source more than it is a recipient in some fields, public health being a leading example, the Thais still see themselves on balance as having further need for the intermediary functions of organized international technical assistance even at their relatively advanced position in the transition from institutional dependence to self-reliance. As imprecise as these notions of dependence and self-reliance are, there is no disputing that Thailand has moved decisively toward intellectual and institutional self-reliance after over a century of deliberate effort to reduce dependence in this regard and that the greatest distance in this move was covered in the twenty to twenty-five years from the mid-1950s to the late 1970s.* There can be no greater demonstration of the impact of the U.S. aid program, along with the institution-building work of the foundations and similar efforts of other donor assistance programs, than this narrowing of the need for further aid for basic institutional development. Successful technical assistance self-destructs as self-reliance spreads from one discipline to another and as dependence is transmitted into the normal processes of intellectual exchange among persons and institutions of equal competence in different countries. In this dimension of the development process the Thailand of the 1950s is now antique.

THE ROLE AND EFFICIENCY
OF GOVERNMENT

Even among thoroughgoing market-oriented countries, where economic assets are largely privately owned and economic activity is left largely to private actors, government has played a key role in the development process. The machinery of government and the behavior and operations of the Thai bureaucracy are somewhat unusual among developing countries. Never having been colonized, the Thais did not start modern development with bureaucratic machinery or a governing structure imposed by a foreign administration. Despite the slow process of bureaucratic reform and modernization that had been started by the Thai monarchy in the nineteenth century, the foreign professionals arriving in the 1950s found a government apparatus that seemed ill-fitted for promoting economic development. As already noted, the aid technicians found that problems of public administration were equally as important as technical aspects in the subject at hand in determining the effectiveness of their projects.

Chapter 4, drawing on the analysis of Morell and Chai-anan, touched on some of the inefficient characteristics of the Thai bureaucracy.

*The appearance of Thai dependency theorists has even eliminated the country's dependence in this subject, an advance of questionable usefulness.

They concluded as of 1980 that the system nevertheless had had "a number of successes" and had given a "high level of support" to the country's economic growth. On the face of it, one would think it unlikely that a society in which the bureaucracy is the central institution and is characterized by behavior, incentive systems, and objectives that are antithetical to legal-rational norms, to considerations of economic efficiency, or indeed to any processes that would undermine the status quo—that such a society could possibly have developed and changed as much as Thailand has since the 1950s, when the classical analyses of this bureaucracy were written. Part of the explanation lies in the decision in the late 1950s (discussed below) to reject the *dirigiste*, or "command," economy role of the state that appeared to be the direction of economic policy in the 1930s and 1940s. But for all those development functions left to the public sector, it is equally clear that the bureaucracy has undergone a major transformation. Only a brief impressionistic account for this view can be given here. Although there have been many studies of facets of public administration in Thailand, the literature to my knowledge has continued to repeat and draw heavily on the classic studies and still lacks a comprehensive analysis of the functioning of the system after a generation of change.

A number of the specific accomplishments of pieces of the bureaucracy attest to operational competence without which the accomplishments would not have materialized. We need merely recall the achievements in health, population, the electric power system, teacher education, aeronautical services, and so on, as examples of public-sector activities in which the RTG has developed performance capabilities adequate to the demands of the development process in each area. These are among Morell and Cha-anan's "number of successes"; these successes are numerous and should not be thought of as selective exceptions to a generally dismal performance.

We have also seen many attempts under the aid program to introduce changes in the bureaucracy as a whole, to make systemic reforms. If one could string together all the activities of projects that helped to correct specific weaknesses, they would add up to an impressive list: budget and accounting reforms, civil service job norms, merit selection criteria for nai amphur, participant training, in-service training institutions and methods, development planning advisory assistance, policy research, interagency seminars, models for interagency coordination of provincial programs, organization and methods function in the Bureau of the Budget, statistical and information systems, monitoring and evaluation functions, project analysis procedures for foreign aid activities, and more. A few projects have worked on core functions of the bureaucracy (development planning, budgeting, national statistical systems, and the like), but the bulk of these activities were developed separately as parts of individual projects in the various sectors. Virtually all technical assistance projects (and many capital projects) of all donors and international development agencies have similar components. But public administration projects per se are usually a minor component of development assistance. For the years for which DTEC has compiled program composition data, public administration took only 2–3 percent of technical assistance. USOM was overwhelmingly the main agency in this field in the early years, still averaging two-thirds of public administration project financing in 1969–1973.

To an observer like myself, who worked with the Thai bureaucracy in the 1950s and returned for a second round in the mid-1980s, the most striking transformation has been in the general orientation of the system. The bureaucracy has swung around from its historic law-and-order and administrative roles to that of a promoter of economic development. Much of the machinery of the RTG now has development as its major raison d'être. Development planning, training and seminars, and development program operations dominate the daily business of government. I would suggest that the U.S. aid relationship in early USOM years had an important role in this transformation in three particular respects.

1. Along with the World Bank, USOM supported the establishment of development planning as a new concept and process for the systematic ordering of public sector investment and operations. The mission subsequently provided training and advisory assistance on and off to NESDB, the agency set up to carry out these functions. NESDB is currently a powerful agency, although it has had its ups and downs of influence and capability. Under Secretary General Snoh Unakul, NESDB turned the drafting of the five-year plan into a consultative exercise that engages a broad spectrum of government and nongovernmental agencies and private sector interests. Through this exercise and NESDB's regular participation in RTG policy review and decision-making processes (and the frequent public appearances of its senior officials), NESDB has developed an educational function intended to convey a sense of participation and better understanding of the ongoing development processes.

2. I cannot demonstrate how important foreign aid may have been, but it was clear in the 1950s that foreign aid acted as a powerful incentive on Thai officials to generate development activities for their

departments and divisions. Any project involving USOM automatically entailed increases, often substantial, in the resources available to a department. In addition to the dollar-financed equipment and the access to incremental local currency from the counterpart fund, a department was in a much stronger position to extract regular budget increases out of the Bureau of the Budget if it could point to the necessity to put up RTG resources to meet USOM's requirements for at least 25 percent matching funds. Vehicles were especially difficult to wring out of the budget staff and, along with foreign training, were powerful incentives for joining up with USOM in development projects. Overseas training was highly valued and more easily funded through aid projects than from normal RTG allocations.

3. The early USOM projects that strengthened the departments and agencies responsible for the country's physical infrastructure helped to raise the so-called absorptive capacity of these units to undertake projects funded with the large resources provided by the World Bank and other international agencies.

There are few development functions of government where effective performance is more important than in the framing of economic policy. In this area the Thai bureaucracy has done very well by international standards. The agencies responsible for macroeconomic policy and planning have developed staff work and policy research capabilities that were virtually nonexistent in the 1950s. In fiscal policy, external borrowing, public sector investment programs, and a whole range of trade and investment policies that affect the efficiency of market operations and of the economy generally Thailand normally ranks among those countries with the least distorting and most effective policy structures.* Especially telling (and interesting to the foreign student of Thai political economy) has been the ability of the bureaucracy, through arcane and opaque decision-making processes

---

*The development economics literature contains a wealth of material on the effects of alternative policies on economic efficiency and the growth performance of developing countries. Policies that are trade-oriented ("outward-oriented" in the jargon) and market-oriented (avoid significant price-distorting interventions that lead to uneconomic investment decisions) have been shown to be fundamental determinants of successful growth experience. One citation from the World Bank will serve to illustrate this point and the relatively efficacious content of Thai economic policy. The Bank ranked thirty-one developing countries according to the degree of price distortion (in exchange rates, wages, prices of manufactured and agricultural commodities, and so on) introduced by government policies. Thailand was second on that list; that is, only one other country had less distortion than Thailand. "A large body of thoretical literature has demonstrated how price distortions result in a loss of efficiency. . . . The average growth rate of those developing countries with low distortions in the 1970s was about 7 percent a year—2 percentage points higher than the overall average. . . . High distortions are associated with low domestic savings in relation to GDP and with low value added per unit of investment [and] also affect growth rates in agriculture and industry, with a marked influence on exports" (World Development Report, 1983, pp. 60–63).

often criticized for their exotic inefficiency, to avoid major mistakes that would have had irreversible long-term consequences. There have been very few white elephants, costly and uneconomic investments that waste large resources and act as a drag on economic growth.

I am trying here to characterize the general trend of government decision-making and operational effectiveness with a very broad brush, comparing the bureaucracy of 1950 with that of 1988 and suggesting how the bureaucracy appears to stand compared with the general run of government in developing countries. It is impossible, of course, to do justice to such broad propositions and comparisons in a treatment as cursory as this must be.* It goes without saying that viewed up close the development management performance of the Thai government over this period has also had deficiencies. It would take me too far afield to explore these at any length, but a brief mention of some examples will give the reader a sense of a few of the problems that have been much debated and where government action and inaction have generated strong criticism.

The delay in the decision-making process has often resulted in the disappearance of ill-advised projects. Delay has also been costly when problems needing prompt attention—for example, the relentless growth of congestion and pollution in the streets of Bangkok—have been allowed to worsen for years, addressed only by palliative and marginal measures. Successive governments have tolerated corruption in high offices. Large-scale corruption appears to have declined over the years (although some would contest this judgment), and Thailand would arguably fall in the middle rather than upper ranks of third world countries on a corruption gradient; still, pecuniary abuse of office remains conspicuous and in too many cases is allowed to distort market conditions and inflate the costs of public sector investment projects. Thai notions and regulations on conflict of interest are loose and give political or bureaucratic insiders wide scope for personal gain even within the confines of the law. Reports on such conflicts are regular grist for the Thai press and feed public cynicism over the integrity of government. As far as the equity of the development process is concerned, there are many critics who feel that government policies, apart from education and health, have suffered sins of omission. Workers' injury compensation is the only piece of "safety net" legislation that has been put in operation; a law empowering the

---

*A good introduction and framework for comparative analysis of economic and managerial efficiency among developing countries can be found in the World Bank's *World Development Report, 1983*," part 2, "Management in Development."

government to establish a social security program was on the books for many years but the implementing legislation was not enacted until 1989. Critics also point to problems of urban slums, crime, prostitution, child labor exploitation, and other social ills that have grown in recent years and have not been accorded high priority in the allocation of public resources or administrative attention. Already noted, the problems of deforestation and other environmental degradation where government policies have been faulted by technocrats and environmental interest groups as neglectful of, if not irresponsible for, the long-run sustainability of the country's economic growth. There are also Thai voices that speak against the consumerism, materialism, and other aspects of behavioral and cultural change brought about or at least facilitated by economic success, problems touched on below.

Much in this list of shortcomings and developmental costs would be familiar to concerned inhabitants of many countries, whether developing or highly industrialized. The Thais are the first to admit that their policymaking process and policy mix could be much better and that government decisions and economic interventions still include an unacceptably high level of response to special interests and of economic detriment. (The Thailand Development Research Institute is doing a major research project on problems of efficiency of RTG development management, including the government's policy formation processes.)[2] Still, the overall judgment that gives high marks to the quality of Thai development policy and to the prudence of public investment policy by international standards is a consensus view I share.

For all the peculiarly Thai inheritance of exotic bureaucratic characteristics, there are also powerful elements of pragmatism, flexibility, willingness to experiment, and indifference to ideology. Economic policy, population policy, and cultural tolerance and integration are three areas where these characteristics have come to dominate the society's direction, with striking consequences for economic development. It may well have been the American penchant for these same pragmatic characteristics that accounts for the role and the rapport with the Thais that the aid mission was able to establish and the relationships that have been maintained despite the much smaller size of the U.S. program in recent years.

FIVE OTHER BROAD ACCOMPLISHMENTS

What emerges are five major accomplishments of the aid program in addition to (and partly as a result of) the development of Thailand's institutional and bureaucratic capabilities.

1. The integrity of the state has been sustained in the face of insurgency and the potential divisiveness stemming from the still incomplete process of bringing divergent ethnic groups and peripheral areas into a consolidated nation-state. How divisive these potentialities might have proven if events had unfolded differently can never be known, nor can debate over the relative importance of the many factors that contributed to the collapse of the insurgency be resolved with "definitive" conclusions. Still, the objectives of the Thai government on these related problems of fundamental security (and economic) importance have been substantially achieved, and the inputs of the aid program were very material to this outcome.

2. The reduction in fertility rates over the past two decades has been described in the demographic literature as a demographic "revolution," the result of one of the most effective population and family-planning programs in the third world. The long-run impact of a substantially lower population growth path is likely to be one of the most important outcomes of the "social engineering" aspects of Thailand's development policies. The demographic change will be one of the basic determinants of the future course of the country's per capita income, employment situation, health status, and environmental condition. On all these counts the marked reduction in fertility is expected to have favorable effects. External aid (of which American-financed technical and commodity inputs comprised one major portion) played an important role in the development of Thai population policy and the design and expansion of the government's family-planning program.

3. The health status of the Thai population, reflected in declining mortality and rising life expectancy rates and in the reduction of the major killer diseases of the past, has improved greatly since World War II. The Thai Ministry of Public Health is recognized as one of the most effective among developing countries. Medical education, major disease campaigns, the development of the rural health delivery system, and the Ministry itself have all benefited from substantial American official and foundation assistance.

4. Although development has proceeded at uneven rates between Bangkok and the rest of the country and from one geographic region to another, poverty overall has been reduced, and income distribution

has remained less skewed than among many developing countries. The concentration of relative and absolute poverty in the Northeast region of the country continues, reflecting the poor resource endowment of the area and the failure thus far of efforts to find technological options with any substantial productive power for Northeast agriculture (apart from the possibilities for the limited irrigation areas). The economic expansion that has occurred in the Northeast owes much to the market access created by the government's heavy investments in the region's road system. The highway and feeder road projects of the U.S. program gave important assistance to these investment programs. Health and education projects since the 1950s also made important contributions to the expansion in social services in the Northeast and the opportunities for Northeasterners to build up human capital. The scope and lasting impact of the aid program's more recent attempts to generate benefits for the poor (apart from health) remain uncertain at this date.

5. The development of Thailand's economic infrastructure—transport and power in particular—has been central to the rapid growth the country has experienced. In the early years of the aid program initial physical investments in key roads and in the air transport and power-generating and distributing systems and technical assistance projects with the government units and agencies responsible for much of the physical and technical infrastructure made significant contributions to the expansion of economic output and to the institutional base for the subsequent investment programs (in which the United States played a diminishing role, as World Bank, ADB, and bilateral donors increased their development assistance).

The aid program's impact on agricultural production is not easy to specify. Some significant measurable effects on rice and corn production and on fish and livestock were achieved in the 1950s and 1960s. The indirect effects of the highway and feeder road programs on opening up new areas for production and transforming previously isolated subsistence production into commercial cultivation for domestic and international markets have been very great. The program helped to create the Bank for Agricultural and Cooperatives, which is now the largest source of finance for agricultural production. Programs with virtually every function of the Ministry of Agriculture (and with Karetsart University and other agricultural schools in the provinces) have made broad contributions to the institutional infrastructure for Thai agriculture. Tracing the effects on agricultural production would not be possible since the project outputs (apart from the occasional case like the seed project and the current Agricultural

Technology Transfer project) are very diffuse and the related inputs from other Thai and foreign assistance sources very numerous. In addition, it must be admitted that much of the growth of agricultural production in the past three decades has proceeded rather independently of the formal institutional structure and that in the case of some important components of that structure (such as the extension services of the ministry) the search for effective configurations and roles has yet to produce satisfactory results.

In an economy where the government leaves the development of the manufacturing sector to private investment decision making and adopts a market-oriented development strategy, an aid program has few options for activities that can have direct leveraged impact on industrial growth. AID sought out some of the few levers that did appear to offer prospects for assisting private sector growth, mainly the Board of Investment and the Industrial Finance Corporation of Thailand, and gave useful support for the creation and development of these institutions. The support to the machinery for public-private sector dialogue over policy and bureaucratic problems looks like an option with substantial leverage, helping to shape systematic, open, and professional relationships in place of the historic personalistic relationships concerned with the welfare of individual enterprises. The ongoing project in science and technology, if successful, should help establish R&D as a significant activity in private industrial development, as compared with its very marginal role at present.

DEVELOPMENT AID:
SOME POLITICAL DIMENSIONS

The relationship between the United States and Thailand in the post–World War II period emerged from a background of good will. Compared to Thailand's history of coping directly with British and French colonial expansion in Southeast Asia and with military encroachment from France (in the nineteenth century) and Japan in 1941 there had been relatively marginal interaction between the two countries. The U.S. stance towards the Free Thai rejection of Bangkok's declaration of war in 1942 and the Truman Administration's actions to prevent the British from imposing severe diplomatic and economic penalties on Thailand as the price of the peace settlement in 1945 served to establish the United States as a country willing and able to give powerful support to vital interests of Thailand, which was then a country of no significant economic or military power in the Southeast

Asian region. The rapid U.S. response to North Korea's invasion of the South in 1950 signaled the American willingness to resist military expansion of Communist power on the Asian mainland and thereby completed the setting for the establishment of the "intimate" postwar relationship with Thailand.

The relationship has been complex, involving external and internal security considerations, military aid, U.S. military operations from Thai territory during the Vietnam War, and long-term development assistance. The mix of these elements has varied over time, as we have seen, in response to changing conditions. Refugees and narcotics trafficking added new dimensions. With the normalization of relationships between China and both the United States and Thailand and the declining likelihood of a Vietnamese military move against Thailand, trade problems have come to the fore as the focus of current interaction between the two allies, although long-term security (military training, logistics cooperation, and the like) and development assistance remain significant components of the relationship.

The relationship has not been free of tensions, of course, and it has even been through periods of great stress, especially when the United States was disengaging from Vietnam and reevaluating the extent and nature of its commitments and interests in the region. This was a time when Thai politics was in a turmoil within which the U.S. relationship was a conspicuous factor, a time when the aid program fell to a low of $7.9 million in 1975.

It is against this background that two schools of thought have developed about the essential nature of the U.S.–Thai relationship. One school continues to see the relationship as based on a meeting of parallel or mutual geopolitical interests. The holders of this view have been described as "the Thai and American academic and foreign-service establishment." The other school, "the new breed of Thai and American political scientists," sees the relationship as one of Thai "dependence" and U.S. exploitation.[3] An attempt to examine the full range of U.S.–Thai relations and the extent to which these two viewpoints illuminate or misconstrue reality would take me well beyond the scope of the present study. The debate, in any case, has centered on the military relationship and the Vietnam War, not on the aid program. Nevertheless, the development aid program has had implications for Thai domestic political affairs (apart from the security aspects per se) and has unavoidably entailed an American involvement inside Thailand not matched by any significant Thai involvement in U.S. domestic affairs. Thus, while I can make no effort to do justice to these issues, I will offer some observations on a few particular aspects of the aid relationship that may serve at least as illustrations of how oversimplification may lead to unsupportable if not erroneous conclusions.

Private Enterprise Policy

Probably the single most important development policy choice by any Thai government in the past forty years was the decision of the Sarit regime around 1958–1959 to repudiate the Thai ethnocentric state *dirigisme*—economic intervention and the creation of state commercial and industrial enterprises to preempt economic development from non-Thai control—that had marked socioeconomic policy since the coup that ended the absolute monarchy in 1932. This decision allowed the private business sector (largely Chinese or sino-Thai at the time) to come forth as the engine of Thai development and set the stage for the later emergence of the business community as a new political force that would make it more difficult for the Thai military to maintain its dominance over domestic political power. Although I can only touch on the factors involved in this policy change (which merits fuller study than it has received thus far to my knowledge), it is important to do so here because of the role the American connection may have played. At the time of the Sarit coup in September 1957, a popular move among the students and general public in Bangkok after a period of instability and a blatantly rigged election, it appeared as if this latest change in the power structure was just another change of personalities. Since Sarit was the head of one faction in the previous government of Prime Minister Pibul, his accession to power hardly appeared to be ushering in a period of fundamental change. (He took over the premiership himself only in October 1958, after recuperating from an operation he had had at Walter Reed Hospital; his takeover was also accomplished in extralegal fashion through declaration of martial law and abrogation of the constitution.) In fact, Sarit represented a different generation from the so-called Promoters of the 1932 coup, which had forced constitutional status on the previously absolute monarchy, and his policies are generally credited with having launched modern Thai economic development with a more purposive and energetic thrust than it had had under previous Promoter governments.*

---

*Prime Minister Sarit's departure from policies of his predecessors was not complete of course. He continued the practice of establishing personal patron-client relationships with prominent business interests and accumulated large assets through extralegal dealings. After his death many of these assets were reclaimed from his estate by the government.

On the political side Sarit imposed stability, not hesitating to use harsh methods, including executions on a few occasions. His most important single political vision was his view that Thailand needed to restore the symbolic and psychological role of the monarchy, a restoration that would also help to strengthen the legitimacy of his own position. The young King Bhumibol Adulyadej turned out to be a person of extraordinary capabilities and political acumen and has been able to bring the monarchy back to a position of importance and veneration, a virtually unique political and cultural phenomenon in the modern world.

Sarit was convinced that the Thai polity could not achieve a restoration of the long historic stability it had lost in the years leading up to the 1932 coup unless his political agenda was reinforced by economic modernization and development.[4] In the light of the dynamic growth performance of Thailand's private sector, Sarit's decision to abandon the Thai version of *dirigisme* appears now to have been farsighted and critical for all the development that has followed. Thai *dirigisme* had always been a uniquely local distillation of Western ideas about the economic role of the state. In the immediate pre- and postwar years there were two strands of thought, two factions within the coup Promoters group (which numbered only forty-nine military personnel and sixty-five civilians). One strand saw the problem of economic modernization in ethnic terms: commerce and industry appeared to be developing largely in the hands of the Thai Chinese (a large fraction of whom were still not Thai citizens before the war), and the only instrument for ethnic Thai economic competition or preemption in these realms was government. The second strand promoted an ill-defined, utopian socialism. The formulators of these programs had derived much of their thinking from their educational experience in Europe, mainly in Paris. The utopian faction did not win power in the event; its intellectual leader, Pridi Phanomyong, was prime minister for only five months in 1946 and was forced into exile in 1947.* The Pibul faction then recovered the reigns of government and continued its pursuit of state intervention in the economy in a mode that might be characterized as bureaucratic capitalism; the bureaucracy spawned economic enterprises, each ministry controlling and managing state enterprises in its sector of responsibility.

Sarit's decision to halt the growth of the state commercial and manufacturing sector was embodied in the legislation establishing

---

*While Pridi's opponents had charged him in the 1930s with being a Communist, his departure in 1947 resulted from factional maneuvering and charges of responsibility for the death of King Ananda (brother of the present King), not from a struggle over economic policy.

the Board of Investment (empowering the BOI to extend guarantees of no government competition to any enterprise set up under incentive arrangements with BOI) and in the first formal RTG development plan in 1961. The factors that appear to have been most important in Sarit's turnaround were 1) he had not been educated abroad or exposed to the Continental intellectual influences that had predominated with the interwar generation of foreign-educated Thai; 2) the principal civilian technocrats on whom Sarit relied, especially the economists led by Puey Ungphakorn, favored a policy of narrowing the role of the state to the development of infrastructure, education, and those other sectors that would not be developed by private economic activity; these advisors had been educated mainly in Great Britain, while the younger generation of postwar economists who manned the new development agencies Sarit created (the planning agency, investment board, budget bureau, and so on) were mainly American educated and market-oriented; 3) in the critical years of this turnaround (1957–1959) the World Bank had a strong presence among Bangkok policy makers; a large Bank team spent a year in Bangkok writing a broad country study and participating in policy discussions; 4) the American advisor John Loftus played a key role, as mentioned earlier, in the government's efforts to salvage the NEDCOL disaster (which had been facilitated by the previous government's willingness to cross the line between the public and private sectors and give guarantees for foreign supplier credits) and in the formulation of economic policies generally; 5) USOM was also directly involved with the creation of the BOI and the drafting of its basic concepts and indirectly, of course, as the financer of Loftus and other advisers.

Beyond this the role of the United States as an active participant or source of influence on Sarit's decision-making is unclear. One Thai view ascribes this influence to the conversations Sarit had with Americans during his convalescence when he is known to have read extensively and reflected on Thailand's conditions.[5] Other Thai and foreign authors attribute the first plan's stress on the private sector to the influence of the World Bank mission (which was "as important in its impact on Thailand's political-economic development as the Bowring Treaty of the mid-1800s," the treaty with Great Britain that opened the country to trade with the West) and the support that mission had from the United States.[6] Another Thai writer, probably the closest student of the personal role of Sarit during these years, has the very different view that the Premier was interested mainly in rural development and left macroeconomic affairs to his technocrats.[7] Yet a fourth source, cites the role of Puey Ungphakorn in having initiated the request of the RTG to the World Bank to send such a mission (that the general economic policy orientation of any such mission would be to favor private rather than government enterprise would have been obvious to any professional like Puey acquainted with the Bank) and in having had a hand in the creation of the BOI and the formulation of its rules of the game.[8]

I cite these different accounts on what might appear to be a point of detail for what they reveal about the difficulties of establishing the facts in questions of the evolution of a government's policy, even for a historically recent event under conditions where government is much more highly personalized and centralized than is the case in the American polity. In my view (which is based not only on experience in Bangkok at the time but on my having seen policy dialogue exchanges in other countries as well) the foreigners served mainly to put ammunition, in the form of foreign prestige and the technical recommendations, into the hands of the senior Thai technocrats who independently wanted to go in that direction. Those authors who see the World Bank report as the source of Thai policies favorable to a market economy and to private (including foreign) capital have overlooked telling evidence: the recommendation to adopt such policies had already been made to the finance minister, before the Bank team arrived in Bangkok in 1957, by an advisory team the minister had constituted comprising four Thai technocrats and John Loftus. (The team had conducted the country's first effort to collate and review all ministerial "development" and capital project expenditure proposals. The review was initiated several months before it was known whether the IBRD mission would actually materialize. The team then wrapped up its exercise in time to present its report to the IBRD group.) There also can be no doubt that Puey's intellectual and moral position in particular was more important to broad policy development formation than any posturing or technical representations of the outsiders. The outsiders were certainly helpful, especially when they were right. But the Thais were always masters in their own house, and to them goes the bulk of the credit, and blame, for what has happened that has been within the capacity of the government to effect.

A close look at Loftus' role illuminates the precise nature of the policy advisor's relationship to RTG policy formation, the contrast between the advisor's intimate involvement in policy deliberation and the nonintervention of the aid mission itself, and the independence of the Thai economic decision process in the midst of so much foreign and international presence. The advice Loftus gave and the influence he exerted were personal. Although his contract required that he submit a semiannual report jointly to the Finance Ministry and USOM, he did not consult the mission on the tasks the minister assigned to him or on the policy initiatives he took, nor did USOM advise or even communicate with him on matters other than those pertaining to U.S. projects in which Loftus was involved (such as selection of officials for advanced training in economics). The ministry occasionally had Loftus work on confidential matters. His reports (on file in the library of the Finance Ministry) identify some of these subjects but disclose none of the confidential details. The effectiveness of a policy advisor who is privy to confidential information rests upon the trust his host country associates have in his loyalty and discretion. There is no sign in the record (nor any instance in my own experience with Loftus and the mission) that this trust was ever violated. Thus, although Loftus was American, there is no basis for asserting that his role was tantamount to a direct U.S. government involved in the substance of Thai economic policy formation. On many issues his advice was ignored, despite his repeated, often bluntly worded, if not scathingly critical, expressions of frustration. Most pointedly, there is no evidence of his having attempted to mobilize USOM or U.S. Embassy support in order to pressure an unresponsive minister of finance.

If this reading of history is correct, a final question of interest for students of Thai–U.S. (or Thai-Western) relations and of modern Thai political economy remains. Why did Puey and his Thai technocratic associates at that time advise Sarit to adopt this fundamental shift away from ethnocentric *dirigisme?* And why have the economic technocrats continued to sustain this policy (albeit with recurrent deviations)? A full treatment of this question would take us beyond the scope of the present study. I can only note here that the compelling evidence leads one to reject explanations in terms of traditional dichotomies of class interest. The disillusionment in Thailand, starting from within the bureaucracy, in the preeminent roles and rights of the public sector derived mainly from a recognition that the private sector would be a more powerful engine of development and that extensive public sector activity, whether in industrial or other operational guises or in regulatory or other market intervention roles, offered opportunities for the unscrupulous (whether public or private sector persons) that could be wasteful of the country's resources and damaging to the general warfare. The NEDCOL experience must be seen in this context as one of the formative episodes of postwar Thai economic policy. The shaping of development strategy during the years leading up to the first development plan took place under the burden the RTG was bearing as it struggled to honor the debts NED-COL had contracted and to sustain the country's reputation for conservative financial and debt management practices. The decision to limit further expansion of a government manufacturing or commercial sector and to invite the international development banks, USOM, and other aid agencies to play a large role in public sector capital projects can be seen in retrospect as related pragmatic responses to the prospect that an unchecked public sector would be detrimental to Thailand's development.

BUREAUCRATIC POWER: CENTER VERSUS PERIPHERY

Thailand is a unitary state, more closely resembling France than the federated structures of countries like the United States or Canada. Governmental authority is highly concentrated in Bangkok, as it is in Paris. Local jurisdictions have only limited local authority. The changwat governors and the nai amphur are employees of the Ministry of Interior. Provincial assemblies have only a minor role and lack taxing authority. Provincial and amphur officials of all ministries (education, health, and so on) report to their supervising divisions in Bangkok. As noted several times above, the U.S. aid mission found the tight control of Bangkok over the implementation of field programs a constraint on the efficiency of execution, and in the context of individual projects it tried to introduce decentralizing arrangements and provincially located institutions. In the 1970s the mission tried to promote a combination of devolution of power to provincial officials and development of processes in which provincial and local planning (of the use of government resources) would be further devolved or opened up to participation by villagers. In the earlier years of the program, however, the transportation and communication activities had been designed to extend the effective reach of the government in order to help consolidate the state. And over the whole history of the aid program the training and institution-building projects helped strengthen the capacities of the Bangkok bureaucratic hub to exercise its governance functions.

The program appears to have had four separate objectives here: strengthening national unity and the physical reach of the central government; strengthening the capacity of (a highly centralized) government to plan and implement development programs; devolution of some decision-making authority from the center to lower jurisdiction officials; participation of villagers in some of the decision-making processes that do take place at local levels. There are several interesting questions about the role of the aid program in the problem of "center versus periphery" in Thailand.* Were these objectives independent initiatives of the U.S. government or, more baldly stated, were they attempts to intervene and alter fundamental characteristics of the Thai polity? Were they local initiatives of the aid mission, or did they represent deliberate U.S. government efforts? Did they have any impact? Were they responsible and intelligent objectives?

Looking at these objectives in the context of the relations between two sovereign states, it seems clear that the center-strengthening and physically unifying objectives of the first two decades of the program were basic to Thai government policy. Devolution of authority for decision-making over matters of implementation was integral to the policy of several ministries with respect to specific programs (such as primary health care) while deliberately eschewed in others (as in agricultural extension). In some cases the mission was out in front of the RTG (in the case of the Lam Nam Oon irrigation scheme, say, where the project's model of local initiative for public-private sector cooperation was subsequently adopted by the ministry); in other cases the mission developed a project in response to an RTG request for assistance in a decentralizing initiative (ARD, for example, and rural development monitoring and evaluation). The Thai government has not had an explicit general policy on devolution. On the one hand the Ministry of Health has pursued a primary health care model that has important decentralizing features; the development of the regional universities has been a very significant beginning to decentralizing the country's intellectual life and strengthening the ability of a few of the smaller cities to attract professionals and people of talent. On the other hand there has been no significant devolution of authority within the Ministry of Interior from Bangkok down to the governors and nai amphur. As far as participation is concerned, there has been some modest expansion in the rural development system, in self-help programs under private voluntary organizations, and in the beginnings of the provincial JPPCC consultation system with the business communities. But participation in national political power and policy

*The terms "center" and "periphery" capture the mix of administrative, technical, and political dimensions involved in the broad context of the structure of governance in Thailand. I have taken the terms and have drawn on a discussion of these issues in a paper by David I. Steinberg, "The Role of External Assistance in the Economic Development and Planning of Thailand: Torques and Tensions in the American Aid Program."

issues hangs on the further evolution of the parliamentary system, an evolution concerning which the aid program has no direct relevance.

The many project-level activities concerned with promoting local technical authority arose within the context of the planning of individual projects over time and not as part of any general U.S. government or aid mission policy regarding devolution. The 1970s projects designed to promote participation (apart from primary health care) appear to have been mission initiatives (not responses to Thai requests) designed to carry out the intent of the 1973 legislation. As we have seen, these initiatives do not appear to have made much of a dent on these dimensions of the Thai polity. In his review of the center-periphery aspects of the Thai aid program, David Steinberg notes that the United States does not appear to have had a consistent policy. He refers to a 1967 review of the program by an internal evaluation staff that observed: "There are occasional references in USOM documents and conferences to 'our policy of promoting decentralization.' It is urged that USOM and Embassy clarify the concept and intentions. The evaluators suggest that 'decentralization' should not be interpreted or risk interpretation as delegation of significant powers to provinces or districts. It is unlikely that Thai officials envision any such departure from the present unitary system. . . . Meaningful villager participation in development and effective coordination of activities at the provincial level and below will be a large and adequate achievement."[10] In Steinberg's summary,

> for the first two decades of U.S. foreign assistance in Thailand, efforts were made to build up centralized authority and power, while in the past decade attempts have been underway to diminish that power (at least as it relates to economic activities) and decentralize authority.[11]

These opposite tendencies at different times were broadly consistent with the policies of the Thai government. Where the occasional specific effort failed or had only marginal impact, the mission was clearly out of line with the intentions of the concerned ministry; the RTG was prepared to tolerate a mission experiment in such cases, but where the Thai authorities were unconvinced, the impact was of no consequence. Given the very much larger resources and role of the aid program in the earlier years and the relatively modest scope of the decentralizing activities of the last decade (again, apart from health), it is not surprising that the upshot was a strong contribution toward national unification and the extension of the effective power and reach of the unitary state, along with significant assistance for certain RTG programs (and their champions) that deconcentrated central power away from Bangkok without altering the essential unitary character of the system.

POWER ON A SMALLER SCALE

An exploration of the political impact of any aid program might be on stronger ground if it approached the subject from the bottom—that is, by identifying the effects of specific program activities on the distribution of power among individuals and groups who are contending within the sector or problem area involved. Consider some of the program's outcomes: the technical capability of specific infrastructure agencies to compete for and utilize large public sector resource allocations; the competence of the "core" financial and development planning units; the resource allocation roles of the assisted financial intermediary organizations; the role of economic researchers in policy debate; the recent creation of new machinery for allocating the country's largest fund for science and technological research; the expansion of small institutions into large organizations with internal hierarchies, big budgets, and wide external relationships and areas of influence; the strengthening of nongovernmental and business organizations. In all of these outcomes the program has been a party to the creation of new power centers, to the diversification of power, and to the relative rise and decline of the position of many individuals.

The assistance the private enterprise projects have been giving to the formation and professional strengthening of the provincial chambers of commerce is particularly interesting in this context. Long after the heyday of the program's institution-building in the 1950s and 1960s, this activity is an example of opportunities that remain for the Thais to draw on external aid to help fill a weak or empty niche in the country's institutional structure. In this case the organizations are unequivocally "peripheral": their membership and their collective interests are separate from and often opposed to those of Bangkok-based interests, private or governmental. The recently formed provincial chambers have already given one striking demonstration of the political life that can emerge from a "technical" institution-building effort. Although, unlike the powerful Thai Chamber of Commerce and Association of Thai Industries (ATI), the new Inter-Provincial Chamber has yet to register and acquire status as a juridical entity, the provincial group succeeded in a lobbying effort in 1987 to remove a provision from draft legislation that would have made it mandatory for all private industrial enterprises and associations to become members of a national apex Council of Industries. The bill had been drafted by the ATI, which would have become the core of the Council. The provincial chambers feared that compulsory membership in the apex would lead to the break-up of the provincial chambers and to further concentration of industrial institutional power in Bangkok. The provincial chambers aired their case publicly through the press and numerous seminars and directly with the legislators from the provinces. While it remains to be seen how successful the new provincial chambers become over time, they show a potential for developing into one of the more significant, decentralized, nongovernmental institutional groups AID has assisted in Thailand. In this case the institutional innovation advances the interests of one of the less powerful economic groups in the country.

The creation or dilution of power is inherent in the process of economic development. Any aid agency involved in creating new capabilities and institutions is a party. It would appear trivial, however, to call this role interventionist. The political powers thereby affected are the other side of the development coin, and they come into being only if the aid activities succeed—which, after all, is the reason the host government seeks aid involvement in the first place.

Nevertheless, there were options that might have been pursued earlier or with more resources—options such as working with Thai nongovernmental organizations or with the labor movement or helping to raise the priority of environmental degradation problems, recognized by the aid mission over thirty years ago but only now being addressed in a meaningful way. My examination of the program up to this point has made no reference to the AID projects that have worked on labor affairs, an omission that reflects the minor role these projects have played and the limited scope for achieving significant leverage in the development of the trade union movement. Between the mid-1960s and mid-1970s the mission undertook three projects in labor administration and training, at a total cost of about $750,000. The projects provided technical assistance and training for the government's Department of Labor, not for the union movement directly. One adviser had a major hand in drafting Thailand's workers' compensation legislation. Others were involved in labor relations law, manpower planning, and other functions of the Department. Since 1972 the Asian-American Free Labor Institute (AAFLI), an arm of the AFL-CIO, has had a small program in Thailand (under an AID centrally funded activity) that works directly with the trade unions. The

AAFLI program has focused on training union leaders and trainers and helping to strengthen membership services, especially credit cooperatives and more recently slum community health services. The training has covered such subjects as collective negotiation and grievance handling. Much of the present leadership of the two (rival) union confederations has participated in these training programs. (The unions have also received substantial assistance from a West German non-profit institution.)

Unions in Thailand have yet to develop into a major institutional or class pressure force. After three years of militant activity—strikes and demonstrations—in the mid-1970s and a short period when unions were outlawed in response, union organization and collective bargaining were reestablished under the 1975 labor relations law. Union leadership has concentrated on bread-and-butter issues rather than on politics, but growth of the movement has been hampered by factionalism. Membership under the two confederations was only about 175,000 in 1987. The strongest unions are in the state enterprises; private sector unions remain much weaker. (It is interesting that the strongest opponents of privatization of state enterprises have been the state enterprise unions, on the grounds that the state firms adhere to minimum wage, work safety, and other labor laws and regulations and that private management might evade these protective measures. For several years, AID/W has been promoting privatization.) The technical assistance provided by AAFLI and other donors has strengthened the union movement, perhaps even helped lay the basis for its eventual emergence as an important economic interest force beyond its current limited role (which is not insignificant for the state enterprises); but the domestic political circumstances that have constrained union growth have also limited the scope for external assistance to advance such an emergence at a more rapid pace.[12]

By not taking such options (assuming the RTG would have concurred), the agency in effect forewent chances (I can only speculate about possible results) to alter the relative institutional and political weight of the interests thus left aside. An examination of the political effects of the program, building up from the actual content, would be more fruitful than speculation at a high level of political generality and might reveal in detail the political fallout generated by the aid program.

If such an empirical examination were done, its overall conclusion would most likely echo the cautious judgment on the aid–political effects questions reached in 1970 by David A. Wilson, an American scholar of Thai affairs:

As is somewhat the case in military assistance ... economic assistance tends to strengthen the political position of those who approach their work rationally and with technical competence. U.S. assistance, together with assistance from other industrial countries, the World Bank, the Asian Development Bank, and the United Nations, stands behind a loose faction of Western trained, rationalist, and technically competent officials in many departments and services. This faction, however, is not a cohesive political power but, rather, represents a coherent attitude toward government. In this way, foreign assistance tends to encourage a greater margin of rationality in any decision.

This influence is only marginal, not dominant. Foreign assistance is only a small fraction of the resources at the disposal of the Thai Government, but this fraction, managed by competent people, has an influence greater than its size. Since it is, for the most part, devoted to change and novelty, the influence in the direction of change is that much enhanced. In the end, however, the leverage of foreign assistance alone is not sufficient to produce major modifications in the relationships of political and military factions, much less modifications in the constitutional structure of the government.[13]

SOCIAL AND POLITICAL STABILITY

Successive administrations have justified aid as an instrument for helping developing countries maintain social stability. It is assumed that economic development promotes stability and that stability inclines a society and its government toward conservative and nonaggressive relations with other countries. The external behavior of states is not easily or consistently explained by this paradigm, of course, but there is enough experience in the pre- and postwar world to lead one to accept it as a useful basis for the relatively rich and stable societies of the West in formulating their relationships with the Third World.

As far as the Thai program is concerned, assistance has been justified year in and year out as likely to be efficacious for promoting regional stability precisely because Thailand already was the most stable country in a turbulent area and because continuing successful economic expansion (and amelioration of poverty conditions) would help sustain that stability. What has been the upshot, and what does the Thai experience say about the development-stability half of the paradigm?

There is no simple answer to these questions. The very concept of stability is imprecise, and, seen from different perspectives, Thailand's recent history can be characterized as stable or revolutionary. The country gave up the economic stability of subsistence isolation when it opened up in the mid-nineteenth century. As a trading economy Thailand has become increasingly exposed to fluctuations in the world economy. The rapid economic growth of the last three decades, urbanization, increase in literacy and education, growth in travel and the rise of new competing economic interests and occasions for adversarial clash, greater opportunities for employment abroad—all these elements of change are altering the content of life in Thailand from month to month, compared with the continuity from one generation to another that characterized the country's earlier history.

Development means change, and if the notion of stability—certainly more highly prized as a social objective in Thailand than in the United States—means anything in this context it must refer to the processes by which the society is resolving conflicts of interest and harmonizing traditional and cultural mores with the behavioral patterns introduced by the exigencies of modern technology and economics and with the values and tastes rushing in from the outside world. Are these processes orderly or violent? Do people seek accommodation and equilibrium, or is the society becoming polarized and divisive? Is tolerance giving way to zealotry?

Compared with the turbulence in much of the Third World, Thailand appears to have maintained a relatively high degree of social stability. Even compared with its own past the country has managed to achieve great continuity. Deep-rooted cultural and religious patterns of conflict avoidance, compromise, and moderation have underlaid the high adaptive capabilities of Thai society. Nevertheless, many Thais deplore the culture changes taking place, and the stridency of the mid-1970s revealed unsuspected potentialities of social conflict, quite apart from the insurgents' program of deliberate destabilization. The apparent coexistence of stability and instability has been described by the historian D. K. Wyatt:

> At first consideration, the Thailand of the 1980s would not seem to be so different from the Thailand of Phibun—or, for that matter from the Siam of King Chulalongkorn. All the central institutions still seem strong: the kingdom is a constitutional monarchy, the bureaucracy pervades almost

every aspect of national life, the military dominates the political sphere, the economy remains predominantly agricultural with a somewhat alien urban business sector, the Buddhist monkhood is accorded special deference, the outlying provinces still are imperfectly integrated into the national economy and society. ... Thailand's rulers hold up to the world an image of the country as an Asian haven of political stability and dynamic economic growth, a nation that almost miraculously has managed to maintain its distinctive cultural identity, its social hierarchy and order, and its Thai and Buddhist values.[14]

Wyatt here describes the half-filled glass of stability. His account ends in 1982. Some of the changes in the few years since then seem to reinforce the picture: the continuity of eight years (1981–1988) under Prime Minister Prem Tinsulananda; the election in July 1988 and the installation of a government (presiding at this writing) headed by an elected member of Parliament; one of the freest presses in the region, which has recently moved into investigative journalism and is bringing more transparency into public affairs; the continuing assimilation of the Sino-Thai; the surge of economic growth since 1986 and the confidence of foreign investors in Thai stability as reflected in surveys and the wave of new investment in Thailand.

But Wyatt also described the half-empty part, the signs of instability and disruption:

This is the same Thailand, however, that within the past decade has seen vicious political violence on the streets of Bangkok and ceaseless labor unrest with strikes and demonstrations previously unknown, involving not only a growing population of factory and other blue-collar workers but also thousands of farmers agitating for land reform and against bureaucratic insensitivity. In a country never distinguished for ideological passion ... the seventies saw a massive outpouring of political sentiment on both the right and the left. The Communist Party of Thailand suddenly appealed to large numbers of young Thai, not just bourgeois Chinese and intellectuals, and the Socialist Party came to seemingly permanent prominence, today regularly contesting parliamentary constituencies. ... When even prominent Buddhist monks took strong public stands on political issues, voicing not only intolerance for the left but even physical extirpation, the polarization was complete, and gone was the old image of the Thai nation as a single, happy, harmonious family-like community, placid in its allegiance to nation, Buddhism, and monarchy. Passions exploded in violence, in public mistrust and suspicion, in demonstrations and assassinations, for three chaotic years from 1973 to 1976, a period of profound importance, the effects of which have shaped not only the Thailand of today but also the Thailand of tomorrow and the day after. (Pp. 277–78)

All students of Thai political affairs agree that the 1973–1976 period was a watershed in Thai history. It had the appearance of an earthquake, suddenly revealing and releasing a complex of social stresses that could not be expressed through the political system as it had operated until then and economic stresses that had arisen in the development process but were not being, or were not seen to be, addressed by the country's development policies and programs. Fifty-six years after the overthrow of the absolute monarchy Thailand has yet to develop a reliable, legitimated system for the orderly transfer of political power. A system lacking predictability and routinized methods for allocating power always carries the potential for destabilizing resort to force, especially where there is no recent tradition of the military confining themselves to the barracks. (In a perspective that would seem paradoxical to Americans, who see adversarial politics as a healthy process that exposes the issues for the electorate, the Thai military has often justified its intervention with the argument that the civilian politicians were creating "disorder.") On the other hand there is a real distinction between the "disorderly" style of the country's politics, with its occasional military coup, and the relative lack of disorder in the body of the society. Economic and social (and foreign) policies generally undergo incremental change rather than lurching or unpredictable shifts, despite changes in leadership. Even in the turbulent years of the mid-1970s Thai society had little of the racial, religious, and ethnic conflict that has generated massive instability in many countries. As of this writing, the economic class conflicts that burgeoned in the 1970s have receded and passions given way to a more Buddhist calm.

It is too early to know how all these events are going to shape the Thailand of the day after tomorrow. But as of 1989 one can argue plausibly that in the wake of the trauma of the mid-1970s the Thais— the farmers, workers, students, the bureaucracy and the military, the intellectuals and the business class—have retreated back to a Buddhist political "middle way" after experiencing the ugly consequences of inadequate accommodation and disordered conflict resolution. Rapid economic growth may well raise the stakes and increase the points of potential conflict as the society develops increasing interest-group differentiation and complexity. What I am commenting on here is not the extent of potential conflict but the manner in which the Thais will work out resolution.

Thailand's failure to develop and adhere to an orderly system for changing and legitimizing rulership makes it impossible, however, to conclude that the return to stability that has been achieved is a firmly established accomplishment. The monarchy remains the final symbol of unity and arbiter of legitimacy, a basis for stability that is at once encouraging because of its effectiveness and a source of anxiety because of the reliance of such a legally powerless monarchical role on the personal characteristics of the individual on the throne. Thus, although the events of the past few years have confounded those who saw Thailand falling into greater disorder, Wyatt's conclusions on this score remain correct:

> Thailand's successes, particularly in what might loosely be called development, while alleviating many persistent social and economic problems, have themselves created new problems, particularly political, to the point where revolution, with all its associated uncertainties and ambiguities, has occurred and is continuing to occur in Thailand. (P. 278)

Revolution with a small "r" is certainly taking place. Thailand no more than any other country can escape the profound changes that are integral to the absorption of modern knowledge, the application of science and technology to a country's problems, communication with the rest of the world, and the pursuit of widening options and material comforts. The issue is not change or no change, but how to deal with the destabilizing effects of successful economic development so that a society can enjoy its benefits and avoid its potentialities for conflict and even chaos. If the search for stability is interpreted in this light, the Thai experience of the past three decades looks reasonably successful. The near descent into chaos in 1976 can be seen as a shock to a society that has always valued moderation and that has drawn back to moderation after staring directly into the face of extreme disorder.

The Thais, like most other poor nations, have chosen to pursue economic development and have sought international aid to help promote the process. Nevertheless, the providers of development assistance are a party to its consequences, and such providers cannot claim some successes in these efforts without admitting some responsibility for their effects, good and bad. In the Thai case at least, as of this writing, rapid development within the context of a reasonable degree of social stability is being achieved, and the American connection in this respect, as I have tried to spell out, can be credited with having made significant contributions to development; to stability, in the restoration of law and order and the undermining of the insurgency; and to the social changes, revolutionary if you will, that are accompanying economic development.

ANNEX TABLES

Annex Tables

Tables A.6 through A.15 list USAID projects under major sectoral and subject headings. These tables are not a complete listing of the 343 development projects USAID has carried out between 1950 and 1988 (including projects active in 1988), aside from the regional and centrally funded projects shown in tables A.1.1 to A.1.4. Omitted are few miscellaneous and minor projects and some accounts (also labeled "projects") that funded overhead and costs of project planning. Also, the table categories are not always mutually exclusive; some projects are listed under more than one table. The figures on U.S. contributions show only dollar expenditures in most of the tables—that is, they exclude local currency expenditures from joint U.S. and RTG contributions, as explained in the text. Data on the USAID program have been drawn from USAID/T annual reports, from the USAID mission's Program Office, and from *Congressional Presentations* of various years. Data on the foundations' programs were provided by the respective foundations, from their files and annual reports. Note that some columns may not add to totals due to rounding. Figures for currently active projects are planned amounts.

TABLE A.1.

U.S. Economic Assistance: Thailand Program—USAID and Predecessor Agencies

| Fiscal Year | Grants | | | | | Other USAID & | Total USAID & |
	Project	Nonproject	Grants Total	Loans	Mission Funded	PL 480	PL 480
				($ million)			
1946	—	—	—	6.2[a]	6.2	—	6.2
1951	8.9	—	8.9	—	8.9	—	8.9
1952	7.2	—	7.2	—	7.2	—	7.2
1953	6.5	—	6.5	—	6.5	—	6.5
1954	8.8	—	8.8	—	8.8	—	8.8
1955	28.8	17.3	46.1	—	46.1	0.7	46.8
1956	10.5	13.0	23.5	10.0[b]	33.5	—	33.5
1957	19.9	4.3	24.2	9.8[b]	34.0	—	35.0
1958	7.3	16.7	24.0	6.9[c]	30.9	—	30.9
1959	8.2	15.9	24.1	21.6	45.7	—	45.7
1960	8.9	14.9	23.8	0.8	24.6	—	24.6
1961	5.8	18.4	24.2	1.9[d]	26.1	—	26.1
1962	13.1	13.3	26.4	—	26.4	—	26.4
1963	16.6	—	16.6	10.2	26.8	—	26.8
1964	12.3	—	12.3	—	12.3	—	12.3
1965	18.7	0.3	19.0	0.4	19.4	0.1	19.5
1966	43.6	—	43.6	—	43.6	0.2	43.8
1967	55.0	—	55.0	—	55.0	0.3	55.3
1968	47.3	—	47.3	3.3	50.6	3.6	54.2
1969	33.5	—	33.5	—	33.5	6.9	40.4
1970	25.1	—	25.1	—	25.1	8.8	33.9
1971	16.2	—	16.2	—	16.2	7.8	24.0
1972	11.0	—	11.0	—	11.0	19.8	30.8
1973	10.4	—	10.4	—	10.4	24.5	34.9
1974	11.5	—	11.5	1.7	13.2	5.8	19.0
1975	2.9	—	2.9	5.0	7.9	5.0	12.9
1976[e]	5.5	—	5.5	5.4	10.9	2.8	13.7
1977	6.9	—	6.9	2.4	9.3	1.0	10.3
1978	3.7	—	3.7	8.2	11.9	3.8	15.7
1979	9.8	—	9.8	7.6	17.4	3.2	20.6
1980	13.8	—	13.8	5.8	19.6	0.6	20.2
1981	14.0	—	14.0	12.2	26.2	8.1	34.3
1982	13.4	—	13.4	17.7	31.1	1.0	32.1
1983	14.8	—	14.8	7.0	21.8	0.5	22.3
1984	13.5	—	13.5	18.1	31.6	22.3	53.9
1985	22.0	—	22.0	10.1	32.1	10.4	42.5
1986	23.0	—	23.0	1.0	24.0	6.9	30.9

TABLE A.1.

U.S. Economic Assistance: Thailand Program—USAID and Predecessor Agencies

| Fiscal Year | Grants | | | | | Other | Total |
	Project	Nonproject	Grants Total	Loans	Mission Funded	USAID & PL 480	USAID & PL 480
			($ million)				
1987	12.9	——	12.9	8.0	20.9	9.9	30.8
1988	20.6	——	20.6	——	20.6	N/A	20.6
TOTALS	$611.9	114.1	726.0	181.3	907.3	153.3	1,060.6

NOTE: USAID/Thailand data has been used wherever available in order to get details of composition not given in AID/W reports. There are differences between Washington and field mission data arising from different treatment of regional funds and deobligations. The AID/W report "U.S. Overseas Loans and Grants" (annual) shows gross obligations, while USAID/T records net obligations—i.e., final amounts available to Thailand after deducting amounts ("deobligations") unused and returned to the U.S. Treasury. The largest difference occurs in 1965: AID/W reports a loan amount of $20.6 million, of which $20.2 was not drawn and was subsequently deobligated.

All figures are on a fiscal year (FY) basis—i.e., they are recorded by the FY in which they were obligated (formally established as a U.S. government financial commitment). For the following reasons FY accounting does not coincide with the matching calendar year: a) the FY ran from July 1 to June 30 (e.g., FY 1960 began on July 1, 1959, ending on June 30, 1960) until 1976, and from October 1 to September 30 thereafter; thus obligations or disbursements of funds during any FY extend over portions of two calendar years; b) although disbursements (actual payments by the U.S. government) of grant funds, especially for personnel and for participant-training costs, take place largely in the FY of obligation, disbursements under contracts for which several years' requirements are obligated in advance and disbursements upon subsequent delivery of goods ordered in any fiscal year stretch over one or more years beyond the FY of obligation; c) FY figures are typically adjusted downward over time to reflect deobligations and other accounting adjustments before the books are closed on a project; deobligations result when a project is left with unspent funds or is changed to delete some originally planned components.

[a] Not a predecessor agency loan.
[b] Includes some nonproject funds. All other loans were for projects.
[c] From Asian Economic Development Fund appropriation
[d] PL 480 Japanese yen loan
[e] 1976 includes the "Transition Quarter" (July–September 1976) at the time the U.S. fiscal year shifted from a July 1 to a September 1 starting date.
N/A = not available

TABLE A.1a.

Counterpart Account: 1951–1986

Cumulative Deposits (baht million)		Percent	Cumulative Withdrawals (baht million)		Percent
U.S. deposits (1955–62)[a]	2,773	36	RTG military projects	704	10
RTG Deposits	4,500	58	USAID Public Safety projects	915	12
Commensurate value of U.S. commodity aid (1950–55)	(358)		USAID development projects	5,729	78
Budget contributions (1956–76)	(4,142)				
Loan repayments, misc.	419	5			
TOTAL Deposits	7,694	100	TOTAL Withdrawals	7,348	100

SOURCES: DTEC; USAID/T Annual Financial Reports.
[a] From nonproject aid, commodity import program.

TABLE A.1b.

U.S. Local Currency Loans in Thailand

Year	Loan	Amount ($ million equivalent)
1954	Agricultural Cooperative Credit	0.4
1956	Northeast Water System Equipment	0.4
1957	Jalaprathan Cement	1.0
1957	Mae Moh Lignite	2.1
1957	Bangkok Power Station	2.0
1960	Bangkok Jute Mill	0.7
1963	Industrial Finance Corporation	0.7
1965	JFK Foundation	0.5
TOTAL		$7.8

NOTE: Between 1954 and 1965 the aid program included nine loans not denominated in dollars. One of these loans, financed from USG holdings of Japanese yen, funded a resource transfer from Japan to Thailand (locomotives) and is therefore listed under tables A.1 and A.20 as performing an aid transfer function comparable with U.S. dollar loans. The remaining eight local currency loans, listed above, did not finance a resource transfer into Thailand; they used baht from the counterpart fund which had been generated (as the sale or "equivalent" value) of externally derived goods and services already provided to Thailand under previous dollar funding. It would be double counting to add such loans into the same aid category as additions to the dollar-financed aid that generated the local currency in the first round transaction.

Two of the loans in table A.1b (cement and the jute mill) were financed from U.S.–owned baht generated from sales of PL 480 commodities. Repayments of these loans reverted to the U.S. Treasury and thus comprised resource transfers back from Thailand to the United States. The remaining six loans were financed from other counterpart funds; repayments reverted to the counterpart account for reprogramming for aid projects, except for the Cooperative Credit project, which was set up as a separate revolving fund.

In the case of the lignite, power, and IFC loans, these baht funds complemented dollar-funded projects.

TABLE A.1.1.

USAID Regional Projects Administered in Thailand

Fiscal Year	Amount ($ million)
1968	2.7
1969	6.3
1970	7.6
1971	7.5
1972	5.0
1973	8.1
1974	5.8
1975	5.0
1976	2.8
1977	1.0
1978	1.6
1979	3.2
1980	0.6
1981	0.7
TOTAL	$58.1

NOTE: Individual projects financed from regional funds are included in other tables, as appropriate, and identified. This table covers the program that was formally designated Regional Economic Development, administered by a USAID office in Bangkok separate from the regular bilateral mission.

TABLE A.1.2.

USAID Centrally Funded Program Activities in Thailand[a]

	1984	1985	1986	1987
	(fiscal years; $ thousand)			
Science and Technology			1,994	1,859
Program in S&T Cooperation			(1,400)	(898)
U.S.–Israel Cooperative Development Research Program			(594)	(749)
BOSTID grants[b]			——	(212)
Agriculture and natural resources			1,600	1,045
Health, population, nutrition			719	324
Private enterprise			689	3,060
Housing and urban development			102	622
Private and voluntary organizations			102	443
Small projects with Peace Corps			55	33
TOTALS	$9,255[c]	8,072[c]	5,261	7,386

[a]Excludes 1) Trade Development Program, which is centrally funded but administered by the Commercial Section of the Embassy, not USAID/T; 2) Housing Guaranty loans (in FY 1984), which are a contingent liability, not appropriated U.S. funds; 3) American Schools and Hospitals Abroad, shown in separate table. Data for years before 1984 not available.
[b]Board on Science and Technology for International Development of the National Academy of Sciences.
[c]Breakdown not available.

TABLE A.1.3.

American Schools and Hospitals Abroad

Grantee	Year	Amount ($ thousand)
Seventh Day Adventist Hospital (Bangkok)	1978	250
	1984	725
	1985	700
	1987	300
		1,975
Payap College (Chiang Mai)	1978	1,980
	1981	1,075
	1982	960
	1983	500
	1984	500
		5,015
Lampang Yonok College (Lampang)	1986	850
	1987	750
	1988	1,000
		2,600
TOTAL		$9,590

SOURCE: ASHA office, AID/W.

TABLE A.1.4.

Trade Development Program: Grant-Financed Feasibility Studies

Year	Subject	Amount ($ thousand)
1984	Lignite power generation—EGAT	350
	Lignite mining	200
	Airport expansion	650
	Computer system—EGAT	200
	Bangkok flood control	450
1985	Coastal waterways	500
	Power generation—Ao Phai, EGAT	280
	Power generation from Bangkok waste	475
	Multipurpose dam—Loei-Upper Pasak	400
1986	Hazardous waste disposal	345
	Radio frequency management	145
	Telephone computer system	200
1987	Bangkok power—EGAT	200
	Power distribution, suburban Bangkok	500
	Petroleum computer system	50
	Railway computerization	100
	Bangkok mass transit	150
	300-MW gas turbine project—EGAT	350
TOTAL		$5,545

SOURCES: U.S. Embassy; USAID/T.

TABLE A.1.5.

Food for Peace (PL 480) Loans/Grants to Thailand

	Title I Loan Sales[a]	Title II Grants to Voluntary Relief Agencies[b]	Total
		($ million)	
1950–1964	1.7[c]	0.7	2.4
1965	——	0.1	0.1
1966	——	0.2	0.2
1967	——	0.3	0.3
1968	——	0.9	0.9
1969	——	0.6	0.6
1970	——	1.2	1.2
1971	——	0.3	0.3
1972	14.0	0.8	14.8
1973	16.0	0.4	16.4
1974	——	——	——
1975	——	*	*
1976	——	——	——
1977	——	——	——
1978	——	*	*
1979–1987	——	——	——
TOTALS	$31.7	5.5	37.2

[a] Tobacco.
[b] Powdered milk and formulated food for programs administered by UNICEF.
[c] 1955: 0.7; 1957: 1.0. Table excludes $1.9 million loan in 1961 for Japanese locomotives financed with U.S.-owned yen from PL 480 sales in Japan.
* Less than $50,000.

TABLE A.2.

Current USAID Program: Active Projects, 1988

Project	Years	Planned Dollar Cost	FY 1988 Obligations
		($ million)	
Agriculture			
Northeast Rainfed Agriculture	1981–88	7.5	0
Seed Development II	1982–89	6.2	0
Northeast Small-Scale Irrigation	1980–89	8.6	0.1
Khon Kaen University Agricultural Research	1983–89	2.2	0
Agricultural Technology Transfer	1984–92	8.3	2.6
Area Development			
Rural Development Monitoring & Evaluation	1984–89	4.0	0
Decentralized Development Management Planning	1981–89	10.5	0
Mae Chaem Watershed	1980–89	9.2	0
Miscellaneous			
Population Planning II	1982–89	17.8	0
Rural Industries & Employment	1986–96	15.6	1.3
Micro-Mini Hydro	1982–89	8.1	0
Emerging Problems of Development II	1985–92	18.0	1.9
Science & Technology	1985–92	35.4	0.4
PVO Cofinancing II	1985–92	6.0	1.0
Management of Natural Resources & Environment	1988–95	44.0	9.6
Affected Thai Villages II	1980–88	32.0	5.0
TOTAL		$233.4	21.9

NOTE: FY 1988 figures exclude (i.e., do not subtract) deobligations of previous years funds; planned costs of projects in final year(s) of implementation, with no FY 1988 new funding, are net of deobligations. About $1.6 million of the obligations during FY 1988 were funded from deobligations—i.e., funds that were obligated in earlier years (for three of the projects in the list) but were found in 1988 to be in excess of actual project needs.

Table excludes centrally funded projects.

TABLE A.3.

Ford Foundation: Major Institutional Grants in Thailand, 1966–1987

Thai Institutions	Grants ($ thousand)
National Institute of Development Administration	3,175
Chiangmai University	2,525
Khon Kaen University	2,274
Central Institute of English Language	1,114
Thammasat University	752
Kasetsart University	506
National Education Commission	468
Chulalongkorn University	453
Social Science Association of Thailand	412
Mahidol University	245
Institute of Population Studies	197
Siam Society	195
Prince of Songkla University	53
TOTAL	$12,174

SOURCE: Ford Foundation, New York.
NOTE: Figures represent sum of numerous individual grants to each institution over the period. Total Ford Foundation grants to all recipients in Thailand were $17,793,000.

TABLE A.4.

Rockefeller Foundation Program in Thailand: Grant Approvals

	Agri- culture	Nutri- tion	Popu- lation	Health	University Development	Number of Field Staff	Number of Fellow- ships Granted
				($ million)			
1922–63	—	—	—	0.2	1.1	—	96
1964	*	—	—	—	0.2	2	11
1965	*	—	*	—	0.3	3	13
1966	0.2		0.2	*	0.8	12	34
1967	0.1	—	*	—	1.7	23	37
1968	0.1	0.1	—	—	2.3	30	25
1969	0.1	0.2	*	—	2.0	33	22
1970	—	*	—	—	2.0	34	15
1971	*	*	*	—	0.3(?)	36	22
1972	*	*	*	—	0.6	28	19
1973	*	*	*	—	0.9	19	15
1974	—	—	*	—	0.9	13	15
1975	—	—	*	—	0.2	9	15
1976	—	—	0.2	—	0.4	7	9
1977	—	—	0.1	—	0.3	5	5
1978	—	—	—	—	0.3	6	7
1979	—	—	*	*	0.3	5	5
1980	*	—	*	*	0.1	3	7
1981	0.1	—	*	0.1	0.1	5	2
1982	—	—	*	0.1	—	3	—
1983	—	—	—	0.1	—	3	—
1984	—	—	*	0.2	—	—	3
1985	—	—	*	0.2	—	—	—
1986	—	—	0.1	0.2	—	—	1
							378

Estimated grants total: $10.0 million

SOURCE: Rockefeller Foundation, files and annual reports.
NOTE: No column totals are given because RF annual reports do not show full funding by country in a consistent manner over the long period covered, especially for field staff and fellowships. In the peak years 1968–1972 total annual expenditures appear to have reached $3–3.5 million.
*Less than $50,000.

TABLE A.5.

Winrock/Agricultural Development Council: Assistance to Thailand, 1955–1985

	Amount ($ thousand)
Teaching, research staff at Kasetsart University	752
Research and teaching grants	85
Fellowships for study in the United States	717
Fellowships at Asian and Australian universities	323
Other seminars, research	178
TOTAL	$2,055
Fellowships for foreign students at Thai universities	$ 210

SOURCE: Winrock/ADC.

TABLE A.6.

USAID Agriculture Projects

Project	Years	U.S. Contribution
		($ million)
Bangkok Experimental Station	1951–53	0.7
Tank irrigation	1951–57	3.8[a]
Forestry	1951–57	0.2
Fishery	1951–57	0.7
Agricultural Programs Administration	1951–57	0.4
Rice Improvement	1951–58	0.2
Extension Education	1951–67	2.4
Crop Improvement	1951–68	1.5
Agricultural Statistics	1952–58	0.1
Agricultural Credit & Marketing	1952–65	1.3
Livestock Development	1952–66	1.0
Kasetsart University	1952–68	1.8
Soil Research Lab	1955–60	*
Soil Fertilization Management	1956–58	0.1
Agricultural Development, Northeast Thailand	1957–60	0.1
Rinderpest Eradication (R)	1956–60	0.1
Rural Youth (4-F)	1955–58	*
Agricultural Leader Training	1960–61	*
Research & Conservation	1959–64	0.3
Plant Protection	1960–65	0.1
Northeast Livestock	1963–68	0.4
Northeast Soil & Water Management	1963–67	0.8
Agricultural Economics	1963–67	0.3
Agricultural Research	1964–74	5.3
Agricultural Economics	1967–74	3.0
Agricultural Development	1965–74	2.6
Agricultural Credit	1968–74	0.2
Farmer Groups	1967–74	1.1
Soil & Water Development	1965–74	1.4
Fishery Development	1968–76	0.5
Livestock Development	1968–74	0.2
Water Development	1968–74	1.2
Agricultural Extension	1968–77	6.8
Highland Development	–77	0.1
Seed Development I	1975–82	3.7
Sericulture	1976–82	1.7
Lam Nan Oon Irrigation (G&L)	1977–86	6.7
Extension (L)	1977–82	2.4
Village Fish Pond Development	1979–82	0.4
NERAD (G&L)	1981–	7.5
Northeast Small-Scale Irrigation (G&L)	1980–	8.6

TABLE A.6. (continued)

USAID Agriculture Projects

Project	Years	U.S. Contribution ($ million)
Agricultural Planning	1981–87	2.2
ASEAN Agricultural Development Planning (R)	1980–87	2.9
Seed Development II (G&L)	1982–	6.2
Agricultural Technology Transfer (G&L)	1984–	5.0
TOTAL		$85.9

[a] Plus counterpart expenditures equivalent to $3.9 million.
G = grant; L = loan; R = regional
* Less than $50,000

TABLE A.7.

USAID Public Administration Projects

Project	Years	U.S. Contribution ($ million)
Public Administration Training	1951–59	0.2
Public Administration Institute (NIDA)	1954–69	1.9
Finance Improvement & Revenue Collection	1955–59	0.1
Community Development	1957–74	3.9
Bangkok City Planning	1959–66	1.4
Civil Service Improvement	1965–73	0.7
Development Administration Training	1965–77	3.1
Northeast Development Planning	1968–76	1.5
Local Government In-Service Training	1968–74	0.8
Economic Policy & Planning	1972–76	0.9
Transfer of Management Skills	1975–81	4.7
Emerging Problems of Development I	1980–86	5.0
Emerging Problems of Development II	1985–92	18.0[a]
TOTAL		$42.2

[a] Planned.

TABLE A.8.

USAID Education Projects

	Years	U.S. Contribution $ millions
Vocational and Technical		
Technical Education	1953–57	*
Agriculture School	1952–58	0.1
Improvement of Technical Education	1955–62	1.6
Vocational Education Development	1952–68	2.2
Vocational Education (with IBRD)	1966–76	3.6
SEATO Skilled Labor (R)	1958–67	1.3
Mobile Trade Training Schools	1966–72	3.5
Technical Training for ARD	1966–71	3.9
SUBTOTAL		16.2
Higher Education		
Chulalongkorn University	1955–62	1.7
Kasetsart University	1952–68	1.8
Asian Institute of Technology (R)	1959–76	9.2
Khon Kaen University	1983–89	2.2
Institute of Public Administration (NIDA)	1954–69	1.9
SUBTOTAL		16.8
Primary, Secondary, and General		
Elementary Education	1953–60	0.5
Secondary Education	1956–60	0.1
Curriculum Development	1952–58	0.1
Supervisory & In-Service Education	1955–58	0.2
Educational Programs Administration	1953–59	0.1
English Language Training (R)	1958–66	1.7
Education Research & Planning	1964–67	*
Teacher Training	1952–76	4.2
Educational Finance	1973–75	0.1
General Education Development	1953–68	2.2
Regional Educational Development (R)	1967–69	0.5
Educational Planning	1964–69	1.5
Hill Area Education	1980–86	1.6
SUBTOTAL		12.8

TABLE A.8. (continued)

USAID Education Projects

	Years	U.S. Contribution $ millions
Nonformal		
Adult Education	1952–58	*
Adult Education	–77	0.2
Rural Training	1964–76	8.0
Nonformal Vocational Education	1979–83	0.4
SUBTOTAL		8.6
TOTAL Education		$54.4

R = regional.
*Less than $50,000.

TABLE A.9.

USAID Transportation Projects

Fiscal Years	Project	U.S. Dollar Funds	Counterpart Funds ($ equivalent)	Total
			($ million)	
	ROADS			
1957–65	Highway Department Operations	1.7	0.8	2.5
1955–65	General Highway Improvement	2.6	12.5	15.1
1951–59	Highway Development	1.8	0.5	2.3
1954–61	Friendship Highway	13.6	6.2	19.8
1957–74[a]	Bangkok-Saraburi Highway	1.9	11.0	12.9
1958–62	East-West Highway	14.6	8.6	23.2
1957–61	Bangkok-Bangkapi streets	——	5.8	5.8
1959–61	Korat-Nongkai Highway	——	12.6	12.6
1959–62	Bridge Replacement	——	6.2	6.2
1963–71	Security Road Program	5.0	4.9	9.9
1964–65	Bangkok-Nakornpathom Highway	——	5.8	5.8
1965	Lomsak-Saraburi Highway	0.4	——	0.4
1960–62	Chumporn-Nakornsrithamaraj Survey	——	0.2	0.2
TOTAL Roads		41.6	75.1	116.7
	RAIL			
1951–57	Railroad Improvement	1.4	0.9	1.5
1955–58	Railway Equipment	1.1	——	1.1
1961	Locomotives (L)	1.9[b]	——	1.9
1957–60	Bangkok-Nongkhai Railroad	0.5	——	0.5
1955–58	Udorn-Nongkhai Railroad	1.3	2.2	3.5
	Repair shop	——	0.3	0.3
TOTAL Rail		6.2	3.4	9.6
	AIR TRANSPORT			
1951–60	Airport Improvement	1.2	*	1.2
1953–74	Aeronautical Ground Services	6.9	8.1	15.0
1955–61	Thai Airways Improvement	1.6	——	1.6
1955–72	Airfield Construction	3.1	9.4	12.5
1955–69	Meteorological Services	0.6	0.1	0.7
1957–64	Aviation Overhaul	0.1	*	0.1
1962–69	SEATO Meteorology Telecommunications (R)	0.4	0.1	0.5
TOTAL Air		13.9	17.7	31.6

TABLE A.9.

USAID Transportation Projects

Fiscal Years	Project	U.S. Dollar Funds	Counterpart Funds ($ equivalent)	Total
			($ million)	
	PORTS			
1951–54	Harbor Development (*Manhattan* dredge)	0.8	0.1	0.9
1959	Bangkok Dredge (L)	1.8	——	1.8
1956–57	Mekong Ferry and Spur	——	0.7	0.7
TOTAL Ports		2.6	0.8	3.4
1957–61	Transportation System Evaluation	0.3	0.1	0.4
TOTAL Transportation		$64.6	97.1	161.7

ᵃIn a few cases the closing fiscal year (i.e., the year of final accounting transactions) is well beyond the year of physical completion.
ᵇLoan in Japanese yen.
L = loan-funded; R = regional.
* Less than $50,000.

TABLE A.10.

Counterinsurgency Projects

Projects	Years	AID Contribution	Counterpart Fund ($ equiv.)	Total
		($ million)		
Counterinsurgency Operations				
Civil Police Administration[a]	1957–76	77.2	41.4	118.6
Village Radio	1966–70	2.1	0.6	2.7
Village Security Forces	1966–71	0.3	*	0.3
CSOC operations[b]	1967–73	0.1	——	0.1
Volunteer Defense Corps	1955–59	0.1	0.9	1.0
50-KV Transmitter	1966–71	0.3	*	0.3
Border Patrol Police	1962–72	6.7	1.6	23.2
SUBTOTAL		86.8	44.5	131.3
Counterinsurgency Development Activities				
Accelerated Rural Development (ARD)	1964–77	63.6	11.7	75.3
Mobile Development Units (MDUs)	1964–76	5.7	0.8	6.5
Mobile Medical Teams	1968–71	0.6	*	0.6
Security Road Program	1963–65	5.1	5.0	10.1
SUBTOTAL		75.0	17.5	92.5
TOTAL		$161.8	62.0	223.8

[a] Included ordinary police activities prior to and not connected with the insurgency.
[b] Communist Suppression Operations Command.
* Less than $5,000.

TABLE A.11.

USAID Health and Population Projects

Projects	Years	U.S. Contribution ($ thousand)
Population		
Vital Statistics	1953	61
Family Planning	1968–73	1,780
Population Planning I	1975–83	8,340
Population Planning II	1983–89	18,370
Centrally funded projects[a]	1984–88	3,760
SUBTOTAL		32,311
Vertical Disease Control		
Malaria Control	1951–57	2,810
Malaria Eradication	1958–71	17,910
Antimalaria Control	1979–84	4,500
(Total Malaria)		(25,220)
Communicable Diseases Control	1952–58	668
Other[a]		47
SUBTOTAL		25,935
Rural Health, Sanitation, & PHC		
Environmental Health & Sanitation	1951–58	919
Rural Health	1952–62	1,159
Village Health & Sanitation	1960–68	1,172
Potable Water Project	1966–69	3,143
Village Sanitation Development Fund	1982–83	26
Rural PHC Expansion	1978–87	6,500
Health & Sanitation Administration	1951–59	866
Comprehensive Rural Health	1961–73	5,042
Mobile Medical Teams	1968–71	642
PHC Operations Research[a]	1983–89	543
Other	1985–88	116
Lampang PHC pilot project	1979–82	400
SUBTOTAL		20,528
Medical Education & Health Training		
Medical Education Development	1951–55	1,480
Chiangmai Medical School	1962–69	5,851
Faculty of Public Health, Mahidol University	1969–74	494
Health Education	1951–59	207
In- and Preservice Training	1952–59	146
Cholburi Training Center	1952–55	585

TABLE A.11. (continued)

USAID Health and Population Projects

Projects	Years	U.S. Contribution ($ thousand)
Faculty of Medicine, Chulalongkorn University[a]	1986–87	133
Other[a]	1985–88	139
SUBTOTAL		9,035
Hospital Services[b]		
Hospital improvement	1951–62	1,604
Police Hospital improvement	1955–61	138
Siriraj Hospital equipment	1955–61	62
Drug and pharmaceutical control	1964–69	112
Mahidol Vaccine Center[a]	1984–87	200
SUBTOTAL		2,116
Health Planning & Assessment		
Health sector assessment	1983	70
Under EPD II project	1985–90	500[c]
Other[a]	1986–89	613
SUBTOTAL		1,183
Nutrition		
Protein food development	1962–72	638
Nutritional disease control	1952–54	129
Nutrition education study	1980–82	16
Infant nutrition & gastrointestinal disease	1985–88	120
Other[a]	1985–88	39
SUBTOTAL		942
TOTAL Health		$92,050[d]

NOTES: Excludes regional health projects (e.g., Asia-Pacific Academic Consortium for Public Health).

[a] Centrally funded. Information on centrally funded projects is incomplete. Projects are implemented by Population Council, Association for Voluntary Sterilization, Family Planning International Assistance, Family Health International, Johns Hopkins Program for International Education in Gynecology and Obstetrics, Program for International Training in Health, Research Triangle Institute, International Planned Parenthood Federation, Harvard Institute for International Development, Mahidol University, Children's Hospital of Buffalo, MOPH, Program for Appropriate Technology for Health, MEDEX, Thai Fertility Research Association, Planned Parenthood Association of Thailand, Population and Community Development Association, TDRI, John Snow Inc., Westinghouse Public Applied Systems, NIDA, Chulalongkorn University Institute for Population Studies, University Research Corporation, and Prince of Songkhla University.

[b] Excludes $9.6 million of ASHA grants shown in table A.1.3.

[c] Budgeted up to January 1987.

[d] Grant-funded except for $4 million malaria loan and $9.9 million population loans.

TABLE A.12.

Poverty Alleviation Projects

	Period	U.S. Contribution ($ million)
1. *Hands-On*		
PVO Cofinancing[a]	1976–	12.0
Peace Corps Impact[b]	1983–	0.2
2. *Site-Specific Area Development*		
Northeast		
Sericulture Settlements (L)	1976–82	1.7
Lam Nam Oon Irrigation (L)	1967–86	6.7
Land Settlement (L)	1979–85	3.7
Northeast Small-Scale Irrigation	1980–	8.6[c]
North		
Mae Chaem Watershed	1980–	9.2
3. *Delivery Systems and Northeast Region-Wide*		
Primary Health Care (L)	1978–87	6.5
PHC Operations Research[b]	1983	0.5
Decentralized Development Management	1981–87	10.6[d]
Rural Development Monitoring &		
Evaluation	1984–	5.0
Agricultural Extension (L)	1977–83	2.4
Agriculture Development (L)	1974–	5.0
Northeast Rainfed Agricultural		
Development	1981–	7.5[e]
Khon Kaen University	1983–	2.2
TOTAL		$81.8

[a] Includes mission and regional funds.
[b] Centrally funded.
[c] Includes $5.8 million loan.
[d] Includes $7.5 million loan.
[e] Includes $4.3 million loan.
L = loan-funded.

TABLE A.13.

AID Grants to Nongovernmental Organizations (NGOs) for Projects in Thailand[a]

Fiscal Year	U.S. NGOs[b]	Thai NGOs	Total
		($ million)	
1976	——	0.5	0.5
1977	0.2	0.4	0.6
1978	1.1	0.6	1.7
1979	1.0	——	1.0
1980	0.1	0.4	0.5
1981	0.6	0.9	1.5
1982	0.4	0.9	1.3
1983	0.1	0.8	0.9
1984	0.2	0.2	0.4
1985	0.2	1.5[c]	1.7
1986	0.2	0.7	0.9
1987	0.1	0.9	1.0
TOTAL			$12.0

[a] Includes funds from three accounts: Operational Program Grants, PVO Cofinancing Project (I and II), Regional PVO Program.
[b] Grants to U.S. NGOs for subgranting to Thai affiliates are included under U.S.
[c] Includes credit line.

TABLE A.14.

Private Sector Projects

Project	Period	U.S. Contribution ($ thousand)
Industrial Technical Advisory Services (IFCT)	1957–64	110
Investment surveys	1960–61	25
Industrial development surveys	1960–62	131
IFCT loan	1964	750
Private sector development (IFCT, BOI, MOI, MOC)	1965–77	2,766
Board of Investment	1966–68	320
Private capital investment (IFCT, BOI, MOC, BOT, NESDB)	1972–76	1,855
Rural off-farm employment assessment	1979–81	500
Private sector in development (BOI, JPPCC)	1983–	3,000
Rural industries and employment	1986–	14,100[a]
Agribusiness loans—Siam Commercial Bank[b]	1982	2,000
Institute for Management Education for Thailand (IMET)[b]	1982	400
Thai Venture Capital Ltd.[b]	1987	3,050
TOTAL		$29,007

NOTE: Table omits some small projects.
[a] Planned level.
[b] Centrally funded.

TABLE A.15.

U.S. FAA–Funded Narcotics Projects in Thailand

Project	Period	U.S. Contribution ($ million)
Narcotics Assistance Unit (in U.S. Embassy)		
Border security[a]	1982–87	7.2
Enforcement[b]	1974–87	10.2
Crop control	1978–87	6.6
Customs	1974–84	5.2
Treatment, rehabilitation	1978–82	1.3
Prevention	1981–94	0.6
Thai Narcotics Control Board	1980–84	0.5
Administration, project support	1978–87	4.1
SUBTOTAL		35.8[c]
AID		
Control, Treatment		
Narcotics enforcement	1974	5.1
Customs improvement	1974	2.1
Drug abuse[d]	1987	0.4
Miscellaneous		0.2
SUBTOTAL		7.8
Crop Substitution		
Mae Chaem watershed development	1980–	10.0
Nine miscellaneous projects		0.2[e]
CROP SUBSTITUTION SUBTOTAL		10.2
AID SUBTOTAL		18.0
TOTAL Narcotics		$53.8

SOURCE: USAID/T; U.S. Embassy, Bangkok.
[a] Military assistance to Royal Thai Army to free border areas of armed groups from Burma engaged in narcotics production and traffic.
[b] Includes helicopters.
[c] Error of addition due to rounding.
[d] Centrally funded.
[e] Information incomplete.

TABLE A.16.

Contributions to Mekong Basin Committee: 1957–1986

Donor	For Pre-Investment Investigations, Planning	For Construction	Total Contribution
	($ million)		
Thailand	27.6	128.5	156.1
U.S.	25.8	20.5	46.4
UNDP	39.6	2.5	42.1
Germany	2.4	38.5	40.9
Japan	3.3	36.3	39.6
Netherlands	10.4	25.3	35.7
Vietnam	6.5	20.5	27.0
EEC	2.4	18.8	21.2
IBRD	——	19.9	19.9
Australia	2.9	13.2	16.1
ADB	——	15.8	15.8
Lao People's Democratic Republic	7.4	7.6	15.0
Cambodia	5.2	9.3	14.5
France	3.3	10.6	13.9
OPEC Fund	——	10.5	10.5
Others	18.7	30.1	48.7
TOTAL	$155.5	407.9	563.3

SOURCE: Mekong Interim Committee, *Annual Report, 1986.*

TABLE A.17.

Water Control Projects in Northeast Thailand Sponsored by the Mekong Committee

Project	Year Completed	Irrigated Area (ha)	Installed Capacity (MW)
Nam Pung	1965	0	6.3
Nam Pong	1966	53,000	25.0
Lam Takong	1970	38,000	——
Lam Dom Noi	1971	24,000	24.0
Lam Pra Plerng	1971	9,760	——
Nam Phrom	1973	0	40.0
Lam Pao	1975	21,300	——
Mun/Chi I	1982	6,500	——
Huai Mong	1986	8,700	——

SOURCE: Interim Committee for Co-Ordination of Investigations of the Lower Mekong Basin, various publications.

TABLE A.18.

U.S.–Financed Mekong Basin Projects in or Concerning Thailand

Projects Under Framework of the Mekong Committee	Years	U.S. Contribution ($ million)
Reconnaissance Study	1956–60	*
River Studies—Hydro Network	1958–62	2.2
Pa Mong Survey	1961–75	13.9
Hydro Network—spare parts (R)	1963–66	0.4
Channel Improvement Analysis	1965–71	0.5
Tributary Study	1964–69	*
Resources Atlas (R)	1965–72	0.5
Mun and Chi River basins study	1966–71	2.7
Basin Development Planning (R)	1970–76	5.9
Ports and Cargo Handling (R)	1971–75	0.2
Three tributary irrigation schemes Lam Pao Lam Takong Lam Phra Plerng	1963–1971	10.2
TOTAL U.S. Contribution		$36.3

R = regional contribution.
* Less than $50,000.

TABLE A.19.

U.S. Military Construction Projects in Thailand

	Length	Date
Road Construction		
1. Bangkok bypass, Routes 304, 311		
Chachoengsao–Kabinburi	96 km.	built 1962–66
Kabinburi–Korat	168 km.	built 1962–68
2. Route 331		
Sattahip naval base–Chachoengsao	127 km.	completed 1968
3. Route 22		
Sakon Nakhon–Nakhon Phanom	54 km	built 1968–70
4. Route 223		
Sakon Nakhon–That Phanom	70 km.	built 1968–70
5. Route 1009		
Chang Thong–Doi Inthanon	48 km.	completed 1976
TOTAL	563 km.	

Airfields
1. Limited provincial airfields improvements—lighting, POL storage, aprons, etc.; built 1961–63.
2. Large-scale improvements and construction of three new fields (U-Tapao, Nam Phong, Kamphaeng Saen); built 1963–68.

Naval Base—Sattahip
1. LST ramps, piers, depot; built 1961–63.
2. Major port development—breakwater, dredged harbor, docks, etc.; built 1963–69.

TABLE A.20.

U.S. Loans to Thailand: 1956–1987[a]

Year	Purpose	Amount
	Completed Loans	
1956	Nonproject, commodity imports	10.0
1957	Mae Moh power (3.3)	
	Aviation overhaul (0.1)	
	Nonproject, commodity imports (6.4)	9.8
1958	Telecommunications	6.9
1959	Metropolitan Electric Authority	19.8
1959	Bangkok dredging	1.8
1959	Meat processing	0.8
1961	Locomotives	1.9
1962	Three irrigation projects	10.2
1965	Lomsak-Saraburi Highway	0.4
1967	Lam Nam Oon irrigation	3.3
1974	Feasibility studies	1.7
1974	Agriculture Development	5.0
1975	Seed Development	3.7
1976	Sericulture Settlements	1.7
1977	Agriculture Extension	2.4
1978	Lam Nam Oon	3.2
1978	Primary Health Care	4.6
1979	Antimalaria	3.9
1979	Land Settlement	3.7
SUBTOTAL		94.8
	Active Loans[b]	
1980	Northeast Small-Scale Irrigation	5.8
1981	Northeast Rainfed Agriculture	4.3
1981	Decentralized Development Management	7.5

TABLE A.20. (continued)

U.S. Loans to Thailand: 1956–1987[a]

Year	Purpose	Amount
1982	Seed Development II	6.1
1982	Population Planning	2.0
1982	Micro-Mini Hydropower	8.0
1982	Agribusiness—Siam Commercial Bank	2.0
1983	Population Planning	7.0
1984	Population Planning	0.9
1984	Rural Primary Health Care	1.5
1984	Rural Development Monitoring Evaluation	5.0
1984	Agricultural Technology Transfer	4.5
1984	Provincial Waterworks	0.1[c]
1985/86	Science & Technology	8.0
SUBTOTAL: Loan agreement amounts, active projects		76.3
TOTAL Loans[d]		$171.1

SOURCES: AID *Status of Loans* report as of December 31, 1986; USAID/T, *Annual Financial Report*, October 1981.

NOTE: Loans are listed by calendar year of signing, not comparable in some cases with the fiscal year basis shown in table A.1. The amounts shown are the final sums drawn by the end of the project, usually less than the original loan agreement amounts. For most loans the interest rate was 2 percent for the first ten years, 3 percent thereafter, for a total amortization period of forty years.

[a] Excludes PL 480, Ex-Im Bank, and miscellaneous others.

[b] Amounts for active loans are original loan agreement figures. Some of these projects are completed; "active" in this table refers to loans for which the expenditures accounts are not yet closed.

[c] Excludes $5.6 million deobligated from loan agreement amount.

[d] As of December 31, 1986, the debt outstanding arising from these loans (taking account of early loans now partially or totally amortized and amounts actually drawn under the active projects) was $68.0 million.

TABLE A.21.

U.S. Military Assistance to Thailand: 1950–1988

Fiscal Year	Grants (MAP)	Credit Financing	Other	Total
		($ million)		
1950	9.7	—	—	9.7
1951	44.8	—	1.9	46.7
1952	31.4	—	0.2	31.6
1953	16.9	—	7.4	24.3
1954	40.6	—	1.9	42.5
1955	42.1	—	3.5	45.6
1956	40.1	—	5.5	45.6
1957	10.0	—	6.2	16.2
1958	2.4	—	11.9	14.3
1959	12.4	—	4.0	16.4
1960	34.0	—	6.4	40.4
1961	52.7	—	8.2	60.9
1962	64.0	—	14.4	78.4
1963	47.8	—	16.7	64.5
1964	28.3	—	7.7	36.0
1965	22.3	—	8.2	30.4
1966	41.7	—	9.8	51.6
1967	59.8	—	9.8	69.6
1968	80.2	—	9.6	89.8
1969	81.7	—	14.7	96.4
1970	87.5	—	22.5	110.0
1971	73.7	—	25.0	98.7
1972	95.9	—	26.1	122.1
1973	40.6	—	22.2	62.8
1974	29.2	—	6.2	35.4
1975	27.6	8.0	6.1	41.7
1976	17.6	36.7	49.6	103.9

TABLE A.21. (continued)

U.S. Military Assistance to Thailand: 1950–1988

Fiscal Year	Grants (MAP)	Credit Financing	Other	Total
		($ million)		
1977	16.0	30.0	1.2	47.3
1978	8.0	29.5	1.1	38.6
1979	1.2	30.0	0.9	32.1
1980	0.6	36.0	0.8	37.3
1981	0.4	53.4	0.8	54.6
1982	4.5	74.7	1.5	80.7
1983	18.5	76.0	1.7	96.2
1984	5.0	94.0	2.2	101.2
1985	5.0	95.0	2.3	102.3
1986	4.8	80.5	2.2	87.5
1987	50.0	——	2.5	52.5
1988	50.0	10.0	2.5	62.5
TOTALS	$1,299.1	653.8	325.4	2,278.3

SOURCE: USAID, *U.S. Overseas Loans and Grants.*
NOTE: Military Assistance Program (MAP) grants financed war material, construction (separate from OICC base construction program described in the text), transport, JUSMAG administration, etc. Credits were for RTG procurement of U.S. military equipment. Other includes costs of training Thai military officers in the United States and acquisition of U.S. military surplus property items. Figures for surplus equipment values prior to 1971 overstated the value substantially. See Caldwell, *American Economic Aid to Thailand*, p. 172, fn. c. Historical data on U.S. military aid appears to suffer from inconsistencies and occasional revision. Data through 1963 were recorded on an annual delivery basis; from 1964, on a program basis. Apart from the differences that delivery versus program would make on the valuation of any one year's military aid, there have been major differences in the recorded cumulative values over long periods. Thus Caldwell shows $977.8 million of military aid for 1951–1971 based on several official sources, including an earlier edition of the annual source used for this table, which shows $1,119.6 million, a difference of $141.8 million, or 15 percent, of Caldwell's figure.

NOTES

1. Background

1. N. H. Jacoby, *U.S. Aid to Taiwan*.
2. *Ibid.*, p. 7; and J. A. Caldwell, *American Economic Aid to Thailand*.
3. Caldwell, *American Economic Aid to Thailand*.
4. U.S. Departments of Commerce, Justice, and State, the Judiciary and Related Agencies, Appropriation Act 1988. PL 100-202, December 22, 1987, p. 156. FY 1988 Continuing Resolution, Sec. 521.
5. International Security and Development Cooperation Act of 1985, Section 315, Minority Set-Aside, *Legislation on Foreign Relations Through 1986* (March 1987), 1:310.

2. Thai-American Relations: Security and Development

1. Vimol Bhongbhibhat et al., eds., *The Eagle and the Elephant*, p. 85.
2. Details on the OICC construction program are drawn from the USMACTHAI/CHJUSMAG, *Command History*, vol. 2; Richard W. Tregaskis, *Southeast Asia: Building the Bases;* and other material provided by the Naval Facilities Engineering Command, Pearl Harbor, and Vice Admiral Wirol Kongchan (ret.) (interview).
3. The full statement is reproduced in Vimol et al., eds., *The Eagle and the Elephant*, p. 186.
4. Heng Liong Thung, "An Evaluation of the Impact of a Highway on a Rural Environment in Thailand by Aerial Photography Methods."
5. *The Nation*, December 9, 1987.
6. The GDP deflator probably understates the extent of inflation in the

prices of the goods and services that comprise the technical assistance content of an aid program. This is evident in the separate "technical cooperation" deflator calculated by the Development Assistance Committee of the OECD. I have not used the DAC deflator because of the difficulty of dividing the aid program numbers between technical and commodity aid and because the series covers only a portion of the time period of this study; the DAC Secretariat reverted to the use of GDP deflators in the late 1970s.

7. Economic Cooperation Administration, *Mutual Security Program, FY 1952 Budget Estimates* (Washington, D.C.: ECA, m.d.), F:89.

8. USAID, *Congressional Presentation, FY 1988*, p. 89.

9. Twatchai Yongkittikul and Paitoon Wiboonchitikula, *Thailand's Transformation Into a Newly Industrialized Country*, pp. 19–21.

10. See, for example, "Asia's New Economic 'Tiger,' " *Newsweek*, July 11, 1988, p. 52.

3. Training

1. Data drawn from USOM, *Participant Training;* and Thavat Vichaidit, *Evaluation of USAID Grants for Technical Assistance to Thailand.*

2. Data from USAID *Congressional Presentations;* and records of the Thai government's Department of Technical and Economic Corporation.

3. USAID, *Congressional Presentations*, program guidance memoranda; DTEC records.

4. Thai Civil Service Commission unpublished records.

5. Likhit Dhiravegin, *The Bureaucratic Elite of Thailand*, pp. 60–69.

6. Thailand–United States Educational Foundation, *Directory of Alumni, 1950–1986.*

7. Rockefeller Foundation, *Annual Reports*, various years.

8. Information provided by Ford Foundation, New York City.

9. Institute for International Education, *Open Doors.*

10. Rockefeller Foundation, *Annual Report, 1986*, p. 19. New York.

11. IBRD, *Review of Bank Technical Assistance to Bangladesh*, 1982.

12. Likhit, *Bureaucratic Elite*, pp. 109, 120.

13. Walter F. Vella, *The Impact of the West on Government in Thailand*, pp. 362–363.

14. IBRD, *A Public Development Program for Thailand*, p. 194.

15. Likhit, *Bureaucratic Elite*, p. 123.

16. *Ibid.*, p. 121.

17. Udom Bausri, "The Influence of John Dewey's Philosophy on Thai Education," p. 86.

18. Although only partial evidence was available, one study in 1968 called brain drain a serious problem that "may go a long way toward offsetting the beneficial effects of technical assistance action" OECD, *Technical Assistance and the Needs of Developing Countries*, p. 15. For some

countries, up to one-third of their students educated in the U.S. did not return home. G. W. Fry, "The Economic and Political Impact of Study Abroad," p. 58.

19. R. J. Muscat, "Evaluating Technical Cooperation," p. 82.

4. Nation-Building, 1950–1959

1. Details on the early history of the program are drawn from J. A. Caldwell and AID (USOM) records and briefing materials, except where indicated. Caldwell drew largely on U.S. sources for information on projects, mainly reports by the technicians who were managing the projects. Other than accounting-type audits and occasional policy reviews, systematic evaluations of project outcomes by independent evaluators became common AID practice only in the 1970s.

2. IBRD, *A Public Development Program for Thailand*, table 11, p. 272.

3. IBRD, *Thailand: Pricing and Marketing Policy for Intensification of Rice Agriculture*, table 3, p. 19.

4. *Ibid.*, p. 18.

5. IBRD, *A Public Development Program for Thailand*, p. 34.

6. Mutual Security Program, *FY 1956 Budget Estimates*, 2:309.

7. IBRD, *A Public Development Program for Thailand*, p. 35.

8. In briefing materials, e.g. USOM, *Thai-American Economic and Technical Cooperation* (March 1965).

9. Jeffrey A. Frankel, "The Impact of U.S. Economic Policies on a Commodity-Exporting Debtor: The Case of Thailand."

10. Jere R. Behrman, *Supply Response in Underdeveloped Agriculture; A Case Study of Four Major Annual Crops in Thailand, 1937–1963*, pp. 43–44.

11. *Ibid.*, p. 47.

12. USOM, *U.S. Economic and Technical Assistance to Thailand*.

13. M. L. Xuchati Khambu, *Memorandum on Water Requirement and Water Control Projects in the Northeast Region of Thailand, 1958*.

14. IBRD, *A Public Development Program for Thailand*, p. 44. The information on the 1980 offer was provided by R. Ralston (personal communication).

15. In King Ramkhamhaeng's famous inscription of 1292, describing the first major Thai state, the King refers to the economy and the basic diet: "In the time of King Ramkhamhaeng this land of Sukhothai is thriving. There is fish in the water and rice in the fields" (quoted in D. K. Wyatt, *Thailand: A Short History*, p. 54).

16. Milton J. Lobell, *The Thai-American Fisheries Project* (cited in Behrman, *Supply Response*, p. 40).

17. RTG, Office of Agricultural Economics, *Agricultural Statistics of Thailand*, 1959 and 1985.

18. R. Muscat, *Development Strategy in Thailand*, p. 101.

19. *Ibid.*, p. 102.

20. Chulalongkorn University, Social Research Institute, *Agricultural Marketing in Khon Kaen Province, Northeast Thailand*, p. 36.

21. Caldwell, *American Economic Aid to Thailand*, p. 85.

22. BAAC, *Annual Reports*, 1976, 1985.

23. USOM, *U.S. Economic and Technical Assistance to Thailand.*

24. Royal Thai Government, Ministry of Public Health, Division of Health Statistics Public Health Statistics (1984), p. 178.

25. Edgar A. Smith, Sombat Chayabejara, and I. A. Ismail, *Thailand Malaria Project Evaluation*, p. 2.

26. This description is drawn from unpublished materials kindly provided by Major R. J. Dunn, Executive Officer of AFRIMS, in Bangkok, 1987.

27. By Section 660 of the Foreign Assistance Act of 1962, as amended. See U.S. Senate, U.S. House of Representatives, *Legislation on Foreign Relations Through 1986*, p. 227.

28. Caldwell, *American Economic Aid to Thailand*, p. 34.

29. USAID accounts show $20.5 million as the cost of the Friendship Highway. The net cost was $15.7 million after deducting the residual value of equipment shifted to work on the East-West Highway, and other adjustments.

30. Behrman, *Supply Response in Underdeveloped Agriculture* p. 57.

31. IBRD, *Thailand Transport Sector Review*, Annex 2, p. 4.

32. See Muscat, *Development Strategy in Thailand*, p. 212–214 for a description of this experience.

33. IBRD, *Thailand Transport Sector Review*, pp. 1–2.

34. Details on the aeronautical projects drawn from USOM, *Aeronautical Ground Services Improvement Project, In-Depth Report.*

35. IBRD, *A Public Development Program for Thailand*, p. 107.

36. TDRI, *Thailand Natural Resources Profile*, p. 134.

37. RTG, National Energy Administration, *Electric Power in Thailand, 1985*, p. 11.

38. IBRD, *A Public Development Program for Thailand*, p. 113.

39. IBRD/NESDB, *Thailand, Issues and Options in the Energy Sector*, p. 14.

40. The following paragraphs draw on the minerals resources chapter of TDRI, *Thailand Natural Resources Profile* pp. 121–43.

41. Caldwell, *American Economic Aid to Thailand*, pp. 35–36. Hereafter references to this work will be given in the text.

42. IBRD, *A Public Development Program for Thailand*, p. 54.

43. The positive correlation of educational attainment and wage levels has been documented for Thailand in TDRI, *Human Resources Management*, pp. 139–153.

44. ILO, *Report to the Committee for Coordination of Investigations of the Lower Mekong Basin on Manpower Related to the Development of the Basin*, pp. 20, 35.

45. IBRD, *Education Sector Policy Paper*, pp. 54–46.

46. IBRD, *Sixth (Secondary) Education Loan*, Staff Appraisal Report, 1982, p. 6.

47. David K. Wyatt, *Thailand: A Short History*, p. 295.

48. Kasem and Smith, *The Public Service in Thailand*; and William J. Siffin, *The Thai Institute of Public Administration: A Case Study in Institution-Building*.

49. D. Axelrod and C. Neher, *Evaluation of Results of Projects Conducted by the Public Administration Service to Improve Management Practices in the Royal Thai Government*.

50. David Morell and Chai-anan Samudavanija, *Political Conflict in Thailand*. Hereafter references to this work will be given in the text.

51. Information on the history of the Mekong Committee, and some project data, drawn from 1986 Annual Report of the Interim Committee for Co-ordination of Investigations of the Lower Mekong Basin, and other materials provided by the Interim Committee secretariat in Bangkok and by UNDP in New York.

52. Royal Thai Government, NESDB, *The Sixth National Economic and Social Development Plan (1987–1991)*, ch. 6, para. 2.1.

5. Counterinsurgency and Development, 1960–1974

1. J. Alexander Caldwell, *American Economic Aid to Thailand* pp. 48–49.

2. Charles F. Keyes, *Isan: Regionalism in Northeastern Thailand*, p. 39.

3. These paragraphs draw substantially on Saiyud Kerdphol, *The Struggle for Thailand: Counter-Insurgency 1965–1985*.

4. David Morell and Chai-anan Samudavanija, *Political Conflict in Thailand*, p. 278.

5. Caldwell, *American Economic Aid to Thailand*, p. 54.

6. *Ibid.*, p. 58.

7. F. J. Moore, et al., *Rural Roads in Thailand*, p. 3. Hereafter references to this work will be given in the text.

8. USAID, Office of Evaluation, *New Directions Rural Roads*, pp. 27–33.

9. USOM, *Impact of USOM Supported Programs in Changwat Sakon Nakorn; Economic and Social Benefits of Roads in the North and Northeast; A Cost-Benefit Study of Roads in North and Northeast Thailand*.

10. Keyes, *Isan*, p. 62.

11. Caldwell, *American Economic Aid to Thailand*, pp. 108–11.

12. USOM Research Division, "Trip Report, Amphoe Loeng Nak Tha, Changwat Ubol," pp. 3–4.

13. Caldwell, *American Economic Aid to Thailand*, p. 150.

14. Morrell and Chai-anan, *Political Conflict*, p. 95. Hereafter page references to this work will be given in the text.

15. Committee for the Ratanakasin Bicentennial Celebration, *Illus-*

trated Handbook of Projects Undertaken Through Royal Initiative; Coordinating Committee for Royal Development Project, *His Majesty King Bhumibhol Adulyadej and His Development Work.*

16. IBRD, *A Public Developmental Program for Thailand,* pp. 3, 160.

17. Allen Rosenfield, et al., "Thailand's Family Planning Program: An Asian Success Story," p. 44.

18. *Ibid.,* p. 45.

19. An example of systematic review of program weaknesses can be found in Royal Thai Government, Ministry of Public Health, National Family Planning Program, *Country Case Studies in Management Development in Population/Family Planning.*

20. Rosenfield et al., "Thailand's Family Planning Program," p. 44.

21. *Ibid.,* p. 45.

22. IBRD, *World Development Report 1987,* table 28.

23. J. Knodel, Aphichat Chamratrithirong, and Nibhon Debavalya, *Thailand's Reproductive Revolution,* p. 6. Hereafter references to this work will be given in the text.

24. Allan Rosenfield (now Director of the Center for Population and Family Health at Columbia University's College of Physicians and Surgeons); Gavin Jones, Professor of Demography, Australian National University; Warren Robinson, Population Adviser, USAID, New Delhi; John Knodel, Population Studies Center, University of Michigan.

25. Allan Rosenfield, in personal conversation.

6. Focus on Poverty, 1975–1984

1. USAID, *Congressional Presentation, 1974, Security Assistance Program,* p. 5.

2. USAID, *Fiscal Year 1975 Submission to the Congress, Asia Programs,* pp. 139–40.

3. USAID, *Congressional Presentation FY 1984, Asia Programs,* p. 163.

4. IBRD, *Current Economic Position and Prospects of Thailand* (August 1970), 1:2–3.

5. IBRD, *Current Economic Position and Prospects of Thailand* (October 1974), 1:59.

6. USAID, Bureau for Asia and the Near East, *Executive Summaries of Evaluations and Special Studies Conducted for AID in Asia in Fiscal Year 1985,* pp. 143–45.

7. *Ibid.,* p. 144.

8. See, for example, Judith Tendler, *Turning Private Voluntary Agencies into Development Agencies: Questions for Evaluation.*

9. M. Anderson and N. Tannanbaum, *An Evaluation of the Co-Financing Project,* p. 32.

10. David Richards, *A Report on the Participation of Thai Non-Governmental Environment and Development Organizations,* p. 7.

11. R. Muscat, *Lam Nam Oon: An Irrigation and Area Development Project in Thailand*, p. vii.

12. USAID, *Executive Summaries*.

13. See, for example, USAID, *Irrigation and Aid's Experience: A Consideration Based on Evaluations*; R. Cassen and Associates, *Does Aid Work?*, p. 125.

14. USAID, Bureau for Asia and the Near East, *Executive Summaries*, p. 156.

15. *Ibid.*, p. 156.

16. Bill Gregg and Uoychai Vattrapoudej, *Seed Development in Thailand and Mississippi State University*, p. 83.

17. Quoted in *ibid.*, p. 64.

18. USAID, *Executive Sumamries*, p. 161.

19. Terry D. Schmidt, Final Project Completion Report, Northeast Rainfed Agricultural Development Project (Bangkok: USAID/Thailand, 1989), pp. 2–3.

20. Details on all the Institute's research and outreach activities are given in its *Report on October 1982–March 1986 Activities*.

21. Pricha Desawasdi et al., *Collection and Analysis of Research Information on Primary Health Care Activities*.

22. Wichit Mathurospas, Chaloem Varavithya, and Nicholas H. Wright, *Rural Primary Health Care Project, Final Evolution Report*. Bangkok, USAID, 1986.

23. Chalongphob Sussangkarn, Teera Ashakul, and Charles Myers, *Human Resources Management*, pp. 167–168.

24. UNICEF, *The State of the World's Children*, p. 66.

25. Chalongphob, Teera, and Myers, p. 178.

26. One citation from the large literature on health interventions and their effects in developing countries will suffice to illustrate this point. The closing remarks of a seminar held at the Pan American Health Organization in 1989 contain the following observations about the uncertainty of the benefits that flow from improvements in water potability and sanitation systems: "One assertion that has emerged clearly as a policy position is that even now one cannot be highly specific about the linkages between interventions in water supply and sanitation systems and health. There are sufficient grounds to assert that improvements in potable water supply are a good thing and that it is not necessary to push much further in order to justify the consideration of significant investments to improve rural water supply for health purposes—subject to a couple of conditions. . . . it is probably a mistake, in most instances, to think of water supply and sanitation as being a distinct sector of work having no close relationship to what is done in other aspects of rural development, including agriculture, transportation, health, and the like." USAID, *The Impact of Interventions in Water Supply and Sanitation in Developing Countries*, p. 158.

27. Medhi Krongkaew, "Institution Building and Economic Development: A Lesson from Rural Public Works Administration in Thailand," p. 13.

28. USAID, *Congressional Presentation, FY 1986*, p. 200.

29. IBRD, *Thailand, Income Growth, and Poverty Alleviation*, p. ii. Hereafter references to this work will be given in the text.

30. Medhi Krongkaew, *Industrialization, Employment, Poverty and Income Distribution of Thai Households* and *Poverty and Income Distribution in Thailand, 1975/76 and 1981*.

31. For a close study of northeast villages and the nature and sources of variation in ecosystems and economic condition, see Khon Kaen University–Ford Foundation Cropping Systems Project, *Tambon and Village Agricultural Systems in Northeast Thailand*.

32. Kosit Panpiemraj, *Rural Thailand: Economics of Poverty*.

33. Thanet Noraphoompipat, *Poverty Problem in Rural Development Planning*.

34. USAID, *Congressional Presentation, FY 1986*. pp. 149–151.

7. Thailand in Transition: New Roles for Foreign Assistance

1. N. W. Temple, *Thoughts on the Future Role and Strategy of USAID in Thailand*, p. 28.

2. *Ibid.*, p. 29.

3. USAID/T, Project Paper, *Private Sector in Development Project* (Bangkok: 1983), p. 1.

4. Fred Simmons et al., *Thailand: An Economy in Transition*, p. 76.

5. Taken from the terms of reference for the evaluation, May 1987, based on *Private Sector in Development Project Paper*, 1983.

6. Anek Laothamatas, "Business and Politics in Thailand; New Patterns of Influence," p. 451. Hereafter references to this work will be given in the text.

7. R. J. Muscat et al., *USAID Assistance for Remote Sensing in Thailand*.

8. The Aid Experience in Perspective

1. Alexander Caldwell, *American Economic Aid to Thailand*, pp. 90–92.

2. TDRI, *Management of Economic and Social Development: Proposed Research Plan* (January 1987).

3. See Clark D. Neher's review of two recent books on Thai–U.S. relations, p. 197. The two books are K. D. Jackson and Wiwat Mungkandi, *United States–Thailand Relations;* and R. Sean Randolph, *The United States and Thailand: Alliance Dynamics, 1950–1985*.

4. Thak Chaloemtiarana, *Thailand: The Politics of Despotic Paternalism*, pp. 278–85.

5. Ukrit Patamanam, pp. 229–312.

6. Grit Permtanjit, "Political Economy of Dependent Capitalist Development," Ph.D. diss., Univ. of Pennsylvania, pp. 108, 116.

8. The Aid Experience in Perspective

7. Thak, *Thailand*, p. 230.

8. Puey Ungphakorn, *A Siamese for All Seasons*, p. 46.

9. John A. Loftus, *Annual Report on the Economy of Thailand* (1957).

10. David I. Steinberg, "The Role of External Assistance in the Economic Development and Planning of Thailand: Torques and Tensions in the American Aid Program," p. 13.

11. *Ibid.*, p. 14.

12. For an account of Thai union history, see Bevars D. Mabry, *The Development of Labor Institutions in Thailand.*

13. David A. Wilson, *The United States and the Future of Thailand*, pp. 159–60.

14. Wyatt, *Thailand: A Short History*, p. 277. Hereafter references to this work will be given in the text.

BIBLIOGRAPHY

Anderson, M. and N. Tannanbaum. *An Evaluation of the Co-Financing Project*. Bangkok: USAID/T, 1983 (mimeo).

Anek Laothamatas. "Business and Politics in Thailand: New Patterns of Influence." *Asian Survey* (April 1988), vol. 28, no. 4.

Axelrod, D., and C. Neher. *Evaluation of Results of Projects Conducted by the Public Administration Service to Improve Management Practices in the Royal Thai Government*. Bangkok: DTEC/USAID, 1983.

Baldwin, W. Lee and W. David Maxwell. *The Role of Foreign Financial Assistance to Thailand in the 1980s*. Lexington, Mass.: D. C. Heath, 1976.

Behrman, Jere R. *Supply Response in Underdeveloped Agriculture: A Case Study of Four Major Annual Crops in Thailand, 1937–1963*. Amsterdam: North-Holland, 1968.

Caldwell, J. Alexander. *American Economic Aid to Thailand*. Lexington, Mass.: D. C. Heath, 1974.

Cassen, Robert and Associates. *Does Aid Work?* Oxford: Clarendon Press, 1986.

Chalongphob Sussangkarn, Teera Ashakul, and Charles Myers. *Human Resources Management*. Bangkok: Thailand Development Research Institute, 1986.

Chulalongkorn University. Social Research Institute. *Agricultural Marketing in Khon Kaen Province, Northeast Thailand*. Bangkok: 1980.

Chamberlain, James R. *Emerging Problems of Development: An Evaluation*. Bangkok, USAID, 1983.

Chamberlain, James R. *The Northeast Small Scale Irrigation Project: A Management Review.* Bangkok: USAID, 1985.

Committee for the Ratanakosin Bicentennial Celebration, BE 2525 (1982). *Illustrated Handbook of Projects Undertaken Through Royal Initiative.* Bangkok: CRBC, 1982.

Coordinating Committee for Royal Development Project. *His Majesty King Bhumibhol Adulyadej and His Development Work.* Bangkok: CCRDP, 1987.

Darling, Frank C. *Thailand and the United States.* Washington, D.C. Public Affairs Press, 1965.

Frankel, Jeffrey A. *The Impact of U.S. Economic Policies on a Commodity-Exporting Debtor: The Case of Thailand.* Berkeley: Second U.S.-Thailand Bilateral Forum, University of California, November 1985 (mimeo).

Fry, G. W. "The Economic and Political Impact of Study Abroad." In Elinor G. Barber et al., *Bridges to Knowledge: Foreign Students in Comparative Perspective.* Chicago: University of Chicago Press, 1984.

Girling, John L. S. *Thailand: Society and Politics.* Ithaca: Cornell University Press, 1981.

Gregg, Bill and Uoychai Vattrapoudej. *Seed Development in Thailand and Mississippi State University.* Bangkok: USAID, 1987.

Grit Permtanjit. "Political Economy of Dependent Capitalist Development." Ph.D. dissertation, University of Pennsylvania, 1981.

Hawaiian Agronomics (International), Inc. *Development Impact in the Northeast.* Bangkok: 1987.

Heng Liong Thung. "An Evaluation of the Impact of a Highway on a Rural Environment in Rural Thailand by Aerial Photography Methods." Ph.D. dissertation, Cornell University, 1972.

Hicks, Norman. *Economic Growth and Human Resources.* World Bank Staff Working Paper no. 408. Washington, D.C.: 1980.

IBRD (International Bank for Research and Development). *A Public Development Program for Thailand.* Baltimore: John Hopkins University Press, 1959.

IBRD. *Current Economic Position and Prospects of Thailand.* Washington, D.C.: 1970.

IBRD. *Current Economic Position and Prospects of Thailand.* Washington, D.C.: 1974.

IBRD. *Education Sector Policy Paper.* Washington, D.C., 1980.

IBRD. *Review of Bank Technical Assistance to Bangladesh.* Washington, D.C.: 1982.

IBRD *Sixth Education Loan.* Staff Appraisal Report. Washington, D.C.: 1982.

IBRD. *Thailand: Pricing and Marketing Policy for Intensification of Rice Agriculture.* Washington, D.C.: 1985.

IBRD. *Staff Appraisal Report, National Agriculture Research Project.* Washington, D.C.: 1980.

IBRD. *Thailand: Income Growth and Poverty Alleviation.* Washington, D.C.: 1980.

IBRD *Thailand Transport Sector Review.* Washington, D.C.: 1984.

IBRD. *World Development Report.* Washington, D.C.: various years.

IBRD. National Economic and Social Development Board. *Thailand: Issues and Options in the Energy Sector.* Report of the Joint UNDP/World Bank Energy Sector Assessment Program, 1985.

Institute for International Education. *Open Doors.* New York: IIE, 1979 and various years.

Interim Committee for Co-Ordination of Investigations of the Lower Mekong Basin. *Annual Report.* Bangkok: 1986.

International Labor Organization. *Report to the Committee for Coordination of Investigations of the Lower Mekong Basin on Manpower Related to the Development of the Basin.* Geneva: ILO, 1960.

International Planning and Analysis Center. *Report on Cargo Preferences.* Washington, D.C.: IPAC, 1985.

Israel Association for International Cooperation, The. *Thailand Country Evaluation Report.* Jerusalem, 1984.

Jackson, Karl D. and Wiwat Mungkandi, *United States–Thailand Relations.* Berkeley: University of California Press, 1986.

Jacoby, N. H. *U.S. Aid to Taiwan.* New York: Praeger, 1966.

Kasem U. and R. Smith, *The Public Service in Thailand.* Brussels: International Institute of Administrative Sciences, 1954.

Keyes, Charles F. *Isan: Regionalism in Northeast Thailand.* Cornell Thailand Project, Data Paper 65. Ithaca: Cornell University Press, 1967.

Khon Kaen University–Ford Foundation Cropping Systems Project. *Tambon and Village Agricultural Systems in Northeast Thailand.* Khon Kean: 1982.

Khon Kaen University. Research and Development Institute. *Report on October 1982–March 1986 Activities.* Khon Kaen: 1986.

Knodel, J., Aphichat Chamratrithirong, and Nighon Debavalya. *Thailand's Reproductive Revolution.* Madison: University of Wisconsin Press, 1987.

Kosit Panpiemraj. *Rural Thailand: Economics of Poverty.* Bangkok: NESDB, 1980.

Likhit Dhiravegin. *The Bureaucratic Elite of Thailand.* Bangkok: Thai Khadi Research Institute, Thammasat University, 1978.

Lobell, Milton J. *The Thai-American Fisheries Project.* Completion of Assignment Report. Bangkok: USOM, 1957 (mimeo).

Loftus, John A. *Reports on the Economy of Thailand.* Ministry of Finance. Bangkok: various, semi-annual 1956–1962 (mimeo).

Mabry, Bevars D. *The Development of Labor Institutions in Thailand.* Ithaca: Department of Asian Studies, Cornell University, 1979 (mimeo).

Medhi Krongkaew. *Industrialization, Employment, Poverty, and Income Distribution of Thai Households.* Bangkok: TDRI, 1987.

Medhi Krongkaew. "Institution Building and Economic Development: A Lesson from Rural Public Works Administration in Thailand." Paper prepared for Seventh Biennial General Meeting on Commonalities and Complementarities in the Asia and Pacific Region. ADIPA, 1987.

Medhi Krongkaew. *Poverty and Income Distribution in Thailand, 1975/76 and 1981.* Bangkok: Thammasat University, 1986 (mimeo; in Thai).

Moore, F. J., C. T. Alton, H. L. Lefferts, Suthep Soonthronpasuch, and R. E. Suttor. *Rural Roads in Thailand.* Project Impact Evaluation no. 13. Washington, D.C.: USAID, 1980.

Morell, David and Chai-anan Samudavanija. *Political Conflict in Thailand.* Cambridge: Oegelschlager, Gunn and Hain, 1981.

Muscat, Robert J. *Development Strategy in Thailand.* New York: Praeger, 1966.

Muscat, R. J. "Evaluating Technical Cooperation." *Development Policy Review* (March 1986), vol. 4, no. 1.

Muscat, R. J. *Lam Nam Oon: An Irrigation and Area Development Project in Thailand.* AID Evaluation Working Paper no. 46. Washington, D.C.: USAID, 1982.

Muscat, R. J., K. Craib, R. Ellefsen, and M. Willard. *USAID Assistance for Remote Sensing in Thailand.* Diamond Springs: Resources Development, 1983.

Nation, The. Bangkok, various dates.

Neher, Clark D. Reviews of books by Jackson and Mungkandi and by Randolph, in *The Journal of Asian Studies* (February 1988), vol. 47, no. 1.

OECD (Organization for Economic Cooperation and Development). *Technical Assistance and the Needs of Developing Countries.* Paris: OECD, 1986.

Pricha Desawasdi et al. *Collection and Analysis of Research Information on Primary Health Care Activities.* Bangkok: Ministry of Public Health, 1984.

Puey Ungphakorn. *A Siamese for All Seasons: Collected Articles by and about Puey Ungphakorn.* Bangkok: Komol Keemthong Foundation, 1984.

Rambo, A. Terry, Charan Chantalakhana, Manu Seetisarn. *Mid-Term Evaluation Report: Farming Systems Research Sub-Project, Khon Kaen University Research Development Project.* Bangkok: USAID, 1986 (mimeo).

Randolph, R. Sean. *The United States and Thailand: Alliance Dynamics, 1950–1985.* Berkeley: University of California Press, 1986.

Rhatigan, D. J. and Pisanu Sunthraraks. *Final Evaluation of Private Sector in Development Project.* Washington, D.C.: TvT Associates, 1987.

Richards, David. *A Report on the Participation of Thai Non-Governmental Environment and Development Organizations in USAID's Proposed Management of Natural Resources and Environment for Sustainable Development Project.* Washington, D.C.: International Institute for Environment and Development, 1987.

Roberts, G. L. et al. *Thailand Land Settlements Projects Evaluation*. Bangkok: USAID, 1984.

Rockefeller Foundation. *Annual Reports*. New York, various years.

Rosenfield, Allan, A. Bennett, Somsak Varakamin, and D. Lauro. "Thailand's Family Planning Program: An Asian Success Story." *International Family Planning Perspectives* (June 1982), vol. 8, no. 2.

Roth, A. D. et al. *Evaluation of Mae Chaem Watershed Development Project*. Washington, D.C.: Development Alternatives, Inc., 1983.

RTG (Royal Thai Government). Bank for Agricultural and Cooperatives. *Annual Reports*. Bangkok: various years.

RTG. Bureau of the Budget/USOM. *Evaluation Report, Second Joint Thai–USOM Evaluation of the Accelerated Rural Development Project*. Bangkok: USOM, 1966.

RTG. Ministry of Public Health. National Family Planning Program. *Country Case Studies in Management Development in Population/Family Planning*. Bangkok: no date.

RTG. Ministry of Public Health. Division of Health Statistics. *Public Health Statistics*. Bangkok: 1984.

RTG. National Economic and Social Development Board: *A Profile of Rural Development Conditions in Thailand in 1986*. Bangkok: 1987.

Royal Thai Government. National Economic and Social Development Board. *The Sixth National Economic and Social Development Plan (1987–1991)*. Bangkok: 1987.

Royal Thai Government. National Energy Administration. *Electric Power in Thailand, 1985*. Bangkok: 1985.

Royal Thai Government. Office of Agricultural Economics. *Agricultural Statistics of Thailand*. Bangkok: Various years.

Royal Thai Government. Secretariat of the Prime Minister. *Final Report*. Bangkok: Technical Assistance Team of the Decentralized Development Management Project (DDMP), 1986 (mimeo: translation).

Siayud Kerdphol. *The Struggle for Thailand: Counter-Insurgency 1965–1985*. Bangkok: S. Research Center Co., 1986.

Siffin, William J. *The Thai Institute of Public Administration: A Case Study in Institution-Building*. Pittsburgh: University of Pittsburgh, 1967 (mimeo).

Simmons, Fred, M. B. Allen, A. W. Dunlap, G. M. Lecce, T. F. Miller, P. K. Monk, and R. C. Young. *Thailand: An Economy in Transition*. Bangkok: USAID, 1982 (draft).

Solem, Richard Ray. *Small Farmer Perspective on Development: Village Survey in Northeast Thailand*. Washington, D.C.: USAID 1988 (mimeo).

Steinberg, David I. "The Role of External Assistance on the Economic Development and Planning of Thailand: Torques and Tensions in the American Aid Forum." Paper prepared for U.S.–Thailand Bilateral Forum, University of California and Chulalongkorn University, 1985.

Smith, Edgar A., Sombat Chayabejara, and I. A. Ismail. *Thailand Malaria Project Evaluation*. Bangkok: USAID, 1985.

Stavrakis, Eileen and Alexandra Panehal. *Final Evaluation of the Thailand Integrated Improvement for the Urban Poor*. Bangkok: USAID, 1985 (mimeo).

Suchitra Punyaratabandhu-Bhakdi. *Managing Energy and Resource Efficient Cities: Mini-Evaluation Report*. Bangkok: USAID, 1985 (mimeo).

Temple, N. W. *Thoughts on the Future Role and Strategy of USAID in Thailand*. Bangkok: USAID/T, 1983 (mimeo).

Tendler, Judith. *Turning Private Voluntary Agencies into Development Agencies: Questions for Evaluation*. Washington, D.C.: USAID, 1982.

TDRI (Thailand and Development Research Institute). *Human Resources Management*. Bangkok: 1986.

TDRI. *Thailand Natural Resources Profile*. Bangkok, 1987.

Thailand–United States Education Foundation. *Directory of Alumni, 1950–1986*. Bangkok, 1986.

Thak Chaloemtiarnana. *Thailand: The Politics of Despotic Paternalism*. Bangkok: Thai Khadi Institute, 1979.

Thanet Noraphoomipat. *Poverty Problem in Rural Development Planning*. Bangkok: Thai Khadi Research Institute, Thammasat University, 1981 (in Thai).

Thavat Vichaidit. *Evaluation of USAID Grants for Technical Assistance to Thailand*. Bangkok: National Institute of Development Administration, 1979.

World Bank, The, *see* IBRD.

Tregaskis, Richard W. *Southeast Asia: Building the Bases*. Washington, D.C.: GPO, 1975.

Twatchai Yougkittikul and Paitoon Winboonchitikula. *Thailand's Transformation Into a Newly Industrializing Country*. Bangkok: Thailand Development Research Institute, 1987.

Udom Bausri. "The Influence of John Dewey's Philosophy on Thai Education." In J. Indorf, ed., *Thai-American Relations in Contemporary Affairs*. Singapore, 1982.

Ukrit Patamanam, "Influence of International Agencies and Foreign Governments on Thai Economic Policy. In Rangsan Thomapornpan and Somboon Sikritprachai, eds., *Dependency Theory and Thai Socio-Economy*. Bangkok: Thai University Press, 1985 (in Thai).

UNICEF. *The State of the World's Children*. New York: 1986.

United Nations Development Programme. *Development Cooperation*. Bangkok: various years.

USAID. (U.S. Agency for International Development). *Congressional Presentation*. Washington, D.C.: various years.

USAID (Bureau for Asia and the Near East.) *Executive Summaries of Evaluations and Special Studies Conducted for AID in Asia in Fiscal Year 1985*. Washington, D.C.: 1986.

USAID. *The Impact of Interventions in Water Supply and Sanitation in the Developing Countries*. Proceedings of a seminar held at the Pan American Health Organization March 25–26, 1980. Washington, D.C., 1981.

USAID. *Irrigation and AID's Experience: A Consideration Based on Evaluations.* Program Evaluation Report no. 8. Washington, D.C.: 1983.

USAID. (Office of Evaluation.) *New Directions Rural Roads.* Washington, D.C.: 1979.

USAID. *U.S. Overseas Loans and Grants.* Washington, D.C.: 1986.

U.S. Senate. U.S. House of Representatives. *Legislation on Foreign Relations Through 1986.* Current Legislation and Related Executive Orders, Joint Committee Print, Committee on Foreign Relations and Committee on Foreign Affairs. Washington, D.C.: GPO, 1987.

USMACTHAI/CHJUSMAG. *Command History.* Honolulu: 1976.

USOM (U.S. Operations Mission). *Aeronautical Ground Service Improvement Project, In-Depth Report.* Bangkok: 1970 (mimeo).

USOM. *Annual Financial Reports.* Bangkok: 1965 ff.

USOM. *A Cost-Benefit Study of Roads in North and Northeast Thailand.* Bangkok: 1966.

USOM. *Economic and Social Benefits of Roads in the North and Northeast.* Bangkok: 1966.

USOM. *Impact of USOM Supported Programs in Changwat Sakon Nakorn.* Bangkok: 1967 (mimeo).

USOM. *Participant Training.* Bangkok, 1969 (mimeo).

USOM. *RGT/USOM Economic and Technical Project Summary, FY 1951–1972.* Bangkok: 1973 (mimeo).

USOM. *Thai-American Economic and Technical Cooperation.* Bangkok: March 1965.

USOM. *Trip Report, Amphoe Loeng Nal Tha, Changwat Ubol.* Bangkok: 1967.

USOM. *U.S. Economic and Technical Assistance to Thailand.* Bangkok: no date.

USOM. *USOM and ARD: The First Ten Years.* Bangkok: 1973 (mimeo).

Vella, Walter F. *The Impact of the West on Government in Thailand.* Berkeley: University of California Press, 1955.

Vimol Bhongbhibhat et al., eds. *The Eagle and the Elephant: 150 Years of Thai-American Relations.* Bangkok: United Production, 1982.

Wilson, David A. *The United States and the Future of Thailand.* New York: Praeger, 1970.

Wyatt, D. K. *Thailand: A Short History.* London: Yale University Press, 1984.

Xuchati Khambu. "Memorandum on Water Requirement and Water Control Projects in the Northeast Region of Thailand, 1958." Bangkok: Royal Water Irrigation Department, 1958.

INDEX

Academics, overseas training and, 50, 56-59
Accelerated Impact Program, 197-99
Accelerated Rural Development (ARD), 121, 160-70; counterinsurgency and, 42; Highway Department and, 166-67; overseas training and, 68; projects, 186
Additionality, 5
Affected Thai Village program, 253-54
Affirmative action, U.S. policy on, 14
AFL-CIO, 286
African countries, per capita aid to, 31
Agribusiness, U.S., 237
Agricultural Technology Transfer project, 212, 273-74
Agriculture, 44, 187; annual flooding and, 24; advances in, 13; aid effects on, 10; ARD and, 164; comparative advantage in, 47n; contract farming and, 205, 211n; cooperatives, 83-85, 130; corn corps, 75-77; credit and marketing and, 85; diversification of, 2; extension systems, 77, 232; fertilizers and, 73, 194; fisheries, 80-81; income from, 73; irrigation projects, 78-80; livestock, 81-83; marketing coops, 130; modernization projects,

77-80; output growth, 191-92; overseas training and, 52, 58-59; poultry, 82; productivity in, 71, 72-73, 192, 208; research and, 72, 195, 209-16; rice output, 72-74; slash-and-burn system, 24; soil quality and, 194; technology and, 77, 209-13, 273-74; training in, 78, 79, 114: USAID and, 71-86, 273-74: U.S. competition and, 74-75; vocational schools and, 114; *see also* Irrigation; Northeast region; Water projects
Agriculture Development Council, 58-59
Agroville concept, 159n
Air transportation system, 103-6; airfield improvements, 21-23, 104-5; military construction program, 25; Thai Airways assistance and, 106; U.S. aircraft imports and, 36
American Schools and Hospitals Abroad, 32, 34
Anderson, M., 200
Anek Laothamatas, 243-44, 245-46
Animal disease vaccines, 212
Anti-Communist Act (1952), 22
Aphichat Chamratrithirong, 181

STUDIES OF THE EAST ASIAN INSTITUTE

The Ladder of Success in Imperial China, by Ping-ti Ho. New York: Columbia University Press, 1962.

The Chinese Inflation, 1937–1949, by Shun-hsin Chou. New York: Columbia University Press, 1963.

Reformer in Modern China: Chang Chien, 1853–1926, by Samuel Chu. New York: Columbia University Press, 1965.

Research in Japanese Sources: A Guide, by Herschel Webb with the assistance by Marleigh Ryan. New York: Columbia University Press, 1965.

Society and Education in Japan, by Herbert Passin. New York: Teachers College Press, 1965.

Agricultural Production and Economic Developments in Japan, 1873–1922, by James I. Nakamura. Princeton: Princeton University Press, 1966.

Japan's First Modern Novel: Ukigumo of Futabatei Shimei, by Marleigh Ryan. New York: Columbia University Press, 1967.

The Korean Communist Movement, 1918–1948, by Dae-Sook Suh. Princeton: Princeton University Press, 1967.

The First Vietnam Crisis, by Melvin Gurtov. New York: Columbia University Press, 1967.

Cadres, Bureaucracy, and Political Power in Communist China, by A. Doak Barnett. New York: Columbia University Press, 1968.

The Japanese Imperial Institution in the Tokugawa Period, by Herschel Webb. New York: Columbia University Press, 1968.

Higher Education and Business Recruitment in Japan, by Koya Azumi. New York: Teachers College Press, 1969.

The Communists and Peasant Rebellions: A Study in the Rewriting of Chinese History, by James P. Harrison, Jr. New York: Atheneum, 1969.

How The Conservatives Rule Japan, by Nathanial B. Thayer. Princeton: Princeton University Press, 1969.

Aspects of Chinese Education, edited by C. T. Hu. New York: Teachers College Press, 1970.

Documents of Korean Communism, 1918–1948, by Dae-Sook Suh. Princeton: Princeton University Press, 1970.

Japanese Education: A Bibliography of Materials in the English Language, by Herbert Passin. New York: Teachers College Press, 1970.

Economic Development and the Labor Market in Japan, by Koji Taira. New York: Columbia University Press, 1970.

The Japanese Oligarchy and the Russo-Japanese War, by Shumpei Okamoto. New York: Columbia University Press, 1970.

Imperial Restoration in Medieval Japan, by Paul Varley. New York: Columbia University Press, 1971.

Japan's Postwar Defense Policy, 1947–1968, by Martin E. Weinstein. New York: Columbia University Press, 1971.

Election Campaigning Japanese Style, by Gerald L. Curtis. New York: Columbia University Press, 1971.

China and Russia: The "Great Game," by O. Edmund Clubb. New York: Columbia University Press, 1971.

Money and Monetary Policy in Communist China, by Katharine Huang Hsian. New York: Columbia University Press, 1971.

The District Magistrate in Late Imperial China, by John R. Watt. New York: Columbia University Press, 1972.

Law and Policy in China's Foreign Relations: A Study of Attitude and Practice, by James C. Hsiung. New York: Columbia University Press, 1972.

Pearl Harbor as History: Japanese-American Relations, 1931–1941, edited by Dorothy Borg and Shumpei Okamoto, with the assistance of Dale E. A. Finlayson. New York: Columbia University Press, 1973.

Japanese Culture: A Short History, by H. Paul Varley. New York: Praeger, 1973.

Doctors in Politics: The Political Life of the Japan Medical Association, by William E. Steslicke. New York: Praeger, 1973.

The Japan Teachers Union: A Radical Interest Group in Japanese Politics, by Donald Ray Thurston. Princeton: Princeton University Press, 1973.

Japan's Foreign Policy, 1868–1941: A Research Guide, edited by James William Morley. New York: Columbia University Press, 1974.

Palace and Politics in Prewar Japan, by David Anson Titus. New York: Columbia University Press, 1974.

The Idea of China: Essays in Geographic Myth and Theory, by Andrew March. Devon, England: David and Charles, 1974.

Origins of the Cultural Revolution, by Roderick MacFarquhar. New York: Columbia University Press, 1974.

Shiba Kōkan: Artist, Innovator, and Pioneer in the Westernization of Japan, by Calvin L. French. Tokyo: Weatherhill, 1974.

Insei: Abdicated Sovereigns in the Politics of Late Heian Japan, by G. Cameron Hurst. New York: Columbia University Press, 1975.

Embassy at War, by Harold Joyce Noble. Edited with an introduction by Frank Baldwin, Jr. Seattle: University of Washington Press, 1975.

Rebels and Bureaucrats: China's December 9ers, by John Israel and Donald W. Klein. Berkeley: University of California Press, 1975.

Deterrent Diplomacy, edited by James William Morley. New York: Columbia University Press, 1976.

House United, House Divided: The Chinese Family in Taiwan, by Myron L. Cohen. New York: Columbia University Press, 1976.

Escape From Predicament: Neo-Confucianism and China's Evolving Political Culture, by Thomas A. Metzger. New York: Columbia University Press, 1976.

Cadres, Commanders, and Commissars: The Training of the Chinese Communist Leadership, 1920–45, by Jane L. Price. Boulder, Colo.: Westview Press, 1976.

Sun Yat-Sen: Frustrated Patriot, by C. Martin Wilbur. New York: Columbia University Press, 1977.

Japanese International Negotiating Style, by Michael Blaker. New York: Columbia University Press, 1977.

Contemporary Japanese Budget Politics, by John Creighton Campbell. Berkeley: University of California Press, 1977.

The Medieval Chinese Oligarchy, by David Johnson. Boulder, Colo.: Westview Press, 1977.

The Arms of Kiangnan: Modernization in the Chinese Ordnance Industry, 1860–1895, by Thomas L. Kennedy. Colo.: Westview Press, 1978.

Patterns of Japanese Policymaking: Experiences from Higher Education, by T. J. Pempel. Boulder, Colo.: Westview Press, 1978.

The Chinese Connection: Roger S. Greene, Thomas W. Lamont, George E. Sokolsky, and American-East Asian Relations, by Warren I. Cohen. New York: Columbia University Press, 1978.

Multiarism in Modern China: The Career of Wu P'ei-Fu, 1916–1939, by Odoric Y. K. Wou. Folkestone, England: Dawson, 1978.

A Chinese Pioneer Family; The Lins of Wu-Feng, by Johanna Meskill. Princeton: Princeton University Press, 1979.

Perspectives on a Changing China, edited by Joshua A. Fogel and William T. Rowe. Boulder, Colo.: Westview Press, 1979.

The Memoirs of Li Tsung-Jen, by T. K. Tong and Li Tsung-jen. Boulder, Colo.: Westview Press, 1979.

Unwelcome Muse: Chinese Literature in Shanghai and Peking, 1937–1945, by Edward Gunn. New York: Columbia University Press, 1979.

Yeman and the Great Powers: The Origins of Chinese Communist Foreign Policy, by James Reardon-Anderson. New York: Columbia University Press, 1980.

Uncertain Years: Chinese-American Relations, 1947–1950, edited by Dorothy Borg and Waldo Heinrichs. New York: Columbia University Press, 1980.

The Fateful Choice: Japan's Advance Into South-East Asia, edited by James William Morley. New York: Columbia University Press, 1980.

Tanaka Giichi and Japan's China Policy, by William F. Morton. Folkestone, England: Dawson, 1980; New York: St. Martin's Press, 1980.

The Origins of the Korean War: Liberation and the Emergence of Separate Regimes, 1945–1947, by Bruce Cumings. Princeton: Princeton University Press, 1981.

Class Conflict in Chinese Socialism, by Richard Curt Kraus. New York: Columbia University Press, 1981.

Education Under Mao: Class and Competition in Canton Schools, by Jonathan Unger. New York: Columbia University Press, 1982.

Private Academies of Tokugawa Japan, by Richard Rubinger. Princeton: Princeton University Press, 1982.

Japan and the San Francisco Peace Settlement, by Michael M. Yoshitsu. New York: Columbia University Press, 1982.

New Frontiers in American-East Asian Relations: Essays Presented to Dorothy Borg, edited by Warren I. Cohen. New York: Columbia University Press, 1983.

The Origins of the Cultural Revolution: II, the Great Leap Forward, 1958–1960, by Roderick MacFarquhar, New York: Columbia University Press, 1983.

The China Quagmire: Japan's Expansion of the Asian Continent, 1933–1941, edited by James William Morley. New York: Columbia University Press, 1983.

Fragments of Rainbows: The Life and Poetry of Saito Mokichi, 1882–1953, by Amy Vladeck Heinrich. New York: Columbia University Press, 1983.

The U.S.-South Korea Alliance: Evolving Patterns of Security Relations, edited by Gerald L. Curtis and Sung-joo Han. Lexington, Mass.: Lexington Books, 1983.

Discovering History in China: American Historical Writing on the Recent Chinese Past, by Paul A. Cohen. New York: Columbia University Press, 1984.

The Foreign Policy of the Republic of Korea, edited by Youngnok Koo and Sangjoo Han. New York: Columbia University Press, 1984.

State and Diplomacy in Early Modern Japan, by Ronald Toby. Princeton: Princeton University Press, 1983.

Japan and the Asian Development Bank, by Dennis Yasutomo. New York: Praeger, 1983.

Japan Erupts: The London Naval Conference and the Manchurian Incident, edited by James W. Morley. New York: Columbia University Press, 1984.

Japanese Culture, third edition, revised, by Paul Varley. Honolulu: University of Hawaii Press, 1984.

Studies of the East Asian Institute

Japan's Modern Myths: Ideology in the Late Meiji Period, by Carol Gluck. Princeton: Princeton University Press, 1985.

Shamans, Housewives, and Other Restless Spirits: Women in Korean Ritual Life, by Laurel Kendall. Honolulu: University of Hawaii Press, 1985.

Human Rights in Contemporary China, by R. Randle Edwards, Louis Henkin, and Andrew J. Nathan. New York: Columbia University Press, 1986.

The Pacific Basin: New Challenges for the United States, edited by James W. Morley. New York: Academy of Political Science, 1986.

The Manner of Giving: Strategic Aid and Japanese Foreign Policy, by Dennis T. Yasutomo. Lexington, Mass.: Lexington Books, 1986.

China's Political Economy: The Quest for Development Since 1949, by Carl Riskin. Oxford: Oxford University Press, 1987.

Anvil of Victory: The Communist Revolution in Manchuria, by Steven I. Levine. New York: Columbia University Press, 1987.

Single Sparks: China's Rural Revolutions, edited by Kathleen Hartford and Steven M. Goldstein. Armonk, N.Y.: M. E. Sharpe, 1987.

Urban Japanese Housewives: At Home and in the Community, by Anne E. Imamura. Honolulu: University of Hawaii Press, 1987.

China's Satellite Parties, by James D. Seymour. Armonk. N.Y.: M.E. Sharpe, 1987.

The Japanese Way of Politics, by Gerald L. Curtis. New York: Columbia University Press, 1988.

Kim Il Sung: The North Korean Leader, by Dae-Sook Suh. New York: Columbia University Press, 1988.

The Indochina Tangle: China's Foreign Policy, 1975–1979, by Robert S. Ross. New York: Columbia University Press, 1988.

Japan and the World, 1853–1952, edited by Sadao Asada. New York: Columbia University Press, 1989.

Anarchism in Chinese Political Culture, by Peter Zarrow. New York: Columbia University Press, 1990.